The Feminist War on Crime

The Feminist War on Crime

THE UNEXPECTED ROLE OF WOMEN'S
LIBERATION IN MASS INCARCERATION

Aya Gruber

UNIVERSITY OF CALIFORNIA PRESS

University of California Press
Oakland, California

© 2020 by Aya Gruber
First Paperback Printing 2021
Library of Congress Cataloging-in-Publication Data

Names: Gruber, Aya, author.
Title: The feminist war on crime : the unexpected role of women's liberation
    in mass incarceration / Aya Gruber.
Description: Oakland, California : University of California Press, [2020] |
    Includes bibliographical references and index.
Identifiers: LCCN 2019049549 (print) | LCCN 2019049550 (ebook) |
    ISBN 9780520385818 (paper) | ISBN 9780520973145 (epub)
Subjects: LCSH: Women—Crimes against—Law and legislation—United
    States. | Women prisoners—United States. | Feminist criminology—
    United States. | Criminal justice, Administration of—United States.
Classification: LCC HV9469 .G78 2020 (print) | LCC HV9469 (ebook) |
    DDC 364.601—dc23
LC record available at https://lccn.loc.gov/2019049549
LC ebook record available at https://lccn.loc.gov/2019049550

Manufactured in the United States of America

28 27 26 25 24 23 22 21
10 9 8 7 6 5 4 3 2 1

For Misa,
a feminist

CONTENTS

ACKNOWLEDGMENTS

When I embarked on this project in 2014, I had been writing on feminism and criminal law for well over a decade. I had authored numerous law review articles on discrete topics of gender violence, and I thought I might put those articles together as a critical reader of sorts. For years, subjects like mandatory arrest and affirmative consent were familiar academic territory, and I had long managed and marshaled arguments on them. As I started writing, it became increasingly clear that my past scholarship on feminist criminal law reform offered pieces of a puzzle, but after so many years and thousands of pages written, I was not yet able to fit them together as a complete picture. Or to invoke another analogy, the feminist war on crime was like a Seurat painting, and I had too few points and stood too close to them. It dawned on me that to see the big picture I had to go back to the origins of my own torn feelings about being a feminist and an incarceration critic and interrogate why I harbored certain beliefs, made certain presumptions, and had certain intuitions. The book became less about rehashing things I had already said and more about using my unease at particular feminist arguments, policies, and discourses as a starting point and sleuthing to fill in the blanks. Each time I tracked down a history, legal argument, or personal tale a fuller picture emerged. By the end, I was able to step back, address my torn feelings, and feel confident that the picture I have and the stances I take are not reactionary or instinctive but products of long reflection and exhaustive (exhausting) research.

So how do I thank everyone who contributed to a project a lifetime in the making? Let me start at the very beginning and thank Samuel ("Shark Doc") Gruber, my father. He was a visionary in his field of shark behavior and biology and was never afraid to break the rules or challenge the orthodoxies. He instilled in me the desire to pursue knowledge and justice, fight against the odds, and stand by my beliefs in the face of powerful opposition. He was so proud of me and looked forward to reading the book, but he passed away in April 2019 just as I was finalizing the manuscript. Dad wasn't perfect—he was often bellicose and quick-tempered—but his life-affirming presence filled an enormous space in the world, and I miss him every day. I also cannot overstate the influence of my mother, Marie Hirata Gruber, who spent her childhood years in a Japanese internment camp at Heart Mountain, Wyoming. Her past gave me personal insights on the harms of government detention and carceral policies that trade on images of dangerous enemies and inscrutable foreigners. Her present continues to give my sister Meegan and me faith in just how strong women are—how they can survive poverty, horrific racism, and adversity and live fully in the moment, while never forgetting the past.

Before leaving the past, I also want to express my gratitude to the law professors and public defender mentors who set me on this path of discovery. During law school, the professors who guided me in developing the ideas that decades later became this book included Duncan Kennedy, Elizabeth Schneider, Alan Dershowitz, and the incomparable Charles Ogletree. Duncan Kennedy, in particular, played an outsized role in the development of my scholarly identity, and I cannot thank him enough. A number of mentors at the D.C. Public Defender Service shaped my thinking on law enforcement and incarceration, including James Forman Jr., Rudy Acree, Tamar Meekins, and Ron Sullivan. I also thank my supervisor at the Federal Public Defender in Miami, Mary Barzee.

Numerous colleagues selflessly devoted time to helping me develop and refine the ideas in this book, including Aziza Ahmed, Kim Bailey, Kathy Baker, Bennett Capers, Amy Cohen, Donna Coker, Erin Collins, Frank Rudy Cooper, Justin Desautels-Stein, Karen Engle, Joe Fischel, Jacob Gersen, Cynthia Godsoe, Lakshman Guruswamy, Sharon Jacobs, Kate Mogulescu, Karen Pita Loor, Alice Ristroph, Carol Steiker, Deb Tuerkheimer, and Corey Yung. I owe a special debt of gratitude to Janet Halley, whose examinations of gender and law and open, searching, and honest approach to "unspeakable" topics long inspired me. While writing the book, I was fortunate enough to have her direct scholarly, and emotional, support. I benefited enormously from presenting a chapter of the book at one of her inimitable "salons." Jeannie Suk Gersen also greatly influenced my analysis and moved me to reach out to a broader audience. She gave me invaluable encouragement, especially at the end of the project. Paul Butler was an early and enthusiastic supporter of the project and provided me with astute advice on book publishing.

Jorge Esquirol has, for fifteen years, been my mentor in all things academic. I would not be the scholar I am today without his steady presence in my life.

I am especially appreciative of the colleagues who took the time to read the entire manuscript. Leigh Goodmark was a wonderful resource throughout, and I am happy we have been in mutual conversation for years. Jennifer Hendricks endured my seemingly endless queries about the nature of feminism, what it means to be a feminist, and the like. Ben Levin gave me vital feedback on earlier drafts, and his insights figured prominently in a major reorganization. Ahmed White spent countless hours reading drafts and engaging me in meaningful discussions of their contents. I am glad to be just two doors down from his office.

This book received substantial support from the University of Colorado Law School's former dean Phil Weiser and current dean Jim Anaya. It was financially supported by several law school summer stipends and a Gilbert Goldstein grant for a half-semester leave. This book was also my sabbatical project in spring 2018. The book would never have come to fruition without the tireless work of the library staff and faculty. In particular, Jane Thompson was an amazing ally and provided incomparable help. Many faculty administrative liaisons had a hand in this project, and Wei-Joan Udden and Kelly Ilseng assisted in proofing. I thank Kelly for being such a dependable, competent, and congenial administrative liaison as I wrote the book. I also profited from the input of my law school colleagues, especially those who attended the 2018 faculty-staff colloquium where I presented the Introduction.

My liaisons at University of California Press also deserve the highest praise for their support and flexibility. I appreciate that the press took a risk on a book that is undoubtedly more controversial and emotion-provoking than many other academic monographs. My editor Maura Roessner believed in and championed this project from the start. She pushed me to the limits of my writing abilities and imagination, and this process has at many points been painful. But the final product is all the better for it, and in retrospect, I wouldn't have it any other way. I also thank Madison Wetzell for marshaling me through the unfamiliar book publishing world with a deft hand. Book agent Cecelia Cancellaro was an enormous asset during the initial stages of the process, just as private editor Linda Gorman was at the final stages.

I benefited considerably from presenting portions of the book at conferences and faculty colloquia. I thank those who provided commentary at the 2018 and 2019 Law and Society Conferences, the 2019 American Association of Law Schools Conference, the 2018 CrimFest Conference, the 2019 University of

Nevada–Las Vegas (UNLV) Law Race, Gender, and Policing Conference, the 2018 Harvard Law School Fighting the (Q)arceral State Conference (particularly D Dangaran and Anna Nathanson), and the 2018 Harvard Law School Prison Legal Assistance Panel (particularly Regina Powers). I received helpful feedback from the faculties of the University of Kansas Law School, Pace Law School, Chicago-Kent Law School, and Harvard Law School. My thinking evolved significantly during my participation as an adviser in the American Law Institute's (ALI) Model Penal Code Sexual Assault Project, and I am grateful for the leadership of ALI reporters Stephen Schulhofer and Erin Murphy.

The people who most inspired me to write the book and most influenced my thinking on it have been my students. So many students in my criminal law courses over the last several years engaged me in meaningful dialogue, particularly on the topic of sexual assault. Without those conversations this would be a very different, and less insightful, book. I am especially appreciative of the students in my 2018 Criminal Law in Context Seminar at Colorado and my 2017 Feminism and Crime Control Seminar at Harvard Law School, who were assigned to read portions of the book and whose input proved extraordinarily beneficial: Angel Ankers, Charmaine Archer, Kaitlyn Beck, Jenny Braun, Paola Campos, Ani Chabin, Sarah Diebler, Rachel Fleder, Michael Gannon, Conrad Glover, Sarah Gutman, Ben Hecht, Whitney House, Daniel Insulza, Kelly Joyce, Margaret Kettles, Nicole Kleiman-Moran, Lyndsay Lyda, Miranda Mammen, Caragh Nimmo, Regina Powers, Morgan Pullan, Tallis Radwick, and Jay Trujillo. Several research assistants contributed to the research and editing of this book. I give a heartfelt thank-you to Leah Travis, Jack Hodge, Alan Bickings, David Wilner, Chelsea Lauwereins, Tallis Radwick, and Whitney House. Emma Johnston provided me with skillful assistance and was a terrific conversant and sounding board. Undoubtedly, one of the most important people at the revising stage was Ariane Frosh. Her knowledge of contemporary feminism runs deep, and her enthusiasm for the project was palpable.

Finally, Brett Fisher and Misa Fisher-Gruber are the foundation upon which this project—indeed all my life's projects—stand. They bore the weight of my all-nighters, deadline stress, and self-doubt. Brett, we went through so much, and I could never have done this without your succor and love. I need to tell you that more often. Misa, to answer your question: Yes, there will be a time when Mommy isn't always typing and the book is finished. That time, my love, is now.

Introduction

When I was a law student and an aspiring criminal lawyer, I always felt mired in a feminist defense attorney dilemma. On the one hand, I was intimately familiar with the harms of sexual assault and firmly believed that gender crimes reflected and reinforced women's second-class status. On the other, I was involved in public defense and anti-incarceration work and had come to regard the prison as a primary site of violence, racism, and degradation in society. I faithfully studied and trained to represent indigent defendants against the awesome power of the state, but I did so with a nagging sense of dread at the prospect of defending batterers and rapists.[1]

That sense quickly abated after I became a public defender and witnessed firsthand the prosecutorial machine processing domestic violence (DV) and sexual assault cases. I felt a sense of disillusionment that the feminist movement I so admired played such a distinct role in broadening and legitimizing the unconscionable penal state. As an academic, I was increasingly concerned that women's criminal law activism had not made prosecution and punishment more feminist. It had made feminism more prosecutorial and punitive. Cases like the following involving my client Jamal and his girlfriend Britney made me lose faith in the possibility of feminist criminal "justice." Subsequently, I continued to dread defending batterers, but I did so for other reasons completely.

JAMAL AND BRITNEY

It is the year 2000.[2] I am a junior public defender in Washington, D.C., standing in the early morning courthouse, already buzzing with activity.

Uniformed D.C. metro police lounge in groups, swapping stories and laughing among the grim-faced, confused defendants and their wide-eyed children. Inscrutable US marshals with military crew cuts enter courtrooms, accompanied by young, gray-suited prosecutors. I wait for my client Jamal, who at nineteen is childlike to me, with his teen Disney-show face, neatly done-up plats, and cool Nike kicks. Because of his immature penchant for missing appointments, I have given him my home number—he is the only client who has ever gotten that number. Years later, I will entertain a hazy memory of his 4:00 a.m. call to say, "What's up," just as I will have ephemeral recollections of the bright orange plastic chairs lining the D.C. Superior Court hallway and the smell of late-night sweat in the holding cells. Yes, Jamal will stick out in my mind, but not because his case is particularly outrageous or quirky. Jamal's case is notable for its similarity to so many run-of-the-mill domestic violence cases that do not make headlines.

I am at the courthouse for the civil protection order (CPO) portion of Jamal's case. Jamal was arrested ten days earlier after his eighteen-year-old girlfriend Britney reported that he punched her and threw a plate at her. Prosecutors have lately adopted the tactic of subpoenaing DV defendants to testify at these quasi-civil hearings, without notice to their attorneys. Much can be at stake with a CPO, such as loss of one's home, expansive stay-away restrictions, alcohol abstention, and loss of parental rights for up to two years. Defendants often attend the hearings unrepresented, and if they refuse to testify there, judges summarily issue the onerous CPOs. Worse, some defendants take the stand and subject themselves to rigorous cross-examination, without ever consulting an attorney or understanding their right to remain silent. I am here to make sure that does not happen to Jamal.[3]

A few minutes before we enter the courtroom, Britney shuffles up. She is equally cute and colorful, squeezed into stretch jeans, with platform flip-flops, and yellow shoulder-length braids. She asks if I am Jamal's attorney, and I reply in the affirmative. She says, "The other lady told me I have to be here, but I didn't want to come." She goes on to explain that she and Jamal live together with their baby in a project called Lincoln Heights—a place, incidentally, where a young man like Jamal is lucky to make it to age nineteen without a severe criminal record or drug habit. Britney tells me that she called the police only because "I was mad and wanted him out of the house." Even if Britney preferred the police not to arrest, police had to do so under D.C.'s mandatory arrest law.[4] Britney explains that she does not want to pursue charges and will not comply with a no-contact order. Then, in a more hushed tone, she asks, "What if I just leave and stay gone—will they drop the case?"

So here I am, straddling the line between zealous advocacy and obstruction of justice. The answer to Britney's question is likely "yes," given that judges routinely dismiss cases when victims fail to appear on the trial date. By this point in my life as a public defender, I am used to DV victims asking what will happen to their boyfriends in court, how they can spare them from jail, and the like. I could give Britney a realistic assessment of the DV court process, but I hesitate, recalling with distaste the time in law school a fellow defense clinic student advised his DV client and girlfriend to marry so that she could assert marital privilege and avoid testifying. I say, "I can't tell you what to do," but also mention that I can take her statement.

Just as I am finishing my sentence, a young woman rushes up and inserts herself between Jamal, Britney, and me. She is blonde, no more than twenty-four, with a hip haircut and an enormous diamond engagement ring. "Domestic violence clinic student," I think to myself. She demands, "What are you doing talking to *my* victim, and why is your defendant near her? He's violating the no-contact order!" From the DV advocates' perspective, defense attorneys are extensions of abusive men, there to intimidate and coerce victims into lying or disappearing. I tell the advocate that Britney approached us to say that she wants to drop the case and stay with Jamal. The advocate replies, "I'm *sure* she told you that."

Britney turns to the woman and protests, "I don't want to be here, and she (pointing to me) said I could leave." Yikes. I am thinking about a recent hubbub where a well-known defense attorney was frog-marched through the courthouse in handcuffs, accused of obstruction of justice for attempting to take a statement from a reticent sexual assault complainant. "No, I told her that I could not give any advice," I reply defensively, "but as you can see, she does not want to pursue this case." The advocate snaps, "We'll see about that. Come on, Britney we need to talk, away from *them*." With that, she leads Britney away through the sea of humanity gathered in the bustling hall. Ten minutes later, we are all seated at counsel table. I listen as the judge orders a renewable one-year CPO, including requirements that Jamal leave the apartment and have no contact with Britney or the baby. Britney keeps her eyes locked on the table below.

I never get to take the statement, but the day before Jamal's criminal trial Britney calls to say she is not coming. She says she tried to tell the "domestic violence lady" to drop the case but could not reach her. True to her word,

Britney is a no-show. Instead of moving to dismiss the case, however, the prosecutor says he is prepared to go forward on hearsay, specifically, Britney's initial "excited utterances" to the police (a tactic generally regarded as unconstitutional after a 2004 Supreme Court decision).[5] Jamal decides not to risk a jail sentence and agrees to a guilty plea and deferred sentencing. In D.C., first-time DV offenders can plead guilty to assault and have the sentencing hearing postponed for several months, during which they must pay fines, go on probation, and complete "rehabilitative" programs. If the defendant satisfies conditions and stays out of trouble, the case is dismissed. If he does not, he is immediately sentenced on the DV conviction. The judge defers Jamal's sentencing for nine months, prescribing conditions including twenty-seven domestic violence classes and ten anger management classes, at eight dollars a pop.[6]

A month later, I receive notice that Jamal has violated the terms of his probation. Apparently, Jamal was turned away from several of the mandated classes because he could not pay. We go to court, where the judge finds Jamal in violation, enters the DV conviction, and sentences Jamal to one hundred days in jail. Jamal serves his time, while Britney struggles to pay for the apartment and baby by herself. (They never did comply with the no-contact order.) Jamal moves home after his release, but the couple eventually lose their eligibility for public housing because of Jamal's conviction. That conviction will be the first of several over the next couple of years, none for domestic violence. As for Britney, the last I hear, she is moving from place to place—and still with Jamal.

There is much to say about Jamal's case and the feminist laws and policies that govern it. For now, I want to emphasize one particularly salient characteristic of the case: it is representative. Jamal is not a falsely accused victim of a biased system, and in fact, he likely did assault Britney. Britney is neither a liar nor a serially tortured battered wife, but a woman constrained by her race, gender, and circumstances to a less-than-ideal relationship. This is not a story of heroes and villains.

The characterology of Jamal's story is thus unusual in feminist storytelling. Popular feminist commentary on subjects like rape and trafficking often meticulously detail horrific cases of brutality and the utter trauma of victims. The focus on spectacular violence that "speaks for itself" also underlies the common feminist sensibility that injustice lies in the state's failure to adequately punish male offenders. However, simplistic cases of particularly brutal but easily avoidable gender violence are the exception. Crime-and-feminism cases are like Jamal and Britney's. They live in the interstices, in the spaces where the ideas of gender equality and social justice must constantly be reimagined and readjusted.

When compared to evocative stories of women's torture and death, Britney and Jamal's tale appears mundane. She was not injured; he faced a misdemeanor charge. But make no mistake. Britney, Jamal, and their baby suffered brutality—the brutal conditions of entrenched poverty, racial inequality, homelessness, and despair. Britney had called upon the police for aid in her domestic dispute with no clue of the unstoppable penal machine she would trigger. Jamal's criminal contacts put him in constant peril of incarceration and fomented his *civiliter mortuus*, his civil death. This is an American tragedy, representative of many cases touched by feminist reform. This is feminism's tragedy.

As a feminist, woman of color, defense attorney, and survivor, I have personally and professionally grappled with the issue of feminism's influence on criminal law for decades. With this book, I hope to engage the new generation of energized feminists. This group of contemporary thinkers, ranging from generation-Z students to younger millennials, entered adulthood during and after the media preoccupation with campus rape in the early 2010s. For clarity's sake, I will call this group "millennial feminists" and their views "millennial feminism." Millennial feminists came of age in an era of political engagement, sexual liberation, and mass incarceration and thus harbor a fresh perspective on DV and sexual assault. Millennial feminism exists, as I once did, in an uncomfortable equilibrium of distaste for gender crimes *and* punishments. On one side of the scale is a Black Lives Matter–informed belief that policing, prosecution, and incarceration are racist, unjust, and too widespread. This side abhors the practice of putting human bodies in cages. On the other is a #MeToo–informed preoccupation with men's out-of-control sexuality and abuse of power. This side wants to get tough.

The puzzling result is that, today, those most vocal about prison reform are also often the most punitive about gendered offenses, even minor ones like over-the-clothes sexual contact. Despite a burgeoning political consensus that the US incarcerates too many people, uses criminal law as the solution to too many problems, and maintains horrific prison conditions, feminists continue to champion novel penal laws and expanded carceral regimes to address the gender issues that appear on their radars. Invoking "sexual predators," or even mentioning the name Harvey Weinstein or Brock Turner, stops conversations about eliminating pretrial detention, lowering sentences, and abolishing the inhumane sex offender registration system. Despite the vocal chorus against mandatory minimum prison sentences, in 2016, California enacted new mandatory minimums for sex offenses, and in 2017, Iowa enacted new mandatory minimums for domestic violence offenses.[7] One is left to wonder how feminism became a legitimator of penality in an era of declining faith in criminal punishment. How did the feminist antiviolence agenda become so tethered to the tough-on-crime position? How come gender crime gets a carve-out from or even veto over criminal justice reform?

This book analyzes complicated stories of feminist advocacy and penal reform in an effort to explain how we got here and suggest how we can do better. In past decades, feminists were rightly concerned about gender violence, and they made philosophical and strategic choices about how to address it. These were hard choices. They were contested choices. They were choices under conditions of uncertainty, political pressure, and cultural change. But it becomes clear that powerful feminist subgroups repeatedly chose criminal law. Their reform agendas expanded police and prosecutorial power, emphasized criminals' threat to vulnerable women, diverted scarce resources to law enforcement, and ultimately made many feminists soldiers in the late twentieth-century war on crime. The chapters that follow reveal just how much feminism shaped the modern criminal system and how much participation in the criminal system shaped modern feminism.

Let me clarify that the term *feminism,* like *liberalism, Marxism,* or *Christianity,* denotes a blanket category with numerous permutations, many of which I discuss as the book proceeds. Contemporary discourse often presumes that feminism is a unitary concept and that all feminists have similar core beliefs. For men on the far right, feminists are "#MeToo man-hating morons"—or so said an online comment about me after I wrote an op-ed on the Kavanaugh hearings.[8] For many millennials and gen-Z'ers, feminism is likewise a straightforward proposition—it is about preventing and punishing men's bad sexual and intimate behavior. Most schools of feminism share the basic tenet that a person who belongs to the category "woman," whether by biology or social construction, is vulnerable to unique discrimination that the law should remedy. However, feminist theory and practice have always been heterodox, encompassing a range of ideas about gender, biology, equality, state power, and economic distribution.

Certainly, not all feminist theories invoke or support criminal law, and not all those who favor unrestrained prosecution of gender crime are feminists. In the 1970s, as the battered women's and antirape movements grew, different feminists with different commitments vied for control of the narrative and agenda. Some feminists prioritized formal equality, while others sought radical substantive justice. Some abhorred domesticity, while others celebrated motherhood. Some saw sexuality as a tool of patriarchy, while others regarded sex as radically liberating. Some feminists allied with state authorities, and indeed, some *were* state authorities. Others regarded the state as something to be rapidly torn down. In many ways, the feminist war on crime is a feminist civil war.

Throughout the 1980s and '90s, powerful feminist groups identified lax policing of abusers and rapists as *the* gender justice issue, and feminism rapidly became "carceral," meaning incarceration-centric. Sociologist Elizabeth Bernstein coined the term *carceral feminism* in 2007 to describe late twentieth-century feminism's commitment to law and order and "drift from the welfare state to the carceral state as the enforcement apparatus for feminist goals."[9] There were, to be sure, dissenting voices expressing alarm at feminism's carceral drift, but they were muted by law-and-order messages from within and outside feminism. By the close of the millennium, the stalwart suit-wearing SVU prosecutor who throws the book at rapists had replaced the bra-burner as the symbol of women's empowerment.

Then, around 2010, something profound happened. Enough evidence amassed to produce a liberal consensus that US mass incarceration is one of the great human rights tragedies of our time. National and international human rights groups decried the inhumane conditions of US prisons, now significantly maintained by for-profit corporations. The Supreme Court even weighed in, excoriating California for the conditions of its overcrowded prisons in the 2011 case *Brown v. Plata*.[10] The Black Lives Matter movement and books like *The New Jim Crow* did much to publicize the endemically racialized nature of policing, prosecution, and punishment.[11] Although there was and remains public appetite for political law-and-order talk, the war on crime is not the bipartisan issue it once was. "Criminal justice reform" to soften the system's sharp edges has become a uniting political issue. Liberals see decarceration as a humanitarian mandate, and conservatives view it within the frames of fiscal responsibility and liberty.[12]

In the 2010s, feminists increasingly questioned the movement's historical embrace of criminal law. People listened when black feminist scholar Beth Richie argued that feminist criminal law reform helped create the "prison nation" that renders poor women of color particularly vulnerable to violence.[13]

Rape reformers began to describe prison not as a solution to but as a *site of* sexual violence. Victims' advocates started to reconsider the dogma that harsh criminal punishment is invariably good for all victims. Professor and advocate Leigh Goodmark argued that the incarceration-separation model of DV reform reflects an "essentialist" construction of the victim as a helpless, middle-class woman, who necessarily benefits from state criminal intervention. The model therefore often disserves poor women of color.[14]

However, the 2010s also brought prolific media coverage of a campus rape epidemic. Female college students hoisted their mattresses in symbolic protest of rape, showing the weight rape puts on victims' shoulders. Students agitated for reforms to campus rules and regulations to prevent and remedy student sexual assault.[15] Protest rhetoric veered toward the punitive— punishing and exposing "serial rapists." Still, many student activists did not want their fervor for campus reforms to put more people in jail. As society's outrage over sexual assault grew, the question became whether millennial anti-incarceration sentiments could still steer law and policy makers away from the tempting solution of broadened criminalization.

And then the #MeToo tsunami washed over social media in 2017. By this time, the feminist protest movement initiated during the campus rape crisis had already grown exponentially in the wake of the election of Donald Trump, "groper-in-chief." The public soon became entranced by the twenty-four-hour news cycle coverage of #MeToo's "national reckoning," lauded by the press as America's "cultural revolution." #MeToo's messages are broad, diverse, and often conflicting. For many, the movement is about employment justice and workplace sexual harassment. For some, it is diffuse support for women's political and social empowerment. However, much of #MeToo discourse is punitive and carceral. The movement arose in the wake of explosive reports of movie mogul Harvey Weinstein's predatory abuse of Hollywood's brightest female stars, and one of its functions has been to label his and other powerful men's misconduct as "real" rape.[16] #MeToo called on women to show solidarity through confessing sexual victimhood, and they did so by publicizing a range of experiences from the extreme (violent rape) to the seemingly mundane (wolf-whistling, overenthusiastic hugging).

As the #MeToo media storm over women's sexual victimization reached a fever pitch, feminism literally came into fashion. The 2017 Dior Spring show featured $700 "We should all be feminists" T-shirts.[17] Magazines such as *Teen Vogue*, once devoted to prettiness and proms, now extensively cover politics and protest.[18] That pop culture purveyors have replaced articles on how to court a man with stories about how to bring a man to court is impressive and in ways positive. There are, however, real dangers of this reclamation of female political identity in a time of fear and anger around sex crimes. The #MeToo era reinvigorated the declining feminist inclination to fight sexism through strict law enforcement. "Zero tolerance"—more unforgiving than intolerance—resurfaced as women's political rallying cry.[19]

To be sure, it is natural, even instinctive, to advocate more criminal enforcement in the face of rape crisis statistics and stories of abuser impunity. There is a deeply ingrained American punitive impulse, originating from the media and government's relentless focus on horrific criminality, that leads even progressive incarceration critics to advocate for strict prosecution of those whom they see as the worst of the worst (corporate CEOs, white supremacists).[20] However, in the rush to punish bad apples, real and imagined, we tend to forget that the criminal system is culturally ordered, technocratic, and beholden to specific political forces. Feminist criminal law reforms have always operated within the context of larger social phenomena, from slavery to sex panics.

Historians and critical race theorists have shown in exacting detail "the centrality of race to the political history of rape," as historian Estelle Freedman put it.[21] Chapter 1 of this book recounts how rape law and policy enabled a lynching epidemic in the post–Civil War South. This race-rape connection persists. Candidate Donald Trump launched his campaign with racialized rape fearmongering, declaring that Mexicans immigrants were rapists and promising to protect American women with a wall. Later, he justified his administration's horrific treatment of asylum seekers as deterrence of migrant caravans, where women were "raped at levels that nobody has ever seen before."[22] Zero tolerance necessarily occurs against the backdrop of rape law's racist past and present.

Many #MeToo devotees know that the US penal system is a site of racial and socioeconomic inequality. Nonetheless, in the zeal to fight sexual misconduct, millennial feminists abandon their liberal (in the double sense of "progressive" and "respecting individual rights") commitments. Their Bernie Sanders, AOC-style commitment to labor rights, for example, becomes a casualty in the battle against sexual harassment. In the avalanche of op-eds on #MeToo, one remains in the forefront of my consciousness. The *New York Times* published a piece by Elizabeth Nolan Brown, founder of "Feminists for Liberty," about the November 2017 ouster of newsman Matt Lauer for sexual harassment.[23] It asserts that corporate managers are particularly adept at handling sexual misconduct because they can summarily terminate employees in response to public pressure. #MeToo is thus an argument for *capitalism:* "The modern American capitalist system ... has delivered social justice more swiftly and effectively than supposedly more enlightened public bodies tend to. As we observe and adjust to the sociosexual storm we're all in, let's appreciate the powers and paradigms making it possible: feminism, but also free markets."[24]

If past is prologue, there are costs to getting caught up in #MeToo's heady solidaristic moment—in the pleasure of a reckoning that inflicts pain on male oppressors. In the shadow of this cathartic letting, policy is forming, political players are adapting, and strange bedfellows are forming coalitions. Although feminists imagine that expanding punishment and contracting due process will get at the untouchable power brokers who appear immune from law, the distributional reality is not so neat. Rich and powerful men have the corrupt influence to evade even toughened laws, placing the burden of increased criminalization on the poor minorities who form the policed segment of the population. Today, many feminists regret that feminist law-and-order policies contributed to a carceral regime that disserves marginalized people, including women.

#MeToo in fact originally had little to do with law enforcement and was part of a grassroots program to aid women. In 2006, Tarana Burke quietly started the "'me too' movement" as part of her social service program Just Be, Inc., which "focused on the health, well-being and wholeness of young women of color."[25] Remarking that the "me too" mantra "started in the deepest, darkest place in my soul," Burke recounts an emotional conversation with a girl at a youth camp who confided that she had been sexually abused by her stepfather: "I could not find the strength to say out loud the words that were ringing in my head over and over again as she tried to tell me what she had endured. I watched her put her mask back on and go back into the world like she was all alone and I couldn't even bring myself to whisper ... me too."[26]

Ten years later, the Weinstein story broke in a *New Yorker* article by Ronan Farrow, himself the scion of Hollywood royalty embroiled in sexual assault controversy.[27] Public thirst for stories about Harvey's latest outrage proved insatiate, and the Twitterverse lit up with righteous condemnation of his abusiveness and of his perversity. Within this milieu, television star Alyssa Milano tweeted out her own "me too" message. It had a different, more empirical purpose: "If all the women who have been sexually harassed or assaulted wrote 'Me too.' as a status, we might give people a sense of the magnitude of the problem."[28] This simple message connected idiosyncratic acts of Hollywood degradation among the most privileged to the experiences of every woman, transforming clickbait into a feminist political movement.

The tweet created a sense that sexual assault is utterly omnipresent. The first three responses to Milano's tweet included two revelations of child molestation and this: "Standing in a line for food when a man took unwanted pictures of my chest. I was shocked."[29] Both types of conduct are objectionable, but they are extremely different. Attempts to differentiate among the credibility of allegations, the nature of the conduct described, or the historical context in which incidents occurred were shot down as victim-blaming, rape-culture arguments. Actor Matt Damon, who had a history of tone-deaf comments, made a reasonable #MeToo remark: "There's a difference between patting someone on the butt and rape or child molestation. Both of those behaviors need to be confronted and eradicated without question, but they shouldn't be conflated."[30] The comments were promptly met with social media disgust, and he was scolded to keep his Damonsplaining mouth shut. Former girlfriend Minnie Driver elaborated, "The time right now is for men just to listen and not have an opinion."[31] A chastened Damon made a vow to "get in the back seat and close my mouth for a while."[32]

Lost in this girl-versus-boy celeb fracas was Burke's original intention to support the invisible, resource-less survivors. Also lost was Burke herself—Milano was initially credited for the catchphrase. Upset women of color on Twitter had to "out" Burke as the originator. Burke eventually responded, "In this instance, the celebrities who popularized the hashtag didn't take a moment to see if there was work already being done [and] sisters still managed to get diminished or erased."[33] Burke's hope that the public would focus on the work already being done on behalf of vulnerable women was in vain. The public's appetite was still for salacious stories of rich and famous men tormenting their female (and male) ingénues. It showed little interest in women-of-color survivors who faced obstacles caused by entrenched racial discrimination and socioeconomic marginalization.

One by one the famous men fell. Accusations against them ranged from forcible rape to "creepy" behavior. Some accusations were anonymous, and some involved half-century-old events, but all were reported in titillating, repulsive detail. That men received discipline without due process gave women little pause. After all, many were public figures with plenty of money to cushion a demotion or termination. #MeToo supporters remained resolute as progressive darling Senator Al Franken resigned in December 2017, even though the accusations against him had the whiff of partisan opposition research and involved misconduct a universe apart from Weinstein's. Some Democrats protested that instead of bringing needed perspective, progressives had made a political calculation to eat their own to maintain a useless moral high ground against Republicans, who would just write off allegations against conservative politicians as fake news. Meanwhile, a single accusation was enough for liberals to condemn their political heroes and artistic icons.[34]

And then came the Aziz Ansari story.

"GRACE" AND AZIZ

The story appeared on Babe.net, a Rupert Murdoch–funded news-tabloid website dedicated to "girls who don't give a fuck" and "the pettiest celebrity drama."[35] The site prides itself on its young staff—the average age is twenty-three and no reporter is over twenty-five—one of whom, Katie Way, broke the Ansari story.[36] Way, the author of such classics as "Here's What Your Go-To Drunk Food Says about What Kind of Hoe You Are," describes in chair-squirming and ineloquent detail a sexual encounter between Ansari and twenty-two-year-old photographer "Grace." The upshot of the story is that Ansari "violated" Grace by engaging in sexual contact despite her "verbal and non-verbal cues to indicate how uncomfortable and distressed she was."[37]

The story, as told by Grace only, begins with her excitement at dating a celebrity and her hope that Ansari would be like his TV persona. The dinner itself was unremarkable. It is what happened afterward that Way considered newsworthy. The couple retired to Ansari's house, where they started making out and undressing. When Ansari went to get a condom, Grace said, "Whoa, let's relax for a sec, let's chill." They went back to kissing and then engaged in various sexual activities, which Grace claimed followed her attempts to "move away from him." Grace told Ansari, "I don't want to feel forced because then I'll hate you, and I'd rather not hate you." He replied, "Oh, of course, it's only fun if we're both having fun." Grace, satisfied with the response, watched TV with Ansari, hoping "he might rub her back or play with her hair." Instead, Grace recounts, "He sat back and pointed to his penis and motioned for me to go down on him. And I did. I think I just felt really pressured." The foreplay escalated toward intercourse until Grace stated, "I really don't think I'm going to do this," and Ansari replied, "How about we just chill, but this time with our clothes on." They did. Eventually, Grace decided to leave, at which time Ansari hugged her and gave her a "gross" "aggressive" good-bye kiss. "I cried the whole ride home," Grace laments.[38]

The day after the sexual encounter, Grace "reached out to her friends, who helped her craft a message to tell Ansari how she felt about the date." It admonished Ansari for ignoring Grace's "clear non-verbal cues" and expression to "slow it down." The following day, Ansari sent a text to Grace saying he enjoyed meeting her, which was met with Grace's carefully crafted message. Ansari responded, "I'm so sad to hear this. All I can say is, it would never be my intention to make you or anyone feel the way you described. Clearly, I misread things in the moment and I'm truly sorry."[39]

The article unleashed a tempest of controversy. Some in the media took the article not so much as a criminal indictment of Ansari (though it accused him of "sexual assault") as a comment on the woeful state of "normal" sexual encounters.[40] Others like journalist Caitlin Flanagan advanced a racial critique. She declared the Babe article "3,000 words of revenge porn" and mused, "I thought it would take a little longer for the hit squad of privileged young white women to open fire on brown-skinned men."[41] Perhaps the most forceful critique came from HLN anchor Ashleigh Banfield, a vocal #MeToo cheerleader. Banfield objected that Grace's characterization of botched sex as assault served to undermine the seriousness of rape and threaten the #MeToo movement. With her signature glare, Banfield looked into the camera and spoke directly to Grace: "You had an unpleasant date. And you didn't leave. That is on you. And all the gains that have been achieved on your behalf and mine are now being compromised by allegations that are reckless and hollow." She concluded, "The only sentence [Ansari] deserves is a bad case of blue balls, not a Hollywood blackball."[42]

HLN invited author Katie Way to be a guest on the network, but she declined through an invective-laden email, which Banfield read on air: "The way your colleague Ashleigh (?), someone I'm certain no one under the age of 45 has ever heard of, by the way, ripped into my source directly was one of the lowest, most despicable things I've ever seen in my entire life. Shame on her. Shame on HLN. I hope the [ratings] made that burgundy lipstick, bad highlights, second-wave feminist has-been feel really relevant for a little while."[43] Way's screed then took a Trumpian turn: "No woman my age would ever watch your network. And I will laugh the day you fold."[44]

Banfield warned that labeling as rape this "bad date" where Grace "could have left" and wanted Ansari to be a "mind reader" would make feminists look ridiculous. Critics were indeed shocked at the suggestion that Ansari's persistence was coercion and that he had to ensure Grace's enthusiastic participation. They failed to realize the ship had sailed long ago.

During the media storm over campus rape, the national rallying cry was "Only yes means yes." Senator Kirsten Gillibrand, who built her political brand during the campus rape crisis, dismissed the Banfield-style "bad date" claim in 2014. Accused students, she said, "are not dates gone bad, or a good guy who had too much to drink," but "repeat offenders" who should be "facing a prosecutor and a jail cell."[45] College codes already specified that verbal persistence can be "coercion." One administrator averred that asking more than *once* can be coercive.[46] Moreover, by the time of the Ansari story, the "Yes means yes" message, also known as "affirmative consent," had been absorbed into university policy and criminal law. Affirmative consent's express purpose is to intervene in Ansari-like scenarios by creating a determinate method of attributing responsibility for miscommunication. To determine whether it was rape when she says she didn't want sex and he says he thought she did, just look for the "yes" (or its functional equivalent). Even sexual assault laws without an affirmative consent component do not require victims to say "no" or leave, as Banfield indicated.[47]

This is all to say that the text of many current sexual assault statutes makes what Grace said Ansari did a *crime*. Feminists criminal law scholars routinely argue that police and prosecutors should enforce affirmative consent laws to the letter, always believe victims, and refrain from weeding out cases before trial. Unlike a celebrity, the poor men of color who come within the purview of this aggressive prosecution of overbroad rape laws will not garner Banfield-style public support. Ansari faced a career hitch, but these men, as Gillibrand demanded, will face a jail cell.

Some critics attribute the seismic shifts in sexual assault law and policy to public fascination with the sexuality of "privileged young white women." In turn, they argue, young (white) feminists have embraced a neopuritanical stance toward sex, revoking the previous generation's support for sexual liberation.[48] To be sure, there is a sense that gen-Z women think that sartorially challenged, poorly coiffed, "boomer" feminists-of-a-certain-age should keep their outdated sexual liberation to themselves. They should leave it to the younger generation to decide whether workplaces need to be "sanitized" of sexuality,[49] whether sexual communication should be managed by apps, and how to understand the current "sex recession." However, puritanism does not really capture the phenomenon. Babe.net prides itself on its irreverence toward sexual mores. Millennial feminists participate in "slut walks," and, at the same time, call the actual commercial sex engaged in by marginalized women "modern-day slavery."

This reasoning on sexuality can appear incoherent or alternatively female supremacist, delegating to men the criminal risks of casual, misguided, or subversive sex. I see it differently. The tension between over-the-top sexuality and intolerance for imperfect sex reflects contemporary feminists' *struggle* to embrace sexual liberation while simultaneously critiquing a hazardous sexual terrain where the burdens of open sexuality fall disproportionately on women. Unfortunately, the existing criminal law discourse of devastating victimhood, righteous indignation, and punishment as "justice" provides a ready-made vocabulary for women's unease with the disparate nature of sexual liberation. The existing criminal system provides a ready-made remedy in the form of prosecution, conviction, and prison. Condemnation of men's newly branded criminal conduct and calls for just deserts multiply on social media until feminists' thoughtful efforts to grapple with a complex issue appear as little more than pitchfork-bearing vengeance, demonstrating that #MeToo has lost its way.

Millennial feminists can yet articulate their complex beliefs about gender, sex, and violence outside of the criminal law framework. They need not adopt the refrain of some earlier feminists that sex is mostly something that heterosexual cisgender men weaponize to subordinate heterosexual cisgender women. They need not view policing, prosecution, and punishment as the most promising avenue toward gender equality. However, without an alternative, the criminal law discourse of evil men versus vulnerable women thrives, albeit uneasily, among this generation steeped in pluralism and keenly attuned to the complexities of gender, sex, and social power.

This book seeks to provide an alternative by offering a framework for protesting gender violence without the individualist and punitive logic of criminal law. It sketches a path for moving past the current banality of simply protesting men's evil. The book examines historical feminist reform efforts to show that the connection between the feminist antiviolence agenda and incarceration is not natural, inevitable, or desirable. To be clear, the point is not to criticize feminism as inherently punitive or, alternatively, to defend its role in mass incarceration as mere co-optation, but to diagnose. The chapters identify internal and external factors that entangled feminism with mass incarceration. Some of the punitive outcomes were intended, and some were not. Some programs were co-opted, and some were not. The following chapters tell a rich story of feminists' simultaneous participation in and resistance to institutions of power and show how their reforms exacerbated larger inequalities even as they produced gender justice in individual cases.

Before proceeding to the format of the book, let me add a caveat. Much of its language presumes the gender binary, male and female. Throughout, I generically refer to abusers and rapists as "he" and victims as "she." This is not to signal that gender and sex are biologically determined, that women cannot engage in violence and men cannot suffer it, or that same-sex violence is trivial. To the contrary, I hope this book will illuminate the dark side of feminism's tendency to adopt "man-versus-women" as a given, characterize violence as a product of individual men, and account poorly for intersecting identities. The language is gendered because feminists, throughout time, have viewed domestic violence and rape as a matter of *women's* inequality. It would be confusing, if not impossible, to discuss feminism's contribution to criminal law using gender-neutral pronouns. There are innumerable linguistic choices I have made for clarity and flow, and to keep within the language of a discussion (e.g., *victim* versus *alleged victim* or *survivor, domestic violence* versus *intimate partner violence, prostitute* versus *sex worker*). These choices are not intended to be substantive, and I use terms even as I critique them.[50]

The chapters are organized roughly chronologically. Chapter 1 discusses early feminist ("first-wave") efforts to fight rape and domestic violence. These efforts took place over decades, beginning in the antebellum period and extending into the Progressive Era, and include the prohibition and purity movements, age-of-consent reforms, and the white slavery crusade. Much of this reform occurred as southern states invoked antirape law and policy as the primary ground for killing blacks at wartime levels. Chapter 2 moves forward to the 1960s and the dawn of the "second wave" of feminism. It details how radical '60s feminism departed from its antiauthoritarian, antiracist roots to ally with "the Man" in fighting DV. "Antipatriarchy" feminists successfully battled antipoverty activists for control of the narrative, characterizing DV as a phenomenon of sexist men emboldened by weak laws rather than one of economic inequality and racism. Chapter 3 highlights a particularly influential group of feminists, "legal feminists," who in the late 1970s reconceptualized battered women's interests as a right to the arrest of batterers. They successfully litigated for pro- and mandatory arrest policies and defended those policies in the face of evidence of their criminogenic and racially disparate effects. In the process, feminist activism transformed policing.

Chapter 4 moves into the eighties and discusses a narrative shared by feminists and conservative crime control enthusiasts involving innocent white female victims brutalized by monstrous offenders. It examines how feminist activism on DV and rape influenced and, in turn, was influenced by an increasingly punitive victims' rights movement. Chapter 5 details feminists' efforts in the '80s and '90s to configure "date rape" as "real rape." In doing so, they systematically expanded the list of sexual behaviors labeled rape and narrowed procedural protections for accused sex offenders, within a system that was increasingly draconian because of a panic over "predators." The last two chapters are situated in contemporary times and work through some of the tensions within millennial feminism highlighted above. They examine the grassroots and bureaucratic feminist efforts spawned by the campus rape crisis and highlight the danger that, despite millennial feminists' distaste for mass incarceration, their outrage against campus predators and endorsement of "crime logic" will not be confined to campus and will have carceral consequences.[51]

At times, the chapters read like a brief against feminism. But as a feminist myself, I too believe that the movement, in the long arc of history, has been a force for good. Nevertheless, this is my argument—perhaps manifesto—on how feminism has shaped and has been shaped by the penal state, and how it can do better. The stories of the many feminists who labored for gender justice completely outside of the criminal system, while extremely important, are not this story. This book is also not meant as an exhaustive history, and it inevitably leaves out many stories, individuals, and facts. I have highlighted the chronicles, connections, and claims that add up to a billboard-sized "proceed with caution" sign.

I conclude by suggesting a "neofeminist"—as opposed to post- or non-feminist—approach to gender harm and violence. This approach holds that sexual misconduct and battering constitute pressing social problems that reflect and reinforce women's subordination and concedes that offenders' impunity exacts a social price. At the same time, neofeminism is acutely conscious that criminal law causes real injuries and views feminist participation in the penal system with a jaundiced eye. It is also mindful that gender is one of multiple intersecting sites of hierarchy, along with class, race, and economic status. Methodologically, neofeminism involves a "distributional" approach to law reform. Feminists all too often adopt backward-looking justifications, rehashing the details of the horrible crimes that provoked their reform efforts instead of looking ahead to how the laws will operate in the world as it exists: a world of racialized overpolicing and overimprisonment. Thus I propose the following as a basic tenet of modern feminist thought: Criminal law is a last, not first, resort.

These neofeminist principles and methodologies provide some guideposts to modern women's movements. Feminists should not propose new substantive offenses or higher sentences for existing gender crimes. Feminists should oppose mandatory arrest, prosecution, and incarceration. Feminists should ensure a strict line between college discipline and criminal sanction. Feminists should support sexuality education over sexual assault fearmongering. Feminists should stop characterizing violence as a function of evil men rather than social decay. Feminists should expend their capital on reforms that provide material aid to the women most vulnerable to violence. Feminists should topple powerful abusers through political action, not through allying with criminal authority that disproportionately harms the disempowered.

The following chapters pose many hard questions and provide no easy answers. Instead, they offer a theoretical, legal, and rhetorical tool kit to enable those concerned about DV and rape to thoughtfully engage the tough issues. I hope the book will free feminists to imagine new approaches to gender violence. I hope it will free criminal justice reformers and policy makers from the fear of offending an imagined carceral feminist sensibility and will remove one more barrier on the long road to unmaking mass incarceration. I hope it will help shift the winds so that feminism sails in the direction of greater justice, not only for women.

ONE

The Opening Battle

FIGHTING PATRIARCHY WITH PURITY

The battle against sexual and gender-based misconduct is the feminist fight du jour, and it feels thoroughly modern. In recent years sexual misconduct has monopolized the attention of media, lawmakers, feminist theorists, and bloggers. Unsurprisingly, contemporary law reformers are biased to overvalue present efforts, believing that these will *finally* address long-existing social ills that were never sufficiently tackled. They characterize reform as the overdue fix to persistent problems rather than the latest factor in a complicated drunkard's walk of colliding rules, cultural changes, political reactions, and social evolutions and devolutions. Rape exists as a national emergency now, feminists assert, because our sexist society historically tolerated it and past antirape efforts were feckless or failed. Domestic violence (DV) persists because criminal assault law never garnered the strength to counter the eighteenth-century legal principles of "coverture" (married women abdicate legal rights to their husbands) and "chastisement" (husbands have license to physically discipline wives).[1]

The simplistic telling of American DV and rape law history as one of underenforcement, that is, the failure of law and legal actors to appropriately penalize male offenders, prefigures a common modern sensibility that feminists must always support stricter policing, prosecution, and punishment of gender crimes. History, however, is not so neat and not so linear. Past sexist norms and patriarchal laws permitted and *punished* sexual and domestic misconduct, depending on the context. Rape law's past is one of *selective* enforcement, including overenforcement, depending on the gender, marital status, class, and race of those involved in the sexual encounter. Accordingly, as historian Marybeth Hamilton Arnold cautions, "A feminist politics that sees sex throughout history as simply a force for women's exploitation is a dangerously simplistic politics."[2]

Another frequent presumption is that gender crime persists because past feminist efforts to strengthen criminal law were few, feeble, and failed. However, the feminist war on crime is as old as American feminism itself. Concerns over rape, prostitution, and domestic abuse lay at the very heart of the early women's movement in the mid-nineteenth century (the "first wave" of feminism), and they played no small part in suffragists' quest for voting rights. Nor were feminists' anticrime efforts in vain. Turn-of-the-century feminists found success in securing antirape legislation and statutes that criminalized sex trafficking and prostitution. Feminist activists' preferred remedy for DV—alcohol abstention—became a national priority, ushering in the Prohibition Era. The need to enforce these nascent regulatory regimes led to the expansion of the US Border Patrol and the FBI.[3] First-wave feminists' early battle against crime may be overshadowed in the legal literature by second-wave reforms, but it indelibly colored feminist theory and practice and continues to influence feminist law reform today.

SEX, POLICING, AND SEX POLICING

Crack open any criminal law textbook in the United States and you will find centuries-old rape cases that paint the victim (called the "prosecutrix") as a vindictive liar or an unchaste manipulator. Until recent decades, rape law contained peculiar and exceptional legal hurdles to conviction. In rape cases, it was not enough that the defendant violently forced sex; the victim had to "resist to the utmost."[4] In rape cases, jurors could not rely on victim testimony as proof; there had to be "independent corroboration."[5] In rape cases, judges routinely gave a warning adopted from the writings of seventeenth-century jurist Sir Matthew Hale that rape "is an accusation easily to be made and hard to be proved" (the "Lord Hale instruction").[6] In rape cases, prosecutors had to introduce evidence that the victim had made a "fresh" complaint, that is, had reported the rape to officials within a short period of time.[7]

The common thread among these doctrines appears to be "the cherished male assumption that female persons tend to lie," in famed feminist Susan Brownmiller's words.[8] For decades, rape statutes required prosecutors to introduce independent corroboration of the victim's claim. Because there are rarely eyewitnesses to rape, corroboration usually came in the form of serious injury. Thus the requirement had the effect of rendering noninjurious rapes totally legal. One court of appeals rationalized the requirement: "The corroboration requirement provides an essential safeguard" because "complainants all too frequently have an urge to fantacize [*sic*]."[9] One might take some comfort if this statement came from a mid-1800s rural court. But this observation of the epidemic of rape-fantasizing women comes from the federal court of appeals in Washington, D.C.—the famed D.C. Circuit—in the 1974 case *U.S. v. Wiley*.[10]

One of the most disturbing archaic rape rules required that women physically resist rape "to the utmost," even at their peril.[11] Resistance was not only embedded in the notion that women lied but also reflective of the social equation of women's value with their aversion to sex. The idea was that a properly chaste woman would consider ravishment (by a nonspouse) as a fate worse than death and fight tooth and nail against it. These irregular principles thwarted rape prosecutions and discouraged victims from reporting. It is no wonder that feminists regularly take them as proof positive that the American legal scheme was deliberately constructed to license men to coerce women into sex at whim.[12]

The male sexual license account, however, does not tell the full story. Early American sex regulation was puritanical at its core. In fact, in fascinating studies of the highly sex-regulatory and patriarchal Puritan settlements, legal sociologists discovered that officials believed women's rape accusations and aggressively prosecuted rapists, alongside fornicators.[13] From the eighteenth through the early twentieth century, rape law formed an integral part of a complex web of restrictions and permissions that policed intercourse, procreation, and marriage. It accompanied fornication and adultery statutes to restrict lawful sex to marriage and simultaneously make all marital sex, even forced intercourse, lawful.[14] Even sex workers, unlike wives, could legally claim rape, although they faced near-impossible obstacles to conviction. The Iowa Supreme Court opined in 1911, "Of course, a common prostitute may be raped; but it is not so likely that [defendant's] act is by force and against her will."[15] In addition, murder laws carved out an "honor defense" for husbands who killed men for "invading their property" by engaging in sexual relations with their wives.[16]

It is also important to note that early rape law was shaped by not just the prosecution of men for sexual assault but also the prosecution of *women* for adultery and fornication. For these female defendants, a claim of rape could be the difference between imprisonment and freedom. It is a well-documented phenomenon that state actors disbelieve defendants' protestations of innocence.[17] Judges routinely warn jurors that testifying defendants have a self-protective motive to fabricate.[18] Thus rules like corroboration may have stemmed less from the assumption Brownmiller identified, that women were prone to lie out of vindictiveness, and more from typical law-and-order notions that defendants, including female adulterers, would lie to exculpate themselves. Law professor Anne Coughlin suggests, "The objectionable elements of the rape offense could have been produced not by the law's special hostility towards women, but rather by its ordinary hostility towards defendants who seek to be excused from criminal liability."[19] It was *after* the demise of legal penalties for fornication and adultery that courts turned toward sexist rationales for the doctrines, such as the claim that women "fantacize."

Feminist commentators also regard the Lord Hale instruction to carefully scrutinize rape complaints, which was widely adopted into American law, as proof of a prevailing societal presumption that women were vindictive liars. Upon closer examination, however, the instruction was confirmation not of old English law and society's rape tolerance but of Hale's (perhaps misogynistic) view that jurors were too inclined to *believe* women, prematurely judge defendants, and hastily convict out of revulsion for the sex crime. The "heinousness of the offense," Hale warned, could "transport[] the judge and jury with so much indignation, that they are over hastily carried to the conviction of the person accused."[20] This was especially problematic because rape was "punished by death."[21]

Indeed, far from being sex and rape tolerant, eighteenth and nineteenth-century US laws widely prescribed capital punishment for rape, and society had little tolerance for men's or women's unorthodox sexual behavior. Marital norms, class distinctions, and notions of purity and chastity ruled the rape issue. To be sure, chastity expectations prevented many women, not just prostitutes, from accessing victimhood status. Poor, lower-class, and minority women and those who defied social conventions or feminine expectations were labeled "unchaste" and unrapable by law. The label applied even to serving-girls as young as seven.[22] At the same time, lower-class men who raped married, helpless, or high-class victims faced convictions and harsh sentences. Applying chastity standards to a woman charged with fornication produced a consistently sex-restrictive result: the "unchaste" woman was denied the rape defense, and the law incentivized women's chastity. Applying it to a man charged with rape produced an inconsistent result: it encouraged women to be chaste but tolerated male sexuality. In the end, early legal leniency toward men who raped "unchaste" women may have reflected society's desire to strictly circumscribe women's sexual behavior, even at the *cost* of licensing male sexuality.

The picture of a nineteenth-century America filled with licentious men who forced sex and enjoyed the protection of a rape-loving society is thus largely a false portrait. However, the libertine seducer is not just a product of feminist imagination. Popular European culture and British penny press writings did introduce nineteenth-century Americans to the iconography of high-class seducers and their coquettish paramours. Estelle Freedman notes that by then, "the older Puritan emphasis on the sinfulness of both men and women had been supplanted by a narrative of male conquest of willing female partners."[23] As social tolerance for the seductive rake grew, feminists became increasingly concerned about vulnerable girls being lured with false promises of marriage or affection, ruined, and forced into a life of prostitution. As early as 1793, Mary Wollstonecraft highlighted the problem in *A Vindication of the Rights of Woman:* "Many innocent girls become the dupes of a sincere affectionate heart ... and ... are ... *ruined* before they know the difference between virtue and vice," she warned. "A woman who has lost her honour imagines that she cannot fall lower. . . . Prostitution becomes her only refuge, and the character is quickly depraved by circumstances over which the poor wretch has little power."[24]

Inspired by such writings and by liberal movements like the antislavery movement, educated white middle-class American women in the mid-nineteenth century joined the "burgeoning social reform efforts to improve American society by opposing intemperance, vice, and slavery," Freedman writes.[25] Once they started pursuing larger social goals, women ran up against the extreme limits on their legal and political power. By necessity, the women's movement had to prioritize women's diminished political rights. Enfranchisement soon became a primary purpose of the movement, and in 1848 at Seneca Falls, American feminism was born. "Because women do feel themselves aggrieved, oppressed, and fraudulently deprived of their most sacred rights," Elizabeth Cady Stanton wrote in the Seneca Falls Declaration, "we insist that they have immediate admission to all the rights and privileges which belong to them as citizens of the United States."[26] Historian Ian Tyrrell remarks that at the end of the nineteenth century, women in the Women's Christian Temperance Union (WCTU) retained an instrumental view of suffrage as a means of securing the political power to protect "purity, sobriety, and honor."[27] These activists often exhibited polite contempt for the lower-class women and women of color involved in voting rights agitation.[28]

Throughout the latter nineteenth century, as women's organizations pursued suffrage, abolition, and temperance, Mary Wollstonecraft's warning about the ills of seduction remained at the forefront of many activists' minds. Women's groups championed robust enforcement of the tort of seduction, where a woman, or rather her male family members, could pursue monetary damages against men who falsely promised nuptials to procure sex. The criminal law agenda against seduction, and ultimately prostitution, largely came about after the formation of the WCTU in 1874. In Frances Willard, who became president in 1879, the WCTU found an indefatigable, captivating, "do everything" leader. Under her direction, the WCTU established a formal Social Purity Department, and by 1892, the union was far and away the nation's most robust feminist organization. It had branches in every state, all major cities, and thousands of localities, and it had ten times the members of the National Women's Suffrage Association.[29]

Books on the WCTU and Willard crowd library shelves, and there are varied explanations for why the early feminist movement prioritized moral purity in its political agenda. One common, and somewhat trite, observation is that the WCTU was simply the embodiment of uptight Victorian moralism. Others regard feminism's turn to purity as a reflection of the mood of the larger society, which was moving into an era of social engineering and social hygiene. There is ample evidence, however, that the purity agenda was more intentional—and more feminist. First-wave feminists were particularly concerned with women's predicament of political disempowerment outside the home and brutal treatment in the home. Suffragists and temperance activists directed their efforts against a particular icon—the slovenly, undisciplined drunkard who was "a wife beater, child abuser, and sodden, irresponsible nonprovider."[30] Susan B. Anthony identified the problem in her 1895 Social Purity speech:

> Though women, as a class, are much less addicted to drunkenness and licentiousness than men, it is universally conceded that they are by far the greater sufferers from these evils. Compelled by their position in society to depend on men for subsistence, for food, clothes, shelter, for every chance even to earn a dollar, they have no way of escape from the besotted victims of appetite and passion with whom their lot is cast. They must endure, if not endorse, these twin vices, embodied, as they so often are, in the person of father, brother, husband, son, employer. No one can doubt that the sufferings of the sober, virtuous woman, in legal subjection to the mastership of a drunken, immoral husband and father over herself and children, not only from physical abuse, but from spiritual shame and humiliation, must be such as the man himself can not possibly comprehend.[31]

Some of the proposals to fight the drunkard's rule were structural, even socialist. Although Anthony professed fondness for the old economic model of marriage, where women "were occupied with useful and profitable work in the household," she recognized that industrialization had thrust "millions of the women of both hemispheres . . . into the world's outer market of work to earn their own subsistence."[32] Anthony and others, including Frances Willard, called for women's political, economic, and social rights so they did not have to be financially dependent on men and could make a decent wage without backbreaking "toil" or a resort to prostitution. Anthony also famously championed liberalized divorce laws as the solution to women's predicament, courting controversy with some purity crusaders. Frances Willard herself touted an ideal of "homosocial" female-friend relationships, similar to second-wave cultural feminists' embrace of relational intimacy in the 1980s.[33]

Despite their socialist-feminist concerns, temperance activists are not remembered for fighting the "twin vices" of inequality and capitalism. Middle-class Christian sensibilities rose to the top, and the WCTU remained committed to eradicating the vices of sex and alcohol. All that was missing was rock and roll. Or was it? In 1910, social worker and temperance advocate Jane Addams lamented the "public dance halls filled with frivolous and irresponsible young people in a feverish search for pleasure."[34] Dance halls were, in fact, a target of moral reprobation throughout the Progressive Era. The 1912 book *From Dance Hall to White Slavery* decried the "tragedies of the dance" in Chicago.[35] It lamented that five thousand girls were "sacrificed" to prostitution, attributing "their downfall in a greater or less degree to the public dance hall."[36] Such sentiments underlay a spate of proposed regulations to limit the spread of the dance, most of which failed. However, police simply relied on the sweeping delinquency laws aimed at controlling and disciplining promiscuous girls as justification for raiding dance halls.[37]

In any case, if the chief problem identified by Anthony and other feminists was men's sexual and physical violence in the home, why not direct criminal law efforts against marital rape and domestic assault? Whipping wifebeaters at the post did in fact come into vogue in the late nineteenth century, but not because of the WCTU. First-wave feminists instead advocated for the criminal regulation of drunkenness and lust more generally. A critic might say the temperance activists instrumentally used spectacular narratives of domestic abuse and rape as means to the end of social purity. Law professor Reva Siegel has a more measured take: "Temperance protest was simultaneously radical and conservative in tenor. Condemning alcohol provided reformers an outlet for criticizing the social conditions of family life, in the name of protecting the sanctity of family life."[38] My read is that, like the socialist proposals, alcohol prohibition was a *structural* remedy for a root cause of domestic abuse, rather than the Band-Aid remedy of arresting individual offenders. Early feminists well knew that the temporary penalty of a short jail stint would do little to improve the drunkard's wife's condition of poverty, abuse, and degradation. In fact, it might make things worse. Accordingly, the WCTU championed the prophylactic, and authoritarian, program of prohibition. Prohibition laws ended up being so sweeping that, unlike the many criminal prohibitions confined to deviant individuals or discrete groups, they did not last.

With alcohol and sex firmly entrenched as the primary enemies of women, Willard turned to the problem of the libertines who seduced and ruined women. Civil—even criminal—responses to seduction, in Willard's estimation, were not enough to stop the spread of this noxious practice. Rather, the age of consent in rape law—at that time generally ten years—had to be raised so that tolerated seductions could be converted into easily prosecutable rapes. The WCTU's efforts were remarkably successful. In 1885, the age of consent in the states ranged from zero (no cutoff) to twelve years, with most states codifying the age of consent as ten years, reflecting English law. By 1920, all but one state had raised the age of consent to sixteen or eighteen years.[39]

Some historians regard age-of-consent reform as merely another of the WTCU's mechanisms for stopping prostitution and confining sex to the minimum needed for reproduction, both for Christian reasons and because lust was regarded as *male*. Legal historian Jane Larson, however, is more generous to Willard and maintains that, like modern feminists, she saw how seduction and prostitution harmed the women involved.[40] When Willard began her reform campaign, she met strong resistance from male legislators who argued that prostitutes, grifters, and other girls of ill repute would seduce men and use the liberalized rape laws as leverage to extort money. In countering this argument, middle-class temperance advocates found themselves in a solidaristic moment where they had to support not just the young girls preyed on by older men but the lower-class "loose" women that had become the center of male legislators' arguments. This necessitated tempering the temperance agenda of discouraging extramarital sex, deterring low-class depravity, and eradicating prostitution by any means, in favor of a more inclusive program of supporting and protecting unchaste and chaste, poor and middle-class, and black and white women alike.[41]

Unfortunately, this inclusive moment proved short lived. By the dawn of the Progressive Era, Larson observes, age-of-consent activism became "more conservative, nativist, and racist, and lost its feminist bite."[42] The antisex policy that emerged from temperance efforts was anything but female liberationist. The antirape movement took a particularly maternalistic and authoritarian turn, as reformatories for errant girls and women's prisons, filled with and run by women, constituted the sole alternative to the patriarchal and classist sexual and marital order. "And therein," Larson opines, "lies the peculiar paradox of early feminist sexual politics."[43] Whereas a woman's class, race, and adherence to social norms once had determined whether she was freely rapable, it now controlled whether she was free.

One of the greatest barriers to racial and class solidarity within antirape activism was the growing concern with "white slavery" and the "new abolition" movement. At the turn of the century, as the older suffragists and abolitionists passed away, the agenda of temperance and equal rights gave way to stricter social purity movements. By the Progressive Era, the narrative of the seducer who cajoled women into consenting to their own ruin had given way to the narrative of the slaver who captured unsuspecting girls and procured sex through punishment, not persuasion. Although evidence was largely lacking that the women engaged in prostitution were physically coerced, the vision of enslaved young white girls gave the antiprostitution crusade an air of emergency and moral authority. Popular books of the time warned of the lurking dangers threatening girls and their oblivious parents. Pastor Frederick Lehman's 1910 book *The White Slave Hell* described girls' descent into prostitution in polemical and poetic prose, punctuated with photos and rhyming captions, such as "With breaking heart he bids his child farewell, en route to languish in a living hell"[44] and "The iron bars the law decreed must go, today entomb the White Slave in her woe."[45]

For moral purists, the road to slave hell often began with women's undisciplined behavior: "We know that many young females fall victim to their own improper conduct. An excessive love of finery beyond their means, bold and forward behavior in the presence of men, light and frivolous conversation, Sunday walks with merry companions, attending theaters and, singing saloons, keeping late hours and neglecting home duties—all of these are judged to be indications of easy virtue; and, as a rule, the judgment is correct."[46] In turn, the temperance movement prioritized policing young women's imprudent behavior because such was the precursor not just to moral ruination but to physical bondage.

Racial hierarchy was integral to the "white slavery" narrative, as the term implies. Historian Jessica Pliley notes that the term *white slavery* was first applied to prostitution—it had previously been used to describe underpaid white male labor—in an 1830s publication about "Jewish pimps" who entrapped women "in their den of iniquity."[47] In the 1880s, a British journalist published a lengthy "exposé" on the "international slave trade in girls," the titillating and perverse nature of which captured the Western world's attention.[48] British feminists, who had already organized in opposition to Britain's program of regulating prostitution as a public health matter rather than forbidding it as an immoral practice, eagerly promoted the slavery label. One British activist remarked, "English speaking girls ... are systematically sought after, entrapped, and sold into a condition of slavery infinitely more cruel and revolting than negro servitude, because it is slavery not for labour but for lust."[49] American feminists were also receptive to the analogy, converting their moral condemnation for now-abolished chattel slavery to a moral reprehension for prostitution.

The primary racial imagery of sexual slavery involved white girls entrapped by or sold to foreign men, low-class criminals, or ethnic minorities. Within this narrative, as was often the case with temperance narratives, the darker a woman's color, the greater her invisibility. By calling white slavery worse than "negro servitude" because of its sexual nature, activists collapsed the sexual violence exacted on enslaved black women (and men) into less-invasive "labour harm" and simultaneously presented white prostitutes' often nonphysical (financial and emotional) constraints as more dire than the physical torture inflicted on enslaved black people. But these were not the only racialized aspects of the sexual slavery discussion. Class had always played a distinct role in feminist antiprostitution agitation. Temperance activists lamented that lower-class prostitutes, although victims, were also perpetrators of harm. They tempted husbands into debauchery and brought lust and disease into the marital home. Such debauched women needed to be reformed, redeemed, and morally hygienized.

This divide between prostitutes and their rescuers had a particularly eugenicist and assimilationist bent on the US West Coast. In the late 1800s, as the Chinese population in California neared 25 percent and panic around a "Yellow Peril" was in full swing, Asians' perverse sexuality figured prominently in anti-immigrant rhetoric. Such sentiments were not confined to the West and are reflected in the *New York Daily Tribune*'s infamous 1854 statement: "The Chinese are uncivilized, unclean, and filthy beyond all conception without any of the higher domestic or social relations; lustful and sensual in their dispositions; every female is a prostitute of the basest order."[50] California state legislators pressed the "yellow slavery" narrative to secure strict immigration laws. One state newspaper remarked, "Chinese females who immigrate into this state are, almost without exception, of the vilest and most degraded class of abandoned women. These women exist here in a state of servitude, beside which African slavery was a beneficent captivity."[51] The moral repulsion for slavery met with hygiene-based fears of exotic venereal diseases. In 1876, Dr. Hugh Toland, founder of the University of California medical college, testified to San Francisco lawmakers that Chinese prostitutes were the cause of nine-tenths of the syphilis cases in the city and that his white patients "think diseases contracted from Chinawomen are harder to cure."[52] Indeed, the American Medical Association undertook a study on whether Chinese prostitutes were poisoning the nation's blood. Another drawback of Chinese prostitution, one pamphlet warned, was that "comminglingly with Eastern Asiatics . . . creat[ed] degenerate hybrids."[53]

Meanwhile, social purity activists worked to "rescue" the relatively small pool of Chinese women in California. Many of these Chinese émigrés were bonded by contract to be brides, second wives, or concubines and regarded immigration, even under such conditions, as a chance for a better life. Historian Peggy Pascoe makes the interesting observation that "the highly skewed sex ratio in immigrant Chinatowns . . . and the absence of established in-laws, created unusual opportunities for immigrant prostitutes to marry and leave prostitution behind."[54] But because of xenophobic stereotypes policy makers saw Chinese women's "degraded" status as something cultural and innate. A San Francisco police representative testified to Congress's 1876 Joint Special Committee to Investigate Chinese Immigration, "These Chinese women have generally submitted passively and helplessly to this imposition, degradation and slavery, to be sold and bought, and transported at the will of the masters."[55] By contrast, "The white women who are living a degraded life are not quite so easily handled."[56] Law professor Kerry Abrams puts it bluntly: "If Chinese men were innately coolies, willing to indenture themselves into servitude, Chinese women were innately prostitutes, willing to do the same thing in sexualized terms."[57] The narrative connecting sexual slavery to Chinese culture and character fueled the claim that Chinese immigrants were unassimilable. Legislators vowed "to prevent the importation of these female coolies."[58]

In 1874, California amended its laws to give immigration officials power to exclude "a lewd or debauched woman."[59] When the steamer *Japan* pulled into port in San Francisco in August 1874, the immigration commissioner detained the twenty-two Chinese women without children on board, designating them debauched women. The detainees challenged their custody in the California Supreme Court, which upheld the regulation as valid state authority. The hearings were covered by local newspapers, which faulted the women not for their excessive passivity in the face of sexual slavery but rather for their "noisy demonstrations" and "obstinate and saucy" back talk.[60] The *Alta California* reported that "the whole lot were jabbering and screaming at the top of their voices, and it was found impossible to quiet them."[61] The *San Francisco Chronicle* further stated that one woman gave "an awful screech," after which others "bellowed at the top of their lungs," forcing the judge to "stuff[] his fingers in his ears and retire[] to his chambers." The interpreter explained to the reporter that the women were protesting "being kept in prison, saying that they had not killed anybody, stolen anything, or set fire to anything."[62]

The women pursued the case in federal court, and US Supreme Court Justice Field, who was "riding circuit" in the San Francisco federal court, wrote an opinion invalidating the California law for usurping federal power over immigration. If Chinese immigration "is to be stopped," he opined, "recourse must be had to the federal government, where the whole power over this subject lies."[63] Not five months later, Congress passed the 1875 Page Act, which forbade "the importation into the United States of women for the purposes of prostitution."[64] The Page Act was the first federal law to control immigration, and in pressing for the act, its sponsor Horace Page emphasized that China was not sending its best people. America was China's "cess-pool," he lamented, because "she insists on sending here none but the lowest and most depraved of her subjects."[65] Like temperance crusaders, Page emphasized the need to "place a dividing line between vice and virtue" and "send the brazen harlot who openly flaunts her wickedness in the faces of our wives and daughters back to her native country."[66] Abrams observes that "the result of the enforcement of this newly federalized immigration system was not just a reduction in prostitutes, but the virtually complete exclusion of Chinese women from the United States."[67]

The Page Act paved the way for the Chinese Exclusion Act of 1882, which prohibited Chinese laborers from entering the country for a ten-year period.[68] Following the Page Act were also various initiatives to control or prohibit prostitution at the southern and northern US borders and in colonial areas abroad. The Page Act necessitated new systems of monitoring and investigating immigrants and a centralized enforcement system. Historian Eithne

Luibhéid notes that enforcement "strategies, which were pioneered on Chinese women because of fears about their sexuality, gradually became extended to every immigrant who sought to enter America."[69] As detentions under the Chinese Exclusion Act increased, the San Francisco "mission homes" set up by Christian women's groups to rescue prostitutes doubled as detention centers to house Chinese women taken into custody at the border—no doubt a welcome alternative to prison at the docks.[70] Well into the twentieth century, newspaper editorials continued to decry Asian women being "bought and sold into a worse slavery than ever Uncle Tom knew of."[71] Consequently, Pliley observes, "yellow slavery provided a foundation for the development of an American anti-white slavery movement."[72]

By 1910, the antiprostitution crusade was firmly entrenched in mainstream politics, and Congress passed the "White Slave Traffic Act," commonly known as the Mann Act. In urging the act's passage, sponsor James Mann called prostitution "much more horrible than any black-slave traffic ever was in the history of the world."[73] The act made it a crime to transport women across state lines "for the purpose of prostitution or debauchery, or for any other immoral purpose," and it is still in force today, although it now prohibits transportation for "any sexual activity for which any person can be charged with a criminal offense."[74] Infamous and controversial prosecutions under the Mann Act are legion and include the cases of Charlie Chaplin, Frank Lloyd Wright, and Chuck Berry. In 2008, prosecutors flirted with charging disgraced New York governor Eliot Spitzer with Mann Act crimes.[75]

On its face, the Mann Act (and its state law analogues) criminalized traffickers, imagined as ethnic thugs or foreign criminals, not victims, imagined as vulnerable white girls. And yet it was women who bore the primary brunt of criminal law management of commercial sex. Two aspects of feminist white slavery discourse prefigured that the panic would culminate in women's imprisonment. First, irresponsible girls were vulnerable to coercion into sexual servitude "a thousand times worse and more degrading in its consequences and effects upon humanity than any species of human slavery that ever existed in this country," in Mann's words.[76] Vulnerable women therefore required state management for *their own good*. Second, prostitution was not just an individual harm to trafficked women but a rapidly spreading social contagion, with prostitutes as patient zeros, that required containment by the state.

The white slavery discourse slid back and forth between rescue and recrimination, and the regime ended up ensnaring the enslaved. In 1915, the Supreme Court ruled in *U.S. v. Holte* that the government could prosecute a woman under the Mann Act for participating in *her own* transportation for prostitution. Mirroring nineteenth-century legislators' concerns over grifters, Justice Oliver Wendell Holmes pontificated: "Suppose, for instance, that a professional prostitute, as well able to look out for herself as was the man, should suggest and carry out a journey within the act of 1910 in the hope of black-mailing the man . . .—she would be within the letter of the act of 1910."[77] The act clearly applied to women, Holmes reasoned, once we "abandon the illusion that the woman always is the victim."[78]

The role of alcohol prohibition in modernizing and expanding American policing and prosecution is familiar. Less discussed is the white slavery crusade's substantial effect on law enforcement. In addition to systematically increasing immigration control, antiprostitution policies within states and cities played a pivotal role in redefining policing from a horizontal community model to a vertical top-down model and creating new means of criminal management, including widespread surveillance and preventive detention of arrestees.[79] Within three years of the Mann Act's passage, the FBI increased its number of agents fivefold.[80]

Helping victimized young girls was the stated purpose of age-of-consent reforms and anti–white slavery campaigns, but the irony, as Larson notes, is that "in the twentieth century it turned out to be mostly girls rather than men who were placed in state custody in order to prevent underage sex."[81] Law professor Mae Quinn highlights stunning facts about the juvenile detention regime that ultimately grew out of temperance activism:

> A 1912 study of the Los Angeles court system indicated that nearly sixty-four percent of all girls with active juvenile court cases faced charges of "being lewd and dissolute"—compared to boys who overwhelmingly faced theft and burglary charges. . . . A 1916 study of Chicago's juvenile court indicated that while only 21% of charged boys were placed outside of their homes, 51% of the charged girls were sent to institutions. And by 1920, nineteen new reformatories had to be established across the country to handle the explosion of young women being taken into custody and placed outside of their homes.[82]

RAPE AS A RACIAL PHENOMENON

As the story of the Page Act demonstrates, it is not easy to separate first-wave feminists' concerns over sexual victimization from classed and raced concerns over deviant and dangerous sexuality. One of the most infamous prosecutions under the Mann Act was that of boxer Jack Johnson, who in 1908 became the nation's first black heavyweight champion. Johnson not only dethroned the white reigning champion at the height of Jim Crow, he also openly defied segregation laws and norms by dating and marrying white women. The FBI began investigating Johnson as soon as the Mann Act passed. After an unsuccessful attempt to charge Johnson with kidnapping his girlfriend, who denied the claim and shortly thereafter married Johnson, the government successfully prosecuted him in 1913 for transporting his white former girlfriend for "debauch" purposes. A surreal update to the story is that President Trump posthumously pardoned Johnson in 2018 after receiving a call from his friend the *Rocky* actor Sylvester Stallone.[83]

One might reason that rape and sex slavery prosecutions were racist during Reconstruction and Jim Crow because *all* prosecutions were racist at that time. Indeed, during those time periods, the domestic violence issue also served as an arrow in the racist's quiver. Siegel writes:

> During the Reconstruction Era, public interest in marital violence rose as wife beating began to shift in political complexion from a "woman's" issue to a "law and order" issue.... During this period, the Ku Klux Klan took an interest in punishing wife beaters (both white and black), and began to invoke wife beating as an excuse for assaults on black men.... By the 1880s, prominent members of the American Bar Association advocated punishing wife beaters at the whipping post, and campaigned vigorously for legislation authorizing the penalty. Between 1876 and 1906, twelve states and the District of Columbia considered enacting legislation that provided for the punishment of wife beaters at the whipping post. The bills were enacted in Maryland (1882), Delaware (1901), and Oregon (1906).[84]

The contention that rape law was racist because all law was racist, however, underestimates the extent to which southern racial attitudes *constituted* the American concept of rape and to an extent DV. As Estelle Freedman remarks, "The influence of the South on the ways Americans understood rape in the nineteenth century cannot be overstated."[85]

To be sure, marginalized women in the North and West who claimed rape were also mistreated because of their identities. Poor white women were regarded as grifters, not innocent victims. Lawmakers saw Chinese women as culturally inculcated to passive slavery. Their status as perpetual victims made them unassimilable and un-American. But black women in the South had it the worst. It was not just that female slaves could not be victims— their *job* was to submit to rape. After the abolition of slavery, what was once considered black women's duty under slavery became a narrative of their internal disposition. In the eyes of many Americans, black women's sexual nature was innate, just like Chinese women's passivity, but black sexuality was anything but passive. It was lustful, insatiable, and savage.[86]

In the years before the Civil War, savvy abolitionists hoped that publicizing the sexual plight of black women under slavery would draw more white women to the antislavery cause. Indeed, abolitionists often used the literary device of "slave narratives," both written and recited in person, to rally the public to condemn slavery in all its bitter brutality. In 1861, Harriet Jacobs, in consultation with abolitionist activists, published the now-famous *Incidents in the Life of a Slave Girl*. In it, she described the double-edged sword of sexual brutality from the enslaver and jealousy from the southern mistress: "He told me I was his property; that I must be subject to his will in all things. My soul revolted against the mean tyranny. But where could I turn for protection? . . . The mistress, who ought to protect the helpless victim, has no other feelings towards her but those of jealousy and rage. The degradation, the wrongs, the vices, that grow out of slavery, are more than I can describe. They are greater than you would willingly believe."[87]

Jacobs and her abolitionist allies intended the book to appeal to northern white women who at the time embraced a cult of true womanhood.[88] The book accordingly emphasized Jacobs's maternal nature and persistence in staying connected to her children in the face of the family-destroying institution of slavery. It also emphasized her attempts to maintain her chastity in the face of a culture that portrayed black women as wild temptresses. The delayed publication of the book put its distribution at the commencement of the Civil War. This, and the fact that the sexual nature of the text was explicit for delicate white female readers, made the book inconsequential at the time. In modern times, however, it has enjoyed a renaissance as required reading in colleges throughout the country.

The end of formal slavery did little to stem the tide of sexual violations of southern black women. The Jim Crow Era saw a rash of interracial rapes as white men sought to reestablish white dominance and undermine black personhood. At the same time as southern white men weaponized rape against black women's dignity, they utilized antirape laws and policies to terrorize black men and thwart black political power. Tolerance for rapes of black women and rape-based lynching of black men were two sides of the same coin: both stemmed from whites' desire to deny African Americans' bodily integrity and impose de facto slavery. In the Reconstruction Era, lynching of black men for sexual offenses against white women reached epidemic levels. The longevity of such murderous practices is evidenced by the fact that one of the most infamous cases of this kind, that of fourteen-year-old Emmett Till, who was beaten to death for being "uppity" and allegedly whistling at a white woman, occurred in 1955.[89]

Rape-based lynching was so common as to occupy the agenda of prominent Reconstruction Era activists, who asserted that the practice was a prime mechanism for maintaining slavery-era conditions. Frederick Douglass opined in 1895, "Now that Negro insurrection and Negro domination are no longer defensible as an excuse for Negro persecution, there has come in due course another suited to the occasion, and that is the heart-rending cry of the white women."[90] He and other antilynching activists like Ida B. Wells sought to publicize that "white men used their ownership of the body of the white female as a terrain on which to lynch the black male," as scholar Hazel Carby observed.[91] Wells argued that white men's purported "chivalrous" concern with the virtue of white women was a sham. "True chivalry respects all womanhood," she opined, "and no one who reads the record, as it is written in the faces of the million mulattoes in the South, will for a minute conceive that the southern white man had a very chivalrous regard for the honor due the women of his own race or respect for the womanhood which circumstances placed in his power."[92]

As Wells's antilynching activism began to secure support domestically and abroad after she toured Britain in 1894, critics doubled down on the argument that black men's natural tendency to rape required tough legal responses. The racial narrative of rape forged in the fires of southern slavery soon circulated in polite northern society. The *New York Times* ran an op-ed critical of lynching but defending the southern status quo because of black men's propensity for savagery and the pressing need to deter rape: "It is a peculiar fact that the crime for which negroes have frequently been lynched, and occasionally been put to death with frightful tortures, is a crime to which negroes are particularly prone. . . . The existence of a large element of a race especially disposed to this crime makes it a matter of public concern that every possible deterrent should be interposed to the commission of it."[93] The author went on to argue that "a single bestial savage" was all it took for "the whole community to convert itself into a set of bestial savages."[94]

The rape issue put feminists and civil rights activists at odds. During Ida Wells's 1894 trip to Britain publicizing her antilynching efforts, she ended up in a notorious confrontation with, of all people, Frances Willard, who happened to be touring Britain on behalf of temperance. Wells rebuked Willard in British nobility circles, telling aristocratic liberals that Willard had made racially charged statements and encouraged mob justice when she had toured the South in support of her age-of-consent reforms. Willard too made the rounds of the aristocratic tearooms. She accused Wells of harboring antiwoman sentiments and enlisted female members of British high society to help her suppress media coverage of Wells's criticism.[95]

Nevertheless, Willard's past racist statements made her vulnerable to Wells's reproach. Recall that the early women's movement prioritized the problem of domestic violence committed by drunkard husbands. Although feminists' prohibitionist stance was universal—denying all people the drink—the narrative of the dissolute drunkard, like the rapist narrative, was far from race-neutral. Southern policy makers invoked the image of the inebriated woman-beating Negro to champion voting restrictions. In 1895, legislators in South Carolina carefully crafted their disenfranchisement rules to cover "negro crimes," such as wife-beating and attempted rape. Notably absent were crimes then associated with whites, including fighting and *murder*.[96] One Alabama lawmaker explained that adding "the crime of wife-beating alone would disqualify sixty percent of the Negroes."[97]

In 1890, Willard defended Alabama's voting restrictions, and in doing so articulated a vision of black men as sexually potent and procreant drunkards: "The Anglo-Saxon race will never submit to be dominated by the negro so long as his altitude reaches no higher than the personal liberty of the saloon.... The colored race multiplies like the locusts of Egypt. The grog-shop is its centre of power. The safety of woman, of childhood, of the home, is menaced in a thousand localities at this moment, so that the man dare not go beyond the sight of their own roof-tree."[98]

Given such sentiments, some commentators maintain that Reconstruction Era racial terrorism was "aided and abetted ... by white women."[99] Willard's statement was plainly racist, but Wells directed her aiding-and-abetting accusations primarily at a different class of white women. In defending black men from the widespread charge of sexual predation, Wells provided an alternate account involving unchaste white women crying rape after their consensual sexual liaisons with black men were exposed. In her 1892 writings, Wells recounted a story from the *Cleveland Gazette* about a white minister's wife. The wife, fearing that others had discovered her affair with and possible pregnancy by a black man, told her husband she had been raped. Wells went on to say, "There are thousands of such cases throughout the South, with the difference that the Southern white men, in insatiate fury, wreak their vengeance without intervention of law upon the Afro-Americans who consort with their women."[100] Wells accordingly cautioned southerners that the larger public would soon see through the "the old thread-bare lie that negro men rape white women" and counseled that rape accusations reflected "the moral reputation of their women."[101] As one might imagine, the ferocity of the backlash to these public comments knew no limit, and Wells was lucky to survive it.[102]

The idea that philandering white women were accomplices to the lynch mob may ring true to those familiar with the notorious 1931 Scottsboro Boys case. Two working-class white women, Victoria Price and Ruby Bates, had been on a train where several black boys were "hoboing." The women subsequently fabricated (by all accounts) a story that the boys had gang raped them and thereby incited a lynch mob. The story twists and turns, and features Bates as a surprise defense witness in the 1933 trial, recanting the accusation. Price never took back the accusation. The three convicted "boys" were finally pardoned by the Alabama Board of Pardons in 2013, after eighty years. But history here, as everywhere, does not easily produce heroes and villains. Southern white women, married and single, were constrained by a sex regulatory system powered by disciplinary mechanisms ranging from economic ruin and social ostracism to incarceration. Price and Bates did not wield the weapon of criminal authority out of privilege. Rather, a popular explanation for the lie is that they were sex workers who feared their own criminal prosecution under the White Slavery Act.[103]

Historian Martha Hodes details an antebellum-period story that poignantly illustrates how race *and* gender inequality influenced interracial rape cases.[104] In 1825 in North Carolina, Polly, an eighteen-year-old white girl, accused her neighbor "slave Jim" of raping her in the woods. The community rallied around her and paid for the prosecution of Jim. However, Polly and Jim's long-standing affair had been an open secret in the community, and Jim testified that "he had kept her as a wife for several months."[105] Indeed, there was evidence that Polly took refuge with Jim to escape a sexually abusive white master in the house where she was a servant. "Up to a certain point," Hodes states, "local whites had tolerated the liaison," but the rape accusation changed things.[106] Although the trial revealed evidence of the relationship, Polly held steadfast that Jim forced himself upon her. The jury of all white men convicted Jim, more to punish him for the illicit affair than from the belief that he committed rape, Hodes reasons.

Community attitudes began to change a couple of months later when Polly appeared to be pregnant. The governor granted Jim a reprieve from sentencing and stayed further hearings pending the outcome of the pregnancy. When the baby was born "obviously mulatto," the community turned on Polly and rallied around Jim.[107] Polly maintained that she had conceived the child during the rape, but this did little to dissuade critics. Those who now denigrated Polly, however, did not argue that Polly's pregnancy, which would expose the interracial relationship, created a motive to fabricate the rape. Rather, they held to a fallacy about female biology, made all too familiar in recent times by Congressman Todd Akin's 2012 comments at the height of the Republican "war on women": rape victims cannot get pregnant.[108] In pardoning Jim, the governor reiterated the opinion of the "highest authority on medical jurisprudence" that "without an excitation of lust, or the enjoyment of pleasure in the venereal act, no conception can probably take place."[109]

Fast forward to the mid-twentieth century. As Jim Crow gave way to de facto segregation, informal lynching was replaced by sham capital trials. According to historian Danielle McGuire, post–World War II racial activism in the South triggered an uptick in rape-related executions of African Americans.[110] Returning black soldiers with "a new a sense of pride and purpose . . . led campaigns for citizenship rights, legal equality, and bodily integrity," Maguire writes. She goes on, "It did not take long for white Southerners to claim black efforts to gain equality were a mask for more sinister, sexual desires. . . . Black activists in the post–World War II period often joked that 'the closer a black man got to a ballot box, the more he looked like a rapist.'"[111] The author recounts the 1951 case of Willie McGee, who submitted to a sexual relationship with his white female employer "after she threatened to cry rape if he refused her flirtatious advances."[112] The relationship eventually broke down, and McGee was charged with and convicted of rape. The chief justice of the Mississippi Supreme Court dismissed McGee's claim of a mutual affair as a "revolting insinuation" and sentenced him to death. Officials brought a portable electric chair to the courthouse.[113] The execution took place at midnight on May 8, 1951, in front of "an ecstatic, almost all-white audience of five hundred, men, women, and children."[114]

Ann Braden, a white activist, traveled from Kentucky to protest the execution, and she admonished the crowd, "No more innocent men [should] die in the name of protecting southern white womanhood. We have been made a party to this injustice too long."[115] In 1977, civil rights lawyer Ruth Bader Ginsburg echoed these sentiments in an ACLU amicus brief, filed in *Coker v. Georgia,* the case that stuck down capital punishment for rape of an adult woman. In contrast to some modern feminist sentiments, Ginsburg viewed *opposing* rape punitiveness as the distinctly feminist position. She submitted her brief "on behalf of a large segment of the women's legal community who oppose the death penalty for rape as a vestige of an ancient, patriarchal view of women as the property of men."[116] The brief described rape law in the context of interlaced racial and gender hierarchies in the South. Ginsburg argued, "Rape of white women by black men threatened the white man's status by decreasing the value of his sexual possession, and by jeopardizing the purity of his race, and it was therefore necessary to take extreme measures to prevent this result. Lynching was one such measure; and the death penalty for rape—particularly when perpetrated by blacks—was another."[117]

The rape-race nexus has proven durable. Race continues to color whom society regards as a rape perpetrator or victim. A 2014 study of "slut shaming" on college campuses found that shaming female students was common among men and women on campus. Moreover, being targeted for shaming had an *inverse* relationship to engagement in casual sex. Women of higher social status (white sorority sisters) shamed lower-status women (poor minority students), regardless of sexual behavior, to cement their low status. The higher-status women, by contrast, had freedom to engage in sexual experimentation without reputational damage.[118] Awareness of this type of disparity led black feminists to criticize the "slutwalk" protests that were popular in the 2010s. One commentator stated that black women "do not have the privilege or the space to call ourselves 'slut' without validating the already historically entrenched ideology and recurring messages about what and who the Black woman is."[119]

In 2016, Donald Trump infamously launched his presidential campaign with the image of the Mexican immigrant rapist.[120] Trump's anti-immigrant rhetoric borrowed heavily from the writings of right-wing provocateur and self-proclaimed "real" feminist Ann Coulter. Channeling purity sentiments, Coulter once objected to birth control on the ground that it enabled "liberal men" to engage in sexual abuse (birth control "helps Bill Clinton, Anthony Weiner and Dominique Strauss-Kahn").[121] Coulter's 2015 racist diatribe ¡*Adios, America!* invokes feminist tropes in its anti-immigrant fearmongering:

> America is a nation apart from the rest of the world. In no area is that clearer than the treatment of women and children. Latin Americans, Arabs, Asians, and Indians take a distinctly less respectful view of the gentler sex. Even Continental Europeans can't compete with American men. They don't have

the gusto for gang rape, incest, and child rape of our main immigrant groups, but they fall far short of what the English-speaking world considers gallant behavior. It's as if Ted Bundy designed our immigration policies to ensure that the most misogynist cultures go to the head of the line. American employers get the cheap labor, Democrats get the votes, and American girls get the rapes.[122]

Immigrant women are also to blame, Coulter argues, because they are often involved "in the rape or the cover-up."[123]

In sum, feminist criminal reform efforts in the nineteenth and early twentieth centuries reinforced existing and created new hierarchies, even as they provided justice to women. Temperance activists' successful antirape, antiprostitution, and Prohibition efforts derived from a sense of gender justice and from a deep-seated commitment to moral purity and social hygiene. Their rape reforms, formulated to help vulnerable women, operated at a time when race was central to constructions of rapists and victims and rape law was a tool of racial terror. A simple, formulaic approach to rape and DV, often repeated unreflexively, holds that the past was sexist, past criminal law was too lenient, and therefore lenient criminal laws are sexist. But the complexity of the historical relationship between feminist criminal reform and sexism, racism, classism, xenophobia, and puritanism casts doubt on the dogma that strengthening criminal rape and DV law is invariably enlightened. The early feminist crusade against rape and DV, which certainly benefited many women, cannot be separated from the larger purity crusade, which greatly harmed many marginalized individuals, especially women.

TWO

The Enemy

FROM "THE MAN" TO BAD MEN

This chapter of feminist criminal law reform, like so much of the contemporary American story, begins in the late 1960s. It was an era of social, economic, and demographic upheaval, as well as a time of war. From the brew of social anxieties emerged a new political awareness and a new generation focused on class solidarity, antiauthoritarianism, and racial and gender justice. Students, people of color, and women took to the streets to protest the war, segregation, poverty, and unequal rights. Just as civil rights activists ranged in their radicalism from Black Panthers to NAACP leaders, so did activists in this "second wave" of feminism. In the late 1960s and early '70s, those identifying as feminists ranged from equal-rights liberals to welfare rights radicals, lesbian separatists to proud homemakers, and institution-rejecting anarchists to lawyers.

If late sixties radicalism was a strong backlash to 1950s conservatism, the backlash to the backlash—Nixon's war on crime—was even stronger. Crime had long been a political issue, and the racialized "war" analogy predated Nixon. The predecessor Johnson administration had prioritized tackling the socially deleterious effects of poverty through various initiatives, including law enforcement. Johnson's labor department circulated a report entitled *The Negro Family: The Case for National Action,* today known as the infamous "Moynihan Report."[1] The report attributed poverty, crime, and social displacement in segregated urban areas to the "pathology" of black "subculture."[2] As part of the war on poverty, Johnson formed a crime commission whose recommendations culminated in the 1968 Omnibus Crime Control and Safe Streets Act, the "master plan for the national war on crime."[3] But it was Nixon's 1968 campaign that put crime control at center stage of national politics.

At that time, 81 percent of Gallup respondents agreed that "law and order has broken down in this country," and for a majority of these, "negroes" and "Communists" were to blame.[4] Nixon capitalized on social anxieties about scruffy hippies and hostile blacks fomenting civil unrest and ran a campaign ad pledging to protect law-abiding citizens from such "domestic violence."[5] "Let us recognize that the first right of every American is to be free from domestic violence," boomed Nixon's stern voice, accompanied by images of protesters and bloody bystanders. "So I pledge to you, we shall have order in the United States."[6] Nixon reportedly later remarked of the ad, "It's all about those damn Negro-Puerto Rican groups out there."[7] Nixon deftly employed the so-called Southern Strategy, developed during the 1964 Barry Goldwater presidential campaign, which used dog-whistle crime rhetoric to court Dixiecrats to the Republican Party.[8] Infamous Republican strategist Lee Atwater candidly explained in 1981: "You start out in 1954 by saying, 'Nigger, nigger, nigger.' By 1968 you can't say 'nigger'—that hurts you, backfires. So you say stuff like forced busing, states' rights, and all that stuff."[9]

The modern antirape and battered women movements were born in this tumultuous political atmosphere. Between the Progressive Era and the late sixties, there was little feminist action in the criminal arena. Historian Estelle Freedman notes that in the post–World War II period up until the 1970s, most rape law reform came from civil libertarians seeking to narrow criminal regulations out of concern for black defendants and sexual liberation sentiments.[10] Moreover, until the latter twentieth century, the US criminal system contained no specific framework for intimate partner crimes. Domestic assaults and murders were prosecuted under general battery and homicide laws. The state response to "domestic disturbances" often began and ended with the police officer's presence at the scene. With the advent of the modern women's movement, all that changed.

Much of second-wave feminist activism grew out of the leftist sensibilities of the time and opposed Nixon and his law-and-order program. The nascent battered women's movement was radical and antiauthoritarian at its core. In the '70s, battered women's shelters cropped up throughout the nation from the tireless efforts of grassroots activists. One radical ideology that deeply influenced the shelter movement was an intense aversion to the racist, sexist, Vietnam War–supporting state, aka "the Man." Shelters were a subset of a larger radical feminist vision of alternative medical, welfare, and community organizations that could operate outside of the Man's influence.[11] Moreover, shelter feminists saw DV as a phenomenon at the intersection of many interlocking social inequalities that occupied the Left's protest agenda. DV, they believed, was rooted in patriarchy, exploitative capitalism, and race- and class-based subordination.

During this era, the police were the very embodiment of the Man, a "fascist" institution that drew condemnation from progressives of all stripes—from student protesters to civil rights leaders. Accordingly, radical feminists generally regarded criminal law as an oppressive institution where "relationships of domination based on race, class, and sex are continually played out," as shelter feminist Susan Schechter put it.[12] Indeed, the antistate sentiments of shelter feminists also made them reluctant to engage with the bureaucracies of traditional social services that were not involved with the criminal justice system; they too were, in one activist's words, "embodiments of the top-down hierarchical, imperialistic, war-mongering society."[13] Shelter organizers even forwent funding, worrying that the more the state bureaucracy got its hooks into shelters, the less feminist they would be. If shelter activists felt conflicted about allying with the state welfare apparatus, surely they would actively resist the criminal system. Yet within a decade "law enforcement" became the centerpiece of feminist DV activism.

By the 1980s, experts regularly identified the proarrest, proprosecution position as a distinctly feminist position. Writing in 1984, DV victims' lawyer and academic Lisa Lerman contrasted nonfeminist "mediation" models with the feminist "law enforcement" model: "The 'law enforcement' model ... is espoused both by grass roots advocates working with battered women, and by an increasing number of court officials, police officers, and others who provide services to battered women. In general, the law enforcement model advocates formal legal action combined with punishment or rehabilitation of wife abusers. The goal is to ensure the safety of the victim and to give the abuser a clear message that society will not tolerate his continued violence against his mate."[14]

As for the antirape movement, it was not as antiauthoritarian as the shelter movement, but neither was it carceral in nature. In the late 1970s, activists and students came together in "take back the night" (TBTN) rallies to give voice to women's shared fear of prowlers lurking in the dark. TBTN rallies often occurred after high-profile, if statistically rare, murders and rapes of women by strangers. Women rallied on campuses and marched at night through blighted urban areas, claiming their rights to be free of the predators lurking there. However, TBTN policy proposals were practical, not carceral. Protesters called for measures like increased security on campuses and police on the streets, free self-defense classes, and funds for crisis centers. Over time, the marches became less about rape and more about the various "violences" faced by women, including systemic, social, and institutional inequality and state violence.[15]

In certain localities, notably San Francisco, TBTN rallies were more radical. Those protests were about rape, but primarily the rape depicted in pornography. These activists, like temperance-era white slavery crusaders, regarded pornography and prostitution as forms of modern-day servitude that entrapped and devastated the women involved and polluted larger society with their messages about women's sexual subservience. The predator-prey narrative popular in radical TBTN protests would significantly overlap with conservative sex-panic discourse and would play a role in the coming war on sex offenders. Still, the legal reforms that grew directly out of radical TBTN efforts were not criminal but civil ordinances directed at pornographers.[16] The feminist expansion of rape law would come later in the decidedly nonradical 1980s, when feminist lawyers and academics turned their attention to the problem of "date rape." That revolution would happen in books, statehouses, and courtrooms, not in the streets.

Today, second-wave feminism is remembered—fondly or regretfully—for its contributions to policing, prosecution, and punishment. The prosecutorial achievements of second-wave feminism are numerous and include mandatory arrest and no-drop prosecution for domestic violence, criminalization of nonforcible sex, and prosecution-favoring evidentiary rules. By 2000, when I represented Jamal, whom we met in the Introduction, specialized DV courts and their functionaries were a firmly entrenched and growing portion of states' criminal systems. States had widely reformed their arrest laws to encourage and even mandate DV arrests. Colorado law, for example, dictated that "the officer *shall,* without undue delay, arrest" DV suspects.[17] Many jurisdictions boasted detailed DV codes designed to counteract the lenient impulses of state actors and victims. Florida law, for instance, required each state attorney's office to adopt "a pro-prosecution policy for acts of domestic violence."[18] Specialized DV and sex offender regimes engendered a robust for-profit cottage industry, allowing courts to outsource treatment and supervision from their overloaded dockets.[19]

This increased concentration of criminal authority in the intimate realm has had profound effects. Since the 1980s, the population of sex offenders in prison has exploded, even as rape offending has precipitously declined.[20] Arrests for domestic violence have also increased exponentially—with increases in arrests of women outpacing those of men—although arrests have declined overall and violent crime rates have reached historic lows. Today, domestic assaults are more likely to result in arrest, prosecution, and incarceration than nondomestic assaults. Women, who are more inclined than men to be violent in domestic settings versus on the street, have for several years constituted the fastest-growing segment of the prison population. And, in Jim Crow politicians' ultimate triumph of the future, the increased penalization of the "negro crimes" of DV and rape has disproportionately harmed and disenfranchised men and women of color.[21]

The rest of this chapter discusses how, in a few short years, the battered women's movement transformed from a radical antiauthoritarian movement into a propolicing, proprosecution lobby. In doing so, it highlights three different feminist groups that engaged the DV issue in the 1970s and '80s. The first group consisted of leftist antistate feminists and included shelter organizers, socialist feminists, and welfare rights activists. These feminists saw DV in the context of the larger racist, pro-war, capitalist government. Second, there were less radical, but still left-leaning, antipatriarchy feminists, including lesbian separatists and liberal feminists who regarded sexist marriage norms and male economic privilege as the driving force behind battering. Finally, there was a powerful and ultimately triumphant group I call "legal feminists," who pursued their antibattering agenda through law reform and litigation. Legal feminists were civil rights lawyers and victims' advocates, and they analyzed the problem of battering as a failure of the *law,* specifically the ineffectuality of criminal law.

The legal feminist position that stronger criminal punishment is *the* remedy for harmful behaviors categorized as "crimes" is ingrained in contemporary thinking. However, in the early days, few of the feminist and nonfeminist experts viewed criminal punishment as the solution to battering. Sociologists and psychologists, like radical feminists, retained deep skepticism of criminal law's capacity to meaningfully address relationship violence. Often agnostic about the feminist political agenda, these "professional class" experts prioritized resolving relationship conflict over changing societal gender dynamics. Civil libertarians and antiracist activists counseled against aggressive police presence in minority communities. Even many police and prosecutors opined that placing DV within a traditional arrest paradigm would escalate violence and leave women worse off. The lone voices for incarceration at that time were the feminist lawyers and victim advocates, and, owing to a variety of factors discussed below and in the following chapters, they eventually spoke for the battered women's movement.

Let me add the caveat that categorizing is inherently imperfect. There were ideological convergences between the feminist groups, especially between antistate feminists and antipatriarchy feminists. Moreover, individual feminist activists held multiple, even conflicting, views. For example, many legal feminists who pursued criminal law policies also welcomed programs to secure women's economic equality. Nevertheless, radical feminists, who viewed state-enforced social, racial, and economic inequality as main drivers of gender violence, diverged from antipatriarchy feminists, who saw violence as a near-exclusive product of sexism. Antipatriarchy feminists, who wanted nothing to do with masculinist police forces, diverged from legal feminists, who championed proarrest policies. And, as the stories below demonstrate, these divergences mattered.

POVERTY OR PATRIARCHY?

Over the years, I have often spoken on feminism's role in establishing and maintaining mass incarceration, and one of the most frequent questions I get asked is, "Well, if not criminalization and punishment, what are we supposed to do about violence against women?" I generally respond, probably too impertinently, "Give women money." This invariably invokes some form of "Yeah, keep dreaming" response. It is as if feminists have all become cynical realists who regard the original progressive designs of socialist feminists as utopian pipe dreams, not worth talking about. Then the activist or lawyer instinct to "do something" about gender violence kicks in, and we are left with tools of criminal law. However, in the 1970s, antipoverty activism and litigation were very real and very prominent within radical circles, among black feminists, and even in established feminist organizations. Historian Marisa Chappell observes:

> The early 1970s illuminates an extraordinary moment when a significant sector of the American middle class urged federal responsibility for families' economic well-being.... By 1966 a "new sense of hope" had come to many poor people and middle-class activists, for whom an intensifying "urban crisis" signaled a moment ripe for far-reaching reform. In the second half of the 1960s, the Citizens' Crusade Against Poverty brought together over 100 organizations to demand an expanded War on Poverty. Continuing the effort in the early 1970s, the Campaign for Adequate Welfare Reform Now demanded a guaranteed income.... The broad range of organizations fight-

ing for more generous welfare reveals how 1960s social movements and federal activity expanded visions of the possible.[22]

One would think that feminist antibattering activists would naturally drift toward the established antipoverty movement rather than helping create a new crime victims' rights movement.

In fact, early shelter activists' initial battle was to secure funding, unencumbered by the bureaucratic shackles of the state. Sharon Rice Vaughan, founder of the first battered women's shelter in St. Paul, Minnesota, recalls that the shelter effort germinated from women's burgeoning social activist mind-set.[23] Vaughan was part of a feminist "consciousness-raising" group that, after meeting for a year, "looked for a project" to embody their ideological commitments.[24] The group set a long-term goal of establishing Woman House, "a place for classes, workshops, and weekend retreats."[25] More immediately, they decided to provide women resources and information on divorce through a telephone information service for women called Women's Advocates. Phone lines were soon flooded, as the "phone service seemed to be a dumping ground for all kinds of problems."[26] Vaughan remembers, "We found there was one request we could not satisfy: it was a woman calling and needing a place for herself and her children to stay in an emergency."[27] Soon, the Woman House idea morphed from a consciousness-raising center to a battered woman shelter, and Vaughan and colleagues set out to fund-raise for the brick and mortar.

This introduced a dilemma. It was 1973, and the consciousness-raising group viewed "money that supports the Vietnam war [as] 'dirty' money."[28] They decided, however, that using the money for shelter made it "'clean' money, even if it [came] from the government,"[29] and they applied for and received funding from the state's mental health program board. The activists' "stomachs sank" when the board requested that the shelter fall under its organizational umbrella, adopt a hierarchical administrative structure, and change its name, but they "caved in" for the $35,000.[30] Vaughan laments, "In that one moment—the mental health board meeting—we had abandoned the core principle of collectivity. While we were prepared to face and resist the inevitable pressures of outside agencies to mainstream us, ... we were also vulnerable to those pressures and had to make some concessions concerning our future."[31] Later, the complexities of running a shelter created further challenges to the grand egalitarian experiment. It became necessary to set rules, for instance, against stealing, child spanking, and pets, and to divide the labor: "No one wanted to clean the toilets, and almost everyone wanted to do public speaking."[32]

Shelter feminist Susan Schechter tells a similar story of the challenges faced by early antibattering grassroots activists who wanted to maintain independence from the state but needed money.[33] Feminists found themselves in a never-ending quest for funding from the very state administrators and wealthy capitalists they detested and an unending series of painful compromises. One shelter administrator remarked, "I worry we are becoming another social service agency. We have debts for rehabilitation and we're tied to needing money."[34] She went on, "I don't feel we are part of a movement to end violence against women anymore."[35] According to Schechter, many funding agencies "downplayed or discouraged social change"—for example, the federal grant agencies that required shelters to quantify "units of client services" and prohibited using money for community education.[36] The worst instance of this unhappy pattern occurred in 1977 with what Schechter calls the "nightmare in New York City," when shelter residents had to be "certified as battered" by state administrators.[37]

How could battered women—or any woman in need—obtain resources from the state without becoming ensnared in a political and social order that ultimately harmed them? Battered women and shelters, it seemed, were stuck between the unfair capitalist market and the disciplinary welfare bureaucracy. During the 1970s, feminist antipoverty activists sought a third way. These activists characterized welfare as a "right" that should be free from the racist, sexist, and classist mechanisms of social control that invariably accompanied government money and services. They also argued that welfare rights were a far more pressing issue of gender justice than fighting inchoate patriarchy. Johnnie Tillmon, a black feminist and the first president of the National Welfare Rights Organization, observed that women's liberation was "a matter of concern" for middle-class women, whereas welfare was "a matter of survival" for poor women.[38]

Welfare reformers sought to court the burgeoning women's liberation movement to their cause. They argued that the welfare system permanently impoverished women married to low-wage earners. They also highlighted stories of humiliated single mothers, whose cupboards welfare detectives raided for any signs of a man. In a 1972 *Ms.* magazine article, Tillmon reached out to the middle-class women's rights contingent by analogizing the welfare system to a controlling husband:

> The truth is that welfare is like a super-sexist marriage. You trade in a man for *the* man. But you can't divorce him if he treats you bad. He can divorce you, of course, cut you off anytime he wants. The man runs everything. In ordinary marriage sex is supposed to be for your husband. On AFDC you're not

supposed to have any sex at all. You give up control of your own body. It's a condition of aid. You may even have to agree to get your tubes tied so you can never have more children just to avoid being cut off welfare. *The* man, the welfare system, controls your money.[39]

For a time, national women's organizations incorporated antipoverty sentiments into their agenda, although NOW's support was always a bit tepid— the organizers of the 1970 national conference "forgot" to schedule the poverty workshop.[40]

But a rift between the antipoverty and antipatriarchy camp was inevitable. The welfare rights platform conflicted with liberal feminists' insistence that women's equality required escaping the domestic realm into "real" society. Women's libbers had worked hard to describe women as self-sufficient contributing members of society, an image inconsistent with "welfare mothers." Legal historian Martha Davis explains that NOW's leadership remained "fixed on formal, legal equality for those already in the workplace as the proper instrument for addressing women's poverty."[41] As early as 1971, NOW's antipoverty position translated into suing the government to ensure that the compulsory work requirements of work-to-welfare reform were equally applied to women recipients.[42]

The antidomesticity sentiments of mainstream feminists never resonated with black women, whose employment outside their homes did not confer superior social status or political power. Scholar Premilla Nadasen notes that for black women, "To enter the world of work would only reinforce the kind of exploitation and oppression that many of them faced on a daily basis."[43] Single mothers and poor working women wanted to spend more time in *their* homes mothering *their* children. Acclaimed author Toni Morrison's searing 1971 critique reflects this deep divide: "It is a source of amusement even now to black women to listen to feminists talk of liberation while somebody's nice black grandmother shoulders the daily responsibility of child rearing and floor mopping and the liberated one comes home to examine the housekeeping, correct it, and be entertained by the children. If Women's Lib needs those grandmothers to thrive, it has a serious flaw."[44]

The fledgling battered women's movement struggled with similar divisions: activists faced the existential question of whether the movement was about meeting the material needs of battered wives where they were at—what today might be called "harm reduction"—or using the battering issue to disrupt marriage norms, sex roles, and the larger patriarchy. Antipoverty activists like Tillmon were forthright that they did not view compulsory domesticity as the biggest, or even a significant, challenge for marginalized black women. However, women's libbers in the DV movement were skeptical of welfare as a remedy to battering because the family-friendly program could shore up rather than dismantle sexist marriages, thereby cementing women's subordinate roles. Del Martin, whose 1976 book *Battered Wives* is widely credited with launching the battered women's movement, put it bluntly: "The basic problem, as I see it, is the institution of marriage itself and the way in which women and men are socialized to act out dominant-submissive roles that in and of themselves invite abuse."[45]

A true civil rights pioneer, Martin was a founder of the first lesbian political organization in 1955, the Daughters of Bilitis. She worked to integrate the male-dominated gay rights movement and the hetero-dominated National Organization of Women, which had actively resisted the lesbian "lavender menace."[46] Martin's fifty-five-year relationship with her partner Phyllis Lyon has been the frequent subject of celebratory scholarly and political retrospective. Less well known is that Martin was as powerful in the battered women's movement as she was in LGBT rights circles. She remarked in 2002, "A lot of people forget that lesbians started the domestic violence movement."[47]

Martin was a somewhat unlikely candidate for mother of the modern battered women's movement. She had not been battered, had not worked with battered women, and was not a part of the shelter movement. Her interest in the wife abuse problem came about somewhat circuitously through Lyon's job. In 1964, Lyon went to work for the Memorial United Methodist Church as a switchboard operator and became something of a counselor for callers. In the early 1970s, Lyon began receiving calls from abused wives, which piqued Martin's interest in the subject. After Martin and Lyon published their groundbreaking book *Lesbian/Woman* in 1972, Martin turned her attention to the battering issue. Martin had the time, interest, talent, and resources to take a scholarly deep dive into the DV issue and produce a work that caught the attention of lawmakers and the public.[48]

Martin's main ambition in publishing the book was upending the patriarchal structure of marriage. She explained in 1978: "I deliberately called my book *Battered Wives* to focus on marriage as the institutional source and setting in which the violence is initiated and carried out. Although many try to avoid its implications, to me, domestic violence cannot be fully understood without examining the institution of marriage itself as the context in which the violence takes place. The power relationship between husband and wife is culturally determined, and its imperatives necessarily affect other man-woman relationships."[49] Feminists like Martin envisioned the wife abuse issue as a means of toppling the institution of marriage and its sexist domesticity norms. They saw no rationale for preserving violent marriages. For Martin, wives who wanted to stay with abusers were either "immobilize[d]" by fear or under the spell of a Svengali: "A woman with her own money! What can she be thinking when she says she needs a man who takes her money and her will? . . . The fact is, she may not be thinking for herself at all."[50] From this perspective, separation, not welfare, is the answer.

The antipatriarchy camp quickly overshadowed the antipoverty camp, as *Battered Wives* and its searing exposé of the "hidden epidemic" of battering prompted the federal Commission on Civil Rights (CCR) to hold its historic 1978 hearings on "wife abuse."[51] Those hearings would pave the way for various congressional efforts to fund antibattering initiatives and would set forth best practices that influenced states throughout the country—practices that included proarrest procedures. The activists, experts, and interested parties constituting the audience of CCR hearings would soon form the National Coalition against Domestic Violence. Thus, to call that moment in 1978 a watershed is hardly an overstatement. Del Martin was the keynote speaker, leading off the hearings and providing the overview of the wife-abuse problem. Chairman Arthur Flemming lavished introductory accolades on Martin, omitting her lesbian activist credentials in favor of titles such as "Citizens' Safety Task Force of the Mayor's Criminal Justice Council, San Francisco."[52] Martin used that platform to champion the antimarriage version of battered women's activism.

Today, the name Del Martin is associated with marriage—but interestingly, not the *critique* of marriage. In 2004, San Francisco mayor Gavin Newsom began issuing marriage licenses to same-sex couples, an act that helped catalyze the ultimately successful marriage equality movement. Kate Kendell, then executive director of the National Center for Lesbian Rights, called up Martin and Lyon. "This will hopefully be the last thing the movement will ever ask you to do," she said, "but do you wanna get married?"[53] Martin and Lyon were the first same-sex couple to legally marry in San Francisco, their ceremony presided over by the mayor himself. After the exchange of rings and "I do's," "the room erupted in cheers—and tears."[54] But the radical antimarriage Martin may have had the last laugh. "There are lots of old ladies who are friends, but they don't have the right to turn marriage upside down," lamented Campaign for California Families executive director Randy Thomasson. "This was all done to victimize marriage."[55]

Martin hoped that *Battered Wives* would help unify a fractured women's movement. She was all too familiar with feminist internal conflict, since the top leadership of NOW had strongly opposed her joining that organization. "Betty Friedan was such a homophobe," Martin recalled, "As soon as I was on the board she was on the phone to the New York Times saying that lesbians are ruining the movement."[56] Martin predicted that the battering "issue would pull us all together."[57] She "wanted to unite people whatever their class, race, economic status" in the belief that battering was an outgrowth of a sexist marriage system that hurt black and white, poor and rich women alike.[58] Looking back on it in 2002, Martin ruminated, "I was so naïve."[59]

Black feminists were reluctant to endorse the separation model over the welfare model because separation would not work for women without the resources or inclination to leave their spouses. Black women indeed valued the little privacy they had and were not so sanguine about inviting the government into their private spheres. Antipatriarchy feminists regarded marital privacy with opprobrium, believing that "the private is the distinctive sphere of intimate violation and abuse, neither free nor particularly personal," in Catharine MacKinnon's words.[60] Black feminists, in contrast, recognized that "the black body is [already] culturally, socially, and legally hyper-surveyed" and thus that "the black female subject has never been granted the same kind of privacy as the white female, the privacy that some feminists have argued needs to be 'exploded,'" as scholar Jennifer Nash observed.[61]

Moreover, the larger "separatist" antipatriarchy agenda was an uneasy fit for women of color because men of color were allies in the struggle against white supremacy. In 1977, the Combahee River Collective, a coalition of black female theorists and activists, outlined the principles of "black feminism": "We do not advocate the fractionalization that white women who are separatists demand. Our situation as Black people necessitates that we have solidarity around the fact of race, which white women of course do not need to have with white men, unless it is their negative solidarity as racial oppressors. We struggle together with Black men against racism, while we also struggle with Black men about sexism."[62] Finally, black feminists rejected the premise that battering was solely a matter of sexist men and society and highlighted the contribution of racism and economic inequality.

One would think that black women's articulation of this distinct perspective would cause battered women's advocates to rethink the patriarchy-only account of battering. Instead, however, most self-identified DV activists doubled down on the claim that abuse was something that sexist culture encouraged all men to do to all women. Radical and mainstream feminists alike repeated the refrain that abuse occurred equally across race and class lines. Battered women's advocate Georgine Noffsinger testified at the CCR hearings that when it came to DV, there was "no difference" between upper-class women and low-income, minority women.[63] She elaborated, "You can change the scenery, you can change the props, you can change the costume, and you can change the accents if you have to, but it is still the same ugly drama taking place in the $200,000 colonial house in Potomac as in Brooklyn or any place else."[64] Del Martin similarly declared, "The practice of wife beating crosses all boundaries of economic class, race, national origin, or educational background. It happens in the ghetto, in working-class neighborhoods, in middle-class homes, and in the wealthiest counties of our Nation."[65]

Antipatriarchy activists went to great lengths to defend what sociologist Beth Richie has called the "everywoman" claim that all women are equally at risk of DV.[66] Consider the following exchange between Latina shelter feminist Shelly Fernandez and Yale Law–educated feminist judge Lisa Richette at the 1978 CCR hearings. Fernandez spoke on behalf of San Francisco shelter founder Marta Segovia-Ashley, who was unable to attend. Segovia-Ashley had conceived of the shelter La Casa de las Madres in 1974 as a refuge for victimized Latinas. Committed to an egalitarian multicultural environment, La Casa's founders were reluctant to embrace the state bureaucracy and accepted only seed grant money with few strings. However, avoiding hierarchy was a challenge, Fernandez recalled. "In practice, certain people always seem to get a little higher and assume more power," she remarked. "So instead of minority women being oppressed by men in the outside world, they were at one time fairly recently oppressed by Anglo women at La Casa. Strangely enough, they use the same methods as white men."[67]

Fernandez was the first speaker in the "Support Services" portion of the hearings. She approached the microphone and began: "The soil of this cruelty, maiming, and murder is the racism of the Great White Society. This country has systematically discriminated against, humiliated, and degraded certain of its people. These battered people, the poor and powerless, the ethnic minorities, the disenfranchised are the real abused children of the white patriarchy."[68] She then told Segovia-Ashley's life story. Segovia-Ashley first "felt the oppression of the white culture" at five when she was forced by her "cold, indifferent, stoic white teachers" not to speak Spanish.[69] She had difficulty reconciling her warm family life with the "deadness" of the outside world and felt "terror" when she left her house for the white world.[70]

When Segovia-Ashley was sixteen, her stepfather murdered her mother, Seferina. Seferina had come home from working at the coffee packing factory where she was a union shop steward to find her husband drunk . . . again. They began arguing about his drinking. Seferina's husband reached for a bread knife and warned that "if she did not quit putting him down, he would kill her."[71] Seferina yelled back, "Go ahead, kill me, kill me. What difference does it make anymore?"[72] He plunged the knife into her heart and pushed her out of the window to make it look like an accident. "She landed two stories below."[73]

Decades later, attendees at the CCR hearings would hear Segovia-Ashley's surprising description of the man who had brutally murdered her beloved mother: "He was very kind and gentle when I first met him. He courted my mother for a long time, and she considered carefully before she married him. He worked in a steel warehouse. He had incentive and ambition; he wanted to better himself for our sake. He promised my mother the world and in his heart he really meant it."[74] Segovia-Ashley offered her analysis of what transformed her stepfather from doting spouse into brutal killer: "The white world slowly and insidiously defeated my stepfather. He was degraded at the warehouse. Because he was the only Mexican, he was expected to stay after the regular shift and do all the clean-up. He tried to take on more responsibility, but they always promoted the whites. It troubled him that my mother had to work. In our culture, that isn't done. Racism and despair affected him so deeply that within 2 years a man who had enjoyed a glass of wine with dinner was a full-blown alcoholic."[75] In Segovia-Ashley's estimation, the key factors escalating the marital dysfunction were racial discrimination and socioeconomic precarity. She understood her mother's murder "as the final act of a racist society which propelled two people to annihilate each other."[76]

The rest of Fernandez's remarks described La Casa, its mission, and its needs. Fernandez did not excuse the violent men who had terrorized the women at the shelter, but her account of DV was distinctly structural. At the root of it was white supremacy, which caused minority men to engage in what experts have called "compensatory subordination" against women.[77] As she put it, "Racism is the most deadly sickness in our society today; marital violence, which diminishes the spirit and destroys human life . . . is a civil rights issue."[78] For Fernandez, there was one way the federal government could help: "We need money for teaching sheltered children, bilingual[ly] and biculturally. We need money for the day-to-day operation of shelters, ongoing rent, food, furniture, clothing, remodeling, upkeep, and paid staff. We need money for supplemental housing because we are already full. . . . When the hell are you going to do something about it? Or are you going to wait until we, like Seferina, are dead?"[79]

Judge Lisa Richette, who spoke later in the hearing, singled out Fernandez and expressed her vehement disagreement with Fernandez's diagnosis of the causes of DV. Richette's life could not have been more different from Segovia-Ashley's. Richette, a true trailblazer for women in law, graduated from an all-girls' high school and went on to the prestigious University of Pennsylvania. She was one of five women to graduate from Yale Law School in 1952, and she joined the faculty shortly thereafter, teaching criminal law and working with at-risk children. Her influential 1969 text *The Throwaway Children* continues to be taught today.[80] Richette became one of Philadelphia's first female DAs and in a few years one of the city's first female judges. She quickly became famous, presiding over more murder cases than any other judge and regularly drawing headlines for her no-holds-barred judicial style and "designer clothes [that] turned heads."[81] She married lawyer Lawrence Richette in 1958; "The Center City couple, whose fashionable home featured Italian antiques in the Venetian tradition, quickly became trendsetters" and were known for their fabulous dinner parties with Philly intelligentsia and artists.[82]

Richette was a feminist in theory and practice. One colleague recalled that as an attorney, "She once showed up in court wearing a conservative pantsuit. A judge held her in contempt. . . . She took him to the state Supreme Court and won." Soon, "male attorneys were wearing two-tone shirts."[83] She was known to be more outspoken and self-assured than her male jurist counterparts. A former colleague on the bench remarked, "She was flamboyant, outspoken, people respected her judicial acumen. . . . She was her own person."[84] In short, when Judge Richette spoke, people listened.

Richette was not assigned to respond to Fernandez's remarks. That designation went to Minnesota shelter operator Monica Erler, whose response was "I agree with . . . everything that Shelly has said."[85] Erler concurred that battered women, "like other women, need fair income for their labor, decent housing at an affordable price, competent legal advice, dependable child care and other assistance with childrearing."[86] Judge Richette, however, went off topic to critique Fernandez's contention that DV was a racial and socioeconomic phenomenon. "I disagree completely with what Ms. Fernandez said that this is a problem of white society," the judge protested. "It is a problem of human society."[87] To the extent that race correlated with DV, Richette counseled that "black and Chicano women" should resist the sexism "*inherent* in that culture."[88] Insisting on battering's genesis in the larger patriarchy, Richette characterized shelter funding as a "Band-Aid" that could provide only "a conscience balm to a society which tolerates the oppression of women."[89] Like Martin, Richette saw the solution to battering as redefining marriage, which in her view was a "master-slave" or alternatively "parent-child" relationship that led to women's "infantilization."[90] The judge concluded by stressing the need for "new structures, new institutions, new concepts of relationships between men and women" to achieve an "equalitarian society in which sex stereotyping is condemned as surely as racism is condemned today."[91] Her speech roused the crowd to its feet.

Imagine being sociologist Bok-Lim Kim, chairperson of the National Committee Concerned with Asian Wives of U.S. Servicemen, who had to respond to that stirring performance. Kim began, "Well, that certainly is a very hard act to follow, especially for a person for whom English is a second language."[92] With the required deference of a non-native speaker responding to a powerful white woman, Kim called Richette's performance excellent and urged unity between feminists and activists of color. But, like Fernandez, she emphasized the disunity between women of color and white antipatriarchy feminists, noting that "the women's movement and minority groups' struggle for equality have not coalesced to work toward a shared goal."[93] Kim rejected the contention that DV affected all women equally. She emphasized that "institutionalized bias based on race, language, culture and/or ethnic origin . . . has led to the additional oppression and exclusion of minority women and to the conditions of poverty from which they disproportionately suffer."[94] Kim ultimately faulted white feminists for their inattention to the unique needs of minority women, concluding, "I would like this consultation to raise the consciousness of the majority women so that the concerns of minority women also become their concerns. Otherwise this commendable activity may become another case of special group advocacy which, in its insensitivity and nonresponsiveness to minority women, simply serves to perpetuate racism."[95]

Despite such cautions, feminist DV activists stuck with the everywoman account, where everywoman was essentially "a white, middle-class woman," as Beth Richie notes.[96] Perhaps it was a function of familiarity. Noffsinger, for example, had been a well-heeled abuse victim and later became an advocate in her affluent community. Empathy is another explanation: middle-class feminist activists may have imagined how abuse would look in their own lives. Critics like Fernandez, however, were less generous in their diagnosis of why activists pushed the everywoman account, analyzing it as a strategic choice to bet on white. Fernandez remarked that society "is willing to address the issue of marital violence now" because it "now affects white women."[97] Indeed, political scientist Michael Tesler observed in 2016 that Americans' redistributive sentiments vary by whom they imagine as the beneficiary of government aid, with "whites . . . considered 'more deserving' than blacks."[98] The racialization of the ideal victim persists today, as police disproportionately treat black women who report abuse as provocateurs and mutual combatants, rather than as victims.[99]

Whether articulated for ideological, empathetic, or strategic reasons, the everywoman refrain stuck. However, social scientists have now confirmed that poor women of color are, in fact, more vulnerable to the harms of domestic violence *and* to the harms of policing. On the basis of reporting from 1993 to 1998, the number of DV victims from households making less than $7,500 was 445 percent higher than the number from households making $75,000 or more.[100] Studies confirm that people of color are, in fact, disproportionately involved in the ever-expanding, ever-harsher DV carceral system.[101] Nevertheless, as one researcher recently put it, from the time feminists "began to develop domestic violence programs, concerns of Black women were virtually ignored."[102]

The everywoman (white woman) narrative propelled DV reform toward separation and arrest. Imagining the prototypical victim as a rich white woman hiding behind enormous sunglasses at the club prefigures certain remedies. Imagining her as a poor welfare recipient points to radically different ones. Many rich women had networks of wealthy family and friends to whom they could turn after leaving their husbands, unlike the many poor women who necessarily faced destitution. Such wealthy women, according to advocates, stayed in abusive marriages because of their husband's coercive control or the desire to hide the ugly truth about their "perfect" lives.[103]

The promise of welfare would do little to incentivize these victims to leave. One expert at the CCR hearings testified frankly that welfare reform would not help affluent victims because of their "reluctance to reduce their or their children's standard of living" and the "welfare stigma" that "prevented [them] from considering AFDC payments as a potential solution."[104] Money would not break their abuse cycle, making forced separation, through arrest or otherwise, the most promising avenue toward reforming the husband or creating favorable divorce conditions. A 1976 statement of the International Association of Chiefs of Police reflects this reasoning: "The officer who starts legal action may give the wife the courage she needs to realistically face and correct the situation."[105]

Of course, such paternalistic forced separation could hurt poor women whose husbands were less amenable to reform and for whom getting divorce money would be like getting blood from a turnip. Indeed, DV arrest studies would later confirm that arrest can be a good bet for white women and a losing wager for black women. One large-scale study in Milwaukee conducted in the late 1980s showed that arrest reduced violence among white, employed men while aggravating violence among black, unemployed men.[106] The researchers warned, "If three times as many blacks as whites are arrested in a city like Milwaukee, which is a fair approximation, then an across-the-board policy of mandatory arrests prevents 2,504 acts of violence against primarily white women at the price of 5,409 acts of violence against primarily black women."[107]

The everywoman, patriarchy-not-poverty ideology oriented the battered women's movement toward separation as the solution to battering. Nevertheless, antipatriarchy advocates like Del Martin and Judge Richette did not press proarrest policies, favoring instead programs to restructure gender roles and economically empower women in the market. In fact, Judge Richette was hardly the poster child for tough policing. A notably lenient jurist, in the 1970s she came under attack by Philadelphia mayor Frank Rizzo, a Trump-like and Arpaio-like character who had been known as "the toughest cop in America."[108] One of Rizzo's first mayoral acts was publishing a list of lenient judges, including Richette, and his nickname for her, "Let 'em Loose Lisa," became popular among Philly cops.[109] This moniker stuck with Richette for life. In 1998, fresh off his election as NRA president, Charlton "cold dead hands" Heston spoke at the NRA conference in Philadelphia and roused the crowd with the tales of "Let 'em Loose Lisa," whose lenient sentences—as opposed to gun access—caused crime.[110]

In 2007, Judge Richette's storied life ended in a tragedy that made her political project all too personal. Police arrived at Richette's residence after neighbors reported that her forty-nine-year-old son Lawrence, who had a troubled history of antisocial behavior, was disturbing the peace. Police found the seventy-nine-year-old judge (who still presided over cases) in her room bleeding from a cut above her eye and took her to the hospital. Officers sought her assistance in charging her son with DV, but the judge refused to cooperate with the investigation and "vowed she would not testify."[111] Police nevertheless arrested Lawrence for DV simple assault and reckless endangerment, and the bad news did not end there. Judge Richette learned at the hospital that she had advanced lung cancer. She died three days before Lawrence's DV case went to court. Her obituary concludes: "Two days before she died at the hospice, Richette heard her son calling her. She opened her eyes. Her face lit up. 'Oh, Larry, it's so good to see you,' she said in a voice as weak as her frail body. 'I'm so glad you came.'"[112]

Even though antipatriarchy approaches eclipsed antipoverty ones, the antipatriarchy proposals calling for wages for housework, education against stereotyping, and pink-collar reforms would, in fact, serve the interests of marginalized women. But there was yet a third feminist school weighing in on the battering issue. Legal feminists transformed the general claim that patriarchy causes battering to the specific claim that patriarchal criminal *law* is *the* cause of battering. In reconceptualizing DV as a matter of men's uncontrolled criminal behavior, many legal activists systematically denied all other antecedents of battering, even marital norms and gendered economic marginalization. They reduced DV to the phenomenon of violent sexist men emboldened by weak law enforcement. Strengthening law enforcement soon became the primary goal of the battered women's movement, and radical and antipatriarchy feminists' redistributive, gender norm–upending agenda was discarded as yet another leftist pipe dream.

LENIENCY VERSUS WOMEN'S LIBERATION

In the mid-1970s, as antipoverty feminists agitated for welfare rights, shelter feminists navigated their financial issues, and antipatriarchy feminists pushed for socioeconomic reforms, feminist civil rights lawyers and victim advocates pursued litigation and lobbying efforts to compel police to arrest abusers and courts to grant protective orders to victims. For legal feminists, the criminal court was not a fascist arm of the war-mongering state so much as the normalized system in which they operated daily on behalf of their clients. Advocates represented battered women who had against all odds left their batterers, only to find themselves in a complicated and unforgiving legal system. Advocates heard horror story after story from clients about brutal beatings and officer ambivalence and shared clients' rage that the police had not done their jobs.

Legal feminists highlighted egregious cases of police nonchalance, where a badly beaten woman would beg the police to intervene but the officer, because of sexism or incompetence, refused to do so, with the result of her severe injury or death. Activists regularly emphasized the connection between wife abuse and murder; however, the reality at that time was that domestic homicide was exceedingly rare and perpetrated roughly equally by men and women.[113] It is a familiar phenomenon that people tend to focus on cases of extreme, if atypical, violence, leading to a distorted view of the stakes of criminal law and policy. Feminists' preoccupation with spectacular cases gave the entire DV discussion an air of emergency. In an emergency, people do not want wage reform and anti-bias education. They want the police.

Given this orientation, it is understandable how feminist lawyers concluded that police intervention was the missing factor that would have protected their clients. To them, the exigent nature of DV made arrest necessary, and one could deal with larger issues of poverty and patriarchy later. Feminist Terry Fromson explained in 1977, "The elimination of sexist attitudes [is] the primary means to end woman abuse. Changing attitudes, however, is a long and difficult process. Until that change is otherwise effected, emergency measures . . . are desperately needed to protect these women."[114] Still, many advocates' DV clients did not fit the paradigm of the brutalized, proarrest victim. Some victims did not want to separate, or at least did not want their partner arrested. Many DV victims needed money, shelter, jobs, child care, and other material resources before they could afford to separate. There was no shortage of legal work to be done on these clients' behalf that did not involve the carceral state. Many feminist lawyers, including some of the lawyers engaged in arrest litigation, fought for DV victims' rights and interests outside of criminal law.

Nevertheless, legal feminists reasoned that policing was "already at the doorstep" and in desperate need of reform. Indeed, battering often occurred after hours, when social services were unavailable. Battered women were often unaware of nonpolice emergency services, if any existed, rendering the police the first, and often only, responders. To be sure, some feminists bemoaned this situation. Victim advocate Yolanda Bako testified at the CCR hearings that "if our government ever funded women's programs as well as they have the police," then a solution to battering "would be well in hand." Nevertheless, many law reformers were resigned that police departments would always be disproportionately funded, too powerful, and the primary agency involved in DV intervention. Change could come about, they maintained, only by addressing the policing issue.[115]

In 1976, a group of legal aid and civil rights lawyers in New York City filed a landmark class action lawsuit on behalf of battered women, *Bruno v. Codd*.[116] They argued that DV victims had a right to intervention and aid, which the police failed to provide. Articulating a "right" to government aid was, and remains, an uphill battle for any advocate. The US "tradition," according to many jurists, is that rights are "negative," meaning that people have rights only *against* government intrusion. Rights *to* government support are few and far between. American courts and jurists, unlike many of their foreign and international counterparts, rarely recognize "positive" or socioeconomic rights, such as rights to health care, education, and a decent standard of living. Consequently, DV advocates' reconfiguration of government action as a right was, like the welfare rights argument, quite revolutionary in American law.[117]

Feminist lawyers used their keen legal acumen, time, and money to convince courts that battered women had a right to state action. But it was one kind of state action—arrest. Within short order, this right became compulsory, and a battered woman could not waive the "right" to her husband's arrest. The logic of individual responsibility was inherent in the proarrest position. In justifying compulsory police intervention, even against the victim's will, activists had to paint the abuser as ever more despicable and personally responsible. As a matter of natural focus or litigation strategy, feminists gathered and highlighted egregious stories of manipulative and sadistic batterers who engaged in vicious violence and repulsive acts of degradation.

Legal feminists' narrative of bad individual men sat uneasily with antipoverty and antipatriarchy feminists' focus on the structural factors underlying battering. Feminist litigators well knew that focusing on structural causes of battering would suggest structural—not individually punitive—solutions. It therefore became necessary to deny that battering was rooted in economic, psychological, or cultural conditions at all. *Bruno* lawyer Laurie Woods argued, "It is true that jail and the threat of jail have minimal deterrent value where the cause of the underlying crime is economic or psychological. But where, as is argued here, the cause is social, then arrest and incarceration do have deterrent effects."[118] Woods analyzed and rejected noncriminal solutions to DV. "If one believes that men assault women because of job stress," she remarked, "then one would believe that changing the economic conditions and working conditions of men . . . would provide both the short and long-term solution. If one believes the cause to be psychological abnormalities in the man or in the woman, one would look for the solution in counselling for either or both."[119] However, economic conditions cannot be a factor, Woods maintained, because "husbands of all economic levels assault their wives regularly, and women, who typically have fewer economic resources than men, do not assault their husbands."[120] Psychological dysfunction is also not a cause because "half of the men in this country" beat women.[121] But by this logic, *no* external factor, including patriarchy, contributes to DV because within our patriarchal, economically unequal, violent, stressful, racist society, many men do not batter.

Battered women's advocates instinctively recoiled at causal narratives that let abusers off the hook. Even shelter feminist Schechter, an erstwhile socialist, urged zero sympathy for these men, admonishing, "While psychiatric descriptions and personal experiences make us sympathetic toward individual abusers, they cannot erase the fact that batterers are dangerous and that they beat women."[122] Accordingly, in the legal feminist narrative, the cause of battering was a "simple" matter of law failing to control certain men's violent nature: "Men beat women because society and its institutions encourage and permit woman-assault."[123] The solution to battering was also simple: stronger criminal laws. One feminist litigator remarked, "A 'hands-off' attitude by the criminal justice system—and the police in particular—has the effect of sanctioning the batterer's criminal behavior."[124] Within the legal feminist narrative, battering was no longer a matter of men acting out the sexist "script that society has written for them," as Del Martin had observed.[125] It was a matter of a large population of individually violent men in need of state control. According to legal scholar Martha Mahoney, this "focus on individual violent actors concealed both the commonality of violence in marriage and the ways in which state and society participate in the subordination of women."[126]

The battered women's movement's turn toward individual responsibility and law enforcement exacerbated the internal rifts in the movement. Feminists of color, like Fernandez and Kim, had argued vociferously that minority women were differently situated from middle-class white women, had different views of racism and sexism, and existed in a different relationship with the state. Black feminists were particularly resistant to policing as a response to minority women's problems. Nevertheless, much in the way antipatriarchy feminists insisted on the everywoman argument, many legal feminists doubled down on their commitment to law enforcement, as we will see in the next chapter. Professor Donna Coker suggests that the leaders of the DV movement might not have been "aware of the degree to which white privilege protects [whites] from police suspicion and surveillance."[127] Or, as one activist of color put it, "I think White women talked more as if the courts belonged to us [all women] and therefore should work for us where we [women of color] always saw it as belonging to someone else and talked more about how to keep it from hurting us."[128]

Interestingly, the antiauthoritarian shelter feminists, unlike the feminists of color, offered only faint criticism of legal feminists' proarrest efforts. One would think that given shelter feminists' reluctance to take the state bureaucracy's "dirty" money, they would actively resist calling in the "fascist" cops. However, shelter feminists viewed the DV movement's increasing entanglement with law enforcement as less of a "nightmare" than an insoluble dilemma. Schechter, for example, maintained that "punishment in jail reinforces violence and bitterness" and cautioned against giving prosecutors "the power to shape women's futures."[129] She called instead for "a broad-based, progressive political movement, fighting to democratically redistribute resources, power, and control."[130] But quite remarkably, Schechter nonetheless defended carceral DV reform through the simple talking points that tough criminal law "saves lives" and that "criminal sanctions are one of the only tools [women] have to attempt to stop abuse."[131]

That a socialist feminist harbored this step-in-the-right-direction attitude toward criminal policing and prosecution appears surprising. However, it makes more sense when one considers the situation of shelter residents: they had *already left* abusers and were ensconced in managed living. Shelter administrators, faced with an angry husband banging at the door, compartmentalized their skepticism of authoritarianism and viewed the police primarily as free security services. Shelters often had rosy relationships with the very police that radical feminists otherwise excoriated as pigs. One administrator explained: "I would like to say . . . that when the police do answer our calls at Rainbow Retreat, and we depend very, very heavily on them for security since we [have] an open, published address, that we find they're extremely sensitive to the problem. They are very helpful and they are protective, not just to the center itself but also to the women. It's as if once the woman has made a commitment to do something, they are more willing to work with her."[132] Imagine that, in contrast, officers had the kind of adversarial relationships with shelter residents that they often had with black women and uncooperative victims outside the shelter. Imagine that responding officers raided shelters looking for code violations or busting women for drug crimes. Police would cease to be just cost-free security.

Indeed, many shelter administrators had little experience with the dark side of policing, arrest, and prosecution. Vaughan wrote that she and the other "white middle class women" in charge of the St. Paul shelter were "not yet ready for a political analysis of why [we] assume that everyone thinks, lives, feels, acts, and responds the way we do."[133] Shelter feminists' desire for security services and unfamiliarity with policing crashed into their natural philosophical aversion to top-down state power, leaving them conflicted. One shelter administrator recalled, "While we wanted to activate police protection for the abused wherever possible, we were hesitant to support the extension of discretionary powers of arrest so open to abuse, particularly against Third World and low-income people."[134]

Despite these "notable objections that were raised in isolated forums," Beth Richie observes, the law enforcement agenda "went forward largely unchallenged."[135] In hindsight, we might surmise that radical feminists' revolutionary proposals for gender and economic justice were doomed by the changing times—the dawn of the Reagan Eighties. Perhaps it was inevitable that "feminist liberatory discourse challenging patriarchy and female dependency [would be] replaced by discourse emphasizing crime control," as Professor Elizabeth Schneider remarked.[136] Today, those sympathetic to legal feminists' proarrest activism argue that criminal law's takeover was an unintended consequence of the development of the battered women's movement during a political and cultural shift toward neoliberalism and what legal sociologist Jonathan Simon calls "governing through crime."[137]

Ronald Reagan, who assumed office in 1981, was the first president to use the crime issue to radically alter the relationship between government, society, and individual. The so-called Reagan Revolution was a totalizing and long-lasting ideological shift toward laisser-faire market-based logics and away from social welfare. Reagan vowed to, and did, gut government aid programs, deregulate banks and the market, cut taxes, and end labor and trade protections.[138] As President Barack Obama remarked in 2008, "Ronald Reagan changed the trajectory of America."[139]

The revolution is often thought of as economic, but it was deeply ideological, instilling what experts call a neoliberal ethic. Reagan's policies were less about growing or shrinking any given part of the economy than about how the economy *should* operate. For Reagan and think tanks like the Heritage Foundation that supported him, a "good" economy was, by definition, one where private actors pursued maximum profits and capital accumulation with little or no regulation. A "just" economy eschewed "redistribution," presuming that people's current wealth status—whether obtained through birth, work, luck, or favorable government rules—represented the first and fairest distribution.[140] According to political economists, a unique premise of neoliberalism that sets it apart from predecessor liberal economic theories is that healthy economies can tolerate vast disparities of wealth. And, to be sure, since the Reagan Revolution, the wealth gap has widened into a chasm.[141] Economists Thomas Piketty, Emmanuel Saez, and Gabriel Zucman describe the reverse Robin Hood transfer of wealth from the poor to the rich between 1980 and recent years: "The bottom 50% income share has collapsed from about 20% in 1980 to 12% in 2014. In the meantime, [the top 1%] income share increased from about 12% in the early 1980s to 20% in 2014. *The two groups have essentially switched their income shares,* with 8 points of national income transferred from the bottom 50% to the top 1%. The top 1% income share is now almost twice as large as the bottom 50% share, a group that is by definition 50 times more numerous."[142]

How did Reagan and his allies sell an ideology tailor-made for the 1 percent to the other 99? Yes, Reagan could inspire the American-style hope that "anyone can be a millionaire." Yes, he could argue that the money would "trickle down," giving everyone a higher standard of living. It did not—the official poverty level remained the same between 1980 and today, with the reduction in real poverty due exclusively to increased reliance on government aid.[143] However, Reagan's rhetorical ace in the hole was painting the poor as responsible for their own plights and recasting the problems of poverty as products of criminality.

Reagan contrasted lazy criminals with the rest of hardworking, law-abiding America and drew a straight line from liberals' social welfare ideology to the pressing crime problem: "Individual wrongdoing, they told us, was always caused by a lack of material goods, and underprivileged background, or poor socioeconomic conditions. And somehow . . . it was society, not the individual, that was at fault when an act of violence or a crime was committed. Somehow, it wasn't the wrongdoer but all of us who were to blame. Is it any wonder, then, that a new privileged class emerged in America, a class of repeat offenders and career criminals who thought they had the right to victimize their fellow citizens with impunity."[144] The rhetorical move is brilliant in its simplicity. It reverses the moral order, transforming the "underprivileged" into a "privileged class," transforming society's victims into "victimizers." Moreover, following the Southern Strategy, Reagan cast the crime problem in distinctly racial terms. In 1976, his presidential campaign infamously featured a black "welfare queen" who had defrauded the government of tens of thousands of dollars.[145] Reagan's racialized and spectacular crime rhetoric performed the feat of replacing within the American psyche the image of the deserving poor with the image of the black criminal poor. This set the stage for a total transformation of government intervention, replacing the safety net with a metal cage.

Given this massive ideological shift, it makes sense that the part of the battered women's movement dedicated to arresting and punishing bad men would come to overshadow the movement's larger quest for social and economic restructuring to promote gender, class, and racial justice. In fact, by the time feminist reformers coalesced around law enforcement, the political and legal architecture was already in place for the prioritization of criminalization. Johnson's 1968 Crime Bill established the Law Enforcement Assistance Administration (LEAA).[146] As feminists brought the DV issue to light in the late 1970s, the LEAA systematically ramped up funding to states to "increase the number of crime reports and number of successful prosecutions" of DV.[147] By 1980, the last year of the LEAA's existence, its criminal-law oriented family violence funding outpaced all other federal funding to families touched by DV.[148]

Nevertheless, criminal law's takeover of the battered women's movement was not simply an unintended consequence of shifting national politics. Feminist activists responded to *and helped create* society's preoccupation with protecting victims and punishing offenders, as we will discuss further in chapter 4. Moreover, DV lawyers' procriminalization, individual-responsibility position predated the Reagan Revolution, and it grew out of their *feminist,* not conservative, theory and practice. By the late 1970s, DV activists in court had already adopted what Donna Coker terms "crime logic," involving "(1) a focus on individual culpability rather than on collective accountability; (2) a disdain for policy attention to social determinants of behavior; (3) a preference for narratives that center on bad actors and innocent victims; and (4) a preference for removing individuals who have harmed others as though excising an invasive cancer from the body politic."[149]

The crime logic of legal feminists came to overshadow other feminist positions on battering, and "today, for a significant number of feminists, Crime Logic is feminist logic," Coker observes.[150] The battered women's movement's carceral turn influenced the larger American carceral turn, even as it was influenced by it. The next chapter examines how feminist lawyers wholly transformed the DV movement and, along with it, policing more generally.

THREE

The Battle Plan

ARREST IS BEST

In the late 1960s and early 1970s, the police were the frequent targets of leftist reprobation—the war-mongering state personified. Their violence toward protesters, enforcement of racial codes in the South, and retrograde militarization provoked vocal protest in the peacenik era. As one text on policing recounts, "Civil rights and antiwar movements challenged police. This challenge took several forms. The legitimacy of police was questioned: students resisted police, minorities rioted against them, and the public, observing police via live television for the first time, questioned their tactics."[1] Facing a crisis of legitimacy, police departments began to rethink the role of the officers as exclusive crime control enforcers, moving to more "holistic" approaches like community policing. The late 1970s is often called the "Community Problem Solving" era of policing.[2]

In an influential 1979 article, "Improving Policing: A Problem Oriented Approach," law professor Herman Goldstein urged police departments to abandon their myopic focus on interdicting crimes and to recategorize crimes as "problems."[3] In turn, the police could begin "identifying these problems in more precise terms, researching each problem, documenting the nature of the current police response, assessing its adequacy and the adequacy of existing authority and resources, engaging in a broad exploration of alternatives to present responses, weighing the merits of these alternatives, and choosing from among them."[4] The article gives the reader a sense that change was already in the air. "Police in many jurisdictions, in a commendable effort to employ alternatives to the criminal justice system, have arranged to make referrals to various social, health, and legal agencies," Goldstein observed. "By tying into the services provided by the whole range of other helping agencies in the community, the police in these cities have taken a giant step toward improving the quality of their response."[5]

Given the larger focus on improving policing, it is not surprising that feminist and other experts in the 1970s scrutinized police responses to DV calls. Experts across the political and philosophical spectrum recognized the problems of officers failing to respond to DV calls, responding but doing nothing, or intervening in a way that made the situation worse. These experts, however, held diverse and conflicting views on what constituted "effective" police intervention and whether it needed to involve forcible arrest.

In 1976, when feminist lawyers in New York filed *Bruno v. Codd,* which articulated a battered woman's right to her abuser's arrest, many departments favored mediation as the initial response to domestic disturbances.[6] At that time, there was little empirical evidence on whether arrest (as opposed to nonarrest intervention) better prevented injuries, deterred reoffense, or satisfied victims. The legal aid lawyers and constitutional scholars behind the *Bruno* litigation were well aware of the serious burdens arrest imposed, especially on marginalized individuals. They nevertheless presumed that arrest, with all its costs and dysfunctions, was preferable to the current system in which police exercised excessive restraint.[7] *Bruno* attorney Laurie Woods argued that "the best protection for both a woman and her husband [is] to have a police officer armed with a mandatory duty to arrest, intervene."[8] Arrest became the official feminist position, relegating mediation to the province of retrograde sexists.[9]

This chapter examines feminists' persistent belief that arrest was the best way to address DV, despite increasing sociological evidence and scholarly commentary in the 1980s and 1990s to the contrary. I contend that, in addition to the general orientation of legal feminists toward law enforcement, there were two main ideological drivers of their proarrest stance. First, feminists presumed that police reluctance to arrest derived exclusively from officers' antediluvian ideas about marital privacy and husbands' right to physically "chastise" wives. Second, feminists were highly critical of the "neutral" family violence research school championing mediation. Those researchers, feminists maintained, were inattentive to patriarchy, blamed women and men equally for DV, and supported ineffective psychosocial interventions.

I also postulate that feminist DV advocacy shored up the coercive arrest model of policing in an era of declining faith in the model's legitimacy. In pushing for arrest, feminists made sweeping arguments about the appropriate role of the police, such as the claim that police had a duty to arrest whenever there is probable cause. In the face of evidence that arrest could have an "escalation effect" on violence, many feminists did not rethink the proarrest program.[10] Instead, they articulated a series of authoritarian arguments to downplay the evidence, including that mandatory arrest was not harsh *enough* and had to trigger serious carceral consequences. One feminist commentator in 1983 made the remarkable claim that to address DV, law professors should back off from teaching students about civil liberties. The problem of police restraint in DV, she wrote, would be "solved only by a change in the attitudes of legal educators who traditionally have focused on constitutional and other legal limitations on enforcement authority."[11]

OF NEANDERTHAL COPS

In the late 1970s, feminist lawyers, drawing on their experience with a subset of battered clients, concluded that arrest was the optimal way to intervene in DV, as well as what victims wanted. In pursuing impact litigation for proarrest policies, activists moved from speaking for individual clients to speaking for all women. No one can escape the limits of their own perspective, and I have little doubt that the *Bruno* attorneys felt confident that their picture of DV victims' interests was generalizable. Nevertheless, it seems curious that the lawyers did not set out to systematically determine whether and which victims wanted or benefited from arrest. Moreover, they did not care to rely on the sociological evidence that family violence researchers had already produced. Instead, the *Bruno* lawyers collected and presented to the courts affidavits from victims whose cases had specific characteristics: there was extreme violence; the victim wanted the police to arrest the abuser; and the officers told the victim they had no authority to arrest, or worse, defended the abuser.[12] The affidavits painted a picture of total police indifference and nonfeasance, "not because of the merits of the particular case, but apparently as a matter of policy," as the *Bruno* trial court put it.[13] It is unsurprising then that the court described the litigation's ambition as modest—"merely . . . to compel the police to exercise their discretion in each 'particular situation,' and not to automatically decline to make an arrest."[14]

However, granting individual officers "discretion in each 'particular situation'" was not the *Bruno* litigation's ambition. Legal feminists wanted to *limit* officer discretion to decline arrest, which they believed officers were overusing because of sexism. Professor Kathleen Waits put the sentiment bluntly in 1985: "Society cannot rely on [officers] to use their discretion wisely in battering cases."[15] Thus *Bruno* culminated with the New York Police Department signing a consent decree with a written, legally binding, proarrest policy. The decree limited officers' discretion to decline misdemeanor arrests and mandated arrest for felonies and restraining-order violations.[16] In the decades after *Bruno,* activists, lawmakers, and police departments moved to even stricter policies, requiring police to "automatically" arrest in felony and misdemeanor cases alike, regardless of the "particular situation."

To be sure, the *Bruno* plaintiffs and affiants interviewed in connection with the case did, in fact, desire arrest. It makes sense that *they* would regard arrest as best. But such would not necessarily be true of the many antiarrest and arrest-ambivalent victims whom feminist lawyers simply omitted when they formulated the agenda of the entire class of battered women. Yet today, even die-hard policing critics who recognize that proarrest DV policies are harmful and criminogenic regard the current punitive regime as preferable to the "bad old days" of police tolerance. How were feminist lawyers so successful at making the remarkably broad claim that *every* woman benefited from arrest?

Feminist lawyers adopted, or perhaps strategically deployed, an exceedingly narrow account of officers' motivation for, victims' attitudes toward, and the effects of nonarrest. They publicized a one-dimensional story involving sexist male officers influenced by chauvinist law and culture, who refused to arrest abusers because they believed that abuse was acceptable, the woman deserved it, or the matter was personal. Police empathy for abusers, the story went, remained unmitigated even when the woman was beaten and bloodied. This narrative *defined* nonarrest as an exercise of sexism, so that every arrest was an instance of gender justice, regardless of the consequences. In turn, violent male police officers using violent arrest to control violent men was not a pathology of a "fascist" state. It was feminist.

Feminists drew a direct line between 1970s cops' attitudes and the bygone practice of "chastisement," meaning husband's corrective disciplining of wives. In early DV activism, scholars and lawyers regularly referenced English jurist William Blackstone's 1769 commentaries on the husband's right to "give his wife moderate correction" as proof of legal tolerance of wife-beating in eighteenth- and nineteenth-century England and the US.[17] In fact, however, Blackstone characterized chastisement as "old law" that had been superseded and as an "ancient privilege" exercised rarely and only among the "lower ranks" in the Charles I era.[18] Blackstone further noted that by the later era of "the politer reign of Charles the Second, . . . a wife [had] security of the peace against her husband."[19] Further, there is little evidence that US courts and legislatures widely adopted the ancient English rule. In an 1871 Alabama criminal case, for example, the Alabama Supreme Court addressed a domestic violence incident between two "high tempered" married "emancipated slaves."[20] The defense moved to dismiss the charge, citing the right of chastisement, but the court upheld the man's indictment. Noting that Blackstone "confines this brutal and unchristian 'privilege' wholly to the 'lower rank of the people,'" the court ruled that in Alabama "the law for one rank is the law for all ranks of the people."[21] It elaborated, "This distinguished author [Blackstone] published his commentaries above one hundred years ago, when society was much more rude, out of the towns and cities in England, than it is at the present day in this country; and the exercise of a rude privilege there is no excuse for a like privilege here."[22]

Still, for decades, commentators made much of the so-called rule of thumb,[23] citing the 1868 North Carolina case *State v. Rhodes,* where the trial judge was said to be "of opinion that the defendant had a right to whip his wife with a switch no larger than his thumb."[24] This case was by all respects an outlier in American jurisprudence and was quickly reversed and repudiated by the North Carolina Supreme Court. In fact, the smattering of US chastisement cases were "wholly rejected after the Civil War."[25] Nevertheless, second-wave feminists made *Rhodes* and related cases so infamous that they spawned the etymological myth that the phrase *rule of thumb* originated from domestic violence law (it was an agricultural measure). After the landmark 1978 Commission on Civil Rights (CCR) hearings discussed in the previous chapter, CCR chairman Arthur Flemming issued his final report on wife abuse in 1982. It was entitled *Under the Rule of Thumb.*[26]

This is not to say that seventeenth- and eighteenth-century America was "good" on domestic violence. The complicated history of DV in America is recounted in extraordinary detail—better than I ever could—by historians like Elizabeth Pleck and Reva Seigel.[27] What is clear is that the history is not simply one of law and society celebrating men who beat women. Wifebeaters were regularly regarded as dissolute, unmanly drunkards, deserving of condemnation. The legal cases tolerant of DV reflected "a larger cultural tension in nineteenth-century America, one between sympathy for the victims of abuse, especially innocent women, and the perpetuation of traditional hierarchical relationships within the family," writes historian Ruth Bloch.[28] While some state actors turned a blind eye to abuse to preserve the marital order, others called for nothing less than abusers' flagellation. Southern politicians, in particular, welcomed corporal punishment for DV, which they considered a "negro crime."[29] There is accordingly little support for the opening sentence of the *Bruno* opinion: "For too long, Anglo-American law treated a man's physical abuse of his wife . . . as an acceptable practice."[30]

Legal feminists presumed that contemporary cops' leniency stemmed from "rule of thumb," pro-wife-beating sentiments. The sexist-cops story stuck. Today, even critics who lament the many costs of DV policing policies, such as financial burdens, family separation, and exacerbation of violence, speak as though these are new discoveries that could not have factored into the motivations of the Neanderthal officers of the 1970s. To be sure, many of those officers were—and many still are—raging sexists, sympathetic toward battering, or abusers themselves. However, the nonarrest story has always been significantly more complicated than the narrow activist account admits. The CCR collected police testimony between 1978 and 1980 in preparation for the *Rule of Thumb* report. The sentiments expressed by the police are illuminating, and surprising.

Officers did not opine that abuse was legitimate, no big deal, or a private matter inappropriate for government intervention. Rather, they articulated somewhat unexpected explanations for why the "traditional" police functions of crime investigation and bad-guy apprehension worked poorly in domestic violence situations.[31] Police cautioned that the very intrusion into an emotional conflict could escalate the violence, pointing to evidence that DV calls were particularly lethal to first responders. Researchers agreed: "The police officer, if he is unprepared for his function and left to draw upon his own often biased notions of family dynamics and upon his skills as a law enforcer, may actually behave in ways to induce a tragic outcome."[32] Relatedly, the police asserted that arrest could increase the severity of subsequent battering. Moreover, the continuing connection between the DV defendant and victim made the police more concerned than usual about the harsh collateral consequences of arrest. Like first-wave feminists, they worried that arrest caused batterers to lose employment, thereby financially harming victims and putting greater strains on dysfunctional relationships. But the most straightforward and frequent explanation for nonarrest was that *victims* objected. One former police chief explained to the CCR: "Blood is thicker than water is a true thing out here, and it's hard to get the woman to come forward and sign complaints and follow through on it because in many instances it is her source of revenue to keep the family together. And in many instances she loves him. She still does love him."[33]

Of course, sexism played an important, if nuanced, role in the police's distaste for DV calls. The recurring, relational nature of domestic violence put in stark relief the ineffectiveness of their busting-bad-guys model of policing. Officers indoctrinated toward coercive enforcement were reluctant to face the reality that the best response to crisis, even violent crisis, was not always force. When it came to DV, police could not just play their masculine cops-versus-robbers games, and they felt impotent to serve and protect women in the manner they were accustomed to. Accordingly, officers detested taking domestic violence calls because they did "not believe that arresting assailants [would] have any positive results."[34]

The conventional feminist narrative thus misdiagnoses *how* masculinity norms affected officers responding to DV calls. It was not so much that most officers were club-dragging cavemen who high-fived rather than arrested suspects. Instead, officers lamented that the complicated nature of DV prevented them from capturing the criminal in simple superhero style—and from receiving the gratitude of the rescued damsel. Officers came to feel incompetent, out of place, and personally endangered in the face of complex, emotionally explosive, dysfunctional relationships. One explained that the responding officer saw only "an outcropping of a much more deep-seated problem."[35] "It's a police problem when we deal with it, but the cause is not a police problem."[36]

Police ambivalence toward DV arrest, so denigrated by feminists, presented an opportunity for a larger transformation in police self-identity. Instead of functioning exclusively as an us-versus-them roving band of head-busters, police could see themselves as something else—something less authoritarian, less black-versus-white, and more communal. Psychologist and policing expert Morton Bard, channeling the problem-solving sentiments in vogue at the time, testified at the 1978 CCR hearings:

> There are two ways of viewing the role of the police in relation to domestic disturbances: They can be seen as "enforcers of the law" or they can be seen as "managers of human crisis and conflict." If we take the first point of view, the objective of police intervention in a family dispute is simple and clear: to determine whether a law has been broken. If so, arrest and prosecute; if not, do nothing. Although this role definition certainly simplifies things for the officer, it does very little to help the majority of families who call the police.[37]

Bard, a professor at City University of New York (CUNY), had conducted a large-scale "family violence" policing experiment in the late 1960s. It involved creating a special "Family Crisis Intervention Unit" composed of nine black and nine white officers within the Upper West Side police precinct, which at that time served a community of eighty-five thousand mostly working-class African Americans.[38] The officers in the unit attended an intensive four-week training in de-escalation and mediation, involving simulations, reflection, and group sessions with CUNY psychology graduate students. The inception of the project coincided with a wave of popular antipolice activism. A high-profile clash between police and Columbia University students nearly derailed the project, as the CUNY graduate students "could not face" their police consultees.[39] Later, the CUNY chapter of Students for a Democratic Society (SDS) picketed the project, chanting "Pigs Off Campus." But the project forged ahead.[40]

In many ways the training, which aimed to reorient officers away from reverence for violence and binary views of right and wrong, was distinctly *feminist*. Its demasculinizing goals were explicit. Bard explained, "The group sessions restructured the value system of the officers [so they could] deal with the 'masculine mystique' which has helped make police so malleable at the hands of those who have been interested in provoking violence."[41] Bard intended the training to break the cycle of masculine violence and retrospective justification identified by Hans Toch: "Violent men play violent games because their nonviolent repertoire is restricted. This role, which emphasizes physical and social distance, minimal communication, and a we-versus-they attitude, makes it all too easy . . . to view [an officer] in terms of preconceived stereotypes, and to justify his behavior in terms of the stereotype."[42] The training was precisely the reformation of "sexist attitudes" that many feminists identified as the root of DV.[43]

After the DV unit operated for two years, Bard set out to assess the practical effects of the pilot project. The NYPD forbade him to follow up with the 952 families that had interacted with the unit, citing privacy concerns. Nevertheless, Bard found several indications of success. None of the officers were hurt during interventions, and there were no homicides within the families they had contacted. Arrests decreased by 2.5 percent, and there were fewer overall incidents of family assault in the Upper West Side than in a similar precinct. The few follow-up interviews showed that the police and community enjoyed improved relations.[44]

After Bard's work touting the benefits of nonviolent intervention, several police departments incorporated conflict resolution training. Perhaps this could have been a watershed moment in orienting police identity away from aggressive enforcer toward peacemaker. Alas, it was not. As early as 1976, the International Association of Chiefs of Police declared unequivocally that a "policy of arrest [for DV], when the elements of the offense are present, promotes the well-being of the victim."[45] It turns out that the purportedly abuser-loving police officers were all too eager to adopt feminists' proarrest program. Although departments had defended against lawsuits to protect their financial interests, many officers ultimately welcomed the respite from exercising discretion in DV situations. By the 1980s, police chiefs joined feminists in championing proarrest policies. Bard predicted as much at the CCR hearings: "Many police officers long for the very thing that I have heard recommended here today [by feminist activists]. They long for the simple solution that arrest offers. Because of their action orientation and their intolerance for delay in 'doing something,' the intangible quality of negotiation or mediation can be disturbing to some of them. These officers prefer simple and direct action . . . which they see as getting them out of the 'social work business.'"[46]

One is left to wonder whether, in the absence of feminist proarrest litigation and activism, Bard's program to transform officers from hypermasculine authoritarians to calm crisis interveners would have taken off or translated to non-DV policing. It is true that factors from rising crime rates to policing initiatives aimed at maintaining order undermined police departments' institutionalization of mediation, nonarrest, and de-escalation policies. But the influence of feminist theory and practice cannot be ruled out. At the time of *Bruno,* most states' criminal procedure codes prohibited police from making warrantless misdemeanor arrests for crimes not occurring in their presence.[47] The idea was that, in the absence of exigency, misdemeanors were not serious enough to relieve the police of the obligation to obtain permission from a judge to use coercive force. This liberal rule was intended to protect citizens from government overreach. Feminist lawyers, however, regarded it as a technicality that gave cover to sexist police. Today, forty-nine states and the District of Columbia exempt DV misdemeanors from that rule.[48]

Feminist lawyers specifically targeted police departments' novel dispute resolution policies. The Oakland Police Department's 1975 training policy on "dispute intervention" stated, "The police role in a dispute situation is more often that of a mediator and peacemaker than enforcer of the law."[49] It went on, "[When] one of the parties demands arrest, you should attempt to explain the ramifications of such action (e.g., loss of wages, bail procedures, court appearances) and encourage the parties to reason with each other."[50] This policy formed the basis for *Bruno*'s companion class action suit, *Scott v. Hart.*

The plaintiffs argued that the policy violated domestic violence victims' right to equal protection. The police chief responded that the policy applied to *all* misdemeanor assaults. Unfazed, the plaintiffs rejoined that the department's embrace of peacemaking was sexist and discriminatory because it was formulated with DV victims in mind and disparately affected them.[51]

The 1970s police officers' arguments against arrest—safety, the relationship, the high rate of attrition, financial issues, victims' wishes—are currently articulated by *feminist* critics of mandatory DV policies. Yet legal feminists like *Scott* attorney Pauline Gee characterized such arguments as lacking "any rational factual basis" and "not legitimate."[52] Such arguments were mere pretexts to cover Neanderthal cops' intent to "condone wife beating," as another advocate put it.[53] One legal scholar, writing in 1983, catalogued police reasons for nonarrest, which included sexist beliefs but also factors like "the abuser and his family cannot afford the economic impact of time lost from work" and "the spousal relationship may be brought to an end by the intervention of the criminal justice process."[54] The reasons were *all* illegitimate, she opined, because they would not "be acceptable reasons . . . if the complaint was of assault by a stranger."[55]

I cannot help but be nostalgic for that early police reluctance to use force in family dispute situations. We hear case after case where families in crisis or those worried about mentally ill loved ones call the police for help, only to face drug raid–style deadly force. The home remains an acute site of danger for suspects and officers. Sadly, it is hard to imagine a contemporary police trainer making the statement that Phoenix training officer Glenn Sparks made in 1980: "Obviously if we can avoid putting somebody in jail and still solve the situation that is exactly what we want to do in most cases."[56]

FEMINISTS VERSUS FAMILY VIOLENCE RESEARCHERS

Feminists dismissed the many nonsexist reasons police were reluctant to arrest and, at the same time, admitted that "information about the effectiveness of more stringent arrest policies is scant."[57] Feminist lawyers relied on their clients' accounts of how arrest would have helped them and reasoned that other women would similarly benefit. In the feminist (and increasingly police) narrative, arrest would be the wake-up call that finally made the man come to his senses and stop abusing or the woman come to her senses and leave him. One victims' advocate asserted that mandatory arrest made a woman "begin to believe in herself enough to endeavor to protect herself."[58]

At the time of the *Bruno* and *Scott* litigations in the 1970s, significant "family violence" research projects looking into the structures underlying DV were under way and were producing evidence-informed conclusions about how to intervene. They undermined the feminist claim that arrest served as a wake-up call. Researchers found that family violence correlated with internal relationship stressors, such as childbirth and job loss, and external social stressors, such as persistent poverty, racial subordination, and low-class status. They postulated that decreasing these stressors—not adding arrest stress—was the key to reducing violence.[59] Indeed, Bard testified at the CCR hearings, "More often than not [arrest] initiates a judicial process which, experience tells us, has little chance of a productive outcome."[60] Yet legal feminists largely ignored these studies in favor of a costly arrest program that they could only speculate would work.

Legal feminists did not just reject researchers' socioeconomic and psychological accounts of battering. They disdained them. Activists objected to the very term *family violence*, arguing that it hid DV's true nature as a phenomenon of patriarchy-enabled male-on-female violence. Researchers' tendency to approach the DV issue clinically, without reproach for the abuser and the patriarchy, turned feminists off. Much as antipatriarchy feminists resisted black feminists' connection of DV to racism, legal feminists argued that researchers' structural analyses of DV downplayed men's culpability. Feminists eventually condemned the entire structuralist family violence research agenda as simultaneously abuse excusing and victim blaming. This familiar feminist theme persists today. Contemporary feminists argue that states and institutions should not be in the business of regulating structural risk factors for gender crime because "abusers cause abuse" and "rapists cause rape."[61]

Family violence researchers' road to becoming personae non gratae began in the 1960s. Some infamous studies made popular the pseudopsychology claim that battered women are masochists who enjoy abuse. In 1964, a group of male therapists at a clinic in Framingham, Massachusetts, published "The Wifebeater's Wife."[62] The authors, who treated abusers referred to them by the court, chose thirty-seven wives of their patients as study subjects. They ultimately produced a textbook example of the patriarchal psychoanalysis rightly denigrated by feminists. As a "rule," the authors claimed, wives were "aggressive, efficient, masculine, and sexually frigid."[63] Husbands were "shy, sexually ineffectual, reasonably hard working 'mothers' boys.'"[64] The study disclaimed any cultural or socioeconomic causes of abuse, preferring a misogynistic Freudian account: "The periods of violent behavior by the husband served to release him momentarily from his anxiety about his ineffectiveness as a man, while, at the same time, giving his wife apparent masochistic gratification and helping probably to deal with the guilt arising from . . . her controlling, castrating behavior."[65]

By the time family violence researchers Murray Straus, Richard Gelles, and Suzanne Steinmetz conducted their pioneering 1975 Study of Family Violence, feminists' distaste for family violence research was strong. The study, which comprehensively documented abuse involving 2,143 families, significantly raised the DV issue's profile.[66] Beyond cataloguing the extent of DV, the researchers shed light on the social, economic, cultural, and psychological conditions that contributed to abuse. The study found a strong connection between DV and social stressors like poverty, low status, and racial discrimination.[67] The authors also linked violence to the patriarchal family structure, observing that the compulsion to marry and male-dominant marriage dynamics caused conflict. In short, the authors were distinctly critical of sexist marriage norms and women's general socioeconomic marginality.[68]

Feminists nevertheless excoriated the study for one of its empirical findings. The study found that "the rate of female-to-male assault was slightly higher than the rate of male-to-female assault."[69] Antibattering activists regarded this data point as the very pinnacle of victim blaming. Some rejected the statistic out of hand, but that became harder over time as research consistently found significant female-perpetrated intimate violence.[70] The primary feminist critique became that the researchers failed to appropriately contextualize women's violence. Feminists postulated that women's violence was noninjurious, reactive, and justified: women resorted to minor violence in self-defense or in response to a pattern of bad behavior by men.[71]

Straus and coauthors included "injury-adjusted" rates in later studies, which confirmed feminists' assertion that men's assaults more often produced injuries. Feminists felt vindicated in the belief that the entire corpus of family violence research was infected with patriarchy. Straus, however, offered a distinctly *feminist* explanation for why the researchers had previously downplayed injury. They had thought that separating out injurious assaults would diminish the scope of the DV problem:

> A disadvantage of using injury as a criterion for domestic assault is that injury-based rates omit the 97 percent of assaults by men that do not result in

injury but that are nonetheless a serious social problem. Without an adjust-
ment for injury, the National Family Violence Survey produces an estimate of
more than 6 million women assaulted by a male partner each year, of which
1.8 million are "severe" assaults. If the injury-adjusted rate is used, the estimate is reduced to 188,000 assaulted women per year. The figure of 1.8 million
seriously assaulted women every year has been used in many legislative hearings and countless feminist publications to indicate the prevalence of the
problem.[72]

To be sure, the researchers offered explanations for women's violence,
including the insight that marriage norms, poverty, and *women's* inequality
underlay female-perpetrated violence. Straus too hypothesized that self-
defense explained women's violence, although he later came to question this
hypothesis in light of evidence of female-initiated violence and female-
violence-only relationships. In any case, Straus made clear, in the 1976 article
"Sexual Inequality, Cultural Norms, and Wife-Beating," his view that DV
was caused by "the sexist organization of the society and the family."[73] He
concluded that the "sexual inequalities inherent in all of our societal systems
leave *women* locked in a brutal marriage."[74]

Yet as feminists feared, the public soon became fascinated with female-
perpetrated violence. In 1977, Susan Steinmetz published the provocatively
titled *The Battered Husband Syndrome* to counter society's "selective inattention" to husband abuse.[75] "While the horrors of wife-beating are paraded
before the public," she lamented, husband-beating remained "hidden under
a cloak of secrecy."[76] The relatively short piece reviewed the data on the frequency of wife-against-husband violence and discussed reasons why the
husband didn't leave. Steinmetz expressed plenty of condemnation, but it was
against violence, not patriarchy. She critiqued feminists for adopting a sexist
violence hierarchy that protected certain types of violence: male-against-
female violence was horrific, male-against-male was tolerable, and female-
against-male was invisible. The focus on battered wives, Steinmetz concluded,
"overlooks a basic condition of violence between spouses—a society which
glorifies violence if done for the 'right reasons': the good of society, or that of
one's own family. It is critical to shift at least some of the blame from individual family members to basic socio-cultural conditions."[77]

The article received outsized media coverage and was touted hysterically
by feminist-hating men's rights groups. Feminists pushed back, some quite
literally. Steinmetz recalls that she "received some threats of violence, ironically from angry women because I dared report that women could also be

violent."[78] The battered-husband episode indelibly marked family violence researchers as bêtes noires among feminists. Gelles later reflected on that moment in the late 1970s:

> The response to our finding that the rate of female-to-male family violence was equal to the rate of male-to-female violence not only produced heated scholarly criticism, but intense and long-lasting personal attacks. All three of us [Gelles, Straus, and Steinmetz] received death threats. Bomb threats were phoned in to conference centers and buildings where we were scheduled to present. Suzanne [Steinmetz] received the brunt of the attacks—individuals wrote and called her university urging that she be denied tenure; calls were made and letters were written to government agencies urging that her grant funding be rescinded. All three of us became "nonpersons" among domestic violence advocates.... Librarians publicly stated they would not order or shelve our books.[79]

In 1986, Straus and Gelles published a follow-up family violence study.[80] Gelles recalls that when the study showed similar rates of female-on-male violence and failed to prove the self-defense hypothesis, "This round of personal attacks was much more insidious—in particular, it was alleged that Murray [Straus] had abused his wife."[81]

Steinmetz's article was highly condemnatory of *all* family violence, indeed of societal violence in general. But feminists rightly saw the discussion of female-perpetrated violence as perilous to their agenda. Antipatriarchy feminists used the battering issue to spotlight the harms of inequality and sexist gender norms. If men, who had all the power, stayed with violent women, it stood to reason that it was not gender oppression but "mad love" that made women stay with violent men. Now, Steinmetz had explained that male victims faced their own constraints like masculinity norms, financial concerns, and pressure to stay married. Nonetheless, feminists logically surmised that such nuance would be lost on a public apt to believe that female-perpetrated violence meant DV was just a matter of "crazy couples." Indeed, men's rights agitators exploited the research to deny that gender played *any* role in DV, even though the studies found otherwise. Activist Susan Schechter wrote an open letter to Steinmetz: "Your 'evenhanded' research gives people the opportunity to quibble over numbers and allows them to ignore the ... lack of alternatives in women's lives."[82]

The evidence on female-perpetrated violence was particularly challenging to the legal feminist agenda. Recognizing that women commit abuse would entail recognizing that mandatory DV arrest policies could increase arrests of women.

In addition, the Steinmetz study had the potential to undercut the social outrage that gave the battering issue political heft. The image of female batterers and male victims lessened the sense that DV was invariably a repulsive, horrific, and inexcusable crime perpetrated by the powerful against the weak and manageable only by criminal sanctions. Accordingly, many feminist activists took the ostrich approach, disregarding the female-violence evidence as fake data and writing off all of family violence research as sexist pseudoscience.

WHAT IF ARREST IS NOT BEST?

Feminists needn't have worried about public apathy toward battering or sympathy for batterers. By the 1980s, the rehabilitative, interventionist ideal championed by sociologists was giving way to simple incapacitation and deterrence through incarceration as the exclusive way to address crime. Batterers, as one observer remarked, became "the perfect bad guys, enjoying villainous roles in film and on television."[83] Lawmakers and society members, DV activists along with them, traded "violence begets violence" for "an eye for an eye." It hardly mattered anymore whether there would ever be evidence that arrest "worked."

But the evidence that arrest worked did come in 1984, by way of the Minneapolis Domestic Violence Experiment ("Minneapolis Experiment"). Sociologists Lawrence Sherman and Richard Berk published a bombshell report attesting to the proven deterrent effects of arrest.[84] The experiment followed thirty-four officers of the Minneapolis Police Department on their DV calls for about a year. Officers were assigned by lottery to arrest the suspect, send the suspect away from the house for eight hours, or give advice. The researchers tracked those cases, a total of 205, for a six-month period after arrest and found that arrest was most effective at deterring reoffense.[85] The researchers concluded that the data "strongly suggests that the police should use arrest in *most* domestic violence cases."[86] It was a curious systemic suggestion, given that the study found only that randomly distributed arrests were more effective than randomly distributed alternatives. It did not study whether a presumptive arrest *system* was more deterrent than a calibrated arrest system where police would exercise guided discretion, use an arrest checklist, or give victims control.

Sherman and Berk intended the experiment, which had a small sample size and short follow-up period, to be a precursor to more detailed replication studies. The results of those studies came at a rapid pace in the next several years and undermined arrest's deterrent effect. However, in the increasingly crime-obsessed society, the Minneapolis Experiment had made a splash. It eclipsed previous studies, such as Bard's mediation experiment, and would eclipse the more thorough experiments to come. It is still the most famous DV study. In 1984, the year of the experiment's publication, only a few states had enacted DV statutes. By 1991, around half the states had some form of proarrest DV statute.[87] In 1984, 10 percent of police departments had proarrest policies, and by 1989 that number had soared to 89 percent.[88] In a 1985 survey, 71 percent of police department heads reported knowing about the experiment, leading Sherman to remark that the study "did reach a large number of police departments and may have had a substantial—although far from universal—influence on policy."[89] Even the Supreme Court noted the study's influence, stating in 2005, "Emboldened by a well-known 1984 experiment by the Minneapolis police department, many states enacted mandatory arrest statutes."[90]

Feminists brought family violence research back into their good graces, touting the Minneapolis Experiment as vindication of their turn to the penal state. It was objective evidence of feminists' sexist-cop thesis—conclusive proof, as one advocate wrote in 1985, that feminists were right to regard officers' claims that arrest escalated violence as "absurd."[91] A 1986 *Yale Law Review* article relied on the experiment to declare that arrest was "the *most* effective way for police to protect women from further abuse."[92] Citing the experiment, professor Sarah Buel wrote in 1988, "Evidence shows that arrest substantially reduces the number of domestic assaults *and murders*."[93] Of note, the Minneapolis Experiment said nothing about murders, and in fact it was not until 2007 that a study compared domestic homicide rates among states with and without mandatory arrest laws and within states before and after such laws. It found that "mandatory arrest laws are responsible for an additional 0.8 murders per 100,000 people," corresponding to a "54 percent increase in intimate partner homicides."[94] The author hypothesized that arrest had deterred at-risk DV victims from calling the police and supported the hypothesis with evidence that mandatory arrest for child abuse, which is primarily reported by third parties, did not increase killings.[95]

Of course, there were many factors moving lawmakers and police departments toward proarrest policies, including feminist impact litigation and high-profile DV cases. In 1984, Tracey Thurman filed a civil rights lawsuit against the City of Torrington, Connecticut, police department for failing to protect her from her abusive ex-husband, who had stabbed her thirteen times as she waited for police to show up. Tracey had repeatedly called the police on Buck, but police virtually ignored her calls despite Buck's status as a DV probationer under a restraining order.[96] The case spurred intense media coverage and a made-for-TV movie, *A Cry for Help*.[97] It also garnered Tracey a $2.3 million civil award and spurred the 1986 passage of "Tracey's Law," making Connecticut the seventh state to mandate arrest for DV crimes.[98]

Still, the Minneapolis Experiment had an outsized influence on law and policy, and some peculiar facts help explain why. Dr. Sherman was somewhat singular in his belief that "social scientists should generally view publicity-seeking as a duty rather than a vice."[99] Sherman released the preliminary results of the Minneapolis Experiment in an exclusive story in the *New York Times* Science Section.[100] He released his final results over Memorial Day weekend to garner maximum publicity, leading to coverage by three hundred national and international newspapers, the *PBS News Hour*, and the *CBS Evening News*.[101] During the experiment's initial research phase, Sherman had a local public television station film a ride-along with police so that he would have action footage to accompany the eventual release of the experiment's results.[102]

The unusual publicity about and reception of the Minneapolis Experiment caused some concern in sociological circles. Legal sociologist Richard Lempert, recognizing the "excellent" nature of the study, cautioned that its results "have been prematurely and unduly publicized."[103] He explained, "If an anti-cancer drug had been tested instead of an anti-crime drug, substantial additional testing would have been required before the drug was made available for general distribution."[104] Lempert worried about the study's translation to nationwide policy because of the uniqueness of individual police districts and the fact that the study had not separated procedures accompanying arrest (temporary detention, victim services, etc.) from the arrest itself. Perhaps most importantly, the study did not rule out that reports of violence decreased after arrest because victims had been deterred from reporting.[105] Lempert concluded that "police departments that have changed their arrest practices in response to this research may have adopted an innovation that does more harm than good."[106]

Sherman and coauthors acknowledged that the Minneapolis study had been unusually effective at sparking change and that single studies were not a "panacea in either legal or medical research."[107] But he defended his media-seeking actions as part of a virtuous progression in which publicity of the latest science would foster better policy: "Publicity about each new study can focus attention and funding on further research. Should further studies reach different conclusions, publicity about them can influence policies to change yet again. If legal policies are to be based on science, they must be able to change along with the constant evolution of scientific knowledge. Publicity can hasten this evolution."[108] When Sherman penned this defense in 1989, he and his coauthors' replication studies were already undermining the Minneapolis Experiment's prescriptions. His prediction that politicians would evolve in response turned out to be naïve.

Beginning in 1986, Sherman and colleagues conducted studies in five major urban police districts, each with more cases than in the Minneapolis Experiment, comprising thousands of cases followed for several years.[109] That research, in sum, revealed that "arrest often seems to have an 'escalation effect,' aggravating the subsequent violence," as law professor Stephen Schulhofer observed.[110] It turns out that the police reluctance to arrest out of fear of escalating the violence was not so "absurd." In three of the districts, arrest increased DV reoffense overall. Arrest often produced an immediate protective effect but increased violence over time. In Milwaukee, for example, arrest transformed victims' 7 percent chance of an immediate postpolicing beating to a 2 percent chance of a beating after the abuser's release from detention. However, it *doubled* the incidents of violence over the course of a year.[111] The studies confirmed that socioeconomic and racial factors played a role in arrest efficacy. Arrest increased violence among unmarried, unemployed men and "backfired" rather than "deterred" in districts with larger percentages of black suspects.[112] Today, the deterrent effect of arrest remains hotly contested.[113]

By 1992, Sherman and coauthors possessed enough data to proclaim, "Mandatory arrest may make as much sense as fighting fire with gasoline."[114] Less than a decade after the Minneapolis Experiment fascinated the nation, Sherman advanced an anti–mandatory arrest agenda:

> The most compelling implications of these findings is to challenge the wisdom of mandatory arrest. States and cities that have enacted such laws should repeal them, especially if they have substantial ghetto poverty populations with high unemployment rates. . . . It remains possible but unlikely that mandatory arrest creates a general deterrent effect among the wider public not arrested. Even if it does, however, increased violence among unemployed persons who are arrested is a serious moral stain on the benefits of general deterrence. The argument that arrest expresses the moral outrage of the state also appears weak, if the price of that outrage is increased violence against some victims.[115]

Sherman would be frustrated to find that the science policy evolution began and ended with the proarrest Minneapolis Experiment. Whereas Minneapolis made a splash, the replication studies hardly produce a ripple. Sherman expressed disappointment when the Wisconsin legislature passed a mandatory arrest law in 1988 "despite their awareness of the ongoing replication in Milwaukee."[116] He lamented, "If a little medicine was good, a lot was even better."[117]

Into the 1990s, states and localities adopted proarrest policies as if the replication studies did not exist. In 1997, Virginia adopted mandatory arrest legislation based on the recommendation of a twenty-five-member family violence committee.[118] Joel Garner, research director of the Joint Centers for Justice Studies, authored a searing critique of the committee's report. The report "provide[d] virtually no evidence on why mandatory arrest might be useful to the Commonwealth of Virginia nor on the effectiveness of mandatory arrest for domestic violence in other jurisdictions."[119] Instead, it favored a "highly-dramatic anecdote that describes a brutal domestic violence incident for which the police did not make an arrest."[120] The commission's sole scientific proof that mandatory arrest deterred was Buel's 1988 article referencing the now-superseded Minneapolis Experiment. Garner warned that Sherman's Milwaukee study indicated that "arrest will have generally negative effects in jurisdictions like Richmond, with relatively high unemployment and a high proportion of unmarried, intimate partners."[121] Most troubling, the commission's primary justification for mandatory arrest was not protection, deterrence, or even gender justice. It was "fairness" to social work–averse police officers: "A police officer's job is to preserve public order and prevent crime. By placing the burden on the police to decide whether to make the arrest in a domestic violence case, the law asks the officer to serve as a counselor, which he is not trained to do and is beyond the requirements of his position. *It is unfair to the police officer for him to be required to do more than preserve public order and prevent crime.*"[122]

If legislators ignored the new science, legal feminists actively denigrated the researcher they had just celebrated. Advocates had applauded the Minneapolis design, yet Sherman's better-designed but arrest-unsupportive Milwaukee experiment was proof that "advocates of battered women should be involved in designing *any* domestic violence experiments."[123] To be sure, there were many feminists who were already skeptical of the battered women's movement's carceral trajectory and deeply troubled by the results of the replication studies. However, over a decade into the legal battle for arrest and after massive expenditures of political, financial, and academic capital, many feminists regarded proarrest policies as a crowning achievement. In turn, they automatically equated arrest policies with justice and refused to accept the possibility that the arrest crusade had been a mistake. Lisa Frisch, a director at the New York Office for the Prevention of Domestic Violence, called Sherman's public reversal "painful for those of us who have worked long to achieve a measure of justice for battered women."[124] Sherman predicted that his antiarrest, proservices stance would run counter to what feminism had become: "The opposition to mandatory arrest here may frustrate or even anger many tireless advocates who have relentlessly grasped arrest as the preferred police response to incidents of domestic violence. To them, the suggestion that other institutions, such as battered women's shelters, treatment programs for victims and offenders, schools, and welfare agencies, may better serve victims is perhaps blasphemy."[125] Indeed, Frisch blasted Sherman's focus on services "rather than on better victim protection by consistently holding their abusers legally accountable."[126]

Feminist advocates for arrest articulated a grab bag of arguments to dismiss, downplay, and disregard the replication studies. One puzzling argument that was, and still is, made with some frequency by feminist reformers is that mandatory arrest is good for minority *abusers*. Advocates argued that mandatory arrest policies require the police to arrest every suspect and thereby prevent racist police officers from disproportionately arresting black men. Such racial equality-of-punishment arguments are frequently advanced by proponents of tough crime measures like three-strikes laws and mandatory minimum sentences. It is as if reformers believe that black defendants sitting in jail feel great about their protracted sentences so long as white men are also suffering. In any case, if cops are racists, they may actually arrest black abusers *less* frequently because of prejudice against black women. If this is the case, mandatory arrest policies disproportionately *increase* arrests of black men.[127]

When faced with the argument that mandatory arrest policies are particularly bad for minority men, feminists flipped the script. Disproportionately increasing arrests of black men, they maintained, is actually *good* because it confers disproportionate benefits on black women. In the late '70s, arrest advocates anticipated the critique that arrestees "would be predominantly members of racial minorities and of the working class."[128] Today, we might think of this as the New Jim Crow critique. Criminologist Meda Chesney-Lind, for example, remarked in 2002 that "research suggesting that the criminal justice system functions as the new Jim Crow in many poor and marginalized communities of color" should give DV advocates "considerable pause."[129] However, DV advocates rejected the racial critique as "sexist" because "it places the interests of minority men over and above the interests of the minority women who are their victims."[130] In this view, the interests of victims and abusers were invariably in conflict, and arrest was zero-sum. Feminists reasoned that what was good for the goose had to be bad for the gander, and the more minority men suffered, the more minority women healed.

Many advocates continued to advance this argument after Sherman's and others' studies showed that arrest was not always a zero-sum proposition—it harmed men *and* increased violence against women.[131] Moreover, the racial picture was the opposite of the one feminists pushed. Arrest was not particularly protective of black women. Rather, it disproportionately benefited middle-class white women and harmed poor women of color in part *because* it further disempowered poor men of color. Vindicating black feminists' early warnings about the "everywoman" narrative, mandatory arrest policies put minority women at disproportionate risk of future violence, homelessness, financial ruin, deportation, and their own incarceration. One DV service provider summed up the perils of arrest in 2015:

> A lot of victims don't want to call the police because they don't want the abuser to be incarcerated or deported, and they don't want to bring DSS down on their families and lose their kids. In communities of color and immigrant communities these concerns are paramount. Victims are afraid that if they call the police, the abuser will be subjected to a racist system of "justice" that leaves black families devoid of fathers (if he's in prison that also means no child support, no help raising the kids, etc.) and Latino families [are] in fear of having loved ones deported (often back to places they left because of violence and/or economic hardship).[132]

Nevertheless, feminists' presumption that arrest was good for every woman was exceedingly difficult to dislodge. Defending mandatory arrest policies as "mandatory equal protection" in 1996, sociologist Evan Stark argued that such policies "redistributed" the "hoarded resource" of "police service" to women "on a more egalitarian basis."[133] Many advocates persisted in this characterization of arrest as a distributable good, despite the evidence that for marginalized women arrest was often a distributed evil. The more punitive version of the "equal protection" argument was not about distributing arrest "services" to victims equally but about the carceral system inflicting as much pain on abusers as on other offenders. Responding to the replication studies, feminists made the remarkable argument that because the state did not care whether locking up, for example, drug offenders was bad policy, it was unfair and discriminatory to care about the larger effects of locking up abusers. Frisch defended mandatory arrest, arguing, "Our entire justice system fails to deter the majority of socially marginal criminals from committing *any* crime" and yet it "chooses to continue to respond to burglars, armed robbers, drug dealers and muggers even though deterrence is rarely achieved."[134] This quest for punishment equality was all too successful, and today DV arrests outpace nondomestic violence arrests.[135]

Incredibly, many advocates were reluctant to give up on the idea that mandatory arrest policies were good for women in the face of data that the policies increased arrest of men but *multiplied* arrests of women. Legal feminists of the 1970s had ignored sociologists' female-violence statistics at their own peril. The state of California compared DV arrest data from 1988, before mandatory policies, to data from 1998. It found that total arrests had nearly doubled. The arrests of men rose by 60 percent, but women's arrests rose by 400 percent.[136] Another example is Kenosha, Wisconsin, where in 1990, "after institution of a domestic violence mandatory arrest law, women exhibited a 12-fold increase in arrests relative to pre-mandatory arrest."[137] When Connecticut passed "Tracey's Law" in 1986, it became one of a handful of mandatory arrest states. By 2002, Connecticut jails overflowed with women DV offenders, who constituted 30 percent of all domestic violence arrestees.[138]

One theory for why arrests of women increased so dramatically is that officers, like many feminists, adopted the theory that arrest—now of the victim—would function as a wake-up call. Arrest would knock her out of complacency and incentivize her to leave the battering relationship.[139] However, most likely the increase was due to police just being official "enforcers of the law." In mandatory jurisdictions, officers must arrest anyone who commits domestic assault or battery. The conduct prohibited by misdemeanor assault and battery law is notoriously minor, with many codes defining assault/battery as any "unwanted touching" or act with "intent to frighten."[140] When police arrive at a DV scene, often both parties admit to or complain of conduct that meets the legal definition of assault or battery. Mandatory policies rid officers of their discretion, including the paternalistic *aversion* to arresting women.[141]

Still, many DV reformers refused to admit defeat, asserting that mandatory arrest policies could be fixed if policy makers added the caveat that police must determine the "primary aggressor." However, the genie could not be put back in the bottle. Officers arrived on the scene to find two injured parties or just an injured male party, decided that neither aggressor was "primary," and continued to make dual arrests. Worse, the decision whether a woman was a primary or equal aggressor often depended on the woman's minority status or lack of conformity with gender norms.[142] The demographic shift in assault arrests over the past few decades is striking. According to FBI statistics, between 1994 and 2003, the male arrest rate for assault (domestic and nondomestic) fell by 5.8 percent while the female arrest rate increased by 30.8 percent, and for several years women have been the fastest-growing segment of the incarcerated population.[143] Sociologist Jennifer Schwartz, analyzing data from 1980 to 2003, observed, "Rather than women becoming more violent, changes in the *management* of violence increasingly mask differences in the violence levels of women and men."[144] Police, it turns out, heeded the call not to use their discretion to determine which or whose violence did not merit arrest.

Another popular feminist response to the replication studies was that arrest failed to deter abusers only because the prosecutorial processes that followed were not tough enough. Ever reluctant to give up on the law enforcement model, reformers argued that arrest had to be combined with prosecution and meaningful punishment to send the wake-up call to abusers and victims. Advocates clung to the idea that all victims needed was a long enough state-imposed break to come to their senses. In the coming years, battered women's activism would herald systems where a call to the police triggered mandatory arrest, followed by an automatic no-contact order, followed by no-drop prosecution, followed by a conviction with or without the victim's participation, followed by a sentence of incarceration or probation with no contact. For many battered women, this process did serve as the wake-up call that helped improve their lives. However, other women's bond with—or bondage by—the abuser outlasted the spatiotemporal reprieve of a criminal case. Despite the massive legal program to separate DV couples, defendants and victims routinely ignore no-contact orders, and postdetention reunification remains common, and dangerous.[145]

Let me add the anecdotal observation that in more than a few of my cases as a public defender, the client's incarceration served to *preserve* the relationship. One victim told me that during her boyfriend's time in jail he didn't cheat, he didn't take her money, and he wrote the most loving letters. Although she had left him back when he was on release, she decided they would get back together when he finished his sentence. Another case involved a client with felony charges for brutally beating his girlfriend. Shortly after receiving the case, I went to interview her. Her story was heartbreaking, and she said she was leaving for good. I gave a silent prayer of thanks. Indeed, my client was detained pretrial and in no position to prevent her departure. Fast-forward a few months. The victim came to my office looking quite different. Her street clothes had been replaced by a hijab and an abaya (headscarf and cloak). She explained to me that my client had converted to Islam while in jail and had become a peaceful man of God. I was hardly prepared for what she told me next. She had also converted to Islam, so they could marry *while* he was in jail. They were married! She pronounced that she would not show up for trial and hoped the case would be dismissed. I probably should not have, but I could not help myself. "Are you sure about all this?," I asked. She looked at the floor. "I'm sure."

Feminists nevertheless clung to the crime control logic that ever harsher sanctions were the key to preventing men from reoffending. Because most DV cases involved misdemeanors, long-term incapacitation was generally off the table. To be sure, even the most die-hard activists did not endorse a system where a call to the police would trigger mandatory arrest, which, in turn, would trigger a mandatory life sentence. However, the possibility to "stack" (bring multiple) misdemeanor charges enabled prosecutors and judges to give significant time to DV offenders, which was exactly what some feminists envisioned. Back in the 1980s and '90s, the argument that mandatory arrest plus tough prosecution would reduce DV was, much like 1970s feminists' case for arrest, pure speculation. There were no studies of the effect of harsh prosecution and incarceration on DV reoffense. In general, criminologists find it difficult to pinpoint how, why, at which point, and for whom criminal sanctions for any type of offense produce deterrent effects.

Now, twenty-five years later, there is research on the larger DV criminal system, and it predictably presents a complicated portrait of the criminal system's effectiveness in managing human behavior. Each specialized DV system operates in a unique way; each DV couple reacts uniquely to criminal intervention; and it is difficult to disentangle the carceral aspects of a given DV system from its noncarceral aspects like separation, counseling, and victim services. In fact, some studies indicate that any deterrent effects of specialized DV systems come precisely from the material aid, social welfare, and rehabilitative parts of the process, which can be frustrated by the more punitive parts. There is also evidence that decreases in rearrests are due to victims being deterred from reporting.[146]

From thirty thousand feet, all tough-on-crime measures from the last three decades look as if they "worked" because they coincided with the "great crime decline."[147] Most experts, however, agree that incarceration accounted for little if any of the decline.[148] Of note, *arrests* for violent crimes predictably decreased along with the decline in crime rates, although changes in sentencing kept incarceration rates sky high. Domestic violence crime rates similarly decreased, but, owing to feminist reform, DV arrests did not.[149] Today, the studies attempting to substantiate the benefits of carceral DV policies and *finally* answer whether they deter, satisfy victims, and reduce harm crowd Google Scholar. In the meantime, domestic violence defendants crowd the prisons.[150]

Feminists' arrest-and-punish arguments took on a troublingly racialized tone in response to Sherman's Milwaukee findings that DV arrests escalated violence in black communities. Sherman calculated that across-the-board arrest policies reduced violence against white women at the cost of increasing violence against twice as many black women.[151] Instead of rethinking mandatory arrest, some feminists responded with a claim disturbingly reminiscent of the infamous Moynihan Report on the "pathology" of black "subculture," discussed in the previous chapter. Joan Zorza, staff attorney at the National Center on Women and Family Law, responded to Sherman in 1992, stating that the "first and most important" argument against the Milwaukee study was that the "subculture" of poor black men—"society's failures"— made them immune to all but the harshest sanctions:

> That a few hours under arrest fails to deter the abusers who are generally considered to be society's failures is hardly surprising. In some subcultures of ghettoized people, where imprisonment is all too common, a few hours in jail may be seen as only minor irritation, or even a right [*sic*] of passage. We do not consider eliminating arrest for other crimes (e.g., robbery), however, because it may not deter a particular individual or class of individuals. The studies may suggest that to deter more batterers, the stakes may need to be higher, not lower or nonexistent.[152]

Sherman and colleagues had anticipated just such a "demeaning" claim about the pathology of Milwaukee's poor. He cautioned, "The experience of arrest can be humiliating, degrading, and shameful for a lifetime. To describe arrest as too 'weak' a treatment to produce plausible long-term effects implies that the suspects' lives are so awful that they barely noticed or remembered being arrested. Troublesome as ghetto poverty conditions are, ethnographic evidence suggests that arrest is a long-remembered event in that environment."[153] At the 1978 CCR hearings, feminists of color had warned that conditions of poverty, racism, and police violence, not the lack of tough policing, underlay intimate partner violence. Family violence researchers confirmed this diagnosis. Yet some arrest advocates, unwilling to give up their legal victory, were willing to explain arrest's failure to deter black men by invoking racist tropes about blacks responding to only the harshest punishments. Indeed, white southerners at the turn of the century had argued that whipping wifebeaters was "especially suited for black criminals" because of their "inferior culture [that] exhibited no respect for law and order."[154]

In 2015, Dr. Sherman and a colleague followed up on the 1,125 victims involved in the 1988 Milwaukee study. In researching the status of the victims, Sherman was disturbed to find that many had passed away, but not from intimate partner homicide. A full analysis of the data yielded astounding results: "Victims were 64% more likely to have died of all causes if their partners were arrested and jailed than if warned and allowed to remain at home.... Among the 791 African-American victims, arrest increased mortality by 98% ...; among 334 white victims, arrest increased mortality by only 9%.... The highest victim death rate ... was within the group of 192 African-American victims who held jobs: 11% died after partner arrests, but none after warnings."[155] Murder accounted for only three of the ninety-one deaths. The rest were due to "heart disease and other internal morbidity."[156] In making sense of these results, Sherman hypothesized, "There must be something about witnessing a partner's arrest that triggers a physiological response leading to higher rates of death ... but far more so for victims who are African-American than for whites."[157]

Sherman was clearly struck by the long-term racial impacts of arrest. He concluded with a "demographic victim impact statement," imploring Wisconsin to reconsider its mandatory arrest law. "The evidence is clear: African-American victims of domestic violence are disproportionately likely to die after partner arrests relative to white victims," he professed.[158] "The magnitude of the disparity strongly indicates that mandatory arrest laws, however well-intentioned, can create a racially discriminatory impact on victims."[159] However, the DV advocates of 2015 had not evolved away from the proarrest program whose empirical support rose and ultimately fell back in the mid-1980s. There is accordingly a sad irony to the End Domestic Abuse Wisconsin's spokesperson's summary dismissal of Sherman's 2015 follow-up: "Twenty-five-year-old data cannot be used to conclude that domestic violence arrests are dangerous to victims."[160] Ever loyal to the current carceral DV regime, she added, "Thankfully for victims of domestic violence, we don't live in the 1980s anymore."[161]

FOUR

The Weapon

IDEAL VICTIMS

Any child of the 1970s can picture the iconic poster of blonde, leggy Farrah Fawcett wearing a paper-thin red bathing suit and training a girl-next-door smile on the onlooker. Fawcett burst onto the celebrity scene in the 1976 TV series *Charlie's Angels* as the stereotypical jiggly blonde in a show that sparked the phrase "Jiggle TV."[1] Her rise to fame was meteoric, and her feathered hairstyle can be seen throughout high school yearbooks of the time. Fawcett's *Angels* replacement Cheryl Ladd later reflected on the appeal: "She was sexy, but she was giggly and kind of child-like, and, I believe, unthreatening. It was very appealing to men at a time when women were standing up for themselves and their rights."[2]

For all her fame, Fawcett was not taken seriously as an actor until her dramatic turn playing a battered wife in the 1984 TV movie *The Burning Bed*. The movie was based on the real life of Francine Hughes, who in 1977, after thirteen abusive years, set fire to her brutally violent and controlling spouse, Mickey, while he was sleeping. Francine was charged with murder and spent nine months in jail awaiting trial. The jury found her not guilty by reason of temporary insanity. "Temporary insanity—at the time—was not a recognized defense," Hughes's attorney later explained. "It was a hook I used to obtain a not-guilty verdict."[3] Francine's incredible story inspired a biographic novel, which was adapted to a movie script. Fawcett lobbied for the role, but, she explained, "Everyone at the networks said that was not the way the audience wanted to see me."[4] She nonetheless won the part, and the perfect blonde spends much of the movie in bruised-face makeup, with disheveled hair and torn clothes.

The film draws the audience into the cycle of violence, with lulls in the action followed by sudden, unprovoked, and extreme brutality, including violent rape. Throughout, Francine screams, she curls fetally into a ball, she hides in closets—the tension building as Mickey's bogeyman footsteps approach. But she does not fight back. Even in lull moments, Mickey is an execrable character, and Fawcett appears more repulsed by than affectionate toward him.

Mickey's abuse and Francine's captivity are enabled by his family members, with whom they live, the police, and the state government. Francine calls the cops, who do nothing. She goes to the welfare office, where the indifferent bureaucrat tells her it is a police matter. She goes to the DA, who says his hands are tied. She goes to her mother, who sends her back to Mickey. Indeed, the movie has the "right" answers to why she didn't leave. She tried to leave several times, facing resistance from her family and the state. She finally left, only to have *him* get custody of their four children. She divorced Mickey, but he stayed with her, vowing to kill her if she tried to separate.[5]

The Burning Bed was the highest-rated TV movie of the season.[6] Fawcett received several award nominations and finally became a serious actor. Her next movie, *Extremities,* in which she played a rape victim-turned-vigilante, was released to great acclaim.[7] *The Burning Bed* became a symbol of the battered women's movement. It was the first TV show to flash a 1–800 DV hotline number on the screen. It received accolades from feminists and lawmakers alike. In recent times, the movie has taken on a mythological quality as the single event that galvanized the modern battered women's movement. It has been called a "turning point" in women's rights that "left an indelible mark upon society's collective consciousness."[8] In 2017, the *Washington Post* credited *The Burning Bed* "with dramatically altering public perceptions of domestic violence—redefining it as a crime rather than a private affair and spurring the establishment of shelters across the United States."[9]

As the film became a runaway hit, the real Francine, her 1977 trial a few years behind her, was not doing so well. *People* magazine profiled Francine the week of *The Burning Bed*'s release.[10] After the trial, Francine fell into a difficult period of drug use, during which she met and married Robert Wilson, who was on parole from a thirty-year armed robbery sentence. They remained married until his death in 2015. Francine had an especially volatile relationship with her nineteen-year-old daughter Christy, who was twelve at the time of Mickey's killing. A few months before the *People* interview, child protective services contacted Francine about an anonymous report—it appears from Christy—that her youngest daughter was being sexually abused.[11] CPS was unable to follow up because Francine fled the state with the girls, leaving her two sons with Wilson. Thereafter, Francine and Christy's relationship further deteriorated, and Christy told the *People* interviewer that Francine had recently beaten her up. The *People* profile concludes with this melancholy observation: "More than a week after the argument, Christy was still sporting slight bruises under her eyes. The fading shiners seemed frighteningly symbolic of other family wounds—wounds grown deeper, darker and more terrible with each passing year."[12]

The real Francine was imperfect; mercurial, conflicted, and aggressive. Her attorney remarked that the movie was "not very accurate" because Francine was not the "reticent, ... weak person" Fawcett had portrayed.[13] In swapping her *Angel* persona for the battered wife, Fawcett exchanged one iconic raced-and-gendered image—the giggly, sexy girl next door—for another—the brutalized helpless victim.

In the 1970s, feminists widely recognized the importance of centering the victim in discourse and activism. Highlighting victims' stories and experiences was important for practical, educational, and strategic reasons. Feminist advocates, for example, required an intimate understanding of their clients' needs and perspectives. Reformers also highlighted victims' stories to educate a public that, they believed, misunderstood the harm, causes, and magnitude of gender violence. Sometimes activists publicized victims' experiences to dislodge preexisting stereotypes. For example, highlighting a story about a brutally raped sex worker could help to supplant society's tenacious belief that prostitutes can't be raped. Finally, as proarrest advocates well knew, emphasizing the plight of the victim is a winning political strategy.

There were and remain good reasons for feminists to focus on crime victims' needs. Indeed, many feminists tirelessly fight for resources to aid vulnerable and marginalized women. Publicizing victims' plights can also move the public and the state to provide aid and change the structures that make certain women vulnerable to violence. When it comes to criminal law and policy, however, focusing on the crime victim and her devastation is a dangerous tactic. The narrative of violent crime victimhood and what victims want has always had a political valence, and in the 1980s it took on a distinctly neoliberal and carceral bent. The ideal victim in crime-control discourse was an innocent, brutalized, middle-class, white woman or child, who (or whose family) could receive closure only through the swift and severe punishment of the monstrous offender.

The victim label confines women to one identity—the object acted upon by a private wrongdoer. "Any richer sense of the person undermines the claim of victimhood, because victimhood depends on a reductive view of identity," law professor Martha Minow remarks.[14] Sensing that this flattened construction can be constraining and demeaning, many choose the term *survivor* instead. Victimhood narratives also confine the cause of harm to the offender. To illustrate, imagine that the statement "She is a rape victim" describes a poor, undocumented sex worker of color. This individual suffers greatly from sexism, economic unfairness, racism, sex negativity, and xenophobia, but we call her a "victim" by virtue of one individual act done by a single criminal. As Minow notes, victim discourse "divide[s] the world into only two categories: victims and victimizers."[15] Accordingly, the focus on victimhood is already a subtle but powerful redirection away from structural, social, and institutional accounts of harm and toward punishment.

This chapter discusses feminists' complicated engagement with victimhood narratives and victims' rights. In the 1980s, conservative politicians deftly mobilized victim images to score political points by passing popular punitive laws. Feminists also relied on victimhood stories to push their anti-DV and antirape agendas. Feminists invited discourse on, empathy with, and scrutiny of victims, and this had a significant downside. Society was all too willing to scrutinize women victims in ways feminists did not like. The public was receptive to feminist discourse that DV was a horrific and brutal crime that devastated women. Many could not, however, understand why a woman would stay with such a villain. The public was willing to see rape as life-destroying for women and to see rapists as insatiate perverts. Many had a harder time understanding why, in the absence of physical threat, a woman would not just say "no" to her date. When faced with the downsides of centering the victim, feminist commentators often flipped the script, arguing that the focus should be on the "perpetrator's conduct" and not the victim's feelings, character, and actions.

Feminists' attempts to navigate the double bind of focusing and not focusing on the victim led DV and rape reformers down some tricky paths. To maintain the strategic advantages of the victim narrative, feminists had to deal with society's notions of true victimhood. They had to preserve battered women's innocent status and batterers' monstrous status and explain why women stayed without opening the door to arguments that "victims choose abuse." Antirape activists had to preserve rape as an utterly devastating crime and explain away victims' credibility problems without conceding that complaints were *ever* false. As a result, feminist discourse too often portrayed DV victims as terrified, coercively controlled women, who stayed with abusers out of fear or psychological dependence. It too often described rape victims as ruined by sex and their testimonial inconsistencies as products of debilitating psychological trauma.

Feminists' ideal victims thus looked quite similar to the victims imagined by conservative politicians. Both were innocent, anguished, preoccupied with the crime that occurred, and desirous of punishment as justice. Moreover, feminists' reliance on trauma and damaged psychology to explain imperfect victim behavior resonated with sexist cultural stereotypes about hysterical or cognitively defective abused women and ruined rape victims.[16] In addition, the ideal feminist victim, like the ideal war-on-crime victim, was a nonpoor white "everywoman."[17] Women who fell outside of the ideal often were not helped or were even harmed by policies tailored to that everyvictim. The rest of this chapter discusses feminist and conservative victimhood tropes and how those tropes moved feminist reform programs in an authoritarian direction.

CENTERING, CONSTRUCTING, AND CONFINING THE VICTIM

Comparing US and European victims' movements, theorist Marie Gottschalk found the American crime victims' movement to be more influential and punitive than its European counterparts and to be a significant contributor to US mass incarceration.[18] Indeed, experts have called the US victims' rights movement "one of the most important social movements of our time, comparable in its influence on our political culture to the civil rights movement."[19] In the late '70s, nascent victims' rights organizations, inspired by feminist activism on behalf of battered women, agitated for crime victims' rights within the criminal system. "There is little doubt that the women's movement was central to the development of a victims' movement," notes the victims' rights oral history project.[20] It observes that feminists had painted "the poor response of the criminal justice system" as a "potent illustration[] of a woman's lack of status, power, and influence."[21] Victims' rights activists followed suit, arguing that crime victims were not content to be mere cogs in a prosecutorial machine, receiving little in the way of compassion, services, or courtesy. The federal government took notice, and by the mid-1980s it was providing significant funding to support victims' programs within DAs' offices. States also moved rapidly to adopt victims' rights statutes.[22]

Victims' rights were originally conceived of as protection against indifferent and antagonistic *prosecutors*. Victims' rights statutes thus contain provisions requiring prosecutors to give notice of relevant dates (such as trial and parole), to seek victim input, and to provide victim compensation. Some of these statutory provisions had a potential to negatively affect defendants. The right to present a "victim impact statement" at sentencing, for example, created a risk that sentencers would focus on victims' subjective feelings, or worse, social status, rather than defendants' conduct.[23] In theory, victim impact statements could benefit defendants if victims called for compassion in sentencing. In practice, however, victims often "are angry, depressed, and mourning," as one victim of the Oklahoma City bombing explained.[24] Victims' rights discourse, as law professor Elizabeth Joh observes, neither "generates [n]or tolerates narratives in which victims' families can exercise mercy, kindness, or forgiveness towards defendants."[25]

In principle, the movement was about serving the victims caught up in a stressful bureaucratic criminal system and not about unilaterally strengthening law enforcement. However, even in the early years, victims' rights organizations did not champion the interests of victims who wanted to avoid the criminal system altogether.[26] This may have had something to do with the organizations' composition. Gottschalk notes that "activists in victims' organizations tended to be overwhelmingly White, female, and middle-aged—a group demographic that is hardly representative of crime victims in general."[27] She goes on, "These activists generally were more supportive of the death penalty and of the police, prosecutors, and judges than were victims not active in these organizations."[28] So, in theory, victims' rights are not synonymous with crime control. But as legal scholar Markus Dubber observes, "As a matter of fact, the vindication of victims' rights has everything to do with the war on crime."[29]

Recall that Reagan strategically publicized the image of scary brown men to frighten voters into believing that crime, not lack of stable employment or income, was the main problem to be addressed by government.[30] While this tactic whipped up fear, images of victims as brutalized "'blameless,' innocent, usually attractive, middle class, and white" women inspired loathing.[31] The sentimentalized victim provided a rhetorical trump card for conservative policy makers. Whether punishment worked or even was deserved fell out of the equation as society obsessed over victims' trauma and desire for vengeance. Any lingering 1960s-style empathy for defendants—the minorities, protesters, and others who faced the violence of the state—gave way to a reverential sympathy directed toward victims. In turn, as Dubber remarks, "To maintain its fever pitch of hatred, the war on crime need[ed] ever more, and ever more sympathetic, victims."[32] Indeed, President Reagan pronounced the first week of his presidency and a week in every April thereafter "Victims' Rights Week."[33]

The victim image driving the war on crime was very specific. It actively excluded the marginalized men and women, often defendants themselves, who disproportionately suffered from crime but viewed the criminal system with a jaundiced eye.[34] Victims instead were innocent women and children—preferably white—who were subjected to men's unspeakable brutality—preferably sexual. Victims were devastated, angry, and vengeful, and they defined themselves by that one bad moment in life. Victims felt oppressed by insufficiently zealous prosecutors, prying defense attorneys, due process protections, and lenient judges.[35] Victims desired and benefited from greater participation in the criminal process and were satisfied with the sole reward of the perpetrator's incarceration.[36]

Victims also took on an almost deific quality, making the war on crime something of a holy war. The veneration of victims, Minow writes, "reflect[s] an almost religious view of suffering, empowering those who suffer with ... reverence from others."[37] Clinton's attorney general Janet Reno, in a speech supporting the federal Victims' Rights Amendment, called victims "but little lower than the angels."[38] Decades later, candidate Donald Trump picked up on this theme and featured "Angel Moms," the mothers of children killed by immigrants, at his rallies.[39]

Into the 1980s, the victims' rights movement increasingly reflected the tough-on-crime agenda of the politicians who were capitalizing on victims' plights. What started out as victims pursuing their interests in notification, speedy processes, and statement making, regardless of defendants' rights, became victims *defining* their interests as oppositional to defendants' rights. Following the feminist strategy, victim advocates argued that victims had a "right" to swift and aggressive prosecution and easily obtained convictions unobstructed by procedural protections for defendants. Inspired by the equal protection argument made by battered women's activists, victims' rights reformers argued for rebalancing the scales between the "privileged" criminal and the disempowered victim.[40] They characterized the system's prioritization of defendants' constitutional rights over swift punishment as *discrimination*. Former Republican senator and activist Jon Kyl credited feminists for "spawn[ing] a national movement to reform the legal system by recognizing that crime victims ... were a discrete and unserved *minority* that deserved equal justice under law."[41] The strategy worked. The "unstoppable political force" of victims' rights in the 1980s and '90s, lawyer Alice Koskela remarks, "dramatically expanded the rights of crime victims and restricted the rights of criminal defendants, causing a fundamental change in the justice system."[42]

In 1982, Reagan formed the President's Task Force on Victims of Crime and appointed as chair federal prosecutor Lois Haight Herrington, who would later become a general in Reagan's "war on drugs."[43] It should come as no shock that the task force's recommendations did not involve addressing the endemic poverty and inequality that affected the marginalized people constituting the main crime victim population. Instead, asserting that the criminal system had lost "essential balance," the report advocated nothing less than a reversal of the due process regime put in place by the liberal "Warren Court."[44] The task force's recommendations included laws to abolish parole, limit pretrial release, increase penalties for failure to appear, prevent defense attorneys from contacting victims, limit judges' sentencing discretion, require victim impact statements, compel schools to report student crimes, and make arrest records for sex offenses and pornography available to employers.[45] Those versed in criminal procedure will recognize many of these recommendations as current law—law that propelled the US into its current crisis of mass incarceration.

THE IDEAL BATTERED WOMAN

With the media focused on horrific real and fictionalized DV cases, it was inevitable that tough-on-crime politicians would take up battering as a victims' rights issue. In 1984, Haight Herrington organized the Attorney General's Task Force on Family Violence, and its report put even more distance between the anti-DV movement and its antipoverty, antipatriarchy roots.[46] She assembled an unusual cast of characters to weigh in on the most important feminist issue of the time. One unlikely participant was John Ashcroft. At that time Missouri attorney general, Ashcroft used the task force as his entrée into federal governing. He had been a leading figure in the prolife movement, and later, as George W. Bush's attorney general, he would spark a national outcry for subpoenaing thousands of women's medical records to gain information to support antiabortion legislation.[47] Hardly an antiviolence pacifist, Ashcroft is most infamous for overseeing and defending the Bush administration's post-9/11 revival of physical torture.[48]

After serving on the task force, Ashcroft adopted DV as a pet issue, writing and speaking on the need to take it seriously for decades. Yet he was decidedly less serious about protecting Rodi Alvarado Peña, a battered woman who applied for asylum on the ground that the conditions of Guatemalan society kept her trapped in a brutal marriage. In 2004, the Department of Homeland Security recommended to Ashcroft that he grant Alvarado's asylum claim. He refused and stayed the case pending finalization of asylum guidelines—guidelines he never finalized.[49] On July 11, 2018, Trump administration attorney general Jeff Sessions issued a proclamation that domestic violence is not a ground for asylum.[50]

The Family Violence Task Force took a strict law-and-order approach to DV. Its chair, Detroit police chief William Hart, made clear, "A victim of family violence is no less a victim than one set upon by strangers."[51] The task force's report quotes a young DV prosecutor, Jeanine Pirro, in support of this point. Readers might recognize her as currently an uber-right-wing *Fox News* commentator and rabid Trump supporter. Pirro is infamous for her race-baiting commentary about President Obama and Black Lives Matter.[52] In 2016, she defended Trump's boast about grabbing women "by the pussy" and made sure to emphasize her DV activist credentials: "He has always been a gentleman. . . . I know the man, and I can speak as a woman who has fought for battered women, I have crusaded for women my whole career to level the playing field for women who are victims of crime. And I can tell you unequivocally that whatever that locker-room talk was, whatever that frat-house language was, honestly, most Americans get it."[53] Pirro's comments in the 1984 report echoed the task force's larger message that DV was a matter of individual bad men, rather than societal patriarchy or poverty. She remarked, "Many of the people across the country have looked at [DV] as a civil problem, as a family problem, as a social problem. We believe it is a criminal problem and the way to handle it is with criminal justice intervention."[54]

Many battered women's advocates welcomed and touted the report, despite the strange bedfellows. One advocate, for example, lauded the report for "promot[ing] changes so long demanded by women" and relied on the report to argue that law enforcement was necessary even if it did not deter DV.[55] To be sure the report's get-tough approach had synergy with legal feminists' proarrest stance. Like feminists, the report rejected mediation on the ground that it assumed "the parties involved are of equal culpability."[56]

However, feminists' support of the task force becomes more surprising in light of the report's preoccupation with "family values," an ideology antithetical to feminism.

The family values movement that ascended in the 1980s embraced a vision of God-fearing, law-abiding, heterosexual nuclear families, whose labor was divided strictly along gender lines. The movement is often described as a cultural conservative backlash to 1960s radicalism, feminism, black activism, and gay rights. However, as political scientist Melinda Cooper astutely observes, it was simultaneously part of the neoliberal political-economic revolution. The notion of "family responsibility" helped transform welfare "from a redistributive program into an immense federal apparatus for policing the private family responsibilities of the poor."[57] At the same time, "deficit spending [was] steadily transferred from the state to the private family."[58]

The task force report leads off with a quote from Reagan that "building our future must begin by preserving family values."[59] The concluding sentences—the takeaway from the group's extensive study of DV—reads, "America derives its strength, purpose and productivity from its commitment to strong family values. For our nation to thrive and grow, we must do all that we can to protect, support, and encourage America's families."[60] Family values were front and center when Congress, after years of failed attempts by Democrats, made its first appropriation to battered women's services and shelters in 1984. Democratic representative Les AuCoin quoted the family values language from the report and challenged his Republican colleagues to open the coffers: "Being 'pro-family' means more than providing lip service to the needs of those who are crying out for help."[61] The anti-DV movement born out of Del Martin's critique of marriage as heteropatriarchy had become all about preserving traditional matrimony.

The report quotes numerous family values groups, including Concerned Women of America, a formidable force in conservative politics whose influence has since only grown.[62] According to the organization's website, Beverly LaHaye founded Concerned Women in 1978 after she saw Betty Friedan on television. She was "stirred to action" by Friedan's "anti-God, anti-family rhetoric [that] did not represent her beliefs, nor those of the vast majority of women."[63] "Feminism is more than an illness," LaHaye once proclaimed. "It is a philosophy of death."[64] The report quotes another family values activist, "paleoconservative" Allan Carlson of the right-wing Rockford Institute. Carlson has spent his life fighting the "malignant" forces of "feminism, sexual hedonism . . . and militant secularism" and "build[ing] a new culture of marriage."[65] He linked family violence to the breakdown of traditional marital roles and parents' failure to "sacrifice" for their children.[66]

In later years, Ashcroft was open about the domesticity designs of DV law reform. Speaking at the attorney general's 2002 Symposium on Domestic Violence, Ashcroft emphasized "our responsibility—and our privilege—to pass on our values to the next generation of Americans" and explained that DV intervention was necessary to "transform" masochistic female victims into good mothers. Ashcroft recounted a conversation with a former victim: "She said, quote, 'I finally realized the truth, that I was hurting not only myself, but I was hurting my children even more. I was teaching them by example that they deserved to be abused and that violence was acceptable.'"[67] Family values activists stressed *women's* duty to maintain violence-free families, arguing that mothers who tolerated abuse were insufficiently protective. Law professor Elaine Chiu observes, "All too often, conservatives . . . interpret opportunity for action to be the same as control over the abuse, and therefore, believe it is justified to penalize battered women anytime they do not use their opportunities and control to end the abuse."[68]

Indeed, the more attention and resources the government poured into DV law enforcement, the more people blamed women for not taking the opportunity to prosecute abusers, stop the violence, and protect their children. Farrah-Francine may not have had a meaningful chance to escape, but, thanks to feminist reforms, battered women increasingly had a real ability to invoke law enforcement and state prosecution. As proarrest policies and specialized prosecution became the norm, feminists were challenged to explain why battered women continued to stay with abusers rather than calling the police and having them arrested and jailed. Advocates were reluctant to recognize that some victims regarded abuse as one of many concerns in their lives, and perhaps not the most pressing one, to be balanced against others. Doing so, reformers feared, would reinforce that victims *could* leave but *chose* not to.

For many advocates, the way out of this bind was to argue that when victims declined the criminal process, they acted not from free will but as pawns of abusers who exercised "coercive control."[69] Early battered women's advocates rightly observed that many abusers control victims' behavior not just through violence and direct physical threats but also through emotional and financial manipulation. Women in coercive relationships had to constantly calculate the complex costs and benefits of acquiescence and defiance. Thus battered women acceded to abusers' demands, against their will, even in the absence of immediate threat.[70] The problem was that advocates of strong policing and prosecution used the coercive control narrative in a very specific way. They did not invoke coercive control to champion financial and material aid that could help vulnerable women resist controlling men. They did not invoke it to understand what experts have called battered women's "constrained agency" and to support victims as they managed their complex cost-benefit calculations. Rather, coercive control primarily came up when women chose not to cooperate with law enforcement. And its exclusive role was to enable police and prosecutors to ignore that choice.

Advocates offered the coercive control narrative as *the* explanation for victims' resistance to arrest and prosecution of abusers. For example, arrest proponent Laurie Woods argued that if the victim was given control of the arrest decision, "her *real* desire would often go unrealized because she might not feel free to request [the abuser's] arrest."[71] In this view, allowing coerced victims to choose allowed batterers to "control the judicial process."[72] Advocates reasoned that mandatory arrest and prosecution made women safer because abusers could not blame victims for a criminal process over which victims had no control. However, mandatory policy or not, victims still believed arrest and prosecution would put them in greater danger or otherwise disserve them, and they were often right. Mandatory policy or not, abusers still blamed women for triggering their arrests and prosecutions by calling the police. Many victims accordingly stopped calling.[73]

There was a certain hubris in feminist lawyers' belief that they knew how to manage victims' safety better than victims themselves. When faced with empirical challenges to arrest policies, feminists had insisted that policy makers should not focus on deterrence or racial equity but rather should prioritize victims' preferences, with the presumption that victims "prefer arrest to other possible police responses to domestic violence calls."[74] Similarly, in cases of battered women who killed abusers and asserted self-defense, feminists insisted that the *victim* was the expert on her cycle of violence and how to keep herself safe. But DV activists changed their tune when faced with victims who were reluctant to cooperate with law enforcement against batterers. These victims were no experts. They could not be trusted to "tell their stories in ways that accurately describe the violence" because they "often understate the situation, try to protect the batterer, or blame themselves for the violence," as one reformer argued.[75] In a more extreme move, some feminists argued that separation-averse women suffered from "learned helplessness" and had a type of Stockholm syndrome where they protected the abuser at all costs. One commentator went so far as to propose that courts transfer DV victims' decision-making power to legal guardians, as is done with the mentally incompetent.[76]

The feminist ideal of the coercively controlled victim silently wishing for mandatory separation and prosecution downplayed the various structural, economic, and emotional reasons why women rejected separation and prosecution. Domestic partnerships intertwine lives. They merge families and social networks, form economic interdependencies, produce children, and create everyday routines. The untangling of such comingled interests is difficult and often devastating. A DV victim didn't stay just because of "love," which feminists tended to dismiss as a product of psychological dependence or internalized patriarchal consciousness. Rather, she stayed because of the money, the children, her house, her life.

As mandatory arrest led to mandatory separation and no-drop prosecution, ignoring prosecution-averse (and therefore coerced) victims became de rigueur. Prosecutor Donna Wills defended aggressive prosecution, stating, "We need to be able to say that despite a battered woman's ambivalence, we did everything within our discretion to rein in the batterer, to protect the victim and her children, and to stop the abuser before it was too late."[77] Victims' advocate Prentice White wrote in 2004 about his regret over having adopted this rescue ethic. When his client Joan told him of her abuser Mike's behavior, White called in the sheriff while "Joan pleaded with me not to have Mike arrested."[78] "In retrospect," White remarked, "I realized that my reaction was inappropriate."[79] "Like Mike, I was exercising control over Joan's life . . . when I impulsively—and unilaterally—decided that Mike should be prosecuted and Joan needed rescuing."[80]

Into the 1990s, more and more jurisdictions adopted specialized domestic violence systems with aggressive prosecution rules. Within these systems, state actors ignored, subpoenaed, and treated derisively uncooperative victims, even jailing a few on "material witness" warrants.[81] Material witness warrants force witnesses to be present at court on pain of incarceration. The government used them to detain scores of innocent Middle Eastern people after 9/11, compelling one lawyer to call them "a popular device for rounding people up" and "a systematic weapon used against an ethnically identifiable group."[82] Former prosecutor Cheryl Hanna recognized that aggressive DV prosecution policies "may indeed cause women to face financial hardship and to experience real emotional trauma" and that sanctioned victims "may be treated poorly in other legal proceedings such as divorce and custody cases."[83]

She nevertheless defended such policies, including material witness warrants, as necessary to "send a clear message that domestic violence is criminally unacceptable."[84]

This type of message-sending or "expressive" argument gives tough-on-crime lawmakers carte blanche to create any criminal law, no matter how misguided, ineffective, bad for victims, or disproportionate to the crime. They simply say, "This law creates the penalty of [insert exorbitant sentence] to send a message against [insert behavior of contemporary concern]." Touting the expressive value of a criminal sanction relieves the proponent of responsibility for good governance or for owning up to the high social, political, and economic costs of policing, prosecution, and incarceration.[85] Professors Alice Miller and Mindy Roseman have noted feminists' tendency to rely on message sending as a justification for carceral policies and urge instead a "politics of accountability" that factors in "the material deprivations [penal law] entails: the intentional infliction of pain, at a minimum."[86] Another problem is that criminalization sends more than the message that "DV is bad," a message, by the way, that is amply conveyed by many other less painful means. Theorist Bernard Harcourt articulates the point that feminists of color made so many decades ago: "Many contemporary policing and punitive practices ... communicate a racial and political, rather than moral, message—a message about who is in control and about who gets controlled."[87]

Reformers also justified the direct and indirect harm to prosecution-averse women by the rationale that "domestic violence is a crime against society."[88] Channeling Reagan's deft recharacterization of poor street criminals as a "privileged class," battered women's advocates branded individual (often marginalized) men's violence as the oppressive force in society. With battering established as a "patriarchal force," in legal scholar Claire Houston's words, feminists argued that, regardless of the victims' wishes, "allowing [DV] to continue against an individual woman reinforces male control over women as a class."[89] In turn, determining DV criminal policy was not a matter of weighing prosecution-resistant victims' interests against pro–law enforcement victims' interests. It was a matter of weighing prosecution-resistant victims' interests against the well-being of *all* women. In this view, the victim who refused to cooperate was an ally of male supremacy, "an accomplice to her own battering," as feminist psychologist Lenore Walker remarked.[90]

Police and prosecutors' growing practice of overriding and even mistreating noncooperative victims was particularly perilous for poor women of color. To be sure, there are many reasons why white middle-class women avoid prosecution and separation outside of direct coercion. Nevertheless, poor women of color face greater constraints that keep them tethered to violent men and are at greater risk of harm from law enforcement. And, in an ironic twist, middle-class white women are more able to opt out of the carceral system that was created to fit their "everywoman" needs. Studies confirm that "women with income have greater access to resources to assist them in keeping their abuse private; they have the ability to afford private physicians and safe shelters, which results in their being able to escape detection from law enforcement."[91] This is in contrast to the "socio-economically distressed" victims who call the police for aid, only to find that aid has been defined as arrest for decades.[92] Legal scholar Donna Coker remarks, "It is a cruel trap when the state's legal interventions rest on the presumption that women who are 'serious' about ending domestic violence will leave their partner while, at the same time, reducing dramatically the availability of public assistance that makes leaving somewhat possible."[93]

Feminists of color warned from the very beginning that women living in social and racial marginality and economic precarity regarded police and prosecutors not as rescuers but as repressors. In 2015, the ACLU published the results of a survey of over nine hundred DV service providers. The survey asked them to, among other things, "identify the primary reasons survivors do not call or cooperate with law enforcement."[94] Eighty-nine percent of the respondents reported that clients' contacts with police sometimes or often involved a call to child protective services. One provider explained, "Often times if our client calls police a CPS report will be done[,] then the victim of the DV will be investigated for 'failure to protect' the children and can have her children taken away because her partner has been abusive."[95] At-risk women also worried about being arrested for other crimes. One respondent remarked, "Many of our clients were committing crimes (using illegal substances, participating in sex work, had a taser in their possession, etc.) while they were being abused" and were "afraid of being prosecuted."[96] There was indeed reason to fear. A service provider remarked that in her community, "checking victims for warrants is so encouraged, it is part of institutionalized policy."[97] Perhaps the victims most at risk from calling the police are undocumented immigrant women. Beyond triggering an unstoppable prosecutorial machine that leads to their partners' deportation, the victims can also face removal. There are some statutory immigration protections for women who actively cooperate with prosecutors against their spouses, but these are far from guarantees against deportation, especially in the Trump era.

However iconic the image of Farrah Fawcett's battered visage was in the 1980s, there was an even more powerful and jurisgenerative victim image: the child victim of the sexual predator. Relentless news coverage throughout the 1980s and '90s of horrific kidnappings and killings of young children, some by known sex offenders, created a sense of public insecurity—and even terror. Legislatures capitalized on this fear and scored political points by passing sex offender management and punishment regimes that tested the limits of constitutional powers, including mandatory registration and community notification, strict residency restrictions, and, for some offenders, indefinite civil commitment.[98] Many scholars characterize that moment of collective obsession with sexually violent predators as a "moral panic." Sociologist Stanley Cohen explains that moral panic involves "moral outrage towards the actors (folk devils) who embody the problem," abetted by "an exaggeration of the number or strength of the cases, in terms of the damage caused, moral offensiveness, potential risk if ignored."[99] Moral panic thus thrives at the intersection of brutality and ubiquity. It emerges when the public believes that outrageous behavior committed by a discrete deviant group is also widespread. Social anxiety arose from images of brutal child murders committed by deviant strangers together with statistics about the frequency of child sexual assault writ large. In fact, however, the brutal stranger crimes were exceedingly rare, and the more common assaults involved lower-level sexual touching perpetrated by familiars, often by other children.[100]

In the '80s and '90s, media relentlessly covered child kidnappings, rapes, and killings that represented "every parent's worst nightmare." The names Adam Walsh, Jacob Wetterling, Polly Klaas, and Megan Kanka were seared into public consciousness and memorialized in the titles of federal anti–sex offender legislation.[101] Under the theory that some of the crimes could have been prevented had parents been armed with information, legislatures swiftly passed laws to widely register and notify the public about those convicted of even minor sex offenses.[102] This predictably caused even more panic, especially in the internet era when registrants present as red dots littering an online neighborhood map. The all-encompassing dread of stranger danger kept parents up at night and their kids inside during the day. Parents developed a false sense of insecurity in which every playground became a hunting ground and every second of a child's absence became a moment of terror, leading to "the virtual imprisonment of both poor and privileged children in the name of keeping them safer," as legal sociologist Jonathan Simon observes.[103] The sex predator era, remarks criminologist Richard Moran, produced lasting cultural effects in the form of "a generation of cautious and afraid kids who view all adults and strangers as a threat to them and . . . parents extremely paranoid about the safety of their children."[104]

Accompanying this self-imposed exile was a political demand that the government do more to hold the fiends to account. However, existing criminal law left little room for a ratchet-up solution. Murder and child rape could hardly be punished more severely, and rare opportunistic child sex offenses were almost impossible to predict and prevent. Clever politicians nonetheless realized that "doing something" was all it took. Law professor William Stuntz has called such "pathological politics" a primary driver of mass imprisonment.[105] When existing criminal laws already cover the crisis of the day, "legislatures tend to create new crimes not to solve the problem, but to give voters the sense that they are doing something about it," Stuntz explained.[106] Politicians receive "political returns from symbolic legislation."[107] During predator panic, legislatures passed laws tacking more years on to already exorbitant sex offender sentences: for example, Colorado's mandatory sentence of life in prison for nearly all felony sex offenses.[108] These reforms may have been "symbolic," but they affected real people. For sure, they imprisoned violent offenders who brutalized children. But they also imprisoned nonviolent offenders who were children.

John Walsh, the bereaved father of six-year-old Adam, who was kidnapped and murdered in 1981, became a famous TV figure and leader in the war on sex offenders. His popular 1990s show *America's Most Wanted* is an exemplar of the popular victim-perpetrator narrative of the time, as media scholar Elayne Rapping observes:

> [The show] invariably pitted victims of traditional nuclear families against the harrowing images of criminals as antisocial loners and lunatics preying on women and especially children. Michael Linder, one of the series producers, explained the criteria for choosing cases for the series in an issue of *TV Guide:* "A drug dealer who shoots another drug dealer is not as compelling as a child molester or murderer. . . . If a man brutalizes innocent children, that definitely adds points." Such a hierarchy of victimization is a mainstay of the Victims' Rights Movement, which plays upon notions of decent families besieged by violent amoral criminals.[109]

In 2006, Walsh successfully lobbied the US Congress to pass the Adam Walsh Child Protection Act on the twenty-fifth anniversary of his son's death.

Federal sex offender law was already exceedingly harsh by that time, but the Walsh Act symbolically increased already exorbitant federal penalties and broadened eligibility for registration and civil commitment. Standing next to the now-celebrity Walsh, President George W. Bush remarked that "we're sending a clear message across the country: those who prey on our children will be caught, prosecuted, and punished to the fullest extent of the law."[110]

At the time, the president, or at least his lawyers, had reason to know that the act's sentencing provisions were irrelevant to nearly all sex crime arrestees, whose cases were governed by state law. Federal law has extremely limited jurisdiction over individual violent crimes, affecting defendants only in federalized areas like national parks and Indian territory. The federal public defender had warned Congress that Native Americans would bear the brunt of these harsh reforms and that tribes would shoulder the bureaucratic burden of federal sex offender management.[111] In 2006, the year President Bush signed the act, "nearly three-quarters of Federal sex abuse defendants were American Indian or Alaska Native," according to the Department of Justice.[112] These suspects "tended to be younger . . . and less educated" than other accused offenders.[113]

Shortly after the act's passage, news stories began to familiarize the public with the dark side of reform. In 2007, national media broke the story of the hundreds of former sex offenders forced to live in squalid conditions in a makeshift encampment under Miami's Julia Tuttle Causeway.[114] Spurred on by the 2005 rape and murder of nine-year-old Jessica Lunsford in North Florida, antipredator crusaders and politicians championed some of the strictest residency restrictions in the country, banning sex offenders from residing within 2,500 feet of any place where children gathered. In Miami-Dade County, this left the airport, the middle of the Everglades, and highway underpasses.[115]

Internal Miami-Dade Department of Corrections memos revealed that officials instructed registrants to live under the causeway, which lacked water, electricity, and basic sanitation, and even issued them identification cards with "Julia Tuttle Causeway" as the address. The first woman to reside at the encampment, Voncel Johnson, had been convicted of indecent exposure (she says falsely). She told NPR in 2009: "I'm thinking [my probation officer is] bringing me to a three-quarter-way house. But when I got here it was . . . pitch dark. The first thing I saw was men, and I'm the only lady here. . . . I broke down. I'm asking her, 'Why do I have to be here?'"[116] Media and public pressure eventually induced Corrections to clear out the encampment and find temporary shelter for its residents elsewhere. But without a change to the residency laws, the causeway population simply dispersed to other underpasses and the train tracks.[117]

One of the more controversial provisions of the Walsh Act required states to register juveniles as sex offenders. This was a major expansion, considering that in 2009 "juveniles account[ed] for more than one-third (35.6 percent) of those known to police to have committed sex offenses against minors," according to a Bureau of Justice Statistics report.[118] The report further notes, "Early adolescence is the peak age for offenses against younger children."[119] Indeed, kids as young as nine have been registered for acts ranging from innocent experimentation and sexting to serious assaults. Perusing a community circular or clicking on a law enforcement–sponsored website, one might not realize that the scary twenty-four-year-old predator had been a ten-year-old boy when he fondled his cousin.

Recently, juvenile registrants have received some sympathetic media coverage. A 2016 *New Yorker* article profiled their gut-wrenching tales of homelessness, inability to attend school, public shaming, violence, humiliating "medical treatment," and suicide.[120] There is Charla, who was placed on the registry at age ten for pulling a boy's pants down at school and whose photo still appears online under the banner "Protect Your Child from Sex Offenders." There is Anthony, convicted under "statutory rape" laws for consensual sex as a teenager. Years later, the conditions of his sex offender status prohibited him from living with his newborn daughter, and his violations of those conditions landed him a ten-year sentence. There is Leah, who at age ten was convicted of molesting her siblings. During college, she and her boyfriend drove out of state to meet his parents. They stopped at the local police station so that she could fulfill her sex offender notification requirement. The front-desk officer said, "We don't serve your kind here. You better leave before I take you out back and shoot you myself."[121] Finally, there is Joshua Lunsford, the brother of Jessica Lunsford, whose murder spurred the Florida residency restrictions. A few years after Jessica's death, eighteen-year-old Joshua was arrested for heavy petting of a fourteen-year-old. He faced enhanced penalties under Ohio's newly passed "Jessica's Act," which had been championed by his father.[122]

The government intervention imposed on these children is Kafkaesque, involving "youth-shaming" treatments like masturbation logs and penile plethysmography—a process utilizing a machine that physically measures the subject's erection upon viewing sexual images, which was once used in the military to ferret out homosexuals.[123] One pediatric psychologist derided them as "coercive techniques of doubtful accuracy, untested benefit, and considerable potential for harm."[124] Today, the expert consensus is that the draconian sex offender laws did not reduce, and may have increased, sex offending against children.[125] Patty Wetterling, whose murdered son Jacob is the namesake of the 1989 law establishing the federal sex offender registry, became an opponent of juvenile registration. As director of Minnesota's Sexual Violence Prevention Program, she oversaw a 2015 report that called for deprioritizing punitive responses in favor of "taking on the root causes like alcohol and drug use, emotionally unsupportive family environments, and societal norms."[126] Despite such critiques, the sex offender regulations forged in the crucible of panic have been extremely difficult to reverse.

Ask any contemporary feminist, and she will say that feminist antirape agitation had *nothing* to do with the predator line of reform and will deny responsibility for its dystopian results. The feminist fight, she will say, was to take "date rape" seriously, not to focus on stranger-danger predators.[127] But the relationship between feminism and child predator panic is not so easily dismissed. In the 1970s, it was feminists, not conservatives, who spotlighted child sexual abuse and lobbied for legislative change. Professor Leigh Bienen examined feminists' early emphasis on sex offenses against children and their successful efforts to strengthen criminal laws in that arena. She observed, "When feminists began to lobby for changes in the rape laws in the 1970s, recharacterizing sex offenses involving children became a powerful and per-suasive component of both the practical and the political arguments for redefining all sex offenses and for changing the criminal justice system's response to sex crimes generally."[128]

Feminists reconceived of sexual misconduct within families as rape, turn-ing it from incest—a phenomenon of intrafamily psychosexual dysfunction—to rape—a phenomenon of men's predatory sexuality. Feminists drew a straight line between the forcible rape of adult women by strangers and the molestation of children in the home, coining the term *father rape* and urging legislators to abandon the incest legal framework, which did not carry the punitive outcomes and social judgment of rape.[129] Legal scholar Camille Gear Rich observes that "feminist scholars found that these claims about predatory male sexuality resonated well with conservative child welfare authorities who assumed that mothers should play the primary caretaking role."[130] This notion of men as a persistent sexual danger to children exists today, as many a proud feminist critical of gender stereotyping would still be exceedingly reluctant to hire a male babysitter. In the end, "feminists' representations of male sexuality . . . influenced legal decision makers, even as [their] critique of the nuclear family [was] cabined."[131]

Moreover, in the 1970s, the "stranger in the bushes" trope was more feminist than conservative. Years before Adam Walsh's 1981 disappearance sparked predator panic, feminists organized "Take Back the Night" (TBTN) rallies and marches. As noted in chapter 2, there were two strands of this grassroots activism around sexual violence—a more politically moderate college student strand and a radical antipornography strand. The 1970s student activists, unlike contemporary campus rape protesters, were distinctly concerned with the stranger rapist hiding in the shadows, not the drunken date. The initial TBTN rally in Philadelphia was sparked by the 1975 murder of Susan Speeth, a young microbiologist who was stabbed to death by a stranger while walking home at night. Many student rallies followed, usually in response to high-profile stranger rapes or murders.[132] Harvard's 1980 TBTN march, according to the *Crimson,* occurred after "a Harvard student was dragged into the bushes near her dorm and raped."[133]

Like the predator-panicked parents, the TBTN protesters feared the night and the shadowy threat of the sexual deviant prowling there. Most of those in the sexual violence intervention field today recognize that the risk of random violent stranger attack is very low. But fear and fact often diverge. It is a well-established "paradox" that women, who are far less likely than men to be victims, are more fearful of crime. Researchers suggest that women's fear of rape in particular creates a general apprehension of random attack, despite its rarity. This outsized fear of crime is influenced by one's sense that one's living environment is insecure and the perception that one is particularly vulnerable. The latter helps explain why older women, the safest demographic, are the most frightened.[134] Of course, one can rightly blame randomly attacking rapists for creating panic, just as one blames terrorists whose unpredictable acts inspire fear. Fear, however, is as socially constructed as it is instinctual. In the US, interest groups drum up anxiety over foreign terror for their own political ends. Similarly, public fear of statistically unlikely crime, including stranger rape, is as much a function of politics as psychology.

That said, unlike predator-panicked parents, campus TBTN protesters did not call for draconian sentences, and their rallies did not presage a wave of tough-on-rape legislation. Years later, when statutes like the Walsh Act established exorbitant sentences and unprecedented collateral consequences for rape, many feminist antirape organizations opposed them. It is, however, important to note that they did so, not out of civil libertarian concerns for defendants, but from a fear that excessive sentences would lead to *less* punishment overall: excessive sentences would increase dismissals, acquittals, and the number of uncooperative victims.[135] The TBTN activists did converge with antipredator crusaders in their embrace of monitoring—more policing, surveillance, and community notification. Organizers of Harvard's 1980 TBTN applauded the university for improving security and for creating the "House Blotter—a [police] publication describing all crimes that occur each week."[136] They also called on the school to provide floodlights, more police patrols, and regular self-defense classes.[137] But such measures were not extremely carceral, and TBTN rallies rather quickly evolved away from focusing on stranger rape and toward fighting all gender violence, including state violence. Nevertheless, the high-profile TBTN protests of the 1970s raised public awareness of the omnipresent, night-stalking, predator-rapist-killer, the fear of whom "unit[ed] all women."[138]

The other strand of TBTN was the radical movement that emerged on the West Coast. Less concerned about random sexual or nonsexual attacks at night, these protesters directed their efforts against hardcore pornography, considering it a glorification and cause of violent rape and prostitution. They, like temperance activists, likened commercial sex to "modern-day slavery." Feminist efforts to ban pornography in the late 1970s and early 1980s sparked the infamous "sex wars" where antiporn feminists and sex-positive scholars clashed fiercely over the meaning of pornography to women. With signature dramatic flair, legal scholar and activist Catharine MacKinnon compared the hearings on a 1983 Minneapolis antipornography ordinance she drafted to the Nuremberg trials, arguing that the production of "pornography is a traffic in female sexual slavery" and that its "consumption . . . institutionalizes a subhuman, victimized, second-class status for women."[139]

Indeed, the hearings on that ordinance were quite similar to the congressional hearings on sex offender registration, notification, and confinement laws during the predator panic to come. In the predator hearings, agonized parents and their supporters told gut-wrenching tales of loss, the emotional impact of which drowned out any "cold" policy calculations of the harms and benefits of reforms. The legislation became "simply about taking these sick monsters off the streets . . . to try to end the cycle of horrific violence that is every parent's nightmare," as one lawmaker put it.[140] The antipornography ordinance hearings similarly featured a cadre of victims and their advocates, counselors, and supporters recounting heinous, depraved, and violent sex acts, ostensibly related to pornography. To get a sense of the rhetoric, consider this testimony MacKinnon later offered to the Attorney General's Commission on Pornography: "Women in pornography are bound, battered, tortured, humiliated, and sometimes killed. For every act you see in the visual materials . . . a woman had to be tied or cut or burned or gagged or whipped or chained, hung from a meat hook or from trees by rope, urinated on or defecated on, forced to eat excrement, penetrated by eels and rats and knives and pistols, raped deep in the throat by penises, smeared with blood, mud, feces, and ejaculate."[141]

Opponents of the ordinance faced a challenge countering such emotion-provoking narratives. Law professors Paul Brest and Ann Vandenberg observed that the audience at the Minneapolis hearings "reacted passionately against testimony that opposed or even questioned the proposed law. . . . While speaking publicly of their experiences of abuse may have liberated the victims from a suffocating privacy, reliving the experiences was excruciatingly painful. . . . Under these circumstances, any opposition to the ordinance, especially any questioning of the validity of their experiences, was deeply threatening."[142] As with predator reforms, the spectacular narratives of perverse sex and victim suffering drowned out the experts who testified that the link between pornography and rape was, at best, "equivocal."

Sex-positive feminists and many gays and lesbians worried that a preoccupation with "deviant" commercial sex not only was anti–sexual liberationist but also was likely to disparately affect the LGBT community. There was reason to worry. In 1980, the National Organization of Women passed a resolution "to ensure that NOW does not work with any groups which might misconstrue pornography, s/m, cross-generational sex and public sex as 'Lesbian Rights issues.'"[143] The antipornography agitation in Minneapolis gave the police political cover to target gay bookstores and forcefully arrest buyers, to "terrible effect on the gay community."[144] But for MacKinnon, pornography and the sex it depicted represented an existential threat to women. Gay men's freedom from incarceration was a low price for eradicating this life-threatening force. Observing that "the gay male community perceives a stake in male supremacy, that is in some ways even greater than that of straight men," MacKinnon attributed gay men's reluctance to support her ordinance to their "suicidal and self-destructive stance in favor of the existing structure."[145] And indeed, this argument convinced many members of the gay community. One member of the community testified in favor of the ordinance, stating, "Gay men should accept the inconvenience of the world without adult bookstores in order to promote the *survival* of women which is very much threatened by any situation that promotes pornography."[146] Antiporn feminists' narrative of sex regulation as a matter of women's survival would do much work in the criminal arena in the coming decades.

The radical TBTN movement also protested prostitution and, in doing so, reinvigorated the "slavery" trope of the moral hygiene era. In 1979, TBTN participant Kathleen Barry published her popular book on prostitution, *Female Sexual Slavery*. It characterized most commercial sex as slavery, no matter how the woman became involved or the reason she remained in it. "Female sexual slavery is present in ALL situations where women or girls [involved in prostitution] cannot change the immediate conditions of their existence," she proclaimed.[147] Barry rejected the argument made by sex workers and feminists of color that poverty, discrimination, and lack of opportunity led marginalized women into the commercial sex world. That argument, Barry admonished, would "undermine the feminist critique of sexual domination."[148] Further, no reprieve should be given marginalized "black men from the ghetto" because pimping "cannot be justified by someone's economic conditions."[149] Nor could male prostitutes claim equal victimhood status, no matter how exploited, because sex was inherently *gendered*—something that men weaponized against women. Barry counseled, "The victimization and enslavement to which women are subject in male-dominated society find no equivalent in male experience."[150]

For Barry and other "new abolitionists," sex slavery did not require "whips crack[ing] over writhing, naked bodies" but could be just a matter of "subdued business transactions."[151] Thus, among the many horrors involved when a woman was kidnapped, tortured, locked up, and sold for sex, the factor that defined her situation as "slavery" was the commodified sex. This paradigm, sociologist Ronald Weitzer remarks, "depicts all types of sexual commerce as institutionalized subordination of women, regardless of the conditions under which it occurs. The perspective does not present domination and exploitation as variables but instead considers them core ontological features of sexual commerce."[152] Barry's argument that "slavery" applied to "subdued" commercial sex, nevertheless, did not prevent her from regaling exotic tales of foreign kidnapping that bore a striking resemblance to the white slave crusaders' narratives. "Several thousand teenage girls disappear from Paris every year," Barry reported. "The police know but cannot prove that many are destined for Arab harems. An eyewitness reports that auctions have been held in Zanzibar, where European women were sold to Arab customers."[153] New abolitionists, like their old counterparts, regularly depicted sex slavery through lurid and racialized narratives and then simply applied the label to all prostitution. "Legal scholars, lawmakers, advocacy groups and the media ... consistently used an eroticized version of the female 'sex slave' to justify and garner public support for anti-trafficking legislation," noted one expert.[154] These spectacular stories combined with statistics on prostitution to complete the brutality-ubiquity dyad that characterizes moral panic.

Like battered women's advocates, new abolitionists created an ideal slavery victim narrative that could maintain women's devastated status and explain why prostitution was not a "choice." The sex slave, like the battered woman, was invariably brutalized and damaged, and her free will was an illusion. Sex workers, regardless of what false consciousness might lead them to say, were coercively controlled by men—pimps, fathers, or other enablers—and needed rescuing. Moreover, when the "it's for her own good" analysis ran out, new abolitionists were also willing to characterize unruly women, such as sex workers who called prostitution a chosen profession, as "accomplices" to sexually abusive men. One activist remarked in 1987, "When the sex war is won, prostitutes should be shot as collaborators for their terrible betrayal of all women."[155]

Accordingly, radical feminists felt justified in pursuing criminalization policies counter to the wishes and material interests of women in the commercial sex industry. Although some abolitionist feminists gave lip service to partial decriminalization—criminalizing purchase but not sale of sex—their antitrafficking laws and policies, like the social hygiene laws of old, landed many women in jail. Today, antitrafficking raids "save" victims by arresting them and requiring them to meet with "service providers" on pain of incarceration.[156] Prosecutors even counsel that "arresting the victim" is a useful tool in trafficking interdiction because it allows prosecutors to keep tabs on these potential victim-witnesses. Prosecutors applaud a situation where the trafficking *victim* is "required to make periodic court appearances and, in the event that she disappears, prosecutors can seek a warrant for her arrest."[157]

The radical feminists of the '70s and '80s lost the sex wars. The movement was besieged from many sides: by popular sex columnists, civil libertarians, sex-positive and postmodern feminists, a burgeoning sex workers' rights movement, and the ever-expanding, increasingly accepted commercial sex industry. So feminists moved on. Specifically, they moved abroad. Elizabeth Bernstein coined the term *carceral feminism* after observing the negative impacts of Western feminists' efforts to control prostitution in developing countries.[158] Prominent scholars have analyzed the discourses, practices, and ramifications of the international and transnational sex-trafficking regime built by late twentieth-century Western feminism—analyses too detailed to reproduce here.[159] Meanwhile, back at home, prostitution arrests in the 1990s continued apace and in places even increased, despite increasingly liberal sentiments on sex. But this was mostly due to "broken windows" policing policies that encouraged officers to target low-level crimes like "street" prostitution and graffiti, on the (now rejected) assumption that "visible disorder" creates a fertile socio-psychological environment for serious crimes.[160]

In the end, the campus TBTN movement was about sexual predators, but it was not really carceral. The radical TBTN movement was carceral, but it was not really about predators. Nevertheless, both had something to do with the predator panic that shortly followed and culminated in today's repressive sex offender laws. Together, they established rape as a spectacular and devastating, but still common, crime committed by predatory males. Any "tolerated residuum of sexual abuse" posed an existential threat to *all* women.[161] Feminists of the TBTN era were happy to traffic in discourse about cloaked marauders in the night. Radical feminist Andrea Dworkin, coauthor of the antiporn ordinance and infamous for her alliance with Jerry Falwell Jr. against the First Amendment, delivered a speech at a 1979 TBTN rally in Connecticut.[162] Speaking to over two thousand people, she voiced a predator rhetoric that was at once terrifyingly beautiful and beautifully terrifying:

> The policemen of the night—rapists and other prowling men—have the right to enforce the laws of the night: to stalk the female and to punish her. We have all been chased, and many of us have been caught. A woman who knows the rules of civilized society knows that she must hide from the night. But even when the woman, like a good girl, locks herself up and in, night threatens to intrude. Outside are the predators who will crawl in the windows, climb down drainpipes, pick the locks, descend from skylights, to bring the night with them.... They bring with them sex and death.... Once the victim has fully submitted, the night holds no more terror, because the victim is dead. She is very lovely, very feminine, and very dead.[163]

In sum, feminist antibattering and antirape discourse and activism meaningfully influenced the conservative victims' rights and crime control movements of the 1980s and the draconian sex offender laws of the 1990s. However, commentators rarely describe "feminist rape reform" as child sex abuse laws, sexual predator statutes, or antipornography ordinances. Rather, the second-wave feminist war was about date rape, and it was fought in the courts and scholarly literature. In pursuing the claim that "ordinary boys" rape, feminists had to downplay the icon of the stranger in the bushes. At the same time, reformers did not want to jettison the repulsion society had developed for rapists, the sympathy for devastated victims, or the presumption that rape was the ultimate crime. Antirape activists accordingly used increasingly evocative language to describe date rape and significantly broadened the category of men to be deemed "real rapists" and predators.[164] To borrow a phrase from theorist Sharon Marcus, feminists "collapsed the continuum" between violent rape and inadequately authorized sex at the precise time when being branded a rapist meant certain social death.[165] And feminists' prosecutorial achievements operated within a legal apparatus built by moral panic.

FIVE

The New Front

DATE RAPE

From the sex wars to consent, scholars widely recognize that second-wave feminists altered the legal landscape around sexual violence. Most assume that this rape law revolution originated wholly within feminism in the 1980s and that activists *finally* addressed the long-acknowledged problem of men coercing their dates into sex. However, this account leaves out a very important aspect of the '80s antirape movement. It was at core reactionary—a response to the unprecedented upheaval of sexual mores and traditions in the late 1960s and '70s. During the first wave of feminism, casual sex was entirely too taboo to parse. First-wave temperance reformers had no reason to police the boundaries of acceptable sex on a date because there was *no* acceptable sex on a date.[1]

The sexual revolution was a massive cultural transformation. Society moved from temptation avoidance to free love, and it had to sort out the new sexual boundaries—what was good, bad, liberated, sexist, desirable, and immoral. The old distinctions between acceptable and unacceptable sex, once mediated by marriage, crumbled. Lawmakers struggled with sexual modernity and where to draw new legal lines. Much of the action on the legal front was deregulatory. Pushed by progressive activists, including feminists, states widely decriminalized birth control, abortion, fornication, adultery, and sodomy. There was also civil libertarian agitation to protect pornography as speech and even successful sex worker rights lawsuits to legalize prostitution.[2]

Society members, feminists among them, found themselves in a sea of newly liberated sexuality. Because women had been denied sexual subjectivity for so long, the new sexual culture reflected men's preferences and predilections. It rapidly became clear that sexual liberation was at best a double-edged sword for women. The paradigm of male conquest and female submission continued to rule the intimacy dance. In the absence of fornication and adultery laws, the regulation of nonmarital sex became a matter of culture. Women's chastity was governed through an ever more incoherent set of ad hoc norms: "You can wear a tank top but not short shorts"; "Drunk is okay, but sloppy drunk is not"; "Nonmarital sex is fine, but not on a first date." People presumed that women regularly made up rapes for attention, for revenge, or to cover an affair. Feminists reacted accordingly.

The radical take-back-the-night feminists discussed in the previous chapter called for strict regulation of sex, which they viewed as the root cause of male dominance over women. This "dominance feminist" view, like the purity campaigns of old, characterized pornography, prostitution, and male-dominant sexual encounters as devastating to victims and as a social poison to every woman. By contrast, sex-positive feminists ("sex radicals") saw in the revolution promise for women to explore and redefine their previously repressed sexuality. Sex radicals' distaste for any form of sexual regulation gave many feminist commentators pause. Law professor Kathy Abrams critiqued sex radicals for adopting "a surprisingly laissez-faire approach—avoid legal encumbrance, and women may interrogate and re-imagine their sexuality."[3] On the extreme end, prostitution abolitionist Kathleen Barry accused sex radicals of enabling "male leftists [to] continue their sexual abuse of women."[4] A third group of feminists was less concerned about whether sex was inherently dominating or redemptive and was more preoccupied with equality and autonomy. These "liberal" feminists shaped reform in the "classic liberal ideology of privacy, autonomy, and individual choice," as one expert noted,[5] and they called on lawmakers to treat date rape like "real" rape. Together, second-wave feminists *defined* lawful sex in the postrevolution era and determined who among the newly liberated date sex participants was a "bad date" or a criminal meriting imprisonment.

This chapter examines feminists' successful battle to expand rape law and establish proprosecution procedural rules. Dominance feminists hoped to craft a legal regime reflecting that sex was presumptively coerced except under the narrowest conditions of equality, mutuality, and authentic feminine desire. Liberal feminists favored a framework in which sex was lawful so long as there was "consent." Eventually, consent emerged as the preferred regime, and the line between sex and rape was determined not by the defendant's forceful and violent conduct but by the victim's state of mind. State actors, judges, and jurors, in turn, scrutinized rape complainants and their internal desires. Rape reformers, like DV advocates, soon found themselves in the double bind of wanting society to focus and not focus on the victim.

To resolve the bind, antirape feminists championed special evidentiary rules and pushed the narrative of a sex-averse, frozen-in-fright, and easily traumatized victim to explain away victims' testimonial inconsistencies, their consensual behavior, and why they didn't say "no." This victimhood narrative was certainly bad for defendants. It also posed more inchoate risks to women's sexual self-understanding.

COERCION VERSUS CONSENT

A journalist recently asked me why second-wave feminists so readily embraced the criminal system as the solution to sexual violence, given what she understood as feminism's general hostility toward state authority. Indeed, many feminists of the sixties saw the state as war-mongering masculinism incarnate. Theorist bell hooks argued that it was the "Western philosophical notion of hierarchical rule and coercive authority that is the root cause of violence against women."[6] Undoubtedly, the prison is a concentrated site of hypermasculinity and sexual violence. One would therefore think that "feminists, who champion empathy and connectedness," would "extend that same ethic of care to criminal defendants," in Professor Aviva Orenstein's words.[7]

A deeper understanding of feminist dominance theory, as articulated by Catharine MacKinnon, illuminates why dominance feminists saw strict regulation of newly liberated heterosexual sex as *the* feminist battle. Dominance feminist theory begins with the premise that the patriarchy organizes society in a male supremacist order. This idea that law reflects and reinforces male supremacy is a feature of many feminisms and is intuitively persuasive. However, perhaps owing to the hedonistic atmosphere of the time, MacKinnon identified "*sexuality* as the primary social sphere of male power."[8] In her view, "The organized expropriation of the sexuality of some for the use of others defines the sex, woman."[9] Dominance feminists actively engaged state power, despite their recognition that the state was "male," because only it could topple "the most pervasive and tenacious system of power in history"—male sexual domination.[10]

The sex-is-oppression mantra failed to resonate with many women in a sexually liberated world. Indeed, gender oppression was and is overdetermined—a matter of economic inequality, deregulated labor, and social, religious, and cultural mores.[11] Moreover, many women saw sexual pleasure and erotic interest in "ordinary" male-dominant sex. But to MacKinnon, women who desired male sexual pursuit had simply eroticized their own domination. Their desires were "adaptive preferences conditioned by inequalities."[12] Such women were, in the DV legal feminist parlance, "accomplices" to their own sexual exploitation.[13] It followed that the law should place men's predatory sexuality "where it truly belongs, within the context of modern *criminal* violence," as Susan Brownmiller urged.[14]

Translating dominance theory into rape law practice meant codifying the principle that sex is ordinarily oppressive to women and that only narrow conditions of equality can remove sex's inherent stain of male domination. To dominance feminists, "Sex is presumed guilty until proven innocent," as queer theorist Gayle Rubin once commented.[15] Reformers successfully relied on this presumption of coercion to lobby for tougher incest and statutory rape laws. They argued that the inherent power differentials of age and familial authority made sex across those differentials rape per se, regardless of force or consent.[16] Dominance feminists hoped this presumption of coercion would transfer from children to adult women. MacKinnon maintained that "gender belongs on the list of inequalities that, when drawn upon as a form of power and used as a form of coercion in sexual interactions, make sex rape."[17]

In fact, some courts and lawmakers, in the face of egregious cases of adult men who exploited vulnerable children, did expand the definition of coercion generally. In one particularly horrific 1986 Pennsylvania case, the adult male defendant, Nicholas Rhodes, lured an eight-year-old girl away from a playground to a filthy abandoned building. He told her to lie down and then penetrated her, leaving her with significant injuries. Rhodes's defense was an alibi— he said he had been at his mother's house. The jury convicted him of rape, involuntary deviate sexual intercourse, statutory rape, and corruption of minors.[18] Rhodes appealed, and the appellate court affirmed all the convictions, except for rape, which required "forcible compulsion."[19] The appellate court remarked that "there is not one iota of evidence that sexual intercourse was accomplished by forcible compulsion or by threat of forcible compulsion."[20] It concluded, "Although we do not minimize the heinous nature of appellant's act, it seems clear that the act of vaginal intercourse was criminal because of the provisions ... defining statutory rape and not because it was a forcible rape."[21]

The Supreme Court of Pennsylvania reversed and reinstated the rape conviction. The court held that "forcible compulsion" could be satisfied through actions other than physical violence, regardless of whether the victim was a child or adult. Consulting Webster's dictionary, the court interpreted *force* both in its strict meaning of physical compulsion and in its colloquial sense of pressure by "moral, psychological, or intellectual" means.[22] This interpretation was promising for dominance feminists who wanted to outlaw "*all* the forms of force that someone, usually a man, deploys to coerce sex on someone with less power," including "social coercion" and "gender inequality."[23] The court, however, was unwilling to "delineate all of the possible circumstances" where force could be found.[24] Future decisions about coercion would rely on the "totality of the circumstances," including age, mental and physical condition, and relationships of authority.[25]

As dominance feminists called for a broad presumption-of-coercion framework, liberal feminists lobbied lawmakers to treat nonconsensual "date rape" like forcible stranger rape. Recall from chapter 1 that rape law historically contained peculiar legal barriers to prosecution. In the 1960s, at the height of the civil rights protests, the American Law Institute undertook to revise the Model Penal Code (MPC), an influential collection of model criminal provisions that states adopt and reference in interpreting their codes. In revising the rape sections, the MPC drafters were acutely aware of the past and ongoing problem of the overpunishment of black men. They worried about cases like that of Willie McGee, discussed in chapter 1, where the discovery of an interracial affair led white women to falsely accuse black men of rape.[26] As a result, the drafters codified some of the most archaic defendant-friendly rape principles, including the prompt complaint rule, the corroboration requirement, and a Lord Hale–like instruction to "evaluate the testimony of a victim or complaining witness with special care."[27] The MPC also made rape of a "voluntary social companion" a lower-level offense than stranger rape.[28]

In 1986, Susan Estrich, a prominent law professor and rape survivor, wrote a compelling article and book challenging the system that had treated her stranger rape as a "real rape" but failed to do so for date rapes.[29] Back in the 1970s, however, feminist TBTN activists had highlighted the specific terroristic nature of stranger rape, arguing that it was a "conscious process of intimidation by which *all men* keep *all women* in a state of fear."[30] Estrich, by contrast, viewed date and stranger rape as equal, and some reformers argued that date rape was *more* traumatic because of the violation of trust.[31] Liberal feminists successfully prevented the MPC's "voluntary social companion" distinction from being widely absorbed into state law. They also waged a winning battle against the MPC doctrines that treated rape complainants differently from other victim-witnesses. By the close of the millennium, most jurisdictions had eliminated the Lord Hale instruction and the corroboration and fresh complaint requirements.[32]

Liberal feminists are probably best known for orchestrating the consent revolution in rape law. Prior to the second wave of feminism, many rape statutes, like Pennsylvania's, required the offenders to compel sex by force or threat. When a stranger dragged a woman into the bushes, force was clear, but the dating scenario required new legal lines. Feminists highlighted cases where narrow force standards exonerated men who had engaged in intimidation, isolated victims, or surprised victims with sudden penetration, and states responded by broadening their force interpretations, as the court had in *Rhodes*.[33] Liberal feminists, however, wanted the law to move away from force altogether. For them, the crux of rape's harm was not the accompanying violence or the fact that sex is inherently oppressive to women. Rape is harmful, they maintained, because of the violation of "autonomy" that comes from engaging in *unwanted* sexual activity.[34] In liberal feminism, as Estrich noted, the "discussion of rape begins (and ends) with consent."[35]

The consent framework, like dominance feminists' coercion frame, greatly expanded the reach of criminal rape law. In addition to equalizing stranger rape and nonstranger rape, the consent standard labeled as rape behavior that was qualitatively different from forced violent sex. Some criminal law theorists opposed the law treating "the rapist who jumps out from the bushes with a knife" like "the teenage boy who has ordinary intercourse ... without obtaining permission."[36] To this day, liberal commentators, including feminists, offer proposals to "scale" sexual assault and treat nonforcible date rape as a lesser offense.[37] By contrast, dominance feminists denigrated consent for not being tough enough. Culturally compelled, patriarchy-conditioned sex, they argued, would certainly *look* consensual and could even be bargained for. MacKinnon protested, "Consent is a pathetic standard of equal sex for a free people" because "under unequal conditions, many women acquiesce in or tolerate sex they cannot as a practical matter avoid or evade."[38]

Rape law's expansion would proceed primarily in the liberal vein, through consent. Many commentators, including liberal feminists, bristled at dominance feminists' characterization of women's sexual choices as manifestations of internalized oppression. Moreover, dominance feminism's coercion frame was entirely impractical. It did not give lawmakers a clear way to distinguish between rape and "ordinary" sex. MacKinnon herself ruminated, "Perhaps the wrong of rape has proven so difficult to articulate because the unquestionable starting point has been that rape is definable as distinct from intercourse, when for women it is difficult to distinguish them under conditions of male dominance."[39]

In 1994, the Pennsylvania Supreme Court heard a case that tested the limits of its "moral, psychological, and intellectual" construction of force from *Rhodes*. *Commonwealth v. Berkowitz* is probably the most well-known college date rape case of all time, taught for decades in law schools throughout the nation.[40] The parties, college sophomores, were acquaintances with a somewhat flirtatious relationship. On the night in question, the victim "Lisa" had some time to kill while waiting for her boyfriend. She entered Berkowitz's unlocked room and woke him up. Berkowitz invited her to "hang out for a while,"[41] and this is where the stories diverge.

Lisa testified that she was sitting on the floor talking to Berkowitz when he "kind of pushed [me] back with his body. It wasn't a shove, it was just kind of a leaning-type of thing." Berkowitz then straddled and kissed Lisa, who demurred that she had to meet her boyfriend. When Berkowitz started fondling her, she said, "No." When he tried to initiate fellatio, she said, "Let me go." Berkowitz then locked the door and put Lisa on the bed: "It wasn't slow like a romantic kind of thing, but it wasn't a fast shove either. It was kind of in the middle." During the ensuing sexual intercourse, Lisa said no several times, but "softly in a moaning kind of way . . . because it was just so scary." After, Lisa left and found her boyfriend. She tearfully told him what happened, and he called the police.[42]

Berkowitz admitted to initiating intimate contact and acknowledged that Lisa had said "No" several times. However, he claimed that she passionately returned his kisses and "whisper[ed]" no, while "amorously . . . passionately" moaning. Berkowitz said he locked the door for privacy, and the two lay down on the bed, where Lisa helped him undress. During intercourse, Lisa continued to say "No," but it was "moaned passionately." Berkowitz claimed that he understood her protests as token resistance and believed, on the basis of all their interactions, that she had consented to sex. The jurors didn't buy it. They convicted Berkowitz of rape (forcible sex) and indecent assault (nonconsensual sex).[43]

In a widely denigrated holding, the Pennsylvania Supreme Court overturned Berkowitz's rape conviction. The court opined that "forcible compulsion" meant to punish rapists who use physical force beyond the sex itself. Further, the court summarily rejected the claim that Berkowitz's physical pushes, even as described by Lisa, were forcible.[44] The court acknowledged that "psychological coercion" could also be forcible compulsion but declared that it was not present.[45] The court's ruling on force dashed dominance feminists' hopes for a broad coercion standard.[46] When the legislature amended the rape laws in 1995, it codified the "intellectual, moral, emotional or psychological force" construction from *Rhodes*.[47] It did not, however, specify that force included the type of conduct Berkowitz committed.

The *Berkowitz* ruling produced a public outcry. From the Pennsylvania press to the *New York Times,* the case became known as the "'No' is not enough" case. The state chapter of the National Organization of Women organized a protest outside of the courthouse, with president Phyllis Wetherby calling the decision "the greatest favor" to NOW because their phones were "ringing across the state."[48] Outrage at *Berkowitz* unleashed the public's punitive instincts. A letter to the Allentown *Morning Call* entitled "Lock Up Rapists Longer" read: "We are hearing much about the recent decision of the Pennsylvania Supreme Court reversing the Berkowitz rape conviction. I believe the women of this state would do themselves the most good by expending support for, longer, mandatory, non-parolable prison terms for convicted rapists. They would find millions of men who would join them in this cause."[49]

Those who vociferously condemned the case generally failed to mention that the court *upheld* Berkowitz's conviction for nonconsensual sex (indecent assault), and he served six months on that charge.[50] "No," in fact, had been enough to establish nonconsent. Indeed, at the time of the outcry, Pennsylvania already criminalized nonconsensual sex; the jury had convicted Berkowitz despite his no-means-yes argument; the court had upheld the conviction; and Berkowitz was *incarcerated*. Feminist activism in the wake of *Berkowitz* changed only one thing—it significantly increased the sentence for nonforcible, nonconsensual sexual assault. The legislature bumped it up from a serious misdemeanor to a second-degree felony carrying ten years in prison.[51]

MANAGING MYTHS

Consent won the day, so let me explain how it works. At a basic level, to prove nonconsensual sexual assault the prosecution must show that the victim did not consent, meaning she did not want sex to occur. Typically, juries determine a person's state of mind by considering their testimony and any "circumstantial evidence" shedding light on their thoughts. A modern example of circumstantial evidence of consent might be a text saying, "Let's have sex tonight." Second, the prosecution must show that the defendant had intent to commit the crime, known as *mens rea*. To be guilty, the defendant must have some awareness that the victim did not want sex. Juries determine defendants' *mens rea* by looking at their statements and the surrounding circumstances. If a defendant confesses, "I knew she did not want sex," that is great prosecutorial evidence. But this often not the case, and the jury must determine what the defendant knew about the victim's state of mind by an examination of the parties' outward behavior in context.[52]

Having established the rape inquiry as an assessment of the victim's mind-set, feminists became increasingly worried that juries would get that assessment wrong. After mock jury studies demonstrated the influence of "rape myths," feminists feared that jurors were predisposed to believe defendants' claims that the victim really consented and was lying or reinterpreting the event.[53] One problem with this theory was that studies showed that rape myths biased jurors to favor or disfavor a given party, depending on that party's conformity with certain stereotypes. Jurors, for example, were biased *against* defendants who looked like sexual "loser[s]."[54] Nevertheless, reformers pushed unique definitional and evidentiary rules specifically to manage juries' purported antivictim, prodefendant bias. By the mid-'80s, "changes in the legal definition of the crime of rape, with their accompanying statutes directed at limiting the admissibility of evidence regarding the prior sexual history of [the] victim at trial, were enacted in response to vigorous, nationally coordinated lobbying by feminists," Professor Leigh Bienen remarks.[55] Equality between rape and other crimes ceased to be a priority.

Feminists' preoccupation with jury decision-making was likely misplaced. First, mock jury studies revealed that tinkering with legal rules made little difference to sexist mock jurors bent on exonerating the defendant.[56] Perhaps more importantly, mock jurors doubted guilt in mock cases, but real juries apparently did not.[57] The Bureau of Justice Statistics' (BJS) 1990 to 2009 data on felony defendants in the largest seventy-five counties is telling. In 1990, juries rendered guilty verdicts in 98 percent of rape cases, the same as for violent felonies overall. Prosecutors pursued *more* rape prosecutions than violent felony prosecutions overall, with the result that 52 percent of rape defendants received felony convictions, compared to 40 percent of violent felony defendants overall and 31 percent of nonsexual assault defendants.[58] Nineteen years later, in 2009, the picture had changed little. Prosecutors dismissed fewer cases across the board, but guilty verdicts remained the rule, rendered in 97 percent of rape trials and 98 percent of violent felony trials. The rape felony conviction rate, at 57 percent, was still higher than that of violent felonies overall (49 percent) and nonsexual assaults (39 percent).[59] As might be expected, rapists consistently received higher sentences than the run of violent offenders.[60]

The action, it appears, was on the arrest and prosecution front. And, indeed, experts warned that definitional and evidentiary reforms geared toward jurors would do little to increase the number of convictions because police and prosecutors exercised total discretion over charging and thus "control the doors to the courthouse."[61] I should note, however, that the BJS data did not reveal prosecutorial hostility toward rape cases. Prosecutors consistently dismissed *fewer* rape cases than violent crime cases on average. Nevertheless, rape reformers took a different path than DV advocates and did not propose mandatory arrest and prosecutorial no-drop laws or seek to craft specialized rape courts.[62] They focused their reforms on trial.

Turning to the definitional reforms, feminists imagined that juries were eager to believe the Berkowitzes who claimed that no meant yes, although the actual *Berkowitz* jury rejected that claim. Feminists filed "No means yes" under rape myths and advocated rules to prevent defendants from making that claim. "One of the most common . . . myths," remarked one feminist, "is that 'no' does not always mean 'no.'"[63] However, studies performed during the second wave and today attest that "No means yes" is a real phenomenon. In a widely publicized 1988 survey of female Texas college students, approximately 40 percent of respondents reported that they had engaged in "token resistance."[64] The authors attributed this "rational" behavior to the sexual "double standard" that existed for women.[65] The good news is that sexual partners are quite attuned to when protest is token and passivity is receptivity and when those actions signal unwillingness.[66] But the fact is that "no" sometimes—not always or never—means "yes."

Many rape myths are simply defense arguments about the inferences that can be drawn from evidence in rape trials. For example, feminists say it is a "myth" to believe that rape requires resistance. Yet when the victim does resist, the prosecution emphasizes the *guilt* inferences that follow: she did not consent, and he knew it. However, if a defense attorney asks the jury to draw an *innocence* inference from lack of resistance—she consented, or he thought she did—the defense is trafficking in myths. Prosecutors can argue inaccurately that no always means no, but defense attorneys cannot make the accurate argument that it is *possible* for no to mean yes (and that it did in this case). Such a prosecutorial advantage would be outrageous in other criminal cases. Imagine a first-degree murder case where the defense contests premeditation. The prosecution highlights evidence that the defendant brought a gun with him to prove planning and premeditation. The defense responds with an alternative inference, arguing that some people carry their guns all the time and the defendant is such a person. It is hard to imagine the prosecution being able to characterize the "People carry guns" claim as a "myth."

Feminists rationalized the ban on "No means yes" as necessary to counteract juries' belief that no *always* meant yes. Allowing the defense to argue "No means yes," feminists asserted, led to too many unfair acquittals, and preventing those was worth sacrificing the few (or nonexistent) defendants who correctly interpreted no as yes. Feminists offered reassurance that police, prosecutors, and victims themselves would weed out the few cases where no plausibly meant yes. We will see below that this presumption that testing at trial is hardly necessary because the pretrial process accurately eliminates spurious rape claims has become a mainstay of feminist reasoning. Today, the "No means no" rule has been adopted by some states and the US military.[67] As I write this book, the denigrated 1962 Model Penal Code rape provisions are finally being revised. Prompt complaint, corroboration, Lord Hale, and voluntary social companion are out, and "No means no" is in.[68]

"No means no" addressed only the date rape cases where the victim in fact said no, leaving the many cases where the victim did not say no. Feminists worried that juries in such cases would unfairly assume that the victim's silence meant she consented. Accordingly, rape reformers championed the "affirmative consent" standard, which outlaws sex absent a clear "affirmative expression." Affirmative consent is often called "Yes means yes," but there has always been considerable confusion over whether it requires a verbal yes or whether some other expression will suffice. It is unclear whether an "affirmative expression of consent" includes a range of nonverbal conduct, including kissing and petting. Nevertheless, second-wave proponents touted the standard for injecting certainty into the law. Instead of the messy endeavor of divining the complainant's mind-set from the totality of the circumstances, fact finders could simply look to whether there was a "yes" or a functional equivalent. This bright-line rule provided added benefits. Focusing the jury on clear language would make them less tempted to scrutinize the victim's behavior, dress, and sexual history to determine whether she really wanted to have sex (or he thought she did). Only what she said at the moment would matter.[69]

Affirmative consent, however, had a big drawback. Under the standard, rape was no longer unwanted sex; it was any sex—even wanted sex—in the absence of *specific* consent *performances,* whether a "yes," a thumbs-up, or something else. Because many couples, especially those in established relationships, have sex without such communicative rituals, affirmative consent turned a lot of regular folks into rapists. When faced with the critique that affirmative consent criminalized ordinary sex, some proponents simply reversed course and maintained that affirmative consent was not really a reform at all—it allowed defendants to determine consent from the totality of the circumstances. Today, proponents like politics writer Amanda Marcotte toe that line: "The concept of affirmative consent, . . . despite what haters might say, simply means only having sex with someone you know for sure wants to have sex with you."[70] However, reformers had proposed affirmative consent precisely to counter defendants' claims that they were "sure" the passive victim wanted to have sex with them. If affirmative consent is no different from totality-of-the-circumstances consent, it does not in fact inject certainty into the rape case.

Back in the 1980s, some states already defined consent by terms like *active cooperation* and *free agreement* (today, fourteen jurisdictions adopt affirmative consent language).[71] Decades ago, courts grappled with whether this language meant to criminalize unwanted sex or all sex without a sufficient consent performance. Like Marcotte, courts punted. The 1980 case *Wisconsin v. Lederer* involved a defendant's constitutional challenge to Wisconsin's sexual assault statute, which required "words or overt actions . . . indicating a freely given agreement to have sexual intercourse."[72] Lederer argued that the statute was overbroad because it outlawed mutually desired sex when the statutorily required "words or overt actions" were absent. The Wisconsin appeals court disagreed, arguing that it was impossible for a person to have desired sex without "manifesting freely given consent through words or acts": "We know of no other means" by which "two parties may enter into consensual sexual relations."[73] The court avoided the overbreadth objection by characterizing affirmative consent as exhaustive of the ways people agree to sex. However, if "words or overt actions" include *every* way to agree to sex, then "words or overt actions" necessarily include silence and inaction. Sexual consent researchers find that "many men and women passively indicate their consent to sexual intercourse by not resisting, such as allowing themselves to be undressed by their partner, not saying no, or not stopping their partner's advances."[74]

Despite its opacity, affirmative consent emerged as the darling of forward-thinking scholars and lawmakers. In a landmark 1992 case, *State in Interest of M.T.S.*, the New Jersey Supreme Court interpreted the rape provision that forbade intercourse when "the actor uses physical force or coercion, but the victim does not sustain severe personal injury."[75] Noting that the 1978 legislation creating that provision was formulated "by a coalition of feminist groups," the court reasoned that the legislature intended a feminist interpretation of "physical force" as *any* physical contact, even sex itself.[76] However, because all sex involves contact, something had to distinguish unlawful forcible sex from ordinary sex. The court landed on consent as the distinguishing factor. Referencing battery laws that defined force as nonconsensual contact, the court held that the statutory prohibition of sex by physical force really meant the outlawing of nonconsensual sex.

The court's reinterpretation of force as nonconsent landed it right in the middle of the feminist conundrum. The court worried that centralizing the complainant's state of mind would put victims "on trial."[77] Yet it was their very interpretation that made the line between rape and sex a question, not of the defendant's forcible conduct, but of the victim's mind-set. To solve the dilemma, the court engaged in a clever sleight of hand. It stated that under New Jersey law, "Any '*unauthorized* touching of another [is] a battery,'" quoting the case *Perna v. Pirozzi*.[78] The court reasoned that if unauthorized touching is battery, unauthorized sexual touching must be sexual battery.[79] Defining sexual assault as unauthorized contact, rather than nonconsensual or offensive contact, changed the rape inquiry from whether the complainant really wanted sex to whether she certified it *ex ante*. But was it true that New Jersey criminalized *all* human contact—a handshake—in the absence of explicit preauthorization?

It was not. Prior to 1978, New Jersey law made only "offensive"—not "unauthorized"—touching a criminal battery. What's more, the very same 1978 legislation that created the sexual assault provision eliminated offensive-touching battery as a crime.[80] It specified that to be criminal, a battery had to involve, not just unwanted touching, but intended or actual *injury*. The New Jersey Superior Court noted in *State v. Cabana* that the legislation reflected that "mere offensive touching is not sufficiently serious to be made criminal."[81] If "offensive" touching was not even a crime, where did the *M.T.S.* court get the idea that "unauthorized" touching was? The case the court relied on, *Perna v. Pirozzi*, it turns out, was a *civil* lawsuit brought by a patient who had consented to surgery by one doctor but was operated on by a different one. The full language of the quote selectively used in *M.T.S.* reads, "A surgeon who operates without the patient's consent engages in the unauthorized touching of another and, thus, commits a [noncriminal] battery."[82] The fact that *Perna* declared surgery without preauthorization a civil wrong hardly meant that any touching in the absence of advanced permission was a *crime*.

Criminalizing sex unless it has the kind of preauthorization required for surgery would make a lot of ordinary sex rape. So how did the *M.T.S.* court deal with the question of whether New Jersey outlawed desired but insufficiently "authorized" sex? Like the *Lederer* court, it punted. The court's mystifying explication of affirmative consent was "words or . . . actions that, when viewed in the light of all the surrounding circumstances, would demonstrate to a reasonable person affirmative and freely-given authorization."[83] The court's statement on *mens rea* hardly clarified things: "If there is evidence to suggest that the defendant reasonably believed that such permission had been given, the State must demonstrate either that defendant did not actually believe [this] or that such a belief was unreasonable."[84] After all that legal wrangling, the questions remained: Which words and actions indicate "affirmative" authorization? Does kissing count? Do silence and passivity count? Can the defendant conclude that "permission had been given" from any circumstance?

Given all the confusion, it was difficult to know whether affirmative consent standards criminalized wanted sex without a "yes," as critics feared, or just made it easier to prosecute unwanted sex, as some proponents contended. A perusal of affirmative consent's role in M.T.S.'s conviction reveals that the standard may serve another function altogether—a difference-splitting function. When fact finders hear "he-said, she-said" cases and do not know whom to believe or support, affirmative consent allows them to err on the side of conviction. Fifteen-year-old C.G. lived with seventeen-year-old M.T.S., a family friend, in C.G.'s mother's house.[85] C.G. testified that on the night in question she fell into a "heavy" sleep and awoke to find M.T.S. having sex with her.[86] M.T.S. testified in contrast that the pair had engaged in consensual kissing, petting, and undressing. He then "stuck it in" and thrusted a few times before C.G. told him to stop.[87] The judge found "that the couple had been kissing and petting, had undressed and had gotten into the victim's bed and then had sex."[88] The judge nonetheless convicted M.T.S. because the penetration "went too far" and there was no consent "to the sexual act itself."[89] The judge found C.G.'s testimony totally false and, at the same time, felt comfortable convicting M.T.S. because C.G. apparently had not performed some required, if unspecified, affirmative consent ritual.[90]

When I teach rape, I pose a close-case hypothetical based on a real story where the parties were drunk; she says he forced sex but has massive credibility problems; and he can't remember anything. I was repeatedly surprised when students said, "I don't know what happened, so under an ordinary consent standard I would acquit, but under affirmative consent I would convict." To acquit the defendant of nonconsensual sex, the students had to totally disbelieve the complainant, but once they discredited the complainant there would be no basis for concluding that affirmative consent was lacking. It finally dawned on me that the students were splitting the difference, like the *M.T.S.* trial judge. They rejected the complainant's testimony that sex was forced, and they could not conclude that sex was unwanted. Nevertheless, they surmised that, whatever happened, the sex (like most sex) probably lacked a "yes" performance. They understood affirmative consent as "When in doubt, convict."

Affirmative consent proponents called it a myth to believe that silence and passivity *ever* meant acquiescence, even though "numerous studies have demonstrated that the preferred approach to signal consent for both women and men tends to be nonverbal instead of verbal," as researchers Terry Humphreys and Mélanie Brousseau remarked.[91] Proponents' challenge was to explain why. In the absence of force, couldn't an unwilling person "just say no"? Like DV advocates who were reluctant to acknowledge that victims stayed with abusers for a variety of reasons other than coercive control, antirape activists knew to avoid explanations that opened the door to victim blaming. Admitting that the victim did not say no because she did not want to argue, she was tired and decided to get it over with, it all happened so fast, she felt embarrassed, or it was too late to leave could make the sex look more like an unpleasant encounter than criminal rape.

Affirmative consent proponents settled on an explanation for passive acquiescence similar to learned helplessness in DV. Proponents asserted that women do not say no to sex because they have "frozen in fright," have gone into "tonic immobility," or have experienced "psychological infantilism."[92] These characterizations of adult female behavior are repeated with disturbing frequency in the feminist literature. Hearing the term *tonic immobility* applied to adult human women for the first time gave me a start. My father, a marine biologist, discovered the phenomenon of tonic immobility in sharks in the 1970s. When he turned them over on their backs, they went into a state of catatonia to such a degree that he could surgically implant a transmitter in them.[93]

In the late 1970s, psychologists began to describe the fight-or-flight impulses that people have upon experiencing sudden violence and threat to their lives. To this day, antirape activists cite to a 1976 article by Martin Symonds, an NYPD police officer-turned-psychologist, on rape victim psychology.[94] Symonds's article states that in his research on violent crime victims, he "noted" that some responded to a life-threatening situation with "fear bordering on panic" that caused "traumatic psychological infantilism."[95] He explained that in the face of a gun, "learned behavior seems to evaporate, and the victim responds with the adaptive and innate patterns of early childhood."[96] Symonds compared it to a phenomenon where "animals, particularly young ones, expose the most vulnerable parts of their bodies to the aggressor."[97] Symonds hypothesized that such behavior must also be characteristic of rape victims because, as feminists insisted, "Rape is a crime of violence."[98] However, Symonds and other researchers were clear that frozen fright is a potential reaction to "sudden unexpected violent crime."[99] To be sure, the theory of psychological infantilism might explain a woman's passive or even active compliance with a home invader, a sudden attacker, a rapist with a weapon, or someone threatening violence. Yet, when such facts are present, it is highly doubtful that a jury would find sex consensual "because she didn't say no."

Affirmative consent proponents problematically relied on frozen fright to explain away victims' failure to say no and apparent compliance in nonforcible, not-sudden, nonviolent dating situations, characterizing paralysis as a "typical" and "common" response of women in sexual situations.[100] One legal scholar declared in 2015, "Women, generally being the physically weaker of the sexes, are particularly prone to tonic immobility when faced with male aggressors."[101] But women are not typically driven to catatonia by a date moving from second to third base, and panic-based paralysis is an extremely unlikely reason for silence in that context. Now, there could be an unusual case where a woman was making out with her date, suddenly became overwhelmingly frightened because of a past trauma, and thereafter feigned willingness. However, without some outward sign of fright, the defendant would have no reason to know sex was nonconsensual. Rape reformers point out that panicked women might cry, curl up fetal, and go lifeless during sex. Yet in such a scenario there would be plenty of evidence of nonconsent without an "Only yes means yes" rule.

Feminists also rationalized "No means no" and "Yes means yes" because they *wanted* no to always mean no, and only yes to mean yes. Feminists endorsed using painful, racially disparate criminal enforcement to incentivize people to adopt aspirational sexual communication ideals not in widespread practice. They argued that it is "easy" to get a "yes" and that if people fail to do so, jail is their own fault.[102] But social science cast doubt on the ease of breaking with entrenched sexual practices. Open sexual communication comes at an emotional and psychological cost, and not just for women. Studies show that people of both sexes have strong incentive to eschew direct expression of sexual desire to avoid awkwardness and embarrassment and "save face" in the event of rejection.[103]

Moreover, criminal punishment, with its embedded biases and idiosyncratic distributions, is a particularly poor way of fomenting widespread sexculture change. Despite feminists' and prosecutors' understanding of consent as a "yes," the public of the 1980s and '90s regarded affirmative consent as radical and unrealistic. Media forums as prominent as *Newsweek* and *Saturday Night Live* hyperbolically ridiculed it as a "sex contract."[104] Even many of the liberal feminists who championed date rape reform said affirmative consent took it too far. To be sure, some of the aforementioned consent studies attesting to the popularity of nonverbal, passive agreement were performed in Canada, decades after the country had formally adopted affirmative consent as the law of the land.[105] Similarly, contemporary studies in the US show that students familiar with affirmative consent rules recite but do not implement "Yes means yes."[106]

Feminists also championed evidentiary reforms designed to counteract jurors' perceived prodefendant and antivictim biases. After the demise of formal requirements for victim chastity and credibility, these became embedded in culture. For instance, the phenomenon of "slut-shaming," which seems so 1982, has proven enduring.[107] Second-wave reformers worried that jurors would wrongly infer that victims with sexual pasts had a "propensity" for consensual sex and therefore must have consented to sex with the defendant.[108] Worse, jurors might not care about consent at all, believing that loose women deserve rape. There were ways to face these problems head on by educating jurors on chastity norms, fine-tuning jury selection, allowing experts to testify that consent is event and person specific, and compelling judges to instruct on myths. Reformers, however, emphasized novel rape shield laws that excluded from the trial, among other things, victims' past sexual conduct, dress, marital status, and other "prejudicial" behavior.[109] Prior to the rape shield revolution, evidence laws already required judges to exclude irrelevant and unduly prejudicial sexual conduct evidence. Rape shield laws did not just direct judges to take special care in assessing the relevance of sexual conduct evidence. They made *independently* relevant evidence presumptively inadmissible unless it fell into defined exceptions.[110]

Some feminists defended shield laws by claiming that they "champion[]" women's sexual autonomy."[111] The argument was that women refrained from being sexual actors because doing so came with the "tax" that in the event of a rape their sexual escapades would be paraded in court and the rapist would go free. Rape shield laws, therefore, made women comfortable with being sexual because they removed this tax.[112] However, it is doubtful that attenuated anxiety over a hypothetical rape trial is what constrains women's sexual behavior. Rather, it is women's internalization of the norm that "loose" behavior is immoral, risky, and undesirable that thwarts female sexuality. In this sense, rape shield laws support rather than undermine chastity norms because they welcome jurors to retain prejudices against loose women but shield them from knowing whether *this* victim was loose.

Many feminists rationalized rape shield laws not as sexual liberation but as protection against the trial becoming a "second rape." MacKinnon articulated the most extreme version on this argument, maintaining that the laws ensured that victims "do not become pornography in court."[113] In her view, exposing a woman's sexual past was not just humiliation but courtroom pornography. Rape reformers' narrative that exposing a woman's sex life is devastating and ruinous resonated with male lawmakers committed to the very chastity-unchastity divide that liberationist feminists abhorred. In 1978, Congress passed the Privacy Protection for Rape Victims Act, following a wave of state reform. Supporters in Congress, including young senator Joe Biden, "concentrated on how degrading and embarrassing it was for women to have to discuss publicly their private sexual affairs," Professor Michelle Anderson notes.[114] Biden insisted that shield laws were required to prevent the trial from being as "degrading as the rape itself."[115] Feminist reformers agreed that procedural reform was vital because women's anxiety over a trial by ordeal kept them from reporting rape. Ironically however, it was feminists and their allies who publicized through spectacular narratives that rape trials necessarily involve public humiliations, or "second rapes," that produce lifelong trauma.

Criminal litigation is undoubtedly stressful to victims. From rape exams to subpoenas and cross-examinations, victims endure unpleasant, adversarial, and time-consuming processes with the only potential reward being a pound of the offender's flesh. The problem is that feminist reformers took criminal prosecution as a given—the default when sexual misconduct occurred. Only a few commentators recognized that "what little the criminal justice process actually offers [rape] victims does not meet their primary needs at the time it is offered."[116] The most aggressive assaults on defendants' due process rights will not fully eradicate litigation's costs to victims, and the fact that rapists face long jail terms means that even the most conservative proincarceration jurists cannot make rape trials rubber stamps. Today, adjudicators in noncriminal forums like campus disciplinary proceedings experiment with summary processes that some courts have called a "a sham" in which the accused is "guilty based on the accusation rather than the evidence."[117] But the criminal process cannot fully spare rape victims distress, and prosecutors' insistence that engagement in prosecution is healing and provides closure has always been suspect. Particularly troubling about feminists' logic in defending rape shield laws is the assumption that ridding the rape trial of only its *sexual* aspects returns the criminal prosecution to being a presumptively beneficial pursuit of justice.

To be sure, rape shield laws did not render all rape trials "shams," but they did prejudice accuseds whose defenses implicated the complainants' past sexual conduct. Such defense theories might include that the complainant fabricated rape to cover an adulterous relationship or to conceal being sexually active from conservative parents. Such defenses do not contend that rape victims are generally sluts and liars but that *this* complainant had a specific sex-related motive to fabricate. Many trial judges had no problem applying rape shield laws in a way that prevented defendants from mounting a specific defense.[118] In the 1987 Michigan case *People v. Lucas,* the court of appeals overturned the defendant's conviction because the trial court, applying shield laws, prevented the jury from knowing that the complainant and defendant had been in a romantic relationship and had broken up just before she accused him of rape.[119] One 1986 Alabama appellate case justified broad application of shield laws through interesting phraseology: the law "was meant to shield the female victim of forcible sexual perversion or rape against such penetrative efforts made by [the defense], which, if upheld, would likely lead to many other successful penetrative efforts."[120]

In advocating for rape shield laws, feminists insisted that jurors should not judge litigants solely on their sexual proclivities. Yet in the midst of '90s predator panic, an alliance of women's rights activists, concerned citizens, and tough-on-crime politicians pushed through a novel federal evidentiary rule, Rule 413, exempting sexual assault defendants from the general rule that prior bad acts are not admissible to prove current behavior.[121] The idea of the general rule is that bad acts are so prejudicial that they lead jurors to judge defendants (and other witnesses) solely on their past behavior rather than the facts at hand. The law does not tolerate imprisoning people regardless of the evidence that they committed the crime at hand, simply because the jury disliked their character. After the 1995 passage of Rule 413, federal defendants' prior crimes generally remained inadmissible to prove a "propensity" to commit crime, but juries were invited to scrutinize the pasts of sex crime defendants.

Advocates have rationalized Rule 413 on the ground that past sexual misconduct is uniquely predictive of future sexual offending. Thus its "probative" or truth-seeking value outweighs the danger that the jury will convict the defendant, regardless of the facts of the case, because they think he is a pervert. However, rapes are *less* likely to be repeat offenses than other crimes, and there is no prior bad acts exception for high-recidivist crimes like burglary.[122] In addition, jurors are *more* likely to be revulsed by and prejudiced against defendants with past rape allegations than defendants with other criminal records. Because past sexual assault evidence has such low evidentiary value and such high potential for prejudice, the legal community uniformly objected to Rule 413. The congressional Advisory Committee on Evidence Rules issued a formal report opposing the rule, which was unanimous save for a dissenting vote from the prosecutor's representative.[123]

Finally, feminists worried that jurors would be too quick to presume that rape complainants were more likely to be liars than average victim-witnesses. The public debate over rape complainants' credibility in the '80s was so contentious that it spawned a cottage industry of studies and scholarship on false rape allegations. False rape statistics range from Susan Brownmiller's famous 2 percent to criminologist Eugene Kanin's infamous 41 percent rate from his examination of rape cases in one small town.[124] Most studies over the last few decades put the false reporting rate somewhere between 5 and 10 percent.[125] Thus feminists were absolutely right to insist that jurors presume that rape victims, like other witnesses, are credible unless there is specific evidence of their untruthfulness.

The problem is that attorneys must test the credibility of every witness, even if people generally tell the truth in court. Prosecutors and defenders "impeach" adverse witnesses by probing their pre- and post-event behavior, bringing up contradictory statements, highlighting memory failures, and the like. The rape victim is the prime prosecution witness to the crime. It would be defense malpractice not to ask questions like "If he raped you, why did you tell your boyfriend nothing happened?"; "How do you remember the rape when you were too drunk to remember any other details of the night?"; and "Why did you keep hanging out with a rapist?" No doubt, feminists look at these questions as "rapey," victim-blaming inquisitions. However, if rape trial processes stray from typical credibility testing only for rape victims, it amounts to a presumption that rape complaints are invariably true, otherwise known as a presumption of guilt. A familiar feminist refrain is that no woman would go through the ordeal of reporting rape unless she were telling the truth, implying once again that trial is not really necessary. Yet willingness to go through an ordeal demonstrates only a complainant's vehemence, which may be directly or *inversely* related to truthfulness.

Such anti-impeachment sentiments do not exist outside of the rape context. In a murder case, no one would fault the defense attorney for asking the prosecution's eyewitness: "If you saw the murder, why did you tell your boyfriend nothing happened?"; "How do you remember the murder when you were too drunk to remember any other details of the night?"; and "Why did you keep hanging out with a murderer?" Of course, in the rape and murder scenarios there are plausible answers to all these questions: "I didn't tell my boyfriend because I was afraid of the repercussions"; "I was drunk, but the event stood out in my mind because it was shocking"; and "I hung out with him because I did not want to face what happened." Feminists, however, worried about jurors being too inclined to accept the impeachment of rape victims in particular.

To counter this purported prejudice, feminists called in experts to explain why rape victims' inconsistencies, memory problems, and postevent behavior should not affect their credibility. The explanation feminist experts settled on was simple and singular: rape victims are traumatized.[126] Extraordinary pathological trauma, not ordinary circumstances, explained rape victims' behavior and testimony. In this narrative, rape victims, unlike other witnesses, do not have typical memory decay, do not make typical misstatements, and do not have typical reasons for not reporting or continuing with life as usual. Instead, rape victims are too psychologically devastated to report, too traumatized to remember critical facts about the rape (or so traumatized that they remember only the rape), and so psychologically damaged that they seek intimacy with the rapist. Undoubtedly, this is true of *some* victims, just as some battered women are perpetually threatened and psychologically damaged. But most rape victims do not seek out their rapists for sex. Most rape victims are surprisingly psychological resilient. Most rape victims have ordinarily functioning memories. Among those who suffer trauma, the effects are individual, idiosyncratic, and dynamic.[127]

Nevertheless, just as battered women's syndrome was compatible with ingrained notions of hysterical women, "rape trauma syndrome" reflected popular views that women were "ruined" by rape (and even imperfect sex). The trauma narrative resonated with judges and juries, and trauma became a prosecutorial trump. Increasingly, prosecutors and experts focused on the "typical" trauma behavior of rape victims rather than explaining why *this* victim acted the way she did, traumatized or not. This only served to exacerbate state actors' and jurors' tendency to scrutinize rape victims' appearance and demeanor for signs of devastation. And judging credibility on who "looks" ruined by rape has unpalatable racial, aesthetic, and class implications. Victims, in turn, knew to tell a story to the police, prosecutors, and others that was consistent with their having been traumatized. Today, prosecutors have specific policies on how to handle rape victims' desires to "embellish" their stories to fit a traumatic rape narrative.[128]

THE SEXUAL COLD WAR

By the end of the 1990s, consent and rape shield laws were the norm, and several states had affirmative consent statutes on the books.[129] With feminist- and predator-driven rape reforms firmly entrenched in law and policy, the battle over rape reform became a scholarly cold war. Feminist prosecutors and victim advocates argued for ever narrower consent definitions and stricter rape shield laws. Critics from within and outside of feminism were distressed that feminist reforms expanded rape law's reach just as predator panic was exponentially increasing the negative consequences of a sexual offense conviction. During this time, progressive feminists, civil libertarians, and race critics produced compelling academic critiques of the carceral moves antirape feminists had made.

Feminist critics like Judith Butler lamented that "feminism ha[d] become identified with state-allied regulatory power over sexuality" and worried about reforms' negative effects on women and sexual minorities.[130] However, unlike DV victims, rape victims were not being jailed on material witness warrants and forced to participate in prosecutions. Rape victims were not arrested as "mutual rapists" because they also failed to procure affirmative consent. Rape victims were generally not financially and emotionally tied to rapists, and jailing the rapist did not harm them. Rape reform, while a losing proposition for men, seemed to spare women carceral consequences. This was exactly the zero-sum calculus dominance feminists intended: "Equality means someone loses power."[131] Yet, as critics pointed out, the distribution of gendered power in society is not so simple and polar. "Some women are the mothers, daughters, or sisters of men facing retributive justice, even as some women are the victims of male violence; some women are the victims of other women's violence," Professor Martha Minow remarks.[132]

Critics within feminism were primarily concerned with how rape reform, with its frightened, traumatized victim narrative, disciplined women's sexuality. Sex-positive feminists lamented that second-wave reforms' intervention into the post–sexual revolution milieu had stunted the authentic evolution of women's sexuality in favor of older conservative notions of (white) women's natural sex aversion. It threatened to cement women's relationship to sex as one of fear, apprehension, disgust, risk aversion, and devastation. Feminist discourse, queer theorist Janet Halley observed, left for women "two options": "coerced" and "fearful" male-dominant sex or "infantile," "entirely feminine" sex.[133] Rape reformers' utopia appeared to be a world where sex was accompanied by verbal negotiation, overt agreement, and frequent double-checking. For sex radicals, this was positively dystopian. Theorist Katherine Franke remarked, "To evacuate women's sexuality of any risk of a confrontation with shame, loss of control, or objectification strikes me as selling women a sanitized, meager simulacrum of sex not worth getting riled up about in any case."[134] Moreover, affirmative consent standards reinforced the cultural norm that men were sexual pursuers, responsible for obtaining permission, and women were chaste gatekeepers, who presumptively withheld it.

In the dominance feminist view, women who were relatively unbothered by past experiences with subtly pressured, unenthusiastic, age-differential, or submissively kinky sex needed to raise their consciousness and see themselves as victims. Accordingly, "the feminist discourse of sexual truth," as Halley characterized it, established the good feminist's relationship to sex as anxious and regretful, not positive or transgressive.[135] This move served to reinforce the harmful cultural norm that sex is a shameful, risky, and freighted proposition, particularly for women. Given that sex's meaning is socially constructed, Halley argued, feminists' "discursive production of pain . . . may be responsible for at least some of the trauma that real women really experience in their real lives."[136]

Some feminists, as might be expected, strongly resisted the critique that feminist discourse risks producing the very sexual trauma that activists highlight as a key component of women's subordination. Professor Robin West, for example, protested that "the injury of rape is done by rapists, not texts, and is done to the jawbone, the pelvis, the reproductive organs, the stomach, the skin, the eyes, the vaginal walls, the anus, and the psyche."[137] Of course, pleasurable, hotly desired, carefully negotiated sex can injure vaginal walls, just as fun nonsexual physical activities can cause muscle pain. Yet, "the exercise of *erotic* capacity, intelligence, curiosity, or creativity all require pretexts that are unnecessary for other pleasures, such as the enjoyment of food, fiction, or astronomy," as sex radical Gayle Rubin remarked.[138]

Indeed, antirape activists, like the *M.T.S.* court, frequently analogized sex to surgery: a painful invasion that required informed consent.[139] Dominance feminist Andrea Dworkin once remarked, "The slit between [a woman's] legs ... which means entry into her—intercourse—appears to be the key to women's lower human status."[140] Critics pointed out that this insistence that women's bodies are traumatized by sex's surgery-like invasion overlapped with not-so-feminist regulatory designs over women's bodies. Indeed, antiabortion activists have also advanced the claim that the crux of rape is the physical invasion of the vagina, an *inherently* traumatic act. One family values activist and former Trump administration official remarked that because of "physical and psychological post-procedural trauma ... the effects of abortion are very similar to the effects of rape."[141] Feminists' construction of sexual intercourse as physical trauma justified only by interests as weighty as medical necessity and procedures as rigid as medical consent is strikingly similar to religious notions of sex as immoral, degrading, and justified only if for procreation within marriage. In recent years, the group Ascend, formerly the National Abstinence Educators Association, rebranded its education program "sexual risk avoidance" and pressed that abstinence was the key to preventing sexual assault. Ascend specifically targeted LGBTQ teens for abstinence indoctrination, arguing that they were at the highest risk of sexual assault.[142]

Second-wave rape reform also engendered strong critiques from civil libertarians and race theorists. Critics objected that in a predator-panicked era, rape reforms expanded the reach of the draconian rape law regime and simultaneously made it harder to defend against rape allegations. Affirmative consent especially troubled incarceration critics because of its potential for overcriminalization. Indeed, some affirmative consent proponents openly tout the standard's overbreadth. One of them applauded affirmative consent for "creat[ing] an equilibrium where too much counts as sexual assault" because it provided uber-incentive to be careful about sex.[143] For decades, most in society have enjoyed sex in technical violation of the affirmative consent standard. Proceeding with sex upon nonverbal and passive signaling, men and women have regularly engaged in what "enlightened" laws categorize as felonious conduct meriting lengthy incarceration. Civil libertarians accordingly fretted that everyone was at the mercy of police and prosecutors who had the power to enforce yes-means-yes to the letter. That said, affirmative consent never did spawn a sex police making sure that everyone got to yes, as some critics feared. Instead, it hung out on the books, and to this day how it is enforced remains unclear.[144]

But critics have voiced concerns not just about overenforcement but also about *selective* enforcement. Affirmative consent laws gave prosecutors and police wide discretionary authority over ordinary sexual actors. Experience shows that when laws forbid acts routinely performed by many people (e.g., loitering and trespass), police and prosecutors restrict their enforcement to certain geographic areas and certain people. In turn, most citizens remain blissfully unaffected by overbroad criminal regulation. Expansive sex regulation, it follows, disproportionately burdens already policed populations, permitting privileged actors to enjoy yes-less sex with abandon.[145]

Critical race theorists also highlighted the risk that the broadened and toughened sex-offense regime would disproportionately affect black men. Studies performed in the 1980s found that black-defendant, white-victim rape cases resulted in higher sentences than rape cases with other racial combinations. Researchers explained that "when blacks violate white victims . . . the high sexual property value attached to the white victims and the racial fears of authorities can justify severe treatment."[146] Another study found that "race, age, and gender will interact to influence sentencing because of images or attributions relating these statuses to membership in social groups thought to be dangerous and crime prone."[147] Indeed, the percentage of black men in the convicted rapist pool has always far exceeded their population percentage, and blacks' rate of incarceration on rape charges is several times higher than whites'.[148] Black rape defendants have never enjoyed the privileged status in the eyes of judges and juries that feminists have assumed accused rapists generally enjoy. At the same time, feminists' efforts to shield jurors from victims' sexual history have done nothing to undercut the *presumption* of black women's unchastity. Race shield laws were never part of the revolution.[149]

We might ask, as we did in the DV context, whether rape reform "worked." To be sure, measuring reform's deterrence of "rape" is so difficult because the definition and understanding of rape is dynamic. Increases in official reporting and even in identifying victimhood on surveys may have more to do with increased awareness than increased offenses. Despite this, data from the Bureau of Justice Statistic's (BJS) annual National Crime Victimization

Surveys do show a steep decline in "rape and sexual assault" over the last several decades from approximately nine hundred thousand in 1993, the first year of the survey, to just under four hundred thousand in 2017, the latest year.[150] This decline, however, was unlikely due to harsh criminal sanctions, whether feminist or predator panic based. As discussed in chapter 3, experts believe only a small fraction of the crime decline can be attributed to incarceration, and there are no studies attesting to the direct deterrent effects of feminist reforms like rape shield laws.[151]

In fact, it is difficult to know whether rape reform even led to more prosecutions and convictions. Studies performed in the 1990s showed few or modest effects on prosecution rates, although some found that reforms increased reporting. As one expert noted, "Despite the intense effort that has gone into rape law reform, we have insufficient and conflicting information about the difference that these laws make for victims, for the criminal justice system, and for the treatment of women generally."[152] The BJS felony defendant statistics show that by 1990, DAs already prosecuted more rape defendants than violent criminals on average, and juries consistently convicted them. Nevertheless, those data also show that over time prosecutors increased the proportion of rape cases they pursued to conviction, from 59 percent in 1990 to 76 percent in 2009, yet conviction rates remained solidly high.[153] This might indicate that feminist trial reforms secured convictions in "closer" cases, although the phenomenon of increasing prosecution rates and consistently high conviction rates was true of other violent crimes.[154] Strikingly, whether because of feminist trial reforms, predator panic–based sentencing reforms, or a combination, between 1990 and 2013, despite a steep decline in sexual offenses, the portion of the prison population serving time for sexual offenses increased by 675 percent.[155]

Whether or not rape trial reforms directly increased the sex offender prisoner population, feminist rape (and DV) agitation played a significant indirect role in expanding the carceral state in the 1990s. The violence against women issue gave moral cover to the liberal politicians who sought to wrest the politically popular crime issue from conservatives. In one of the more notable political maneuvers, 1992 Democratic presidential candidate Bill Clinton successfully ran on a tough-on-crime platform. During the election, crime rates were peaking, and Clinton saw crime control as the bridge to moderate and conservative voters. The infamous "Clinton Crime Bill" (The Violent Crime Control and Enforcement Act of 1994) was a signature achievement of Clinton's administration.[156] (Ironically, by the time it went into effect, crime rates were already in decline.) The *Washington Post* expressed surprise that "the Bush ('41) campaign ceded the crime issue to Clinton, even though a tough-on-crime stance had been one of the key reasons for Bush's success in 1988."[157]

Indeed, Democrats widely considered Michael Dukakis's 1988 presidential run against George H. W. Bush to be disastrous. During the campaign, Bush ran the infamous race-baiting Willie Horton ad, conceived of by Southern Strategy architect Lee Atwater.[158] As governor of Massachusetts, Michael Dukakis had furloughed (temporarily released) convicted murderer Willie Horton so he could attend a funeral. Once released, Horton fled and committed serious crimes, including the rape and murder of a white woman. The Bush campaign ran a TV ad featuring a mugshot of Horton—a "very scary looking, disheveled, wild-eyed black man," one expert observed—with the message, "Weekend prison passes; Dukakis on crime."[159] Dukakis lost by a landslide. In the wake of that defeat, Democratic senators Joe Biden and Chuck Schumer feared the "Hortonizing" of the entire Democratic Party.[160] They hatched a coordinated plan—not dissimilar to the Southern Strategy— to court moderate voters by making Democrats the party of law enforcement in an era of racialized hysteria over crack. Biden had previously authored the Anti-Drug Abuse Act of 1986, which established the infamous 100–1 disparity in sentences for crack and powder cocaine offenses.[161]

Biden and his allies introduced the 1991 version of the Crime Bill as part of this effort to appropriate the crime issue. "If they have a bill, then they can't demagogue crime," he remarked.[162] The "Biden-Schumer strategy," as one insider called it, was successful.[163] By 1992, polls showed that the public had gone from viewing Democrats as relatively weak on crime to regarding the parties as virtually even.[164] Supporting the 1994 Bill, Biden remarked, "The liberal wing of the Democratic Party is now for sixty new death penalties. . . . The liberal wing of the Democratic Party has 70 enhanced penalties. . . . The liberal wing of the Democratic Party is for 100,000 cops. The liberal wing of the Democratic Party is for 125,000 new state prison cells."[165]

In 1994, Clinton signed the bill, declaring, "This bill puts Government on the side of those who abide by the law, not those who break it; on the side of the victims, not their attackers."[166] Channeling previous administrations' sentiments on gangs and urban black pathology, Clinton lamented, "Too many kids don't have parents who care. Gangs and drugs have taken over our streets and undermined our schools."[167] The bill, among other things, created the "three-strikes" rule, eliminated parole, applied the federal death penalty to sixty offenses, created a slew of mandatory minimums for drug and violent crimes, increased sentences for offenses ranging from child pornography to drunk driving and telemarketing scams, created a national sex offender registry, and gave victims of sexual abuse and violent crimes the right to make victim impact statements at sentencing.[168] It should come as no surprise that the prison population doubled by the end of Clinton's administration.[169] In 2014, former White House official Jeremy Travis stated that he and other supporters needed to "look in the mirror and say, 'look what we have done.'"[170] Speaking in 2015 at an NAACP conference, Bill Clinton apologized for the bill, saying that it had "set a trend" toward mass incarceration and admitting, "We were wrong."[171]

Today, feminists still celebrate the bill, or at least a portion of it: Title IV, the Violence Against Women Act (VAWA). Although often held up as a stunning liberal victory, VAWA was no less carceral than the rest of Crime Control Bill. VAWA drastically increased penalties for substantive federal sex offenses and other gender crimes. VAWA's largest appropriation was grant money to states to encourage "more widespread apprehension, prosecution, and adjudication of persons committing violent crimes against women, including "implement[ing] mandatory arrest or proarrest programs."[172] Many of VAWA's material aid provisions had a punitive bent. Restitution went only to victims of *convicted* rapists and abusers, and deportation protection required active cooperation in a qualifying prosecution.[173] Thus some scholars regard VAWA as the very exemplar of carceral feminism.[174]

However, one clearly noncriminal provision of VAWA created a new "civil right" against gender violence and authorized individuals to sue a person who had committed "a crime of violence motivated by gender and thus depriv[ing] another of the right declared."[175] Immediately, the (overwhelmingly male) conference of state chief justices objected, arguing that the right would be "invoked as a bargaining tool within the context of divorce negotiations" and would therefore "impair the ability of state courts to manage criminal and family law matters traditionally entrusted to the states."[176] In 2000, the Supreme Court, over vociferous dissent, agreed. It struck the remedy down as an abuse of federal regulatory power in *U.S. v. Morrison*.[177] Feminists vehemently protested. The general public, by contrast, was surprisingly unfazed by this wholesale judicial assault on a popular bill. It had always viewed VAWA as "about 'rape' rather than about 'civil rights,'" law professor Judith Resnik writes.[178] Because gender violence had been so thoroughly established as a matter of "private and individual, rather than public and group-based [behavior], it was hard for some to accept the category shift," another scholar noted.[179] Of course, *Morrison* left intact VAWA's *criminal* authority.

The gender violence issue allowed Clinton to please liberals with a pro-woman agenda while reaching across the aisle with crime control. In his 1995 address to kick off Domestic Violence Awareness Month, Clinton lauded the "brilliant" Crime Bill and touted VAWA as "a peculiar part of the genius of the crime bill . . . because it combines tough sanctions against abusers with assistance to police and to prosecutors and to shelters."[180] Undeniably, the inclusion of VAWA convinced some liberals to support the very illiberal bill. Vermont congressman Bernie Sanders, a well-known leftist, had voiced serious reservations about the bill's harsh and neoliberal nature: "Through the neglect of our government and through a grossly irrational set of priorities, we are dooming today tens of millions of young people to a future of bitterness, misery, hopelessness, drugs, crime, and violence. And, Mr. Speaker, all the jails in the world—and we already imprison more people per capita than any other country—. . . will not make that situation right. We can either educate or electrocute. We can create meaningful jobs, rebuilding our society, or we can build more jails."[181] Sanders was right that the bill was in direct opposition to social welfare. Clinton was open about his plan to "cut the Federal work force over a period of years by 270,000 positions to its lowest level in 30 years and take all that money to pay for this crime bill."[182] Clinton went on, "The savings will be used to put 100,000 police officers on the street [and] to build prisons to keep 100,000 violent criminals off the street."[183]

Sanders, a vocal prison critic, was nonetheless a fan of VAWA. "I have a number of serious problems with the crime bill," he explained, "but one part of it that I vigorously support is the Violence Against Women Act."[184] VAWA and the assault weapons ban were enough to convince Sanders to vote for the bill—three strikes and all. In the 2016 Democratic presidential primary, he faced criticism for that vote. Former attorney general Eric Holder charged that Sanders "has not acknowledged or apologized for his vote."[185] The Sanders campaign fought back with a press release stating that although Sanders had objected to the bill's "mass incarceration and death penalty provisions," he had "supported [it] to protect women."[186]

As the millennium turned, there was growing awareness that feminists' criminal law success was a poisoned gift, or at least a double-edged sword.

American youth were adopting an increasingly sex-positive, antiracist, and antiauthoritarian outlook. Perhaps young feminists would heed the sexual cold war warnings of critical scholars. But then in the 2010s, the controversy over campus rape exploded, and the warnings were buried under an avalanche of rape anxiety and righteous indignation.

SIX

From the Sexual Cold War
to the New Sex Panic

In the 2010s, the rape issue reemerged, exploding into popular and scholarly discourse and gaining far more attention than the second-wave rape discussion had. Reminiscent of the media frenzy over child predators, the campus rape crisis gained a virtual monopoly on feminist, media, and public attention. Susan Brownmiller even dubbed the campus antirape movement the "fourth wave of feminism."[1] The young women just starting to define their political identities were swept up in this solidaristic protest against campus predators. Feminism *became* fighting sexual predators and enlisting institutional authority to do so. The cautions from scholars that rape reforms had entangled the feminist liberationist project in mass incarceration were lost in the raw emotion and media-driven fury of the campus antirape movement. Young activists doubled down on, and even expanded, some of the most problematic principles of second-wave rape reform.

RAPE'S REEMERGENCE

The beginnings of the campus rape's full occupation of the millennial feminist agenda—and the moral high ground—began in 2010. The Center for Public Integrity, in concert with National Public Radio, published an "extremely powerful" 104-page report and aired a multiepisode exposé on the "nightmare" of campus rape (collectively, CPI report).[2] The report featured stories of easily preventable and poorly remedied campus sexual assault. One was the story of the rape, in 2004, of University of Wisconsin student Laura Dunn by two fellow crew team members: "That night, Dunn was drinking so many raspberry vodkas that they cut her off at a frat house party. Still, she knew and trusted the two men who took her back to a house for what she thought was a quick stop before the next party. Instead, she says they raped her as she passed in and out of consciousness."[3]

Dunn reported the incident to the university and the police over a year later. The state ultimately declined to pursue a criminal case. The university, after a nine-month investigation, found that Dunn's claims could not be sufficiently substantiated and took no action.[4] Dunn then filed a complaint against the university with the Department of Education (DOE). She argued that the university had violated Title IX of the Education Amendments of 1972 (Title IX), which prohibits universities receiving federal funds from sex discrimination, including sexual harassment. Until recent years, Title IX was primarily known as the legal vehicle for equal funding of women's college sports programs. Today, the term *Title IX* is shorthand for university discipline of sexual misconduct.[5]

Dunn argued that the University of Wisconsin had mishandled her sexual assault claim by, among other things, taking too long to investigate and relying on police interviews instead of conducting their own. The DOE found there was "insufficient evidence to conclude that the University subjected [Dunn] to discrimination based on sex as alleged."[6] This finding, according to the CPI report, showed the DOE to be a "feeble watchdog" whose inaction sent a message that the government did not take rape seriously.[7] Conspicuously left out of the CPI report were the multitude of issues that raised doubts about the accused students' guilt. According to the DOE's letter closing the investigation, Dunn made inconsistent statements, had memory lapses, stated that a portion of the encounter was consensual, and acknowledged continued sexual relations with one of the alleged rapists.[8] Further, Dunn told a detective that the men had admitted the rape to two witnesses, but when the detective contacted them, the witnesses said that neither of the men nor Dunn had ever mentioned the incident.[9]

The fact that the complaint had serious issues certainly does not mean that no assault occurred, that the university used correct procedures, or that it or the DOE ultimately came to the right conclusion. The problem is that the CPI report failed to mention any evidence that undermined the "extremely powerful" nature of the exposé. The muddy and contested reality of that case fit poorly into a story intended to provoke moral outrage about institutional complicity in rape culture. Report author Kristin Jones denied that the complicating facts from the DOE letter were relevant at all. Asserting that trauma often leads victims to be intimate with rapists, the author maintained that the continued sexual contact between Dunn and the accused was not worth mentioning.[10]

The CPI report won the prestigious Peabody Award for broadcast journalism and a Kennedy Award for human rights reporting. Obama's newly appointed head of the DOE's office of civil rights, Russlynn Ali, was listening. Attributing cases like Dunn's to Bush-era negligence, she vowed to address the "plague" of campus sexual assault.[11] With the stroke of a pen she did just that and changed the legal landscape in the process. Shortly after the NPR report, Ali released the 2011 "Dear Colleague Letter" (DCL), setting forth administrative guidance on how to interpret and implement the federal legislation.[12] In a few short years, it would be known as "*the*" Dear Colleague Letter.

The DCL begins by citing a statistic from a 2007 Campus Sexual Assault Study ("CSA Study") that "1 in 5" students experience sexual assault and issuing a "call to action."[13] It takes an expansive view of gender discrimination and makes clear that universities discriminate unless they vigorously pursue every claim of student sexual misconduct, on or off campus. The letter delineates how universities should handle these cases, which to a large extent consists of cataloguing the rights *not* due to the accused. Schools cannot send sexual assault cases to mediation, they cannot use a standard higher than preponderance of the evidence, and they cannot allow face-to-face confrontation. The letter's general message is that the accused's "due process rights" are not grounds to "restrict or unnecessarily delay the Title IX protections for the complainant."[14] The letter was novel in its insistence that administrators' disciplinary punishment of students was as an essential component of gender equality in education. After issuing the letter, the DOE ramped up its investigation of and enforcement against institutions for failing to adequately address sexual assault. In the "era of enforcement" between 2011 and 2019, the government brought 502 cases against universities under Title IX.[15]

On the heels of the NPR report, the media regularly reported on campus rape. In 2013, the press covered the troubling Jameis Winston case. Florida State University, the Tallahassee police, and the Florida state attorney hushed up a credible rape allegation against Winston, FSU's star quarterback. After a sham investigation, the state attorney went against the complainant's wishes and closed the case without charges. Nine days later, Winston became the youngest person to win the coveted Heisman trophy.[16]

Receiving substantially more national press was the case involving Columbia University undergraduate student Emma Sulkowicz. In 2014, Sulkowicz used a "performance art" piece to bring attention to campus rape in general and her own case in particular, which the university had resolved in favor of the accused, Paul Nungesser. The performance, entitled "Carry That Weight," involved Sulkowicz hefting a twin mattress—the "scene of the crime"—around campus. The campaign engendered communal mattress-carrying rituals in colleges throughout the nation.[17] The popularly dubbed "mattress girl" went on to win the National Organization of Women's "Woman of Courage" award and to attend Obama's 2015 State of the Union Address as a guest of Senator Kirsten Gillibrand.[18]

Just before Sulkowicz and Nungesser's 2015 graduation, Nungesser sued Columbia for supporting Sulkowicz's "outrageous display of harassment and defamation."[19] In July 2017, after much legal wrangling, Columbia settled with Nungesser and issued a statement: "Columbia recognizes that after the conclusion of the investigation, Paul's remaining time at Columbia became very difficult for him and not what Columbia would want any of its students to experience. Columbia will continue to review and update its policies toward ensuring that every student—accuser and accused, including those like Paul who are found not responsible—is treated respectfully and as a full member of the Columbia community."[20]

One of the most a memorable media moments came on November 19, 2014, when *Rolling Stone* magazine published the explosive nine-thousand-word article "A Rape on Campus: A Brutal Assault and Struggle for Justice at UVA."[21] In it, author Sabrina Erdely describes in excruciating detail a violent gang rape perpetrated on a University of Virginia freshman by seven fraternity brothers. The story gripped a nation already concerned with campus rape, and it went on to be the most-read noncelebrity article in *Rolling Stone's* history.[22] Its publication fomented massive campus protests and forced UVA's associate dean of students and Sexual Misconduct Board director Nicole Eramo to resign. The administration suspended all Greek organizations, including the accused fraternity, which was vandalized the day after publication and whose members received death threats.[23]

Erdely had read the temperature of the country on the campus rape issue, and before starting to investigate she pitched her article about a horrific campus rape and callous administrative indifference. Now she just had to find the facts that fit the narrative. Erdely consulted with former sex crimes prosecutor and activist Wendy Murphy, who had a well-established reputation for antirape zealotry:[24] she had once compared the accused—and innocent—students in the Duke Lacrosse rape case to "Hitler."[25] Erdely and Murphy chose the University of Virginia, *Playboy* Magazine's number one "party school," as the focus of the soon-to-be exposé.[26] Erdely shortly produced a story that, two years later, the magazine's lawyer would describe as "the worst thing to ever happen to *Rolling Stone*."[27]

The article begins with the rape of the protagonist, "Jackie," at the hands of frat boy Haven Monahan (called "Drew" in the article) and his confederates. It meticulously, if not pornographically, depicts the type of brutality that news articles typically summarize as "indescribable":

> There was a heavy person on top of her, spreading open her thighs, and another person kneeling on her hair, hands pinning down her arms, sharp shards digging into her back, and excited male voices rising all around her. When yet another hand clamped over her mouth, Jackie bit it, and the hand became a fist that punched her in the face. The men surrounding her began to laugh.... "Grab its motherfucking leg," she heard a voice say. And that's when Jackie knew she was going to be raped.
>
> She remembers every moment of the next three hours of agony, during which, she says, seven men took turns raping her, while two more—her date, Drew, and another man—gave instruction and encouragement....
>
> As the last man sank onto her, Jackie was startled to recognize him: He attended her tiny anthropology discussion group. He looked like he was going to cry or puke as he told the crowd he couldn't get it up. "Pussy!" the other men jeered.... Someone handed her classmate a beer bottle. Jackie stared at the young man, silently begging him not to go through with it. And as he shoved the bottle into her, Jackie fell into a stupor, mentally untethering from the brutal tableau, her mind leaving behind the bleeding body under assault on the floor.[28]

The article further reported that Jackie's friends "launched into a heated discussion about the social price of reporting Jackie's rape, while Jackie stood beside them, mute in her bloody dress."[29] Her friend "Cindy" lamented, "She's gonna be the girl who cried 'rape,' and we'll never be allowed into any frat party again."[30]

Winding through the article's striking depictions of brutality and collegiate pecking order is a prosecutorial "no-drop" point: schools must do more to prosecute and punish sexual assault, even if against the victim's wishes. Although sympathetic to Jackie's desire not to pursue the matter, Erdely is less tolerant of the university's policy of allowing hesitant victims to control case outcomes. She states, "Like many schools, UVA has taken to emphasizing that in matters of sexual assault, it caters to victim choice.... [But] the sheer menu of choices, paired with the reassurance that any choice is the right one, often has the end result of coddling the victim into doing nothing."[31]

The article directs its strongest fire against Eramo, characterized alternately as a detached bureaucrat and a false savior. The article charges that survivors contacted "Dean Eramo, whom they laud as their best advocate and den mother,'" but that "few ever filed reports with UVA or with police."[32]

Within weeks of its publication, the story publicly fell apart. An ever-expanding trove of information cast doubt on Jackie's narrative and the integrity of Erdely's reporting techniques. Jackie, the evidence indicates, just plain made up the gang rape story.[33] Incredible as it sounds, Jackie *was* the rape ringleader Haven Monahan/Drew. Jackie established the fictional Haven's digital persona to make her crush, Ryan Duffin, jealous. She sent Haven's picture—a picture of some random guy from her high school—to her friends, including Ryan, proclaiming Haven her new crush. The events then turned surreal.

A few weeks before the alleged rape, Jackie asked Ryan to gain intel on Haven's feelings for her by pretending to be a female friend, "Brianna," and texting Haven.[34] Ryan agreed, and Brianna/Ryan engaged in many text conversations with Haven/Jackie. Haven professed his love for Jackie and frustration that she liked some "other guy."[35] Eventually, Ryan texted Haven that he was not Brianna but a male friend of Jackie's. Haven then "realized" Ryan was the "other guy" and castigated Ryan for being distant toward Jackie because she was a "phenomenal" person and terminally ill.[36] Concerned, Ryan texted Jackie, who confirmed, "I'm dying."[37] A week before the "rape," Haven texted Ryan that he had convinced Jackie to go out. The day before, Haven texted, "Tomorrow night I plan on wooing her and, by gum, woo her I will!!"[38] The next night, Ryan found himself comforting a distraught Jackie, who said that the nonexistent Haven made her perform oral sex on several frat guys. Looking back on it, Ryan, who was only seventeen when the texts began, reflects, "I was wondering how I didn't see through it way earlier."[39]

This fantastical tale of teenage digital catfishing would have been easily discoverable if Erdely had contacted any of Jackie's friends or tried to determine whether Haven existed. Erdely defended her decision not to do so because Jackie had said further investigation would cause her trauma. But, in keeping with her criticism of the university's inaction, Erdely's compassion for Jackie's trauma did not stop her from writing the story, despite Jackie's increasing resistance to its publication. Two years later, during Eramo's successful multi-million-dollar libel suit against *Rolling Stone,* Erdely cried when a lawyer read Jackie's text urging a friend not to speak to Erdely because the story was a "witch hunt" and a "disaster."[40]

Erdely was not the only person to take the seemingly traumatized complainant's story at face value. Jackie's story so influenced Emily Renda, UVA's project coordinator for sexual assault misconduct prevention, that she testified about it at a 2014 US Senate hearing.[41] Jackie's trauma would take center stage again during the libel suit, when Eramo's attorney requested to depose Jackie. Calling the request "persecution" and citing "extensive support in the medical literature," Jackie's attorneys stated, "Forcing her to revisit her sexual assault, and then the re-victimization that took place after the *Rolling Stone* article came out, will inevitably lead to a worsening of her symptoms."[42] Eramo's attorney fired back, "The only thing different now is that . . . Jackie will be compelled to tell the truth."[43] The judge ordered Jackie to sit for deposition, where she stated that her PTSD prevented her from remembering most events after the "rape," including what she had told Erdely. In the end, Jackie stood by her rape accusation because "I believed it to be true at the time."[44]

Antirape activists dreaded, and critics hoped, that the public *Rolling Stone* debacle would end the media fervor over campus rape. However, the stage had already been set: a new student movement had coalesced, the bureaucratic machine was in motion, and the public's appetite for campus rape coverage remained whetted. In 2015, activist-directors Kirby Dick and Amy Ziering released *The Hunting Ground,* a searing documentary on the epidemic of campus rape, featuring, among other stories, the Jameis Winston case.[45] The *Washington Post* declared the film "infuriating" and "galvanizing."[46] Schools and legal organizations hosted screenings across the nation, and CNN aired the film in full. Pop-phenom and assault survivor Lady Gaga cowrote the movie's theme song, "'Til It Happens to You." She performed it at the 2016 Oscars, introduced by Joe Biden and surrounded by victims whose bodies bore statements like "not your fault" and "survivor."[47] The wrenching vocals and potent visuals brought the glitterati to tears and spawned headlines declaring the moment "moving," and "inspiring."[48]

Even famed outdoorsman and author Jon Krakauer joined the campus assault chorus, uncharacteristically penning *Missoula,* an invective against rape permissiveness in a small college town.[49] In 2018, Krakauer coauthored a *New York Times* op-ed with Laura Dunn of the 2010 NPR exposé, urging Trump education secretary Betsy DeVos to retain the DCL procedures.[50] By that time, Dunn had gained a measure of fame as an antirape lawyer, activist, and media commentator. After *Rolling Stone* retracted its story and apologized, Dunn gave an interview defending the original story and chastising the magazine for the retraction. Dunn argued that exposing Jackie's "discrepancies" was "blaming the victim" and that the public should continue to believe Jackie because rape victims were frequently "off on some details."[51] *Rolling Stone's* retraction, Dunn argued, was an example of how "rape denialists and apologists will always find some way to say something is untrue."[52]

THE NEW SEX PANIC?

As with the child sex offense panic, the campus rape crisis was based not on changed circumstances but on increased preoccupation with an existing problem. This is quite different from, for example, the societal concerns over sharply rising crime rates that helped prompt the Clinton Crime Bill. Over the past few decades, the national rape rate, including among the college-aged, has followed the declining crime rate, hitting a twenty-year low in 2009, just before the campus rape crisis broke in the media.[53] Studies indicate that rape may be more prevalent among college-aged nonstudents than students.[54] One-in-five/four-type statistics have been around for decades, and older studies counted only "forcible" rape.[55] Indeed, college sex is down in general.[56] In sum, the evidence suggests that female students are safer from sexual assault than ever before.

Nevertheless, media, government, and activist discourse have created the sense that female college students are at constant risk of falling prey to a serial rapist. *Fox News'* September 25, 2014 headline "Every College Parent's Fear: Campus Rape" is more than a little reminiscent of predator panic.[57] In a 2016 poll of female University of Michigan students, 73 percent of respondents reported being "afraid to walk home alone on campus."[58] Adopting a stranger-rape paradigm, two hundred of the students signed a petition for the university to install cameras around campus to help police identify attackers.[59] In response, the university police said they "preferred not to comment about *gendered* security measures."[60] Federally mandated campus crime alerts sent through text and email compounded the sense of ever-present threat.[61] One Northwestern University freshman, reacting to a campus alert that four girls at a fraternity party "were possibly given a date-rape drug," told the press in 2017, "It's scary being a woman on campus, and not knowing what's going to happen to you."[62]

Just as predator panic rested on media stories of horrific child murders combined with statistics on low-level child molestation, the campus rape panic featured spectacular media stories like Jackie's fictional assault combined with statistics on broadly defined attempted and completed sexual misconduct. The "one-in-five" statistic from the 2007 CSA Study and the "one-in-four" figure from a 2015 American Association of Universities study ("AAU Study") became their own self-contained catchphrases.[63] They required no explanation, much less than technical parsing. But there was another wide-ranging rape study that received considerably less attention. The 2014 Bureau of Justice Statistics Assault Victimization Survey ("BJS Study") measured sexual assault rates from 1997 to 2013 in the eighteen- to twenty-four-year-old bracket. It put the student sexual assault rate at less than 1 percent (6 in 1,000).[64]

The studies were methodologically different, but there is a straightforward and nontechnical reason for the divergence: the studies measured different things for different reasons. The BJS Study aimed to document *violent crime* victimization frequency. The study involved detailed interviews of respondents, with the threshold question being a narrow one: "Have you been forced or coerced to engage in unwanted sexual activity?"[65] The CSA Study, by contrast, was a *public health* study intended to explore the link between college drinking and unwanted sexual conduct. The study defined *sexual assault* as touching accompanied by force or "incapacitation," which included "voluntary consumption of alcohol or other drugs."[66]

The CSA Study found that a slightly higher percentage of women experienced sexual assault during college than prior to college.[67] The more profound difference was that the pre-college assaults were split rather evenly between force and incapacitation, whereas college assaults were more than twice as likely to involve incapacitation (11 percent experienced incapacitated assault compared to 4.7 percent for forcible assault).[68] Of the incapacitated assaults, the vast majority were situations where the victim was voluntarily intoxicated.[69] The study confirmed that intoxication plays a significant role in college sexual assault.[70] However, this public health purpose was lost as activists used the study as a "call to action" not to address drinking but to punish rapists.[71]

In the post-DCL era, universities have constructed "climate surveys" that use scientific and lay methods for gathering and processing information. Often the purpose is not law enforcement or public health but something more inchoate. For example, the University of Colorado Title IX office described their 2015 Sexual Assault Survey as intended "to fill gaps in our understanding of the frequency and types of sexual misconduct experienced by CU-Boulder students."[72] The CU survey defined sexual assault as contact ranging from anal penetration to touching *any* "parts of your body in a sexual way." The assaultive "tactics" ranged from "force or having a weapon" to "deception," "emotional threats," and "catching you off guard." With stolen kisses included as sexual assault, it is unsurprising that the study found that about a third of undergraduate women had experienced sexual assault.[73]

There are several forces pushing college climate surveys toward categorizing a wide range of sexual behaviors, from brutal to banal, as rape and sexual assault. The surveys adopt university definitions of sexual assault and misconduct, which are far more capacious than criminal law definitions. Moreover, those who construct the surveys are keenly attuned to problem of "undercounting" where respondents are unwilling to classify their experiences as "rape." Surveys rarely ask whether one has been "raped" or "sexually assaulted." Instead, they ask respondents to check from a list of certain types and circumstances of sexual contact, which researchers predetermine to be sexual assault. Fear of undercounting ensures the list will be long and its content vague and overinclusive.

One might think that, from a policy standpoint, undercounting would be no more problematic than overcounting nonserious events as rape. I asked one of the CU survey authors about it, and she explained that the overbroad questions would be counterbalanced by respondents' natural tendency to avoid identifying minor events like sudden kisses as assault. In addition, any "false positives"—respondents who followed instructions and identified minor incidents—would offset "false negatives"—respondents who did not identify serious incidents.[74] It left me with the impression that the survey was less about measuring *whether* sexual assault on campus was a problem than about furnishing evidence for the administration's predetermination that it was. My impression was confirmed during an open forum on the survey. The Title IX coordinator indignantly dismissed critiques of the survey's methodology because everyone already knew that "we do have a sexual assault problem on campus, a very serious one."[75]

However, 92 percent of the respondents in the CU survey indicated that they had not officially reported the incident, the primary reason being that they "did not think it was serious enough."[76] I asked the survey author why the instrument adopted definitions that evidently did not match up with students' existing perceptions. She explained that the survey was designed to serve an "educational function" and to teach students about what they *should* classify as sex assault. Indeed, the sheer volume of "not serious enough to report" responses did not move the administration to rethink its definitions but instead produced bureaucratic "action items."[77] Those included increasing "recognition of what constitutes sexual assault ('Just Because' campaign)" and "correcting misperceptions about the seriousness of sexual misconduct."[78] The "Just Because" campaign consisted of papering campus with glossy posters proclaiming in the youth vernacular, "Just because she's drunk, doesn't mean she's DTF" and "Just because they're drunk doesn't mean they want to f**k."[79]

As antirape education takes hold, more students will understand their experiences as serious sexual assault. This newfound awareness of victimhood can, in turn, influence survey participation. Authors of the AAU Study found that schools' assault rates correlated to their response rate. This indicated a potential "response bias," where self-perceived victims were more likely to participate in rape surveys than nonvictims. Higher rape rates were found at Ivy League schools and schools with greater proportions of female and graduate students, conditions more compatible with antirape awareness than rape culture.[80] This suggests a feedback loop in which climate surveys produce educational campaigns to orient students as victims, those victims seek out surveys to count their victimization, and the surveys produce ever more alarming statistics.[81]

The results of the surveys are then filtered through media and activist discourse, and the surveys come to confirm, not the social problem of sexist, intoxicant-laden college culture, but a modern *rape* crisis. Colorado's broad "educational" survey intended for the Title IX office's edification produced the headline: "28% of CU-Boulder's Female Undergrads Sexually Assaulted While in College."[82] The labels "rape" and "sexual assault" cannot be disaggregated from their historical meanings. CSA Study author Christopher Krebs noted that surveys ask respondents about "incidents" and not "sexual assaults" precisely because "rape and sexual assault conjure up violent images of someone attacking."[83] This production of politically labeled statistical knowledge, according to law professor Aziza Ahmed, "crystalizes a new commonsense about the way to approach women's rights: through criminal law." Thus "The heavily contested feminist terrain of how to actually address [violence against women] gives way to one strand of feminism."[84] Activists and the media, just like second-wave reformers, purposefully used the "rape" and "sexual assault" labels so the public would see intoxicated or insufficiently authorized college sex as "real rape," with all the horrific connotations it entails. Colby Bruno, senior legal counsel for the Victim Rights Law Center, commented that we should refer to the male students under disciplinary review "as rapists . . . because that's what they are."[85]

Still, some saw through the labels. Journalist Emily Yoffe observed that if campus presidents "truly" believed that rapes were rampant on campus, they would sex-segregate, strictly enforce alcohol bans, and fill campuses with police. "But no college president would suggest such things."[86] To be sure, the statistic that one in four college girls is raped might imply that that many college boys are rapists. However, no one really believed that a significant number of male students—their own sons and brothers—were rapists. And no one had to because the campus rape panic revived predator discourse. Within this narrative, "Serial Rapists Commit 9 of 10 Campus Sexual Assaults," as a 2013 headline screamed.[87] In this account, a small group of cunning repeat offenders exploits the libertine college culture to groom, stalk, and clandestinely intoxicate victims in order to force sex.

The serial college rapist narrative finds support in a 2002 study by sociologists David Lisak and Paul Miller, "Repeat Rape and Multiple Offending among Undetected Rapists."[88] Lisak and Miller sought to fill a gap in studies of sex offender recidivism, which largely examined convicted but not uncharged actors. The authors surveyed 1,882 men (no women), ranging in age from eighteen to seventy-one years old, with a mean age of twenty-six and a half, who were present at an urban commuter college between 1991 and 1998.[89] A small number of respondents, 120 in total, admitted that in their lifetime they (1) used force or threat to achieve sex, or (2) engaged in sex with an unwilling partner too drunk to resist. About 80 percent of the "rapes" fell into the second category. Lisak and Miller found that 63 percent of those "undetected rapists" disclosed repeat behavior, with a median of three rapes per rapist and a mean of nearly six.[90]

Years later, at the height of the campus rape crisis, Lisak's study was understood as irrefutable proof of several propositions: that the virus at the root of the rape epidemic was the serial rapist, that he was not a bumbling student but a manipulative predator, and that anyone accused of a campus rape was more likely to be a serial rapist than an ordinary boy. Harsh and summary disciplinary procedures were therefore warranted because these cunning predators exploited due process and lenient procedures.[91] So how did a single decades-old study of 120 admitted assaulters, ranging from teenagers to the geriatric, morph into a wholesale commentary on who was responsible for the modern student rape crisis?

Theorist Jock Young notes that moral panic is enabled by "the mass media, buttressed by scientific experts and other moral entrepreneurs, and [involves] the mobilization of the police and the courts and other agencies of social control."[92] As campus rape captured the spotlight in the 2010s, activists and state actors relied on the study to deflect criticisms of their punitive, reformist agenda.[93] They had no incentive to emphasize the study's age, its atypical college population, its failure to measure whether the admitted rapists were cunning and manipulative rather than bumbling, and perhaps most importantly, its lack of correlation between being *accused* and being a repeat offender.[94] Study author David Lisak encouraged the revisionist reading of his data and analysis. By the 2010s, Lisak had become a victim advocate and professional expert on campus rape, eventually playing prominent roles in *The Hunting Ground* and *Missoula*.[95] He too recharacterized the study as finding that when a "college girl *reports* a 'date rape' . . . chances are better than 90 percent that the date rape was planned and intentionally carried out by a serial rapist."[96] He too touted the "profile" of the manipulative, calculating, and repeat campus rapist.[97] As an activist consultant and public intellectual, Lisak was attached to the serial predator account of campus rape.[98] In 2015, he would have to defend the fruits of his "moral entrepreneurship"— the narrative of the campus predator—against new science.[99]

Georgia State University sociologist Kevin Swartout and his coauthors, including famed feminist criminologist Mary Koss, published a study in *JAMA Pediatrics* that tested the "campus serial rapist assumption."[100] Swartout, a young and idealistic academic, hoped his research would help university bureaucracies be more effective at preventing sexual misconduct. Using three large sets of incoming male college students with a mean age of 18.5 years and adopting the FBI definition of rape as penetration without consent, the "longitudinal" study surveyed respondents over several years.[101] Its findings were different from Lisak's. A much larger percentage of respondents admitted to rape behavior (nearly 11 percent compared to Lisak's 6 percent),[102] but the vast majority were not repeat offenders.[103] Lisak's study implied that a small group of deviant men consistently offend over time. Swartout's study told a perhaps more disturbing story about first-time sex and sexual acculturation, consistent with the popular characterization of freshman year as the "red zone": "Neither data set supported a cohesive group of men who consistently committed rape across emerging adulthood. The men most likely to commit rape before college were not the men most likely to do so during college. . . . A small group of men who were unlikely to perpetrate before college drastically increased their perpetration likelihood after matriculation."[104] Given that the rapists followed "trajectories" (i.e., high risk in adolescence that decreased by college or low risk in adolescence that increased during college), the authors urged circumspection in the use of the term *campus serial rapist*. They encouraged administrators to be cognizant of how "social controls" like cultural attitudes, peer networks, and alcohol affected perpetrators' decision-making at different times.[105]

Lisak did not take kindly to what was described in the press as a "debunking" of his campus serial rapist theory. He collaborated with Allison Tracy of the Wellesley College Center for Women and his former research partner James Hopper to review the study. They took the unusual step of writing a letter to *JAMA,* the publisher of Swartout's paper, highlighting flaws and urging its retraction.[106] *JAMA* and the authors rereviewed the paper. The authors made some tweaks to the data, which actually bolstered the finding that the admitted rapists were *not* repeat offenders. The publisher, satisfied that the study was methodologically sound and adequately peer reviewed, declined to retract the paper. It offered to publish Lisak and colleagues' response. However, when *JAMA* discovered that they had taken the uncommon step of self-publishing their critique online without peer review, it rescinded the offer.[107]

That was not the end of things. Hopper initiated a research misconduct case at Georgia State against Swartout, an untenured assistant professor. The university conducted the required investigation and exonerated Swartout. Commenting on the end of the investigation, Swartout remarked, "As you would guess—I fully concur with the investigation outcome. This has been a tough process for me and my family, so I do not have any additional comment at this time."[108] Hopper rejoined, "Because GSU, like the authors and the journal editors, has failed [to] step up to the plate, I plan to pursue the other options available to achieve my goals for the good of science, public policy and victims of rape on campus."[109]

DOUBLING DOWN ON CARCERAL LOGIC

With college bureaucrats, social scientists, and the media fully engaged in the fight against campus predators, activists regularly trumpeted the problematic narratives of second-wave rape reform. Campus reformers repeated these truisms—"Yes means yes," rape causes devastating trauma, women freeze in fright, always believe the victim—with an almost religious reverence, but rarely did they reflect that their sacrosanct principles were unabashedly carceral, constructed precisely to counter juror lenience and increase convictions and incarceration. Reformers, for example, insisted that college complainants necessarily "suffer PTSD on the level of veteran soldiers,"[110] which added to the sense that accused students were monstrous offenders. However, it is well established that victims' subjective feelings of trauma are idiosyncratic and do not necessarily track objective offense severity.[111]

The trauma presumption, in university proceedings as in criminal cases, also served as a prosecutorial trump—the ground for administrators to dispense with ordinary investigative and adjudicative techniques. Beyond forbidding cross-examination, some college codes direct investigators to adopt the "trauma-informed" techniques of believing the victim and refraining from uncomfortable questioning, just as Erdely had done with "Jackie."[112] *Rolling Stone* eventually released a self-diagnosis of its epic journalistic failure. It explained that Erdely and her editors' decision not to fact-check Jackie's story was influenced by "social scientists, psychologists and trauma specialists who . . . impressed upon journalists the need to respect the autonomy of victims, to avoid re-traumatizing them and to understand that rape survivors are as reliable in their testimony as other crime victims."[113]

Before the debacle, Erdely never entertained the thought that Jackie's trauma could be grounds to *not* pursue her story at all. Erdely's view, like the view of many activists, was that administrators should encourage and even compel complainants to take action for the good of themselves and all women. College administrators could then try to make proceedings more comfortable for complainants by refraining from meaningfully testing their allegations. Aside from the due process problems with such a practice, victims' participation in even "sham" processes can be taxing. Scientist Patricia Frazier observes that "focusing on the past" and "thinking more often about why the rape occurred is itself associated with more psychological distress."[114] To be sure, Erdely eventually rethought her ethic of pursuing all complaints. "Maybe the discussion should not have been so much about how to accommodate [Jackie]," she reflected, but "about whether she would be in this story at all."[115]

As students and campus bureaucrats increasingly bought into the narratives of campus predators and easily triggered, traumatized victims, "due process" became a dirty phrase. Like crime control politicians, many campus activists came to regard procedural protections as needless "technicalities" that provided a windfall to offenders and harmed victims and the community.[116] Within this ethic, the iconic "Blackstone ratio" that "the law holds it better that ten guilty persons escape, than that one innocent party suffer" fell on deaf ears.[117] Indeed, back during the 2006 Duke Lacrosse rape case, activist Wendy Murphy had railed, "I'm really tired of people suggesting that you're somehow un-American if you don't respect the presumption of innocence, because you know what that sounds like to a victim? Presumption you're a liar."[118] It is strange to hear these sentiments from political liberals. In 2015, Jared Polis, the Democratic congressman from uber-progressive Boulder and now Colorado's governor, articulated an inverse Blackstone ratio. He remarked, "If there are 10 people who have been accused, and under a reasonable likelihood standard maybe one or two did it, it seems better to get rid of all 10 people."[119] Politics professor Caroline Heldman issued a 2013 press release calling accused students' requests for due process "an incredible display of entitlement, the same entitlement that drove them to rape."[120]

One is left to wonder why progressive campus activists assumed that a rights-denying campus disciplinary system would be wholly different from the racist criminal system they regularly protested. College administrators tend to avoid tangling with rich and powerful parents, conferring an undeniable advantage on the more privileged party in a sexual assault dispute. It is well known that primary and secondary school discipline has long been applied disproportionately to marginalized African American children, especially boys. Department of Education data on national primary and secondary education shows that black boys constituted 25 percent of suspended students and black girls 14 percent in the 2015 to 2016 academic year, even though each group made up about 8 percent of the student population.[121] Moreover, black students were a third of the students referred to police, although they constituted 15 percent of the student population.[122]

In 2012, Georgia police made headlines after an officer responded to a report of a juvenile assaulting a school administrator and damaging property. The officer arrived to find a distraught six-year-old black girl, Salecia Johnson, crying on the floor of the principal's office.[123] Apparently, during a tantrum the child had thrown a shelf at the principal's leg. The officer handcuffed the inconsolable kindergartener, forced her into a cruiser, and took her to the station, where she was charged with simple battery and destruction of property. Her aunt came to get the "shaken up" child, who said that the cuffs "really hurt her wrists."[124] Department officials later justified the handcuffing as for the child's "safety."[125]

Given the racially disparate nature of school discipline, the biases linking black men to sexual deviance, and the fact that accused students need expensive attorneys to navigate the complex Title IX process, there is more than a slight risk that colleges' broad disciplinary mandate will disproportionately disadvantage poor and minority students. Law professors Jake Gersen and Jeannie Suk ask, "Is there good reason to think that the unconscious racial stereotyping that may affect police and citizens in decisions to suspect, accuse, arrest, or shoot black men would have no analogue in the pattern of campus accusations and discipline for sexual misconduct?"[126] Policing expert Phillip Atiba Goff puts it succinctly: "Anytime you have high levels of fear and high levels of discretion, you're going to end up with high levels of disparity."[127] When it comes to campus rape, however, concerns over racist and classist disciplinary enforcement have taken a back seat.

Campus rape reformers have rationalized a presumption of guilt because "attending college is a privilege, not a right," as Dunn and Krakauer argued.[128] "We're not talking about depriving them of life or liberty; we're talking about them being transferred to another university, for crying out loud," Polis protested.[129] There is a certain disingenuousness to this argument, given that activists take pains to characterize college as a vitally important experience for women that is ruined by the presence of accused men on campus. Moreover, one might rightly conclude that a sexual assault expulsion imposes more collateral damage than, say, a plagiarism expulsion (and a student would certainly want due process for that). This is especially true in schools that, following some activists' calls, place scarlet letter–style marks on expelled students' transcripts.[130]

Finally, the vision of college sex that emerged from campus antirape discourse was hardly liberating. It often appeared as the very embodiment of sex radicals' dystopian nightmare. College administrators' attempts to construct their misconduct rules as sexy seem artificial, if not laughable. One university pamphlet, *Make Consent Fun,* suggests procuring consent through questions like "Baby, you want to make a bunk bed: me on top, you on bottom?"[131] The last few years have seen the launch of "consent apps." For example, the We-Consent app works like this: "Each partner is prompted to state his or her name, the name of the other partner, and to state explicitly 'yes' to sexual relations. If the second partner is feeling coerced, he or she can state 'forced yes' and the app creates a record of the coercion. The We-Consent™ App records video and audio, which are encrypted, sent initially to cloud storage, and then stored off-line. The recordings are only available to law enforcement, university disciplinary proceedings, or by subpoena."[132]

The company also makes an app called "What About No." The app is designed to counter the pressure women feel in a sexual encounter. When the man asks the woman to have sex, and she is too afraid to say no, she can simply launch the "What About No" app. A white male police officer loudly repeating "NO!" appears on her screen, and she can show it to the man.[133]

Moreover, anxiety over campus rape has returned female students to instinctive fear of crime and fear of the night, even though students have evidenced little concern about the risky but familiar places where date rapes occur. Risky but familiar behaviors also have continued unabated. Student binge drinking rates continue to be alarmingly high.[134] Despite terrible publicity in recent years, sorority and fraternity membership, a documented rape risk factor, has been growing exponentially.[135] Consider this stunning comment from one of my students during a 2014 class on rape. She said that her undergraduate girlfriends informally referred to one of the University of Colorado's fraternities as the "rapey frat" but that despite this dishonorable distinction women *liked* to attend the wild parties there. Female UVA students similarly protested national sorority leaders' post–*Rolling Stone* directive that sisters boycott rush-week parties.[136]

Indeed, risk avoidance has become a dirty phrase in feminism. Once it is established that "rapists cause rape," any proposals that incentivize women to alter their behavior to avoid being harmed are victim blaming. But if rape can be just a matter of intoxication-fueled miscommunication or lack of yes, *someone* must police the cryptic line between desired drunken sex and life-destroying rape.[137] Someone must "ensure" that sex is mutually desired, as California's "Yes means yes" law requires.[138] One need only view the various "peer" messages sent to boys to see whom reformers designate as the party responsible for ensuring appropriate sex. In 2013, YouTube premiered a thirty-second video featuring a young white man pointing to an unconscious attractive white woman and stating, "Hey bros . . . guess what I'm going to do to her?" The video ends with the sober boy covering the girl with a blanket, leaving a glass of water by her side, and proclaiming, "Real men treat women with respect."[139] The clip became the first viral video to win the prestigious Peabody journalism award.[140] Indeed, the image of the responsible, even paternal, male figure protecting the vulnerable drunk girl from ruinous sex has innate masculinist appeal.

On the surface, the Peabody video looks like a typical case: the kids are college students in familiar settings. But upon reflection, it is not so typical. The man is in complete control of his faculties; the woman is unconscious; and there is no ongoing intimate activity. Was the video directed just to predators—men who think it's okay for a completely sober person to have sex with an unconscious person? The video does not depict the more relevant scenario where both parties are intoxicated and actively making out. Its subtle message, however, is that the real man, drunk he might be, has the responsibility to stop the intoxicated woman from having sex. This paternalistic logic underlay Joe Biden's 2014 "It's On Us" video campaign featuring superstar male celebrities admonishing young men to intervene in potential sexual misconduct situations.[141] Announcing the initiative, Biden offered a simple explanation for his long-standing crusade against gender violence: where he came from "if a man raised his hand to a woman you had the job to kick the crap out of him."[142] In a surprising twist, the feminist mantra that rapists cause rapes morphed into a decidedly less feminist notion that *boys* must protect girls from drunk or unwise sex.

Even among student activists who engage in punitive discourse and are committed to being tough on campus predators, many remain vehemently opposed to mass incarceration and reject the premise that the government should manage social problems through criminal punishment. Student activists carry a mattress one day and raise a fist at a Black Lives Matter protest the next. They claim that their efforts to add an array of sexual behaviors to the rape list, to strengthen the trauma narrative, and to presume guilt are limited to civil law and school discipline. They claim that their sex regulatory reforms are not "carceral." However, campus reformers' antipredator logic is the "crime logic," discussed in chapter 4, that legitimates incarceration and encourages policy makers to use criminal law as a tool of social engineering. More importantly, activists are entirely too confident that the antirape juggernaut will be confined safely to campus. As the final chapter demonstrates, crime logic bleeds.

SEVEN

Endless War?

Feminists' more than century-long battle against abusers and rapists is far from over. As with the war on terror, there is an endless supply of frightening bad guys who inspire fear and loathing and have symbolic political meaning. The feminist penal regimes implemented in the 1980s and 1990s are now entrenched institutions overseen by prosecutors, advocates working for the courts, administrators, and for-profit actors with vested interests in their continued survival. Politicians are certainly not apologizing for VAWA as Clinton did for the 1994 Crime Bill that enacted it. Moreover, plenty of feminists, veteran and ingenue, remain committed not just to upholding the existing feminist crime control regimes and closing "loopholes" in them but also to creating new ones—new antitrafficking laws, revenge-porn laws, laws against hosting prostitution ads, laws against coercive control in relationships, laws against stealth condom removal.[1] Emboldened by a modern antitrafficking consensus so powerful that Trump has touted preventing sex trafficking as justification for his wall, prostitution abolitionists have redoubled efforts to criminalize commercial sexual activities.[2]

The punitive logics intensified by the campus rape crisis and the #MeToo movement have already affected criminal law and policy. Campus antirape sentiments have proven a boon to prosecutors eager to implement strict versions of affirmative consent, adopt "trauma-informed" case processing, and expand proprosecution trial rules. Interestingly, some of the most ardent prison critics remain untroubled by this. They proceed as if there were a carve-out to the mass incarceration critique for sexual misconduct—including, or perhaps especially, intoxicated sex or sex without affirmative consent—even though there is no such carve-out for aggravated assault, drug dealing, or even murder. When it comes to these serious but nonsexual crimes, many feminists are willing to exercise empathy for offenders, look to structural causes, and reject state violence as the solution. The exception for sexual offenses is so taken for granted that few feel the need to mention it or stray from the presumption that sex offenders are just a small minority of those swept up in mass incarceration. However, the reality according to a 2015 Bureau of Justice Statistics report on the US prison population is that sex offenders, at 12.4 percent, constitute a higher percentage of prisoners than burglars and nonsexual assaulters (both approximately 10 percent) and nearly as high a percentage as *all* drug offenders (15.7 percent).[3] But because of the silent exception made for sexual offenses, mass incarceration concerns have not diminished political and popular support for carceral feminist activism as it moves ahead full throttle with new criminalization proposals.

YELLOW SLAVERY AND MORAL PURITY, REDUX

In early 2019, the press was all a-twitter with the revelation that the police in Jupiter, Florida, had caught Robert Kraft, the billionaire owner of the New England Patriots, receiving sexual services from two women at the Orchids of Asia Day Spa. The case cast a spotlight on the type of human trafficking interdiction that has become popular among prosecutors (many of whom claim to be "progressive prosecutors") and police departments. In October 2018, Jupiter police detective Andrew Sharp became suspicious of Orchids after he read postings about the spa's sexual services on www.rubmaps.com.[4] He confirmed his suspicions by observing that only men went into the day spa. Sharp directed a health inspector to search the spa, under the pretense of checking to see if the female owner-operators or employees were illegally residing there. The inspector interviewed the women and took pictures of a refrigerator where the staff kept snacks.[5]

Although the inspection report did not find unlawful habitation, Sharp regarded the fridge as smoking-gun evidence that prostitutes were enslaved and forced to live inside a brothel. He directed officers to follow men leaving the spa, wait for the men to commit any minor traffic infraction, and pull them over and question them about Orchids. Apparently, several men admitted to sexual activity like manual stimulation.[6] In January 2019, citing evidence of "trafficking," the police obtained a "sneak and peek" warrant for the spa, after which they faked a bomb scare so they could evacuate the spa and install video cameras inside. For five days officers monitored and recorded activities in the spa in real time.[7]

The police arrested and charged twenty-five men with misdemeanor solicitation.[8] Also arrested and charged were four women who worked at the spa: the owner, fifty-eight-year-old grandmother Hua Zhang, the thirty-nine-year-old manager Lei Wang, forty-three-year-old Lei Chen, and fifty-eight-year-old Shen Mingbi, who gave Kraft the hand job and whose face is now splashed across the web.[9] Announcing the charges in a televised press conference, state attorney for Palm Beach Dave Aronberg began with the observation that human trafficking was "modern day slavery" and "evil in our midst."[10] Aronberg counseled that "the cold reality is that many prostitutes in cases like this [have been] lured into this country with promises of a better life."[11] Aronberg reassured his audience that arrested women could be eligible for expungement of charges or protection against deportation "if they speak up" about trafficking.[12] However, when pressed by the media, Aronberg admitted that the case did not actually involve trafficking. A few months later, an assistant state attorney would confirm in court, "There is no human trafficking that arises out of this investigation."[13] This did not stop the *New York Times* from blaring the headline, "'The Monsters Are the Men': Inside a Thriving Sex Trafficking Trade in Florida," accompanied by a story printed in English and Chinese.[14]

The state promptly offered plea deals involving community service and fines to the men who had been secretly, and likely unconstitutionally, surveilled. The Asian female Orchids employees, by contrast, were hit with an array of felony and misdemeanor charges related to prostitution and profiteering and faced a maximum of fifteen years for the felonies and up to a year for each of the misdemeanors (Zhang and Wang were charged with twenty-six).[15] Unable to post bail immediately, Wang, the former manager, spent six weeks in jail, where inmates asked if it was really her on TV. All the women had various bank accounts and assets frozen for possible forfeiture. Zhang's lawyer, Tama Kudman, attributed the fact that her client was facing decades in prison to racial "stereotypes" of helpless trafficked Asian women, adding that Orchids employees, in fact, "were in their 30s and 40s" and "held multiple massage and cosmetology licenses."[16]

To be sure, the discourse justifying modern-day "brothel" rescue raids is disturbingly reminiscent of the yellow slavery panic of late 1800s, discussed in chapter 1. Trafficking experts Grace Chang and Kathleen Kim write that today, "Symbolically, 'trafficking' has regressed to stereotyped images of poor, uneducated, and helpless young women and girls, forced into prostitution, reminiscent of historical conceptions of 'white sexual slavery' at the turn of the twentieth century."[17] When Detective Sharp's colleague Michael Fenton applied for a warrant to search another Florida massage parlor, Bridge Foot Massage and Spa, he stated in his application that the spa used a "standard Asian model," meaning a "place to operate prostitution under the guise of a massage therapy business."[18]

In 2005, the FBI in coordination with local authorities executed one of the largest prostitution interdiction raids in US history, "Operation Gilded Cage." Between 5 p.m. and 6 p.m. on a Thursday evening in San Francisco, four-hundred-plus officers descended upon Korean-owned massage parlors and businesses suspected of human trafficking.[19] "I thought they were going after Osama bin Laden," said a neighbor. "There were many people running at full speed. I thought there was a terrorist attack."[20] Another bystander saw the rescued women—there were 102 in total—led outside in handcuffs.[21] By the time advocates for the women arrived, the government had already placed most in immigration detention. Officials had already begun sorting out who was a "voluntary" sex worker (immediately deportable) and who was a "trafficked" woman who could cooperate with the government and receive immigration protection. A *San Francisco Chronicle* reporter explained their status: "The women can at any time decide to return to South Korea, although law enforcement officials could then declare them a 'material witness' to the case, forcing them to stay in the United States without any benefits."[22] Indeed, Chang and Kim reported that this was precisely what had happened to one "uncooperative" victim who was "denied ... the ability to return to Korea and held ... in jail as a material witness for the case."[23]

From the second wave to today, antiprostitution feminists have supported, even championed, law enforcement raids to rescue—as in arrest—the primarily poor and minority women engaged in commercial sex. Consider the case of Rhode Island, where from 1980 to 2009 "indoor" prostitution was legal.[24] In 1980, a lawsuit by a sex workers' rights group challenging the felony prostitution law prompted legislative change.[25] The state legislature decided to make prostitution a misdemeanor to promote more widespread enforcement.[26] However, in amending the statute, the legislature deleted the language that made sex for money a crime, leaving illegal only the attendant acts like loitering for prostitution, transporting, and profiteering. Nevertheless, the police continued to raid indoor sex establishments, until a 2003 parlor raid, "Operation Rubdown," led to a state trial court ruling that confirmed that the act of prostitution was not itself a crime and dismissed charges against several women.[27] The case coincided with a wave of public frustration over the growing number of Asian massage parlors in Providence. It spurred several legislative attempts to recriminalize indoor prostitution, which all stalled because of civil libertarian concerns over arresting the women.[28] That is, until 2009, when Democratic House member Joanne Giannini joined with Donna Hughes, a Rhode Island University women's studies professor and activist, and reframed the issue as antitrafficking and gender justice.[29]

Giannini reformulated the prostitution-criminalization bill to include, for those being charged with prostitution, an affirmative defense of being trafficked and introduced it with a tough-on-trafficking bill.[30] This effort drew the attention of the Rhode Island antitrafficking coalition, and although it did not take an official position on recriminalizing indoor prostitution, it held rallies on the eve of the vote to support the entire legislative package.[31] Progressives in the Senate asked advocates why criminalization of the workers was necessary, given the provisions intensifying penalties against traffickers and buyers. Feminist activists and the police responded that it gave the officers the necessary tools to raid brothels, pursue evictions, and force victims to cooperate in prosecutions of traffickers.[32]

The criminalization effort drew strong objections from the ACLU, NOW, and anti–domestic violence groups.[33] "The truth," Hughes rejoined, "is that these very groups are to blame for obstructing efforts to equip police to protect victims of trafficking."[34] Korean spa workers, many using translators, met with legislators to urge them not to pass the bill. Fifty-three-year-old Sunyo Williams asked lawmakers to hold off until her twenty-year-old daughter graduated college. "I need a little more time to help my daughter," she said.[35] Asian workers also testified during the bill's hearing. One thirty-one-year-old explained that providing services to men who are "depressed or who just can't meet girls" earned her far more than the $7 an hour she could otherwise earn with no education.[36] Despite these voices, the bill passed, and now, ten years later, a resolution to study decriminalizing prostitution is under consideration by the Rhode Island legislature.[37]

Also making a resurgence in contemporary feminist discourse are notions of sexual purity. Recall from chapter 1 that early temperance activists sought to control licentiousness because of their Christian beliefs and feminist sentiments that sex is "male." Today's campus rape reform efforts reflect dominance feminists' similarly sex-averse view that intercourse is inherently subordinating and is acceptable only under strict conditions like mutual affection, passionate desire, and clear communication. Feminist commentator Jaclyn Friedman, for example, argues that for sex to be acceptable, "You have to be continually in a state of enthusiastic consent with your partner."[38] Whereas first-wave regulation adopted Christian morality, today's regulatory impulses tend toward sapphic morality, restricting sex to that which produces idealized non-male-dominant female-style pleasure.

Just as temperance moralism combined with progressives' social engineering tendencies to produce purity reforms, modern feminist sentiments on acceptable sex combine with college bureaucrats' natural regulatory tendencies, with the effect of pushing the definition of consent beyond even "Yes means yes." Professors Jake Gersen and Jeannie Suk explain the cycle:

> As nonconsent became the distinguishing feature of illegal sex, schools, parents, advocacy organizations, and the government gave commonsense advice: if there is any ambiguity about consent, stop. Don't take the absence of a no to mean consent. Out of an abundance of caution, avoid ambiguity, get a yes, and avoid the cliff of nonconsent and sexual assault. In short order, however, the extra-cautious strategy of steering clear of the cliff became the new legal definition of consent. Once the line moved, commonsense advice was again to stay well clear of the edge: do not settle for a nod, a smile, or even a yes. Make sure the yes is enthusiastic. . . . Very rapidly, however, the consent line shifted again to make enthusiasm a requirement of consent itself—anything less than enthusiasm is sexual assault.[39]

It is naive to believe that this radical redefinition of rape and consent remains safely ensconced within campus codes and administrative publications. Police and prosecutors across the nation enforce sexual assault statutes that define rape in terms of nonconsent and lack of affirmative consent. They decide what these statutes mean and the types of conduct they prohibit. Influenced by the campus rape crisis and #MeToo movements, they are more likely than ever to adopt the most regulatory interpretation of affirmative consent as "Yes means yes" or clear permission. In January 2018, the National District Attorneys Association of Women Prosecutors Section issued a white paper outlining "best practices" for investigating and prosecuting sexual assault cases. The best practice, it states, is to adopt a "Yes means yes" definition of consent. It explains, "'No means No' has been the contextual framework of sexual assault, both stranger and non-stranger, for decades, but oftentimes prosecutors and investigators find themselves confronted by cases in which a victim has not, in fact, said the word 'No.'"[40] It goes on, "In these cases it is critical that prosecutors and investigators remember that *only* 'Yes' means 'Yes.'"[41]

One might take comfort that prosecutors will not actually pursue cases where sex appears consensual but a "yes" was lacking—that they will still look for signs of force or nonconsent (lifelessness, crying, turning away). However, when there is a policy that *only* yes means yes, it means that prosecutors, per policy, *must* pursue complaints where a "yes" was absent, regardless of the lack of other evidence that sex was nonconsensual. Moreover, if prosecutors are like the *M.T.S.* judge or the students discussed in chapter 5, they will invoke "Yes means yes" as a tiebreaker in favor of prosecution when evidence of nonconsent is weak. Worse, they may selectively pursue "Yes means yes" cases when the defendant appears to be a bad guy or the victim a good girl—factors that easily map onto race, class, and social status. To be sure, researchers note that rape "charging is more likely if the defendant is nonwhite, or if the defendant is black and the victim is white."[42] In the end, we may never know for sure how the "Yes means yes" prosecutorial policy plays out or whether it will ever be checked by a jury. When prosecutors pursue close cases because of the policy, the defendant will likely just plead out to a lesser, even nonsexual, charge to avoid trial for felony sexual assault, with all the risks that it entails.

Current antirape sentiments are likely to affect other aspects of procedure in rape cases. Provictim, trauma-informed investigation and prosecution are the new agenda. When investigators "believe the victim" and act as victim advocates it surely increases the likelihood of conviction, which feminists applaud. But it also increases the risk of false conviction. Criminal defendants lack investigative resources and rely on exculpatory (innocence-proving) evidence produced through meaningful police investigation. If the police decline to examine victims' credibility at all and refuse to pursue all the evidence, such exculpatory information will not be discovered. The 1963 Supreme Court case *Brady v. Maryland* ruled that the prosecution's withholding of exculpatory information from the defendant—in that case, the fact that another person had confessed to the murder—violated Fifth Amendment due process.[43] The Court reasoned that allowing prosecutors to withhold evidence favorable to defendants "casts the prosecutor in the role of an architect of a proceeding that does not comport with standards of justice."[44] Courts have acknowledged that police practices can also thwart defense discovery of exculpatory information and can be unconstitutional.[45]

In this sex-preoccupied moment, we can expect more police and prosecutors to follow "best practices" like those set forth by End Violence Against Women International (EVAWI).[46] EVAWI is a professional training organization that was founded in 2003 by the former head of the San Diego Police sex crimes unit to train police in techniques "to improve outcomes for victims and pursue accountability for their assailants."[47] Since its inception, EVAWI has received over $7.5 million in private and public grant funding, including twenty grants from the Department of Justice's Office of Violence against Women.[48] EVAWI's website has an online training institute with "modules," one of which is entitled "Effective Report Writing: Using the Language of Non-consensual Sex."[49] That directive, written in 2006 and revised in 2019, laments that police reports sometimes document incidents in a way that provide fodder to defense attorneys. It directs police investigators to "anticipate potential defense strategies as much as possible, and include the information necessary to counter them."[50] Effective report writing makes the complainant "appear more 'innocent' in the eyes of prosecutors, judges, and jurors."[51] It also entails "strategies" to "minimize the risk of contradictions" between the complainant's various statements.[52] Think of it as the inverse of police interrogation techniques used on defendants, which are painstakingly crafted to produce contradictions and confessions.

The idea that the police minimize victim contradiction is itself highly problematic, but the actual techniques prescribed are remarkable. The module suggests that when police conduct more than one interview of the complainant, they should issue only one report. Obviously, however, this only minimizes contradiction where the interviews are in fact contradictory. If there are other required documents, for example, a forensic evaluation, the interviewing officer should seek consistency in his report by "consult[ing] with medical professionals to compare the information that was available before and after the forensic examination."[53] Investigators do need to document serious testimonial contradictions, but in such cases they should explore and record the "reasons why victims recall additional details or revise information that was previously provided (e.g., memory impairment, omitting details about unflattering or even illegal behavior, providing inaccurate information so the sexual assault will sound more like 'real rape')."[54]

In the rape crisis era, we can also expect sex crimes prosecutors to find greater success in bending evidentiary rules in their favor. Judges may be more receptive to prosecutors' requests to admit "rape trauma syndrome" evidence. Judges may also be more inclined to apply rape shield laws broadly, with the effect of excluding relevant defense evidence. At the same time, they may give prosecutors free rein to put defendants' reputation on trial. Recall from chapter 5 that in 1995, Congress, over near-universal objection from the legal community, adopted an exception to the ban on evidence of defendants' prior bad acts, but only for sexual assault defendants. The state of Pennsylvania did not follow the federal government's lead and kept the prior bad acts ban for all defendants. But then the Bill Cosby case happened, and "#MeToo [came] to the Cosby courtroom," as Professor Deb Tuerkheimer remarked.[55] In order to permit Cosby's prosecutor to present evidence of his past sexual misconduct, the judge had to narrow Pennsylvania's prior bad acts ban generally—a precedent that negatively affects all future defendants, not just sexual assault defendants.[56]

Perhaps the best example of the translation of Title IX sentiments and measures to the courtroom is the case of Brock Turner, the disgraced Stanford student. Turner rose to instant infamy, giving Bill Cosby serious competition as the poster child for rape. In fact, the 2017 edition of the criminology textbook *Introduction to Criminal Justice* features a picture of Turner's mug shot next to the entry "Rape."[57] *Jezebel* proclaimed, "Brock Turner is Now the Textbook Definition of 'Rape.'"[58] Turner represents millennial feminists' archetype of a bogeyman. In the prevailing narrative, his bad behavior was not a product of a "rotten social background,"[59] marginalization, or mental health issues. It was a product of wealth, race, and male privilege. Years later, as Turner is a registered sex offender banished from society and his victim enjoys professional success and public acclaim, people continue to leave flowers at a makeshift memorial set up where the assault took place.

THE MODEL OF A MODERN CAMPUS PREDATOR

In the early hours of January 18, 2015, passing bike riders saw Turner, a popular student athlete at Stanford, "thrusting" on an apparently unconscious woman behind a dumpster. The bikers, male Swedish graduate students, called out to Turner, who got off the woman and fled. The bikers took chase and subdued Turner until police arrived.[60] From the beginning, the case garnered substantial media coverage because of the unusual nature of a perpetrator being caught in the act, the heroism of the Swedish men, and Turner's and his victims' social status. The 2016 trial and sentencing set media coverage ablaze.

Turner's high-powered attorneys argued that the drunk defendant honestly believed the complainant, "Emily Doe," had consented to what turned out to be digital penetration. The jury, however, was unpersuaded and convicted Turner. The most emotionally charged moment came during the sentencing hearing on June 2, 2016, when Doe read her victim impact statement.

Doe was an aspiring writer and a close friend of Stanford legal history professor-turned-antirape crusader Michelle Dauber, and her emotionally and politically impactful statement reads like a heart-wrenching manifesto in favor of rape trial reform.

At sentencing, Doe dramatically faced Turner and stated, "You don't know me, but you've been inside me, and that's why we're here today."[61] Doe went on to narrate a seven-thousand-word statement of devastation that detailed not so much the crime she could not remember but the aftermath, including the medical examination, media reports, and especially trial. She expressed pointed disdain for the defense team and for Turner's decision to testify in his own defense: "I was assaulted with questions designed to attack me, to say see, her facts don't line up, she's out of her mind. . . . And then it came time for [Turner] to testify and I learned what it meant to be revictimized. . . . To sit under oath and inform all of us, that yes I wanted it, yes I permitted it, and that you are the true victim attacked by Swedes for reasons unknown to you is appalling, is demented, is selfish, is damaging."[62]

By the time of the sentencing hearing, Professor Dauber had already provided *The Hunting Ground* producer Amy Ziering with a written copy of the impact statement. With Doe's permission, Ziering searched for an appropriate news outlet to publish the statement. Ziering consulted her daughter, who told her that *BuzzFeed* reached the "right demographic" for the statement. *BuzzFeed* published the statement in full on Friday, June 3, 2016, the day after the sentencing.[63] The story went viral over the weekend, attracting over eleven million hits in four days.[64] On Monday, HLN anchor Ashleigh Banfield took the "remarkable" and "necessary" step of devoting forty minutes of her hourlong show to reading the statement in full.[65] The statement would go on to be recited on the floor of Congress and performed by women all over the world, establishing Doe's rape as a source of universal female solidarity.[66]

Turner was not in fact convicted of rape. The jury convicted him of three felonies: assault with intent to commit rape, penetration of an intoxicated person, and penetration of an unconscious person.[67] At the time, California law mandated a minimum jail term of three years for "forcible" sexual offenses, but it permitted a term of probation for Turner's nonforcible crimes if a lesser sentence was "in the interests of justice."[68] The case went to the probation department, tasked with preparing a typical presentence recommendation to the judge. The probation department rejected the prosecution's request of a six-year prison term, recommending a sentence that even incarceration critics regard as curiously lenient.[69] It settled on a six-month prison term and three years of probation, with fourteen years if probation was violated.

Judge Aaron Persky followed the recommendation of the probation department and sentenced Turner to six months in prison, with probation and lifetime registration.[70] Outraged, Professor Dauber immediately commenced a recall campaign to remove the judge from office. A few months after the sentencing, Dauber paired up with Facebook feminist "secret society" GRLCVLT and threw a glamourous recall fund-raiser. The professor and celebrity attendees donned custom T-shirts emblazoned with "Fuck Rape Culture" and imbibed mixology cocktails, including "ABrockalypse Now (tequila, lime juice and simple syrup) and Male Tears (a Peroni)."[71] At the fab cocktail party, the wealthy attendees excoriated Persky for giving a "rich" rapist a slap on the wrist (Turner's family had said they are not wealthy and are racked with legal debt). However, it was not Persky but probation officer Monica Lassettre who had made the recommendation. And she had made it on the basis of typical leniency factors, including Turner's young age (nineteen), lack of criminal history, and state of intoxication during the crime.[72] In addition, Lassettre considered the wishes of the victim, who told her, "I want him to know it hurt me, but I don't want his life to be over. . . . I don't want him to rot away in jail; he doesn't need to be behind bars."[73]

By the time of the sentencing hearing, the victim's view of Turner's incarceration had changed. Her impact statement sought retribution, not restraint. Doe attributed the change of heart to Turner's lack of remorse in his probation statement, but some believe she was influenced by the heady publicity surrounding the case.[74] Putting aside the question of whether sentences should be based on the defendant's apology performance, Turner did express remorse to probation. Calling his actions "unforgivable," he stated, "Having imposed suffering on someone else and causing someone else pain . . . I can barely live with myself."[75] He later put it more plainly: "I can't believe I imposed such suffering on her and I'm so sorry."[76] Lassettre in fact cited Turner's "sincere remorse and empathy for the victim" as a reason for her lenient recommendation.[77] Turner was also unequivocally contrite at the sentencing hearing: "I can never forgive myself for imposing trauma and pain on [Doe]. It debilitates me to think that my actions have caused her emotional and physical stress that is completely unwarranted and unfair."[78]

Still, Turner drew fire for insisting that he had not intentionally hurt the victim and that he was not "a predator who [was] searching for prey," as the prosecutor had insisted.[79] Feminist activists were infuriated that Turner did not willingly go along with the prosecution's characterization of him as a monster. It is not altogether unusual for prosecutors to demand that convicted defendants admit to the most heinous versions of their crimes to show they "take responsibility." However, it puts defendants in a double bind. Embellishing their moral reprehensibility to show acceptance of responsibility can influence the judge to levy a harsher sentence.

Commentators seized on the portion of Turner's sentencing statement where he lamented his participation in "the culture surrounded by binge drinking and sexual promiscuity."[80] This statement, in critics' view, was nothing more than a thinly veiled attempt at victim blaming. However, reading the statement in context shows that Turner was trying, however incompetently, to channel the logic of the Peabody-winning video on "real men" discussed last chapter.[81] He wanted his behavior to stand as a warning to men about the risks of college Bacchanal. The "promiscuity" phrase in entirety reads: "I know I can impact and change people's attitudes towards the culture surrounded by binge drinking and sexual promiscuity that protrudes through what people think is at the core of being a college student. I want to demolish the assumption that drinking and partying are what make up a college lifestyle. I made a mistake, I drank too much, and my decisions hurt someone."[82]

But the public had appetite only for the narrative that Turner's actions were a product of his personal immorality, sexism, and privilege. One of the most damning moments for Turner came when his father wrote a letter to the court stating that Turner should not suffer for "twenty minutes of action."[83] Dauber promptly tweeted, "#brockturner father: son not 'violent' only got '20 mins of action' shouldn't have to go to prison."[84] The tweet implied and the indignant social media readership assumed that the word *action* meant "sex," as in "I want some action." The father's statement then served as proof that Turner came from a long line of misogynists. But take a closer look at Dan Turner's statement. Yes, it is full of affluenza-inflected sentiments, such as lamenting that Brock barely ate his favorite "ribeye steak." But the pro-rape stance attributed to Dan appears mistaken. Here is the "twenty minutes" statement in full: "His life will never be the one that he dreamed about and worked so hard to achieve. That is a steep price to pay for 20 minutes of action out of *his* 20 plus years of life. The fact that he now has to register as a sexual offender for the rest of his life forever alters where he can live, visit, work, and how he will be able to interact with people and organizations."[85]

The emphasis is mine, and I do it to illustrate that "action" is more properly read to mean *Turner's* conduct. Now, one might disagree with the notion that offenders should not pay lifetime penalties for a single, but terrible, action. Nevertheless, the statement does not say that Brock was just "getting some action." Rather, Dan was ineloquently channeling the logic of iconic anti-incarceration activist Bryan Stevenson's signature statement, "Each of us is more than the worst thing we've ever done."[86]

Judge Persky's decision to follow probation's recommendation and impose the six-month jail sentence shocked the nation. A Change.org petition supporting the judge's removal garnered over 1.3 million signatures.[87] By contrast, public defenders and other incarceration critics regarded the recall movement with a deep-seated sense of unease. The Santa Clara County public defender Sajid Khan noted "the countless defendants who have suffered relatively harsh sentences in our state [who] fall below any headline" and authored a letter, signed by 116 defenders, opposing recall.[88] Punishing the jurist, it stated, would "deter other judges from extending mercy and instead encourage them to issue unfairly harsh sentences for fear of reprisal."[89] Kahn initially posted the letter on MoveOn.org, which deleted it without explanation, and then posted it on Change.org, where it garnered fewer than five hundred signatures.[90]

Fifty-three of the 180 Stanford Law School 2016 graduates penned an open letter to Professor Dauber, asking her to halt the recall effort.[91] Several of the drafters had been involved in opposing California's three-strikes laws and highlighted their efforts to convince "judges like Aaron Persky to grant early release to men and women serving life in prison because the people of California once believed that our clients' mistakes made them irredeemable."[92] They implored, "If we demand that Judge Persky immediately hand over his gavel for acting on his empathy for this defendant, how can we credibly assure any other judge that her hand need not waver when the human circumstances of a case seem to call for compassion?"[93]

Recall critics' fears were well founded. The recall movement indeed unleashed a tornado of punitive zeal against Turner and college rapists in general. Modern feminist dialogue began to resemble that of the 1990s antipredator right-wingers. What's more, the antipredator contingent had reacted to horrific stories of child murders, whereas the very picture of Turner's drunken mug shot was enough to incite hatred in the blogosphere. Jenn Hoffman, a member of GRLCVLT, authored an article for the popular young women's online magazine *xoJane,* stating that despite Persky's "disregard ... for justice," the "world is actually fairer than we think" because Turner "must register as a sex offender."[94] Hoffman's greatest source of comfort was that Turner had suffered irrevocable public humiliation, if not civil death: "In jail, Turner was shielded from the outside world. In the outside world, he is screwed. . . . Everywhere he goes, he will be known as the poster boy for rape. . . . 'My name is Brock Turner. I'm a rapist' posters have been popping up in cities across the U.S. Brock Turner is a rapist memes exist"— and here Hoffman inserted hyperlinks to the posters and memes.[95]

California was at the time one of two states—the other being South Carolina—that prescribed lifetime registration for all sex offenses with no phase-out process.[96] Turner was put on the registry as a Tier III offender, the highest level. Once an offender is on the registry, he is subject to registration requirements in the locality of his residence. In Turner's case, this means that, among other requirements, he must check in with authorities every three months for life, and, wherever he lives, his neighbors will receive notification.[97] If he moves out of his hometown in Ohio, he could be subject to even more stringent requirements, such as the residency restrictions discussed in chapter 4 that forced Miami registrants to reside under the causeway.

The Turner case's ripples reached far. In August 2016, inspired by Emily Doe, University of Colorado student Kendra Heuer published her victim impact statement.[98] In 2014, after Heuer became drunk at a party, student Austin Wilkerson told Heuer's friends that he would take care of the intoxicated woman. Instead, he had sex with her. The jury convicted Wilkerson of felony sexual assault of a helpless person. Boulder County judge Patrick Butler, following the recommendation of the probation department, sentenced Wilkerson to two years of work-release (release for work during the day and jail at night), lifetime probation, and registration.[99] The noncarceral sentence, combined with publicizing of the victim impact statement, caused a firestorm of backlash from prosecutors, politicians, and social media commentators. However, calls for Butler's removal were in vain, as Colorado does not permit judicial recall.

Heuer publicly disclosed her identity to grace the pages of *People* magazine, along with the likes of Charlize Theron, Queen Rania, and Sheryl Sandberg, as one of their "25 Women Changing the World."[100] *People* noted that Heuer garnered nationwide attention because of "her powerful statement—and the judge's sentence of no prison time."[101] Indeed, critics across the nation vociferously condemned Judge Butler for failing to send a strong message against campus rape. They spent considerably less time grappling with the jurist's reason for avoiding giving a jail sentence. Under Colorado's sex offense sentencing scheme, created during predator panic, any jail sentence he imposed had to be a *life* sentence.[102]

Persky-recall organizer Dauber, an erstwhile liberal, eventually spoke out against her allies' support of lifetime registration and mandatory sentences. Critiquing lifetime consequences, she, like Dan Turner, invoked Bryan Stevenson sentiments: "No one should be defined for the rest of their life by their worst moment."[103] Dauber further stated that she was "no fan of harsh sentencing for nonviolent minority drug offenders . . . that have really fed our mass incarceration problem"; however, "Violence against women is a serious, serious crime."[104] Now that mass incarceration is firmly embedded in the public vocabulary, it is common for policy makers to criticize harsh punishment of "nonviolent drug offenders." However, the stark reality of mass incarceration is that more than half of prisoners are violent offenders.[105] Save for minor drug users, *every* offender in this mass prison system can be said to have committed a "serious, serious crime."

Because of the 1980s predator laws, sexual offenses carry serious, serious penalties. The injustice apparently lay in Persky's discretion to sentence below the fourteen-year maximum of Turner's crimes. Yet the judge and probation department applied discretion in a prototypically progressive way by accounting for factors like age, intoxication, and lack of criminal record that militated against the defendant's culpability and recidivist risk. For Dauber, such factors were illegitimate because campus rapists "are all young, they are all intoxicated for the most part, and they are all high-achieving."[106] However, young and intoxicated rape defendants benefitting from youth and intoxication mitigation are no different from juvenile murder defendants benefiting from the ban on juvenile capital punishment.[107] Recognizing that mitigating characteristics provide leniency to the class of defendants with those characteristics is an observation, not an argument.

To be sure, progressives like Dauber have self-induced myopia about the problematic US prison state when defending harsh criminal sanctions intended to protect minority victims. Take, for example, hate crime legislation, a perennial progressive carve-out. In the face of accumulating evidence that defendants of color are disproportionately subjected to hate crime enhancements, incarceration critics are beginning to realize that criminalizing identity-based animus is a double-edged sword.[108] In fact, the popularity of identity-protecting criminal law has given states another weapon in the enforcement arsenal. In May 2016, the Governor of Louisiana signed the "Blue Lives Matter Law," making Louisiana the first state to treat offenses against "public safety workers" as hate crimes.[109]

Professor Dauber indeed viewed Turner's acts as a hate crime. Responding to the law students' open letter, she queried, "I wonder if they would make this same argument if Turner had been convicted of a violent crime based on race or sexual orientation or gender identity rather than sex."[110] I think the three-strikes project students would have done so and recognized that harsh hate crime laws disproportionately affect racial minorities and ultimately do not promote a more tolerant society. Dauber, however, implied (I believe unfairly) that the students' leniency sentiments reflected, not a general objection to bodies in cages, but a sexist view that severe criminal sanctions are fine for some crimes, but just not for rape. Similarly, Dauber argued that Judge Persky's leniency reflected both his rape-apologetic sexism and his racism. She maintained that Persky, a white former Stanford athlete, had exercised excessive mercy in racial and class solidarity with Turner. Dauber clearly would have preferred that Persky show strong solidarity with the socioeconomically privileged (but nonwhite Asian) Emily Doe, and the victim impact statement was designed precisely to achieve that. As discussed in chapter 4, victim impact evidence shifts focus away from defendants' character and conduct and toward victims' and their families' suffering and social worth. Indeed, studies attest that *victims'* demographic characteristics (e.g., young, white, rich, female, privileged) generally predict punishment levels more than defendants'.[111]

Persky's personal characteristics made him vulnerable to charges of sexist and racist solidarity with Turner, although the same could not be said of probation officer Monica Lassettre, who recommended the sentence. However, was there any specific evidence of Persky's racist, classist, athlete-loving penchant? Dauber pointed to the case of Keenan Smith, a college football player convicted of assaulting his girlfriend, and claimed that Persky had given him an overly light sentence. However, Keenan Smith is black, and he was poor enough to qualify as indigent and get a public defender. Smith's public defender responded to Dauber by noting that Smith's sentence was the result of a plea deal. He remarked, "Judge Persky had nothing to do with this. It was the charging body, the [prosecutor], who determined what sentence he was going to get." He added, "[Dauber] doesn't have a clue what she is talking about."[112]

The Associated Press eventually got around to investigating the sexism, racism, and classism accusations against Persky. They discovered that the judge did have an identifiable sentencing tendency: following probation recommendations.[113] Deputy public defender Andy Gutierrez stated, "From my experience, where most of my clients are from poor socioeconomic backgrounds and from communities of color, Judge Persky has been a fair and decent man."[114] He added that Persky "has gone out of his way to improve our criminal justice system and, where possible, soften the harsher edges of the criminal justice system in regards to its treatment of indigent persons."[115]

District attorney Jeffrey Rosen also initially supported Persky, issuing the statement, "While I strongly disagree with the sentence that Judge Persky issued in the Brock Turner case I do not believe he should be removed from his judgeship."[116] But then Persky presided over the case of Rachel Garcia, who was charged with possession of stolen mail. During jury selection, several people in the venire refused to serve in Persky's courtroom, citing "hardship" because of their distaste for the Turner sentence. "I can't believe what you did," one prospective juror said.[117] Garcia's case never reached the jury. Persky granted the defense's motion for acquittal because the prosecution had not shown the mail was "recent," as required by the charge. Garcia's public defender applauded the judge for fulfilling "his obligation to follow the law and remain neutral despite public opinion."[118] The supervising DA was "dismayed."[119] Persky's lenience toward the indigent Latina defendant proved too much for DA Rosen. The next day, Rosen successfully petitioned to have Persky removed from a pending sexual assault case, stating that his office was "disappointed and puzzled at Judge Persky's unusual decision to unilaterally dismiss" Garcia's theft case.[120]

Reporters remained intent on finding examples of minority defendants treated more harshly than Turner to prove Persky's racism. One of the comparative cases highlighted was that of Cory Batey, a black former Vanderbilt football player, convicted of participating in a gang rape of an unconscious white female student.[121] Security cameras captured Batey and other men vaginally penetrating the incapacitated victim and Batey urinating on her. Batey received a twenty-five-year prison sentence, with a mandatory minimum of fifteen years. One article highlighted the Batey-Turner disparity as proof that "the racial disparity in sentencing for similar crimes is completely out of hand."[122] However, the conclusion of the article was curious. It stated, "America's jails and prisons are overflowing with young black and Latino teenagers who are paying the harshest price possible for their crimes."[123] It was as if the author believed that critiquing Turner's low sentence sent a message that rape penalties should be *reduced* across the board.[124]

Batey's sentence was not in fact a product of racist judicial discretion but of Tennessee's sentencing regime, which prescribes a mandatory minimum of fifteen years for aggravated rape. In Batey's case, the African American judge imposed the lowest mandatory sentence. The judge expressed sadness that the victim, then in graduate school, had suffered great harm. But he also lamented that Batey and the other defendants' lives were essentially over. "After they get out of jail or prison they will be on the sex-offender registry for the rest of their lives," he said. "That's a life sentence in and of itself."[125]

It is hard to believe that those invoking the Turner-Batey disparity intended it as an argument for the "level-down" program of reducing mandatory rape sentences that disproportionately hurt men of color. Few antirape activists said, "Look how lenient Persky was on Turner. We should encourage judges to be that lenient toward similarly situated black defendants." Indeed, the director of the Tennessee Coalition to End Domestic and Sexual Violence criticized Batey's sentence as too merciful, stating, "While Batey has been given a 15-year sentence, the victim has been given a life sentence. She will have to cope with the trauma of this experience for the rest of her life."[126] Within this ideology, the only way to remedy racial disparity was to ratchet Turner-like sentences up to Batey-like sentences. One female college student blogger summed up the Batey-Turner disparity: "Corey Batey is African-American while Turner is white. That is the only difference between these two individuals. Rape is rape. It doesn't matter if the rapist is African American, Hispanic or White; they need to sit in jail for the maximum sentence. The maximum sentence is life—then they will not be a threat to other women in any community."[127]

Reporters also dug up one of Persky's old sexual assault cases involving a poor Latino man. Raul Ramirez was arrested after his roommate called 911 and reported that he had forcibly digitally penetrated her.[128] Ramirez confessed to the penetration, and prosecutors charged Ramirez with sexual penetration by force. The parties agreed to a plea deal involving a three-year sentence, which Persky accepted. The thirty-two-year-old Salvadorian immigrant had no record, and critics charged that Judge Persky, who "oversaw" the plea bargain, treated the two differently because of ethnicity and class. The liberal paper the *Guardian* reported that "if [Persky] wanted to give Ramirez the same favorable treatment, the judge could have utilized his discretion and recommended a less harsh prosecution."[129] Professor Dauber remarked that the case should silence recall critics: "This just shows that our concern about Judge Persky's ability to be unbiased is justified."[130]

However, Ramirez's charge involved "force" and carried a *mandatory* minimum sentence of three years' imprisonment. Judge Persky had no discretion to sentence Ramirez to anything less. The *Guardian* article, incredibly, suggests that Persky was nonetheless biased because he "could have approved or helped negotiate a bargain in which Ramirez only pleaded guilty to the lesser of two charges he was facing—assault with intent to commit rape."[131] Persky, of course, could not approve a plea bargain that was not proposed to him. Nor could he have intervened in the parties' plea negotiations.[132] One might direct criticism toward DA Rosen's office for not offering a lesser charge to Ramirez, as they had with Turner, or for declining to pursue forcible penetration charges against Turner, as they had with Ramirez.[133] In any case, imagine for a moment that Persky had intervened in plea negotiations to convince the prosecution to offer Ramirez a sweetheart deal. Dauber would have used that as further proof that Persky "does not understand violence against women."[134]

In the end, the recallers' race argument was simple: Persky should not have had the discretion to be "unduly lenient" to Turner.[135] Democratic lawmakers in California heard that message loud and clear and took up the Turner issue to exhibit tough-on-rape sentiments and have a badge of liberal credibility. California legislator Susan Eggman called Persky's sentencing determination "baffling and repugnant" and lamented that "it sends a clear message that rape will not be treated seriously."[136] Legislator Cristina Garcia derided Turner's sentence of incarceration, probation, and lifetime registration as a mere "inconvenience."[137] They joined with DA Rosen to convince the state assembly to pass AB 2888, which attached a mandatory three-year minimum to the charges Turner was convicted of.[138] Rosen's rhetoric vacillated between 1980s-style sex panic talk (calling Turner a "predator" and emphasizing the degrading nature of the crime) and mass incarceration–influenced restraint (characterizing the bill as merely "closing a loophole").[139] Rosen said, "Today, a perpetrator at a college party who forcibly rapes a conscious victim will go to prison. However, a different perpetrator at the same party who chooses to watch and wait for a victim to pass out before sexually assaulting her can get probation."[140]

However, AB 2888 does not in fact require "watching and waiting" or even an unconscious victim. It extends the mandatory minimum to "penetration however slight" of an "incapacitated" person. An incapacitated person, in turn, is anyone who is "prevented from resisting by any intoxicating . . . substance, or any controlled substance," even if consumed voluntarily.[141] The defendant is guilty if he honestly but "unreasonably" believed the person he had sex with was lucid enough to consent. Accordingly, AB 2888's mandatory years in prison applies equally to cunning serial rapists who watch and wait for women to pass out cold and to inebriated minority youths who honestly albeit mistakenly believe their awake but drunk date is sober enough to have sex.

In another move to close the Turner "loophole," the legislature passed a bill declaring all forms of penetration (including touching of the labia majora), oral sex, and sodomy to be "rape."[142] Legislators Eggman and Garcia, the Bill's sponsors, explained that the change reflected the seriousness of sexual contact not involving penile-vaginal invasion, thereby protecting LGBT victims.[143] The bill condemns nonconsensual below-the-waist or "third-base" touching as "rape," leaving only above-the-waist fumbling free from serious mandatory prison time and utter moral condemnation.

On September 30, 2016, after Turner's release from jail after serving three months caused another firestorm of outrage, Governor Jerry Brown signed the bills into law. Brown, a dyed-in-the-wool liberal, was careful to note that "as a general matter, I am opposed to adding more mandatory minimum sentences," but that AB 2888 "brings a measure of parity to sentencing for criminal acts that are substantially similar."[144] Today in California, "rapists" subject to mandatory years of incarceration include predators who use force, first-time offenders who do not, frat boys, poor immigrants, those who engage in gang rapes, those who finger intoxicated dates, the purposeful, the unreasonable, white, black, gay, straight, old and young. On June 5, 2018, after years of legal wrangling, scores of headlines, dozens of fund-raisers, and millions of dollars spent, the California voters recalled Judge Persky.[145]

After his release, Brock Turner returned to his home in Ohio. Awaiting his arrival were a group of agitated picketers. They were not, however, the outraged feminists lighting up the internet about rape culture, patriarchy, and the woman's voice. The people inspired to stand outside in anxious anticipation of Turner's arrival were open-carry activists and self-proclaimed anarchists, who bore automatic rifles and other visible firearms. They held signs reading, "Castrate All Rapists," "Shoot Your Local Rapist," and "This Machine [the assault rifle slung across his chest] Kills Rapists." Similar messages appeared scrawled on the sidewalk. One particularly striking photograph captures a large bearded man with a larger semiautomatic rifle, raising a sign declaring, "If I rape Brock, will I only do 3 months?"[146]

The rally organizer, gun activist Micah Naziri, characterized the display as "a militant feminist statement in favor of self-defense of would-be rape victims."[147] Protester Molly Hardin concurred: "It's completely legal to kill a rapist in the act of rape. If [Turner] were to try something like this again . . . we would help protect the city."[148] The group vowed to return to Turner's house at any time unannounced to make him "uncomfortable in his own home."[149] One local mother brought her children to the demonstration. She, too, was unhappy with the Turner family's residence in the neighborhood, describing them as a "cancer" and insisting, "We need to get them out of here."[150] She explained that she had "decided to bring the kids" to give them a reverse-Bryan Stevenson lesson: "to teach them, at a young age, that 20 minutes of wrongdoing to someone . . . can ruin your life forever."[151]

Conclusion

Famed civil libertarian David Cole wrote in 2011 that the United States might finally be "turning the corner on mass incarceration."[1] Cole remarked that "the tragedy of the United States' forty-year incarceration epidemic . . . is old news."[2] The "new news," Cole said, is formerly tough-on-crime legislators' incipient willingness to reduce sentences and embrace "alternatives to incarceration."[3] Change does seem to be in the air. According to the Bureau of Justice Statistics' 2015 report on prisoners, the total number of incarcerated individuals declined by more than 2 percent from 2014.[4] Minorities enjoyed the benefit of this change, with the black prisoner population declining by 3 percent.[5] The latest statistics show the prison rate continuing this very modest path of decline.[6] In the last few years, "criminal justice reform" became a bipartisan issue. The Republican power broker Koch brothers even adopted reducing incarceration as an important pet project. In 2015, Republican senator Chuck Grassley introduced the Sentencing Reform and Corrections Act ("Sentencing Act"), the first serious congressional effort to reduce federal sentences.[7]

However, other forces have muted this across-the-aisle turn to tolerance. In May 2017, Attorney General Jeff Sessions reversed the Obama-era policy that had directed prosecutors to use charging discretion to blunt the force of the draconian federal drug-sentencing regime. Sessions ordered federal prosecutors to vigorously pursue the highest mandatory drug sentences, without retaining even the exceptions that had existed under the Bush administration.[8] In addition, Trump's revival of public loathing of criminals stoked Republicans' long-standing fears of appearing soft on crime. The Sentencing Act stalled in these shifting political sands.[9] But even if the Trump administration's renewal of American lust for punishment had not derailed it, the

Sentencing Act still would not have reduced sentences across the board. The act's compromise for lowering drug sentences was creating new mandatory minimum sentences for domestic violence crimes.[10] And, as we discussed in chapter 4, given the limited jurisdiction of federal criminal law, those penalties would have been distributed in idiosyncratic and unintended ways.

Feminist criminal law discourse, as it did in the 1990s, allows progressive politicians and some self-described "progressive prosecutors" to continue to leverage crime control for political benefit. They can oppose the costly prison problem, while getting tougher on the offenders who liberals agree are the "worst." And for many progressives, when rape and domestic violence criminalization are mentioned, all the problems endemic to criminal prosecution and punishment—racial inequality, prison sexual abuse, inhumane conditions, economic marginalization—simply vanish. Today, feminist criminalization initiatives to broaden rape law, increase DV sentences, and crack down on commercial sex thrive in the way that sex offender laws did during the predator panic.

Millennial feminists can yet transform feminism from a movement that maintains the US as a prison nation to one that actively opposes the penal system as racist, neoliberal, uncivilized, *and* bad for women. It is doubtlessly difficult to maintain an institutional opposition to the prison system in the face of spectacular stories of bad men getting away with brutal crimes against women. Nevertheless, feminists can find space, even during this "cultural revolution" when condemning bad men is all the rage, to direct feminism away from punishment. There will always be horrific crime stories, but we will never incarcerate our way to gender equality and nonviolence. In short, I am asking feminists to recognize that mass criminalization is a paramount problem and to "turn the corner" on the feminist war on crime.

To be sure, recognizing the costs of feminist criminalization can leave the justice-minded feeling hopelessly adrift between toleration of private male violence and complicity with the penal state. Here I offer feminists a three-step path away from criminal law and toward noncarceral gender justice. The first step is to adopt a new theoretical framework, a "neofeminist" approach, that breaks from the orthodox thinking that entangled feminism with mass incarceration. This approach continues to prioritize countering gender violence but rejects feminism's victimization narrative, reliance on criminal authority, and prioritization of (white) women's interests over larger social equality. The second step is to withdraw support for existing and future carceral programs erected in the name of gender justice that produce neither gender equality nor justice. The third step is to redistribute feminist financial, academic, and political capital toward programs that address gender violence *and* counter mass incarceration. Here, I seek only to point feminists in a better direction, not to offer blueprints.

I have previously described "neofeminism" as a new feminism that continues to focus on the problem of women's subordination but is freed from the liberalism, essentialism, and authoritarianism of past movements.[11] Once we see gender violence as part of a complex matrix of intersecting hierarchies, we can move past the instinctive desire to just punish men. The presumption that DV and rape are a matter of what bad men do to innocent women has the effect of rendering "imperfect" victims—victims who stay with abusers, women who engage in sex work, women with their own criminal histories— unworthy of society's concern and aid. A neofeminist approach rejects the dichotomy that women are either passive victims of male behavior or active agents responsible for their own plights. Neofeminism recognizes that women always navigate a complex world of social, cultural, and institutional constraints and make the best choices they can under the weight of oppressive conditions. There is no everywoman. Women's needs are ever-shifting and racially, culturally, and economically contextual.

Understanding the contextuality, complexity, and diversity of women's interests means that deciding on ex ante rules that "serve women" is tricky business. We have seen that feminists' preferred method has been to identify specific gender crimes that have gone unpunished and to propose stricter criminal laws that presumably would have prevented these crimes, much in the way that conservative politicians justified sex offender registration and notification laws. As feminists pushed for ever-stricter laws, they kept this backward-facing position, with an eye squarely trained on the past and the criminals in it. But this reactionary stance ignored some important facts about the operation of law. First, law does not operate linearly but is "embedded in noisy enforcement systems" with complex consequences.[12] In addition, a relentless focus on criminal law as the best, if not definitionally necessary, remedy to social harm obscures the reality that criminal law is also a primary *driver* of social harm.

Thus neofeminism replaces a backward-looking "formalist" approach to law with a forward-looking "distributional" approach where policy proponents contemplate the many interests involved and make evidence-informed predictions about how reform might distribute harms and benefits over time. Critical legal theorists like Jorge Esquirol sometimes describe the enterprise as looking beyond formal rules to the "winners and losers" of a given legal regime.[13] As theorist Janet Halley and coauthors explain in the book *Governance Feminism,* "Basically, you are trying to identify the consequences of a change you could introduce in the status quo, and to decide whether they are 'worth it.'"[14]

Mapping how legal intervention should shift advantages and disadvantages is both an empirical and a normative enterprise.[15] Unlike utilitarians who might see all interests as morally equal, feminists have particular commitments to distributive justice and substantive equality.[16] For feminists, the interests of majority actors (men/whites) in maintaining a monopoly on social and economic power are not coextensive with the interests of minorities (women/people of color) in freedom from subordination. However, instead of working in the mainstream feminist mode and assuming that every move against male power is a move in favor of female empowerment, distributional analysis asks us to examine the conflicts *and* convergences in men and women's interests.

Victims' and perpetrators' interests are not always zero-sum. For example, a battered woman's desire to be free from violence conflicts with her abuser's desire to batter. But as members of a socioeconomically marginalized group the couple may have convergent interests in economic security. As racial minorities they may have convergent interests in freedom from police overreach. As immigrants they may have convergent interests in stemming the tide of anti-immigrant fervor. Many victims and perpetrators have convergent interests in maintaining their marriage and family. Yet domestic violence law, in the name of women's interests, makes it easier for the state to arrest, deny low-income housing, deport immigrants, and impose de facto divorce.[17] Feminist reforms may work in favor of the woman in one area of conflict—abuse (though the punitive model does not necessarily reduce abuse)—but they also can work against her in several areas of convergence.

Finally, distributional analysis counsels that feminists understand that law reform takes place within a larger structural reality, of which patriarchy is only one component. Reforms affect individual interests, but they also reinforce social structures. Poverty, discrimination, and lack of social support are the structural conditions that render poor women of color particularly vulnerable to violence. Racism and pathological politics are the structural conditions that lead politicians to propose and the public to accept military-like repressive conditions in certain neighborhoods. Transphobia is the structural condition that forces trans people out of formal economies and into precarious and illegal forms of labor. Criminal discourses and reforms, with their preoccupation over individual wrongdoing and punishment, reinforce a carceral state that obscures and perpetuates these structural conditions.[18]

This brings us to step two and what not to do. Adopting a neofeminist point of view means resisting the impulse to sensationalize and criminalize the sexist behavior of the day. Women should, of course, protest behavior like sexual harassment, domestic violence, sexual misconduct, "revenge porn," and the like as harmful and subordinating to women. However, they should not characterize even these crimes as exclusive products of individual monstrous men who prey on vulnerable women and need to be caged away from society. Instead, feminists should focus on the cultural, social, and economic circumstances that underlie crimes against women, including patriarchy and sexism.

In recent years, "Yes means yes" became a chant-worthy feminist slogan and the preferred feminist approach to preventing sexual harm. As we saw in chapters 5 through 7, this standard bled out of the campus context into the criminal law, where it is likely to disparately affect minority men. At this very moment, someone is getting arrested, being charged, or going to jail for failing to obtain the requisite authorization for sex. The offender will go to jail, but young people will continue to engage in gendered sexual communication where men are aggressors and women are gatekeepers. Students will say, "Only yes means yes," but men will continue to subtly pressure, and women will continue to "give in."

The symbolic and punitive, but culturally ineffective, affirmative consent revolution has taken up and continues to take up countless hours of scholarly, legal, and activist efforts and has generated a ton of controversy. At the same time, most sexual assault experts have already agreed on a nonpunitive intervention to address sexual assault. Antirape activists, pro-sex feminists, and public defenders alike support "sexuality education" that teaches kids about sexual pleasure, their nascent sexual bodies, and sexual intimacy. Early (as in grade school) familiarity with sexual pleasure and sexual consent, according to experts, can help to prevent miscommunication and the use of alcohol to alleviate sexual anxiety.[19]

To be sure, getting universities, much less grade schools, to implement such sexuality education is truly an uphill battle in a country where a significant and vocal portion of the populace still equates sex with sin. Parents have an innate aversion toward viewing their children as erogenous actors, and they make it known to bureaucrats. Consider the Canadian experience. In 2015, progressive Canadian school administrators proposed a rigorous sexuality education program, including teaching consent, in grade school. The effort failed in the face of intense backlash from outraged parents, who took to the street in droves. Complicating matters, many of those parents were recent immigrants and religious and ethnic minorities, underscoring the tension between feminism and multiculturalism.[20] In the US, the Trump administration is waging war on sex ed, substituting abstinence indoctrination for meaningful instruction. And, as we discussed in chapter 5, this sexual miseducation revolution hides under the guise of mitigating "sexual assault risk."[21]

The sexuality education effort desperately needs the political heft that #MeToo brings. However, by focusing on "Yes means yes" and punitive regulation, millennial feminists may be undermining rather than furthering the educational effort. The Title IX regime has led to freshman orientations involving the ritualized repetition of "an enthusiastic yes."[22] These performances help schools demonstrate that they "take rape seriously." Parents approve of antirape education that counsels that sex is dangerous and should be performed only, if ever, under strict limitations (sober, scripted, within a stable relationship). Warning kids that rape is an ever-present danger with potentially devastating effects has become the new version of warning kids about the horrors of STDs and pregnancy. However, feminists who seek effective rape intervention should be wary. Such education hinders young people from becoming comfortable with sex—comfortable enough to understand their bodies, openly communicate, and forego pre-sex intoxication. Surely, antirape discourse that weaponizes men's sexual organs and regards women's bodies as territory vulnerable to "invasion" is the opposite of the vision of sexuality set forth by seasoned educators.[23]

Moreover, the modern antirape movement often treats sexual discourse as verbal harassment, a trauma trigger, and in extreme cases a "second rape." Educators are supposed to assume that a significant percentage of students are distressed sexual assault victims and to avoid discussions about sexuality and sexual assault, warn students about such discussions, or otherwise police the discussions.[24] However, as noted in chapter 6, trauma is complex, and triggers are unpredictable. No science substantiates that trigger warnings about the content of a discussion reduce trauma, let alone just reciting the phrase "trigger warning" before mentioning something sexual or rape related.[25] As one expert opined, "Requiring trigger warnings in university course syllabi seems a well-intentioned exercise in symbolic politics, in which the terminology of psychology has been enlisted, but its meaning lost."[26] And, in a disturbing twist, it is often pro-sex and anticarceral commentators who face charges of being triggerers. Antirape activists, by contrast, have license to describe sexual brutality in graphic detail—as in the retracted *Rolling Stone* article discussed in chapter 6. This political policing of sex dialogue, whether by feminists or moralists, makes educators afraid and thwarts sexuality education.[27]

"Yes means yes" laws are not the only criminal interventions embraced by the contemporary feminist generation. #MeToo has called for the criminalization of workplace sex, sexting, nonconsensual pornography, clandestine condom removal ("stealthing"), emotionally coercive relationships, and the list goes on. Most of these behaviors are undesirable and problematic, but a regime to seriously criminalize any one of them would have far-reaching distributional effects. My point here is not to go through each and show how criminal reform would harm the vulnerable and increase prison populations. Rather, I want to challenge the instinct that calling for criminalization is the only way to express disapproval of such misconduct. Sexting, bad internet behavior, and problematic relationships are all contemporary issues worthy of serious study, discussion, and intervention. However, for any nuanced and considered dialogue to occur, we need to go beyond the knee jerk impulse to criminalize and incarcerate.

In short, I am asking feminists to adopt an unconditional stance against criminalization, no matter the issue. As famed prison abolitionist Thomas Mathiesen observed, "stance" is important: *"Abolitionism is a stance. It is the attitude of saying 'no.'* This does mean that the 'no' will be answered affirmatively in practice. A 'no' to prisons will not occur in our time, though it may be a guiding ideal for the future. But as a guiding ideal it easily becomes vague and distanced from concrete political commitment. However, as a stance it is viable and important, and it may be quite concrete. [The stance is] a constant and deeply critical attitude to prisons and penal systems as human (and inhumane) solutions."[28] I am asking feminists to stand against the powerful temptation to work within the prison complex—a temptation that often accompanies the sincere desire to combat gender violence.

Mathieson counsels that contemporary intervention into criminal law should come as "negative reform" that dials back arrests, convictions, and sentences.[29] There are indeed many examples throughout this book where "positive" efforts to transform, even soften, the criminal law from within end up fueling the prosecutorial machine. "Better" has come at the expense of "less." As Mathiesen argues, "Rather than helping in constructing 'alternatives' which actually become add-ons to the prison solution, we should see it as our task to strive towards 'shrinking' the system."[30] Indeed, the Trump administration scuttled the aforementioned 2015 Sentencing Act by championing an alternative bill, the "First Step Act," which called for "back-end" prison reforms like good time credit, education, and reintegration. This move prompted the Sentencing Act's sponsor, Iowa Republican Grassley, to write a scathing op-ed on FoxNews.com stating, "The notion that Congress can enact meaningful criminal justice reform by focusing solely on the back-end of the process without addressing the underlying disparities in prison sentencing is naïve and unproductive."[31]

Understanding the dangers of collaborating with the penal state means that sometimes the best thing to do is nothing—to live with the problem rather than invoking a state solution. But millennial feminists are part of a "do something" generation that came of age in an era of renewed activism and protest. Punishing the bad guys and taking down the powerful are agenda items that resonate with this generation. Many imagine that criminalization is "doing something" to produce justice for women. However, the criminal system generally punishes the poor and the powerless and is particularly impotent to dismantle entrenched power structures. Understanding that policing, prosecution, and punishment are largely fixed institutions, with embedded authoritarian and racialized features, shatters the illusion that throwing criminal law at the gender issue du jour is an exercise in gender justice.

So, this brings us to the last step and our last question. How can feminists actively pursue gender justice *and* the end of the American prison state? In the fall of 2018, I spoke at a conference at Harvard Law School, "Fighting the (Q)arceral State," organized by an inspiring group of law students and activists from Lambda Legal, an LGBT rights organization. The attendees were diverse in every sense. They were female and male, gay and straight, trans, cis, and nonbinary. They spanned races, ethnicities, and socioeconomic backgrounds. Many of the conference participants were trans people of color. Now, statistically, trans people of color are victims of private violence at a higher rate than any other demographic group. As a group, they have much to lose in a system that enables gender crime. At the same time, sexual and racial minorities are particularly vulnerable to state brutality and police overreach. This tension, however, has not rendered the students and activists paralyzed by their dilemma like the radical feminists of the 1970s, who abhorred both domestic abuse and the "fascist" police. The students are organizing against gender violence *and* state violence. They know that the neoliberal penal system entrenches marginalized people's vulnerability to private and governmental harm. They know that people without medical, social, mental health, shelter, and child care services are quick to call the police—the only state agency they know of—for aid. They also know that the police intervention often hurts rather than helps marginalized people.

My portion of the conference program involved presenting ideas from this book. I was unsurprisingly asked what we should do next—how feminism could come back from the abyss. I answered as an academic, not an activist. "This book," I said, "can give you a rhetorical tool kit, understanding of history, and theoretical framework to use while you go out and change the world." A couple days later, I received an email that organizers D Dangaran and Anna Nathanson sent to all conference participants. It read, "Thank you so much for joining us for the conference. The passion, the collective knowledge in the room was palpable. But no conference makes life better for people on the inside. This is just the beginning. We must take what we learned, continue to educate ourselves, and ACT!"[32] The email provided a list of action items including protesting corporate investment in the prison industrial complex, taking "action in support of trans people in the wake of the accursed [Trump] memo" that seeks to define trans people out of existence, becoming active in sex worker support, and speaking "to 3 friends or friend members about alternatives to calling the police. . . . Do it now before it's your mom on the news for siccing the cops on a homeless person."[33] The list provided links to local organizations like Black Lives Matter Boston, Sisters Unchained, and Black & Pink Boston.[34]

In the spirit of D's and Anna's "do something" email, let me mention some movements I hope will capture millennial feminist attention as #MeToo has. Millennial feminists should take the policing and prison abolition movement seriously. This does not necessarily mean becoming an anti-incarceration activist, although this could be a good outlet for abundant political energy. It means adopting a firm "stance" against policing, prosecution, and punishment as the preferred solution to gender inequality.

The idea of prison abolition has occupied a prominent place in criminology for decades, especially in Europe. Indeed, Mathiesen wrote "The Politics of Abolition" in 1974. Back then, he believed he "would personally experience the day when prisons were abolished, or at least drastically reduced in size and number."[35] However, in 1986, he noticed a curious phenomenon. As the neoliberal tough-on-crime ideology swept the US and Europe and prison populations began to increase exponentially, social scientists "turn[ed] away from the goal of abolition—more or less as if it were a youthful and confused prank from the late sixties which the middle aged and wise can hardly uphold."[36] In the 1980s, it became increasingly clear "that prisons are a part of the State's apparatus for political repression."[37] This should have led social scientists to redouble their abolitionist theorizing efforts. Instead, they lapsed into "disillusionment and despair."[38]

Today, however, there is a renewed appetite for the abolitionist stance. In 2015, the National Lawyers Guild—the Federalist Society of the Left—adopted a resolution in support of prison abolition. NLG vice president Sharlyn Grace explained, "Calling for the abolition of this profit-motivated system that is designed to maintain racial and economic inequality while relying on individualized punishment as a primary response to social problems falls directly within our mission of protecting human rights over property interests."[39] Young activists' dissatisfaction with repressive Trump-era policies and policing practices ignited movements like Black Lives Matter and "Abolish ICE." Within this ethic, the notion of prison abolition began to trend online and in millennial and gen-Z discourse. These are "not just old Marxist philosophers or Norwegian criminologists [like Mathiesen] but rather a group of young, mostly black lawyers, academics, artists, authors and community organizers," one reporter observed.[40] Alexandra Ocasio-Cortez, a Democratic political star and the youngest woman ever elected to Congress as of November 2018, wrote an online essay linking her Catholic values to prison reform. She encouraged readers to "embrac[e] a growing private prison abolition movement that urges us to reconsider the levels at which the United States pursues mass incarceration."[41]

Still, many consider abolition a worthy, if vague, ideal, so long as we do not actually stop arresting criminals or release all prisoners. Most "reasonable" people regard serious depolicing and decarceration as too radical and fraught with risk, while they pay no mind to the mass incarceration–driven crime, poverty, and dysfunction that they are currently living with. I recall having a discussion with my father several years ago about police brutality and saying that body cameras are not a solution. "Then what is?" he demanded. I replied that cities should drastically decrease the number of officers or should direct officers generally not to stop, frisk, or arrest. Not a very detailed plan, I'll admit. My dad, an erstwhile sixties liberal, replied indignantly, "But if there are no police or arrests, there will be anarchy!" This is not unlike feminists' presumption that without strict DV and rape policing and punishment, there will be an epidemic—or a bigger epidemic—of gender violence.

However, some recent natural experiments dictate otherwise. At the time I had the conversation with my dad, litigation in *Floyd v. City of New York* was well under way. In 2008, the Center for Constitutional Rights filed a class action lawsuit on behalf of thousands of minorities subjected to arbitrary and discriminatory stop-and-frisks by the police. The litigation revealed that stop-and-frisk policies applied disproportionately to blacks and Latinos (who constituted 85 percent of detainees), that many stops lacked any basis for suspicion, and that they were wholly ineffective at uncovering criminal behavior. On August 12, 2013, after years of legal wrangling, federal district court judge Shira Scheindlin issued a historic opinion finding that the NYPD's stop-and-frisk practices violated individuals' Fourth Amendment rights against unreasonable search and seizure and Fourteenth Amendment right to equal protection.[42] The city appealed, and the court of appeals promptly stayed Sheindlin's decision, removed her from the case, citing a proplaintiff bias, and sent the case to a different district court judge.[43]

Then, on January 1, 2014, newly elected mayor Bill DeBlasio, a liberal Democrat, took office. On January 30, he announced that the city would withdraw the appeal and work with the Center for Constitutional Rights to resolve the issue. "We believe in ending the overuse of stop-and-frisk that has unfairly targeted young African-American and Latino men," DeBlasio stated.[44] The stop-and-frisk litigation and its political resolution had a profound effect on policing in New York City. Stop-and-frisks went from a high of approximately 686,000 in 2011 to 11,000 in 2017, a *98 percent* decrease.[45] Far from lapsing into anarchy, the city in 2017 had a crime rate (as determined by CompStat) 17 percent *lower* than its rate in 2011.[46] For decades, New Yorkers had accepted invasive and racist stop-and-frisks under the false presumption that aggressive law enforcement reduced crime.

On July 8, 2016, during a Dallas protest against police killings of unarmed black men, a disgruntled black army vet shot and killed five officers. A few days later, Fox News anchor Megyn Kelly convened a panel of speakers on either side of the Black Lives Matter/Blue Lives Matter divide. In the midst of a very heated discussion, Chicago area activist Jessica Disu mentioned abolishing the police. Disu elaborated, "Demilitarize the police, disarm the police. We need to come up with community solutions for transformative justice." Through audience gasps and a smattering of boos, Kelly replied incredulously, "Who's gonna protect the community if we abolish the police?"[47] The clip of Disu calling for police abolition went viral, garnering over thirty million hits in a month. Disu became the target of threats and trolling, but social media commentators' attempts to ridicule her betrayed their deep sense of panic at her idea.[48] Had Disu been able to answer Kelly's intended rhetorical question over the din, she could have said, "I am."

A 2016 article in *Chicago Reader* profiled Disu and the other women of color at the forefront of Chicago's police abolition movement. In 2015, Tamar Mannaseh established "Mothers Against Senseless Killing" in reaction to yet another killing in her Englewood neighborhood. She and other moms would go to the hotspot street corner every day and set up a barbecue. Kids and adults lined up for the goodies. "It's about cop watching, it's about people watching, but more than anything it's about being seen, being a presence in the community," she told *Reader*. "Nobody wants to come through here shooting if they see 50 kids outside waiting to eat dinner." Mannaseh related an incident where a man had pulled out a gun and she and others had defused the situation without the police. "If we hadn't been here that would have ended so badly," she recalled. Twenty-two-year-old resident Jermaine Kelly noted the difference that Mannaseh had made. "We have our set of gang-bangers here, but their opposition, their rival gangs, don't even ride past when she's here," he remarked. He added that normally on the corner, the police "might jump out and harass us, search us," but now they simply drove past. Kelly summed it up, "Which is better, to be loved or to be feared? And right now love is winning." The article author tried to contact the president of the Chicago Fraternal Order of Police for a comment. She reached his assistant, who laughed: "I doubt he'll want to comment on something so stupid."[49]

Mannaseh's intervention could easily be characterized as a feminist one. She and her "army of moms" substituted their community-oriented interventions for masculinist, hierarchical policing. Nevertheless, many millennial feminists want to fight men's private violence directly, and they might not be satisfied with the broader abolitionist agenda. For them, there are several groups active in the direct fight against DV and sexual assault, but through noncriminal means. The collective "INCITE!," for example, "is a network of radical feminists of color organizing to end state violence and violence in our homes and communities," and its website is a great clearinghouse of information on this brand of activism.[50]

Now in its twentieth year, INCITE! recognized decades ago that violence against women cannot be addressed through state criminal intervention or just through abolitionist efforts to reduce state violence. In 2001, INCITE! issued a "Statement on Gender Violence and the Prison Industrial Complex."

The first part reads like a bill of particulars against the feminist–criminal law alliance. The statement implores: "It is critical that we develop responses to gender violence that do not depend on a sexist, racist, classist, and homophobic criminal justice system. It is also important that we develop strategies that challenge the criminal justice system and that also provide safety for survivors of sexual and domestic violence. To live violence-free lives, we must develop holistic strategies for addressing violence that speak to the intersection of all forms of oppression."[51]

At the same time, the statement expresses skepticism about the "antiprison" movement's commitment to ending DV and rape. Until the movement sets forth strategies "for addressing the rampant forms of violence women face in their everyday lives," it opines, "many women will feel shortchanged." The statement also questions the antiprison movement's complacency in the face of a sexist status quo. The movement's "alternatives," it argues, "often rely on a romanticized notion of communities, which have yet to . . . seriously address the sexism and homophobia that is deeply embedded within them." INCITE! thus calls on activists to "develop community-based responses to violence that do not rely on the criminal justice system AND which have mechanisms that ensure safety and accountability for survivors of sexual and domestic violence." One way is to concentrate on gender violence survivors who are currently in the prison system. Another is to support community programs, social services, and financial programs that target violence but do not involve police intervention or engage in criminal-victim discourses.[52]

In the end, we may never see the day when prisons have been largely abolished, meaningful sex education and community interventions have drastically reduced rape and DV, and police have become friendly security and service providers. But if you had told me in 2011 that six years later stop-and-frisks in New York City would be down 98 percent and Chuck Grassley would be championing a bill to reduce sentences, I would not have believed you. Yes, criminal policies are embedded in local politics, bureaucratic paralysis, and entrenched special interests. Nevertheless, the #MeToo movement has shown us in no uncertain terms that millennial feminists have the power to change things, and quickly.

The punitive nature of feminists' past DV and rape reform efforts is largely a product of a failure of imagination. Focusing rigidly on individual men's bad acts produced myopia on how criminalization would affect the larger and longer quest for gender and other equality. Feminist theorists Ellen DuBois and Linda Gordon once remarked that as feminists advanced through the minefield of sex and politics, they were so busy "looking only to [their] feet to avoid the mines" that they may have "miss[ed] the horizon and the vision of why the advance is worthwhile."[53] Feminists' important crusade for gender justice collapsed into simple carceral politics precisely because it was and remains so difficult to imagine a world where criminal law does not rule the roost. But we must imagine it otherwise. To quote another Norwegian criminologist, Nils Christie, "The size of the prison population is a result of decisions. We are free to choose. It is only when we are not aware of this freedom that the economic/material conditions are given free [rein]."[54]

It is time for feminists to choose.

NOTES

INTRODUCTION

1. I wrote a paper as a law student discussing this dilemma. See Aya Gruber, "Pink Elephants in the Rape Trial: The Problem of Tort-Type Defenses in the Criminal Law of Rape," *William and Mary Journal of Women and the Law* 4 (1997): 206.

2. This narrative is adapted from Aya Gruber, "The Feminist War on Crime," *Iowa Law Review* 92, no. 3 (March 2007): 742–47, 830–33. I changed the name and characteristics of the actual people involved for privacy. The events up until the issuing of the civil protection order happened in Jamal's case, and the post-trial events are an amalgam of events in that and other DV cases.

3. See D.C. Code Ann. § 16–1005(c) (West 2001) (CPO section of the D.C. Code that was in effect); District of Columbia Courts, *Final Report of the Task Force on Racial and Ethnic Bias and Task Force on Gender Bias in the Courts* (Washington, DC: District of Columbia Courts, 1992), 143, reporting that 70 percent of respondents in protection order hearings are unrepresented.

4. See D.C. Code Ann. § 16–1031 (West 2001) (mandatory arrest statute).

5. See Crawford v. Washington, 541 U.S. 36, 68 (2004).

6. See Deborah Epstein, Margret E. Bell, and Lisa E. Goodman, "Transforming Aggressive Prosecution Policies: Prioritizing Victims' Long-Term Safety in the Prosecution of Domestic Violence Cases," *American University Journal of Gender, Social Policy, and the Law* 11, no. 2 (2003): 469, describing DV plea-bargaining process in DC.

7. Sex Crimes: Mandatory Prison Sentence, A.B. 2888, 2016 Leg., Reg. Sess. (Cal. 2016), https://perma.cc/3CCG-NWZJ; An Act Relating to the Criminal Offenses of Domestic Abuse and Unauthorized Placement of a Global Positioning System, and Providing Penalties, H.F. 263, 87th Gen. Assembly (Iowa 2017), https://www.legis.iowa.gov/perma/103020194268.

8. Aya Gruber, "Corroboration Is Not Required," *Hill*, October 3, 2018, https://perma.cc/J8R2-8GQ2.

9. Elizabeth Bernstein, "The Sexual Politics of the 'New Abolitionism,'" *Differences: A Journal of Feminist Cultural Studies* 18, no. 3 (2007): 128–51.

10. Brown v. Plata, 563 U.S. 493, 502 (2011).

11. Michelle Alexander, *The New Jim Crow: Mass Incarceration in the Age of Colorblindness* (New York: New Press, 2010); see also Jennifer Chernega, "Black Lives Matter: Racialised Policing in the United States," *Comparative American Studies: An International Journal* 14, nos. 3–4 (2016): 234–45.

12. Benjamin Levin, "The Consensus Myth in Criminal Justice Reform," *Michigan Law Review* 117, no. 2 (November 2018): 307.

13. Beth E. Richie, *Arrested Justice: Black Women, Violence, and America's Prison Nation* (New York: New York University Press, 2012).

14. Leigh Goodmark, *A Troubled Marriage: Domestic Violence and the Legal System* (New York: New York University Press, 2011).

15. Amanda Hess, "Emma Sulkowicz Inspired Students across the Country to Carry Their Mattresses. Now What?," *Slate: The XX Factor,* October 30, 2014, https://perma.cc/9VFE-JRPC.

16. Ronan Farrow, "From Aggressive Overtures to Sexual Assault: Harvey Weinstein's Accusers Tell Their Stories," *New Yorker,* October 23, 2017, https://perma.cc/3W52-F48U.

17. Rachel Lubitz, "Dior Is Selling a Plain Cotton T-Shirt That Says 'We Should All Be Feminists' for $710," *Business Insider,* March 17, 2017, https://perma.cc/5RXL-9EXN.

18. Samantha Cotter, "I'm Voting to Increase Sexual Assault Education in America," *Teen Vogue,* October 31, 2018, https://perma.cc/2VKB-MXK5.

19. Sheila Weller, "#MeToo's Generational Divide," *Time,* March 12, 2018, https://perma.cc/7PPU-8SD6.

20. See Aya Gruber, "When Theory Met Practice: Distributional Analysis in Critical Criminal Law Theorizing," *Fordham Law Review* 83 (May 2015): 3222; Aya Gruber, "Race to Incarcerate: Punitive Impulse and the Bid to Repeal Stand Your Ground," *University of Miami Law Review* 68 (Summer 2014): 961–1023.

21. Estelle B. Freedman, *Redefining Rape: Sexual Violence in the Era of Suffrage and Segregation* (Cambridge, MA: Harvard University Press, 2013), 2.

22. See "'Drug Dealers, Criminals, Rapists': What Trump Thinks of Mexicans," BBC News, video, August 31, 2016, https://perma.cc/6L86-65JV, for rapist comment; see Veronica Stracqualursi and Elizabeth Landers, "Trump Claims Female Migrants 'Are Raped at Levels That Nobody Has Ever Seen Before,'" CNN, April 5, 2018, https://perma.cc/Z77A-74D3, for caravan comment.

23. Elizabeth Nolan Brown, "NBC Didn't Fire Matt Lauer. We Did," *New York Times,* November 29, 2017, https://perma.cc/NZ7D-Q3MU.

24. Brown, "NBC."

25. Tarana Burke, "Purpose," Just Be, Inc., n.d., accessed October 31, 2018, https://perma.cc/PTX9-PFSE.

26. Tarana Burke, "The Inception," Just Be, Inc., n.d., accessed October 31, 2018, https://perma.cc/KVE5-VCGW.

27. Farrow, "From Aggressive Overtures."

28. Alyssa Milano (@Alyssa_Milano), "If you've been sexually harassed or assaulted, write 'me too' as a reply to this tweet," Twitter, October 15, 2017, https://perma.cc/VG4P-S7WW.

29. Milano, "If you've been sexually harassed," comments below tweet.

30. Felicia Gans, "Matt Damon Faces Backlash after Saying There's a 'Spectrum' When It Comes to Allegations of Sexual Misconduct," *Boston Globe,* January 15, 2018, https://perma.cc/3Y53-H24F.

31. Edward Helmore, "Minnie Driver: Men Like Matt Damon 'Cannot Understand What Abuse Is Like,'" *Guardian,* December 17, 2017, https://perma.cc/CN7B-NKX5.

32. Martha Ross, "Maybe Matt Damon Has Finally Learned to Stop Saying Stupid Things about #MeToo and So Much Else," *Mercury News,* January 17, 2018, https://perma.cc/X54E-4WJH.

33. Zahara Hill, "A Black Woman Created the 'Me Too' Campaign against Sexual Assault 10 Years Ago," *Ebony,* October 18, 2017, https://perma.cc/CJP2-CE89.

34. Naomi Alderman, "The Deep Confusion of the Post-Weinstein Moment," *New York Times,* November 6, 2017, https://perma.cc/CLX5-ZKWF.

35. "Babe Is for Girls Who Don't Give a Fuck," Babe.net, n.d., accessed October 31, 2018, https://babe.net/manifesto.

36. Kerry Flynn, "What Is Babe? Meet the Site That Published the Aziz Ansari Allegation," *Mashable,* January 15, 2018, https://perma.cc/AE8T-BDMU.

37. Katie Way, "I Went on a Date with Aziz Ansari. It Turned into the Worst Night of My Life," Babe.net, January 14, 2018, https://perma.cc/GD5X-P3MH.

38. Way, "I Went."

39. Way, "I Went."

40. Emily Stewart, "Aziz Ansari Responds to Sexual Misconduct Allegations against Him," *Vox,* January 15, 2018, https://perma.cc/22MZ-EUQL.

41. Caitlin Flanagan, "The Humiliation of Aziz Ansari," *Atlantic,* January 14, 2018, https://perma.cc/9X5E-DDAS.

42. Ashleigh Banfield, "Banfield Slams Ansari Accuser in Open Letter," CNN, video, 3:30; 4:18, n.d., accessed October 31, 2018, https://perma.cc/6A2X-YPX3.

43. Maxwell Tani, "Read the Email the Writer behind the Aziz Ansari Sexual Misconduct Story Wrote Slamming an HLN Anchor Who Criticized Her," *Business Insider,* January 17, 2018, https://perma.cc/B3FR-GJY9.

44. Tani, "Read the Email."

45. Kirsten Gillibrand, "We Will Not Allow These Crimes to Be Swept under the Rug Any Longer," *Time,* May 15, 2014, https://perma.cc/CD4E-5TTE.

46. Doe v. University of Denver, Civil Action No. 16-cv-00152-PAB-KMT, deposition of Title IX investigator (on file with author). See also "Prohibited Sexual Conduct: Sexual Misconduct, Sexual Assault, Stalking, Relationship Violence, Violation of University or Court Directives, Student-on-Student Sexual Harassment and Retaliation," Stanford University, March 11, 2016, https://perma.cc

/N9BZ-JDMS ("It is the responsibility of person(s) involved in sexual activity to ensure that he/she/they have the affirmative consent of the other").

47. I discuss affirmative consent in detail in chapter 5, in the section "Managing Myths."

48. See, for example, Mona Charen, "Real Message of #Metoo: The Sexual Revolution Has Not Been Kind to Women," *National Review,* January 18, 2018, https://perma.cc/6YDW-7L7Z.

49. Vicki Schultz, "The Sanitized Workplace," *Yale Law Journal* 112 (2003): 2061–2193.

50. For example, I use *prostitute, sex worker,* and even *women engaged in commercial sex,* although they are all loaded and imperfect terms. I hope I can convey my view that abused women and women engaged in commercial sex are neither total objects of male domination nor atomistic free agents happily choosing to sell sex. They necessarily make choices under personal, social, cultural, and economic constraint.

51. See Donna Coker, "Crime Logic, Campus Sexual Assault, and Restorative Justice," *Texas Tech Law Review* 49 (Fall 2016): 147, 150. I discuss the elements of this logic in chapter 2, in the section "Leniency versus Women's Liberation."

1. THE OPENING BATTLE

1. I discuss the history of chastisement in chapter 3, in the section "Of Neanderthal Cops."

2. Marybeth Hamilton Arnold, "The Life of a Citizen in the Hands of a Woman: Sexual Assault in New York City, 1790–1820," in *Passion and Power: Sexuality in History,* ed. Kathy Lee Peiss and Christina Simmons (Philadelphia: Temple University Press, 1989), 36.

3. See Estelle B. Freedman, *Redefining Rape: Sexual Violence in the Era of Suffrage and Segregation* (Cambridge, MA: Harvard University Press: 2013), 9, arguing that first-wave rape reform is not a story of either "unremitting progress" or a "failed reform movement."

4. See Kinselle v. People, 227 P. 823, 825 (Colo. 1924); People v. Geddes, 3 N.W.2d 266, 267 (Mich. 1942).

5. Matthew Hale, *The History of the Pleas of the Crown,* vol. 1 (Philadelphia: Robert Small, 1847), 635 (Lord Hale instruction).

6. See Michelle J. Anderson, "The Legacy of the Prompt Complaint Requirement, Corroboration Requirement, and Cautionary Instructions on Campus Sexual Assault," *Boston University Law Review* 84, no. 4 (October 2004): 947–48.

7. Fresh complaint transformed the long-defunct "hue and cry" rule requiring victims to alert authorities of felonies into a rule about rape victims' incredibility. State v. Hill, 578 A.2d 370, at 375 (N.J., 1990).

8. Susan Brownmiller, *Against Our Will: Men, Women and Rape* (New York: Ballantine Books, 1975), 369.

9. U.S. v. Wiley, 492 F.2d 547, 550 (D.C. Cir. 1974), citing Coltrane v. U.S., 135 U.S. App. D.C. 295, 418 F.2d 1131, 1135 (1969). See also Allison v. United States, 409 F.2d 445, 449 n.10 (D.C. Cir. 1969)

10. Wiley, 492 F.2d 547.

11. For example, People v. Johnson, 168 N.W.2d 634, 634 (Mich. App. 1969); People v. Warren, 24 A.D.2d 664, 664 (NY 1965).

12. See Anderson, "Legacy"; Brownmiller, *Against Our Will.*

13. David P. Bryden and Erica Madore, "Patriarchy, Sexual Freedom, and Gender Equality as Causes of Rape," *Ohio State Journal of Criminal Law* 13, no. 2 (2016): 331, quoting Lyle Koehler, "A Search for Power: The 'Weaker Sex' in Seventeenth Century New England (Urbana: University of Illinois Press, 1980), 28.

14. See Jill Elaine Hasday, "Contest and Consent: A Legal History of Marital Rape," *California Law Review* 88, no. 5 (October 2000): 1373–1505; John D'Emilio and Estelle Freedman, *Intimate Matters: A History of Sexuality in America* (Chicago: University of Chicago Press, 1988), 27–38.

15. State v. Johnson, 133 N.W. 115, 116 (Iowa 1911).

16. For example, Tex. Penal Code § 1220 (Vernon 1936) ("Homicide is justifiable when committed by the husband upon one taken in the act of adultery with the wife"). See also George Wilfred Stumberg, "Defense of Person and Property under Texas Criminal Law," *Texas Law Review* 21 (1942–43): 35.

17. See Saul M. Kassin, "On the Psychology of Confessions: Does Innocence Put Innocents at Risk?," *American Psychologist* 60, no. 3 (April 2005), https://perma.cc/6J6A-N5EA.

18. See C. S. Wheatley, annotation, *Right to and Propriety of Instruction as to Credibility of Defendant in Criminal Case as a Witness,* 85 A.L.R. 523 (2004).

19. See Anne M. Coughlin, "Sex and Guilt," *Virginia Law Review* 84, no. 1 (February 1998): 8; see also Donald A. Dripps, "Beyond Rape: An Essay on the Difference between the Presence of Force and the Absence of Consent," *Columbia Law Review* 92 (1992): 1781–83.

20. Hale, *History of the Pleas,* 635–36.

21. Hale, *History of the Pleas,* 635–36.

22. Arnold, "Life of a Citizen," 38–50. See also McQuirk v. State, 84 Ala. 435, 438 (Ala. 1887) ("A woman who is chaste and virtuous will be less likely to consent to an act of illicit carnal intercourse than one who is unchaste"); Herndon v. State, 56 So. 85, 87 (Ala. Ct. App. 1991) ("It is competent to impeach the general character of a prosecutrix for chastity").

23. Freedman, *Redefining Rape,* 16.

24. Mary Wollstonecraft, *A Vindication of the Rights of Woman, with Strictures on Political and Moral Subjects* (Dublin: College-Green Press, 1793), 87–88.

25. Freedman, *Redefining Rape,* 34.

26. Elizabeth Cady Stanton, *A History of Woman Suffrage,* vol. 1 (Rochester, NY: Fowler and Wells, 1889), 70–71.

27. Ian Tyrrell, *Woman's World/Woman's Empire: The Woman's Christian Temperance Union in International Perspective, 1880–1930* (Chapel Hill: University of North Carolina Press, 2014), 232.

28. Tyrell, *Woman's World/Woman's Empire,* 231–41.

29. Kenneth D. Rose, *American Women and the Repeal of Prohibition* (New York: New York University Press, 1997), 159n63; Jessica R. Pliley, *Policing Sexuality: The Mann Act and the Making of the FBI* (Cambridge, MA: Harvard University Press, 2014), 21.

30. Ruth Bordin, *Woman and Temperance: The Quest for Power and Liberty, 1873–1900* (Philadelphia: Temple University Press, 1981), 3–4.

31. Susan B. Anthony, "Social Purity," speech delivered at the Grand Opera House, Chicago, March 14, 1895, https://perma.cc/RBE8-TJ88.

32. Anthony, "Social Purity." Compare with Mary Jo Buhle and Paul Buhle, introduction to *The Concise History of Woman Suffrage,* ed. Mary Jo Buhle and Paul Buhle (Urbana: University of Illinois Press, 1978), 21, who note that suffrage advocates like Anthony never constructed a "grand alliance" with working women's groups.

33. See Ruth Bordin, *Frances Willard: A Biography* (Chapel Hill: University of North Carolina Press, 1986), 45–47, citing Carroll Smith-Rosenberg, "The Female World of Love and Ritual: Relations between Women in Nineteenth-Century America," *Signs* 1, no. 1 (Autumn 1975) (describing the "homosocial" framework). See also Eric Burns, *The Spirits of America: A Social History of Alcohol* (Philadelphia: Temple University Press 2004), 124.

34. Jane Addams, *The Spirit of Youth and the City Streets* (New York: Macmillan, 1910), 21.

35. John Dillon, *From Dance Hall to White Slavery: The World's Greatest Tragedy* (Chicago: C. C. Thompson, 1912), 8.

36. Dillon, "From Dance Hall."

37. Mae C. Quinn, "From Turkey Trot to Twitter: Policing Puberty, Purity, and Sex-Positivity," *New York University Review of Law and Social Change* 38, no. 1 (May 2014): 66–72.

38. Reva B. Siegel, "'The Rule of Love': Wife Beating as Prerogative and Privacy," *Yale Law Journal* 105, no. 8 (June 1996): 2127.

39. Mary E. Odem, *Delinquent Daughters: Protecting and Policing Adolescent Female Sexuality in the United States, 1885–1920* (Chapel Hill: University of North Carolina Press, 1995), 14–15, counting statutes.

40. Jane E. Larson, "Even a Worm Will Turn at Last: Rape Reform in Late Nineteenth-Century America," *Yale Journal of Law and the Humanities* 9, no. 1 (January 1997): 71.

41. Larson, "Even a Worm," 65.

42. Larson, "Even a Worm," 66.

43. Larson, "Even a Worm."

44. Frederick Martin Lehman, *The White Slave Hell, or, with Christ at Midnight in the Slums of Chicago* (Chicago: Christian Witness, 1910), 57.

45. Lehman, *White Slave Hell,* 76.

46. John Ashworth, *Strange Tales from a Humble Life* (London: William Bremner, 1863), 4.

47. Pliley, *Policing Sexuality,* 15.

48. Pliley, *Policing Sexuality.*

49. Pliley, *Policing Sexuality.*

50. *New York Daily Tribune,* Friday, September 29, 1854, 4, col. 4, https://perma.cc/F6HN-YL25.

51. George Anthony Peffer, *If They Don't Bring Their Women Here: Chinese Female Immigration before Exclusion* (Urbana: University of Illinois Press, 1999), 79, quoting the *San Francisco Call,* August 25, 1877.

52. Yong Chen, *Chinese in San Francisco, 1850–1943* (Stanford, CA: Stanford University Press, 2000), 86.

53. Chen, *Chinese in San Francisco,* 86. See also Kerry Abrams, "Polygamy, Prostitution, and the Federalization of Immigration Law," *Columbia Law Review* 105, no. 3 (April 2005): 693n330; US Senate, *Report of the Joint Committee to Investigate Chinese Immigration,* 44th Cong., 2d sess., 1877, S. Rep. 689, 14–15, 651–52 (statements of Toland).

54. Peggy Pascoe, *Relations of Rescue: The Search for Female Moral Authority in the American West, 1874–1939* (Oxford: Oxford University Press, 1990), 95.

55. US Senate, *Report,* 148.

56. US Senate, *Report.*

57. Abrams, "Prostitution and Immigration Law," 658.

58. Abrams, "Prostitution and Immigration Law."

59. Abrams, "Prostitution and Immigration Law," 664, quoting 1873–74 Acts Amendatory of the Codes of California § 70, at 39.

60. Abrams, "Prostitution and Immigration Law," 685, quoting Sucheng Chan, "The Exclusion of Chinese Women, 1870–1943," in *Entry Denied: Exclusion and the Chinese Community in America, 1882–1943,* ed. Sucheng Chen (Philadelphia: Temple University Press, 1991), 100, citing *Alta California,* August 28, 1874.

61. Abrams, "Prostitution and Immigration Law."

62. Abrams, "Prostitution and Immigration Law," quoting "A Cargo of Infamy," *San Francisco Chronicle,* August 28, 1874, 3.

63. In re Ah Fong, 1 F. Cas. 213 (C.C.D. Cal. 1874) at 218.

64. Page Act, ch. 141, 18 Stat. 477 (1875) (repealed 1974).

65. Abrams, "Prostitution and Immigration Law," 694.

66. 43 Cong. Rec. Appx. at 44 (1875).

67. Abrams, "Prostitution and Immigration Law," 698.

68. Chinese Exclusion Act, ch. 126, 22 Stat. 58 (1882).

69. Eithne Luibhéid, *Entry Denied: Controlling Sexuality at the Border* (Minneapolis: University of Minnesota Press, 2002), 32.

70. Pascoe, *Relations of Rescue,* 97–98.

71. Pliley, *Policing Sexuality*, 19.

72. Pliley, *Policing Sexuality*.

73. 5 Cong. Rec. H548 (daily ed. January 12, 1910) (statement of Rep. Mann).

74. Mann Act, chs. 393–395, 36. Stat. 825a (1910) (amended May 29, 2015, at 18 USCS § 2421(a)).

75. See Danny Hakim and William K. Rashbaum, "No Federal Prostitution Charges for Spitzer," *New York Times,* November 6, 2008, https://perma.cc /S8T8-DXYV.

76. 5 Cong. Rec. H547 daily ed. January 12, 1910) (statement of Rep. Mann).

77. U.S. v. Holte, 236 U.S. 140 (1915), 145.

78. U.S. v. Holte, 236 U.S. 140 (1915), 145.

79. Marie Gottshalk, *The Prison and the Gallows: The Politics of Mass Incarceration in America* (Cambridge: Cambridge University Press, 2006), 50–60.

80. Jessica R. Pliley, "Why Is It Congress Seems Concerned with Families Only When Sex Trafficking Is at Issue?," *George Washington University History News Network,* December 7, 2014, https://perma.cc/6NZM-JTHW.

81. Larson, "Even a Worm," 65.

82. Quinn, "Turkey Trot," 74.

83. Pliley, *Policing Sexuality,* 101–3; ESPN.Com News Services, "Jack Johnson Pardoned for Violation of Mann Act in 1913," ABC News, May 24, 2018, https:// perma.cc/W7MX-9VZT.

84. Siegel, "Rule of Love," 2136–37.

85. Freedman, *Redefining Rape,* 27.

86. See Dorothy Roberts, "The Paradox of Silence and Display: Sexual Violation of Enslaved Women and Contemporary Contradictions in Black Female Sexuality," in *Beyond Slavery: Overcoming Its Religious and Sexual Legacies,* ed. Bernadette Brooten and Jacqueline Hazelton (London: Palgrave Macmillan, 2010), 41–60.

87. Harriet Jacobs, *Incidents in the Life of a Slave Girl* (Boston, 1861), 45.

88. See generally Barbara Welter, "The Cult of True Womanhood, 1820–1860," *American Quarterly* 18 no. 2 (July 1966): 151–74.

89. Safia Samee Ali, "Justice Department Considering Reopening Emmett Till Murder Case, Family Says," NBC News, April 6, 2017, https://perma.cc/YER3– 4KTV.

90. Frederick Douglass, *Why Is the Negro Lynched?* (Bridgewater, MA: J. Whitby and Sons, 1895), 13.

91. Hazel V. Carby, "'On the Threshold of Woman's Era': Lynching, Empire, and Sexuality in Black Feminist Theory," *Critical Inquiry* 12, no. 1 (Autumn 1985): 270, summarizing Ida B. Wells, *Southern Horrors: Lynch Law in All Its Phases* (New York, 1892).

92. Ida B. Wells, *The Red Record: Tabulated Statistics and Alleged Causes of Lynching in the United States* (Chicago: Donohue and Henneberry, 1895), 7.

93. "British Anti-lynchers," *New York Times,* August 2, 1894, https://perma .cc/4MU6–3MS7.

94. "British Anti-lynchers."

95. Maegan Parker, "Desiring Citizenship: A Rhetorical Analysis of the Wells/Willard Controversy," *Women's Studies in Communication* 31, no. 1 (Spring 2008): 63–68.

96. Francis Butler Simkins, *Pitchfork Ben Tillman, South Carolinian* (Baton Rouge: Louisiana State University Press, 1944), 297.

97. Jimmie Frank Gross, "Alabama Politics and the Negro, 1874–1901" (PhD diss., University of Georgia, 1969), 244. See also Andrew L. Shapiro, "Challenging Criminal Disenfranchisement under the Voting Rights Act: A New Strategy," *Yale Law Journal* 103, no. 2 (November 1993): 537–66.

98. Ida B. Wells, "Mr. Moody and Miss Willard," *Fraternity,* May 1894, 16–17.

99. Angela Harris, "Race and Essentialism in Feminist Legal Theory," *Stanford Law Review* 42, no. 3 (February 1990): 600.

100. Ida B. Wells, *Southern Horrors: Lynch Law in All Its Phases* (New York, 1892), https://perma.cc/4S8T-NA8C (e-book).

101. Wells, *Southern Horrors.*

102. Jonathan Markovitz, *Racial Spectacles: Explorations in Media, Race, and Justice* (New York: Routledge, 2011).

103. See generally Dan T. Carter, *Scottsboro: A Tragedy of the American South* (Baton Rouge: Louisiana State University Press, 1969). See Pliley, *Policing Sexuality,* 172–73; Paul D. Moreno, *The American State from the Civil War to the New Deal: The Twilight of Constitutionalism and the Triumph of Progressivism* (Cambridge: Cambridge University Press, 2013), 202–3.

104. Martha Hodes, *White Women, Black Men: Illicit Sex in the Nineteenth-Century South* (New Haven, CT: Yale University Press, 1999), 39–48.

105. Hodes, *White Women, Black Men,* 42.

106. Hodes, *White Women, Black Men.*

107. Hodes, *White Women, Black Men,* 47.

108. Todd Akin, "The Jaco Report: Full Interview with Todd Akin," interview by Charles Jaco, Fox News, August 21, 2012, television broadcast, 3:57–4:30, https://perma.cc/GJM7-JUMG.

109. Hodes, *White Women, Black Men,* 48.

110. Danielle L. McGuire, *At the Dark End of the Street* (New York: Random House, 2010), 52–58.

111. McGuire, *At the Dark End,* 52, 54.

112. McGuire, *At the Dark End,* 58.

113. McGuire, *At the Dark End,* 59.

114. McGuire, *At the Dark End,* 60.

115. McGuire, *At the Dark End.*

116. Brief of the ACLU et al. as Amici Curiae, at 9, Coker v. Georgia, 433 U.S. 584 (1977) (No. 75-5444) 1976 WL 181482 (U.S.) (1976), 14, 16.

117. Brief of the ACLU, 16.

118. Elizabeth A. Armstrong, Laura T. Hamilton, Elizabeth M. Armstrong, and J. Lotus Seeley, "'Good Girls': Gender, Social Class, and Slut Discourse on Campus," *Social Psychology Quarterly* 77, no. 2 (June 2014): 117. The authors found that "slut

discourse was ubiquitous among the women we studied." Also, because high-status women's "definitions prevailed in the dominant social scene," low-status women were the ones "vulnerable to public shaming."

119. Susan Brison, "An Open Letter from Black Women to SlutWalk Organizers," *HuffPost,* September 27, 2011, https://perma.cc/57Z3–66VP.

120. Janell Ross, "From Mexican Rapists to Bad Hombres, the Trump Campaign in Two Moments," *Washington Post,* October 20, 2016, https://perma.cc /QWZ6-PTF3.

121. Caroline May, "Coulter on Feminism: 'All Pretty Girls Are Right-Wingers,'" *Daily Caller,* February 10, 2012, https://perma.cc/J2EJ-P3UD.

122. Ann Coulter, ¡*Adios, America!: The Left's Plan to Turn Our Country Into a Third World Hellhole* (Washington, DC: Regnery, 2015), 143.

123. Coulter, ¡*Adios, America!,* 145.

2. THE ENEMY

1. Office of Policy Planning and Research, "The Negro Family: The Case for National Action," US Department of Labor, March 1965, https://perma.cc /M285-ZR7M.

2. Michelle Alexander, *The New Jim Crow: Mass Incarceration in the Age of Colorblindness* (New York: New Press, 2012), 45; see also Elizabeth Hinton, *From the War on Poverty to the War on Crime: The Making of Mass Incarceration in America* (Cambridge, MA: Harvard University Press, 2016), 55–60.

3. Marie Gottschalk, *The Prison and the Gallows: The Politics of Mass Incarceration in America* (Cambridge: Cambridge University Press, 2012), 85.

4. Alexander, *New Jim Crow,* 46.

5. Alexander, *New Jim Crow,* 47, quoting Nixon ad.

6. Alexander, *New Jim Crow,* 47, quoting Nixon ad.

7. Alexander, *New Jim Crow,* 47, quoting Nixon.

8. Alexander, *New Jim Crow,* 42.

9. Rick Perlstein, "Exclusive: Lee Atwater's Infamous 1981 Interview on the Southern Strategy," *Nation,* November 13, 2012, https://perma.cc/W35E-GRJF.

10. Estelle B. Freedman, *Redefining Rape: Sexual Violence in the Era of Suffrage and Segregation* (Cambridge, MA: Harvard University Press, 2013), 272.

11. Sharon Rice Vaughan, "The Story of Shelter," in *Violence against Women in Families and Relationships,* ed. Evan Stark and Eve Buzawa (Santa Barbara, CA: Praeger, 2009), 2.

12. Susan Schechter, *Women and Male Violence: The Visions and Struggles of the Battered Women's Movement* (Cambridge, MA: South End Press, 1982), 177.

13. Vaughan, "Story of Shelter," 2.

14. Lisa G. Lerman, "Mediation of Wife Abuse Cases: The Adverse Impact of Informal Dispute Resolution on Women," *Harvard Women's Law Journal* 7 (1984): 70.

15. Freedman, *Redefining Rape*, 278–80, discussing TBTN marches; Barbara C. Burrell, *Women and Politics: A Quest for Political Equality in an Age of Economic Inequality* (New York: Routledge, 2018), 126, on the origin of TBTN; Anne Valk, "Remembering Together: Take Back the Night and the Public Memory of Feminism," in *U.S. Women's History: Untangling the Threads of Sisterhood,* ed. Leslie Brown, Jacqueline Castledine, and Anne Valk (New Brunswick, NJ: Rutgers University Press, 2017), 186–203.

16. See generally Laura Lederer, ed., *Take Back the Night: Women on Pornography* (New York: William Morrow, 1980). I discuss the TBTN movements in detail in chapter 4 in the section "Predators and Prey."

17. Colo. Rev. Stat. Ann. § 18–6–803.6 (West).

18. Fla. Stat. § 741.2901(2).

19. See Laurie S. Kohn, "The Justice System and Domestic Violence: Engaging the Case but Divorcing the Victim," *N.Y.U. Review of Law and Social Change* 32 (2008): 213–15 and nn109–10, citing statutes and observing that forty-nine states and the District of Columbia permit warrantless arrests in DV cases. In 2011, the American Bar Association reported that nineteen states and D.C. have mandatory arrest policies (Alaska, Arizona, Colorado, Connecticut, D.C., Iowa, Kansas, Louisiana, Maine, Mississippi, Nevada, New Jersey, Ohio, Oregon, Rhode Island, South Carolina, South Dakota, Utah, Washington, and Wisconsin); six states have preferred arrest policies; and the remaining twenty-five states give officers discretion, although some states, like New York, mandate arrest for felonies. American Bar Association Commission on Domestic Violence, "Domestic Violence Arrest Policies by State," updated June 2011 https://perma.cc/V5QW-K369. A 2009 survey from the Center for Court Innovation identified 208 specialized DV courts across thirty-two states, significantly more than the 150 DV courts identified in their 1999 survey. Melissa Labriola, Sarah Bradley, Chris S. O'Sullivan, Michael Rempel, and Samantha Moore, "A National Portrait of Domestic Violence Courts," Center for Court Innovation, New York, December 2009, https://perma.cc/APR3–7D64. For a discussion of for-profit companies managing the consequences of carceral regimes, see Laura I. Appleman, "Cashing In on Convicts: Privatization, Punishment, and the People," *Utah Law Review* (2018): 579–638; Sarah Stillman, "Get Out of Jail, Inc.," *New Yorker,* June 23, 2014, https://perma.cc/F7AU-RGJG.

20. Sourcebook of Criminal Justice Statistics Online, table 6.0023.2013, https://perma.cc/3MBL-35RW, showing a prison population percentage of 0.8 in 1990 and 6.2 in 2013. Both the FBI Uniform Crime Reports and National Crime Victimization Survey show steep declines in rape rates from the mid-1990s to the 2010s. See chapter 5, note 150.

21. I discuss statistics on race and DV in the text accompanying notes 100–102 of this chapter. See also David Hirschel, Eve Buzawa, April Pattavina, Don Faggiani, and Melissa Reuland, "Explaining the Prevalence, Context, and Consequences of Dual Arrest in Intimate Partner Cases," National Criminal Justice Reference Service, May 2007, 61, table 4:32, https://perma.cc/RM6L-WBD5, for a comprehensive nationwide arrest study showing that police arrested in 48 percent

of intimate partner violence cases, 34.6 percent of stranger violence cases, and 28.1 percent of nondomestic relations violence cases and that the assault victim being an intimate partner raised the chance of conviction by 67 percent.

22. Marisa Chappell, "Rethinking Women's Politics in the 1970s: The League of Women Voters and the National Organization for Women Confront Poverty," *Journal of Women's History* 13, no. 4 (Winter 2002): 157.

23. Vaughan, "Story of Shelter," 2–8.

24. Vaughan, "Story of Shelter," 1.

25. Vaughan, "Story of Shelter," 5.

26. Vaughan, "Story of Shelter," 2.

27. Vaughan, "Story of Shelter," 2.

28. Vaughan, "Story of Shelter," 5.

29. Vaughan, "Story of Shelter," 5.

30. Vaughan, "Story of Shelter," 5–6.

31. Vaughan, "Story of Shelter," 6.

32. Vaughan, "Story of Shelter," 7.

33. Schechter, *Women and Male Violence,* 94–95, 127.

34. Schechter, *Women and Male Violence,* 94.

35. Schechter, *Women and Male Violence,* 95.

36. Schechter, *Women and Male Violence,* 127.

37. Schechter, *Women and Male Violence.*

38. Johnnie Tillmon, "Welfare Is a Women's Issue," *Ms.* magazine, spring 1972 (reprinted in *Ms.* magazine, spring 2002), https://perma.cc/FH6D-C5TV.

39. Tillmon, "Welfare."

40. Tillmon, "Welfare."

41. Martha F. Davis, "Welfare Rights and Women's Rights in the 1960s," *Journal of Policy History* 8, no. 1 (January 1996): 157.

42. Chappell, "Rethinking Women's Politics," 165.

43. Premilla Nadasen, "From Widow to 'Welfare Queen': Welfare and the Politics of Race," *Black Women, Gender and Families* 1, no. 2 (Fall 2007): 66.

44. Toni Morrison, "What the Black Woman Thinks about Women's Lib," *New York Times,* August 22, 1971, https://perma.cc/3YGB-HCX9.

45. Del Martin, *Battered Wives* (San Francisco: Glide Publications, 1976), 11.

46. Stephanie Gilmore and Elizabeth Kaminski, "A Part and Apart: Lesbian and Straight Feminist Activists Negotiate Identity in a Second-Wave Organization," *Journal of the History of Sexuality* 16, no. 1 (January 2007): 96.

47. Del Martin, "From 'Lesbian/Woman' to 'Battered Wives,'" *Women's eNews,* March 27, 2002, https://perma.cc/474L-SZ52.

48. Martin, *Battered Wives;* Dianna Lee Johnson, "A Narrative Life Story of Activist Phyllis Lyon and Her Reflections on a Life with Del Martin" (master's thesis, Grand Valley State University, 2012), 99, https://perma.cc/K5L4-T7UF.

49. US Commission on Civil Rights (hereafter CCR), *Battered Women: Issues of Public Policy* (Washington, DC: US Government Printing Office, 1978), 3–4, https://perma.cc/EE3R-MFUW.

50. Martin, *Battered Wives,* 85.

51. CCR, *Battered Women,* iv.

52. CCR, *Battered Women,* 2.

53. Anne Hull, "Just Married, after 51 Years Together," *Washington Post,* February 29, 2004, https://perma.cc/H7BS-X6UF.

54. Rachel Gordon, "Couple of 55 Years Tie the Knot—Again," *SF Gate,* June 17, 2008, https://perma.cc/T34Q-7AK4.

55. Hull, "Just Married."

56. Annelise Orleck, *Rethinking American Women's Activism* (London: Routledge, 2015), 169.

57. Martin, "From 'Lesbian/Woman.'"

58. Martin, "From 'Lesbian/Woman.'"

59. Martin, "From 'Lesbian/Woman.'"

60. Catharine A. MacKinnon, *Toward a Feminist Theory of the State* (Cambridge, MA: Harvard University Press, 1989), 168.

61. Jennifer C. Nash, "From Lavender to Purple: Privacy, Black Women, and Feminist Legal Theory," *Cardozo Women's Law Journal* 11 (2005): 319.

62. Combahee River Collective, "Combahee River Collective Statement," 1978, 4–5, https://perma.cc/WNB8-TYN8.

63. CCR, *Battered Women,* 28.

64. CCR, *Battered Women,* 28.

65. CCR, *Battered Women,* 4.

66. Beth E. Richie, *Arrested Justice: Black Women, Violence, and America's Prison Nation* (New York: New York University Press, 2012), 90.

67. CCR, *Battered Women,* 105.

68. CCR, *Battered Women,* 99.

69. CCR, *Battered Women,* 99–100.

70. CCR, *Battered Women,* 100.

71. CCR, *Battered Women,* 100–101.

72. CCR, *Battered Women,* 101.

73. CCR, *Battered Women,* 101.

74. CCR, *Battered Women,* 100.

75. CCR, *Battered Women,* 100.

76. CCR, *Battered Women,* 101.

77. For example, Frank Rudy Cooper, "Understanding 'Depolicing': Symbiosis Theory and Critical Cultural Theory," *University of Missouri Kansas City Law Review* 71 (Winter 2002): 367; Nancy Ehrenreich, "Subordination and Symbiosis: Mechanisms of Mutual Support between Subordinating Systems," *University of Missouri Kansas City Law Review* 71 (Winter 2002): 276.

78. CCR, *Battered Women,* 101.

79. CCR, *Battered Women,* 107.

80. Lisa Richette, *The Throwaway Children* (New York: Delta, 1969).

81. Kitty Caparella, "Prominent Judge, Civic Giant Lisa Richette Dead at 79," *Philadelphia Inquirer,* October 29, 2007, https://perma.cc/9557-MZ54.

82. Caparella, "Prominent Judge."

83. Caparella, "Prominent Judge."

84. Caparella, "Prominent Judge."

85. CCR, *Battered Women,* 108.

86. CCR, *Battered Women,* 113.

87. CCR, *Battered Women,* 128.

88. CCR, *Battered Women,* 130 (emphasis added).

89. CCR, *Battered Women,* 128.

90. CCR, *Battered Women,* 129.

91. CCR, *Battered Women,* 133.

92. CCR, *Battered Women,* 133.

93. CCR, *Battered Women,* 134.

94. CCR, *Battered Women,* 134, quoting the Statement of the Minority Women's Caucus of the 1977 International Women's Year Convention.

95. CCR, *Battered Women,* 136.

96. Richie, *Arrested Justice,* 92.

97. CCR, *Battered Women,* 101.

98. Michael Tesler, "Trump Voters Think African Americans Are Much Less Deserving Than 'Average Americans,'" *Huffington Post,* December 19, 2016, https://perma.cc/E5BR-7W43.

99. Michelle S. Jacobs, "The Violent State: Black Women's Invisible Struggle against Police Violence," *William and Mary Journal of Women and the Law* 24 (2017): 47.

100. Matthew Durose, Caroline Wolf Harlow, Patrick A. Langan, Mark Motivans, Ramona R. Rantala, and Erica L. Smith, "Family Violence Statistics: Including Statistics on Strangers and Acquaintances," Bureau of Justice Statistics report, 2005, 38, https://perma.cc/5GXN-Z5SC.

101. Durose et al., "Family Violence Statistics," 38. See also Donna Coker, "Shifting Power for Battered Women: Law, Material Resources, and Poor Women of Color," *U.C. Davis Law Review* 33 (2000): 1016.

102. Robert L. Hampton, Jaslean J. LaTaillade, Alicia Dacey, and J. R. Marghi, "Evaluating Domestic Violence Interventions for Black Women," *Journal of Aggression, Maltreatment and Trauma* 16, no. 3 (2008): 332.

103. CCR, *Battered Women,* 170–72.

104. CCR, *Battered Women,* 172.

105. R. Emerson Dobash and Russell P. Dobash, *Women, Violence and Social Change* (London: Routledge, 1991), 127.

106. Lawrence Sherman, Janell D. Schmidt, Dennis P. Rogan, and Douglas A. Smith, "The Variable Effects of Arrest on Criminal Careers: The Milwaukee Domestic Violence Experiment," *Journal of Criminal Law and Criminology* 83, no. 1 (Spring 1992): 137–69.

107. Sherman et al., "Variable Effects of Arrest," 160.

108. Wayne King, "Tough Cop Falters: How Rizzo Has Slipped," *New York Times,* February 4, 1974, https://perma.cc/5E2M-3N6Z.

109. Caparella, "Prominent Judge."

110. Donald Janson, "Rizzo's First Year: Crime Off Slightly," *New York Times,* January 7, 1973, https://perma.cc/7SXL-7P3W; MaryClaire Dale, "Charlton Heston Rant Leads Court to Toss Murder Conviction 20 Years Later," *USA Today,* March 2, 2017, https://perma.cc/2CWB-CQYD.

111. Caparella, "Prominent Judge."

112. Caparella, "Prominent Judge."

113. CCR, *Battered Women,* 5.

114. Terry L. Fromson, "The Case for Legal Remedies for Abused Women," *New York University Review of Law and Social Change* 6, no. 2 (Spring 1977): 142.

115. CCR, *Battered Women,* 67.

116. Bruno v. Codd, 396 N.Y.S.2d 974, 976 (N.Y. Sup. Ct. 1977).

117. See DeShaney v. Winnebago County Dep't of Soc. Servs., 489 U.S. 189, 195–96 (1989) (holding that the Due Process Clause "cannot fairly be extended to impose an affirmative obligation on the State"). Cf. Leandro v. State, 488 S.E.2d 249 (N.C. 1997) (finding that the North Carolina Constitution provides a substantive right to education).

118. Laurie Woods, "Litigation on Behalf of Battered Women," *Women's Rights Law Reporter* 5 (Fall 1978): 12.

119. Woods, "Litigation," 11.

120. Woods, "Litigation," 11.

121. Woods, "Litigation," 12.

122. Schechter, *Women and Male Violence,* 211.

123. Schechter, *Women and Male Violence,* 211.

124. Pauline W. Gee, "Ensuring Police Protection for Battered Women: The Scott v. Hart Suit," *Signs* 8, no. 3 (Spring 1983): 562.

125. CCR, *Battered Women,* 11.

126. Martha R. Mahoney, "Legal Images of Battered Women: Redefining the Issue of Separation," *Michigan Law Review* 90 (October 1991): 12.

127. Donna Coker, "Foreword: Addressing the Real World of Racial Injustice in the Criminal Justice System," *Journal of Criminal Law and Criminology* 93 (Fall 2003): 831.

128. Ellen L. Pence and Melanie F. Shepard, "An Introduction: Developing a Coordinated Community Response," in *Coordinating Community Responses to Domestic Violence: Lessons From Duluth and Beyond,* ed. Melanie F. Shepard and Ellen L. Pence (Thousand Oaks, CA: Sage Publications, 1999), 7, quoting a legal advocate interview of September 19, 1995.

129. Schechter, *Women and Male Violence,* 178, 175.

130. Schechter, *Women and Male Violence,* 176.

131. Schechter, *Women and Male Violence,* 176.

132. CCR, *Under the Rule of Thumb: Battered Women and the Administration of Justice* (Washington, DC: January 1982), 20, https://perma.cc/2HSG-8ZAP.

133. Vaughan, "Story of Shelter," 10.

134. Schechter, *Women and Male Violence,* 178.

135. Richie, *Arrested Justice*, 83.

136. Elizabeth M. Schneider, *Battered Women and Feminist Lawmaking* (New Haven, CT: Yale University Press, 2000), 183.

137. Jonathan Simon, *Governing through Crime: How the War on Crime Transformed American Democracy and Created a Culture of Fear* (Oxford: Oxford University Press: 2009), esp. 1.

138. See Michael Allen Meeropol, *Surrender: How the Clinton Administration Completed the Reagan Revolution* (Ann Arbor: University of Michigan Press, 2000); Melinda Cooper, *Family Values: Between Neoliberalism and the New Social Conservatism* (Brooklyn, NY: Zone Books, 2017).

139. "In Their Own Words: Obama on Reagan," *New York Times* (captured April 21, 2019), https://perma.cc/4LJ6-GTED.

140. Wendy Brown, *Undoing the Demos: Neoliberalism's Stealth Revolution* (Brooklyn, NY: Zone Books, 2017).

141. Emmanuel Saez, "Striking It Richer: The Evolution of Top Incomes in the United States," *UC Berkeley,* September 3, 2013, 7, fig. 1, https://perma.cc/FR58-ZVP2.

142. Thomas Piketty, Emmanuel Saez, and Gabriel Zucman, "Distributional National Accounts: Methods and Estimates for the United States," National Bureau of Economic Research Working Paper 22945, December 2016, 3, https://perma.cc/AF6S-3DJD.

143. Office of Human Services Policy, "Poverty in the United States: 50-Year Trends and Safety Net Impacts," US Department of Health and Human Services, March 2016, 8, https://perma.cc/CG4Z-F3F9.

144. Ronald W. Reagan, "Remarks at the Annual Conference of the National Sheriffs' Association in Hartford, Connecticut," Ronald Reagan Presidential Library and Museum Archives, June 20, 1984, https://perma.cc/SU8G-V6A4.

145. "'Welfare Queen' Becomes Issue in Reagan Campaign," *New York Times,* February 15, 1976, https://perma.cc/GZG6–3U68.

146. See Gottschalk, *Prison and the Gallows,* 85, describing the LEAA.

147. Schechter, *Women and Male Violence,* 187, quoting an LEAA staff person's testimony to the Commission on Civil Rights.

148. Schechter, *Women and Male Violence,* 186.

149. Donna Coker, "Crime Logic, Campus Sexual Assault, and Restorative Justice," *Texas Tech Law Review* 49 (Fall 2016): 147, 150.

150. Coker, "Crime Logic," 159.

3. THE BATTLE PLAN

1. Carol A. Archbold, *Policing: A Text/Reader* (Thousand Oaks, CA: Sage Publications, 2013), 38.

2. See Michael Palmiotto, *Community Policing: A Policing Strategy for the 21st Century* (Gaithersburg, MD: Aspen, 2000), 28–29.

3. Herman Goldstein, "Improving Policing: A Problem-Oriented Approach," *Crime and Delinquency* 25, no. 2 (April 1979): 236–58, 242, https://perma.cc /ZV87-QYQH.

4. Goldstein, "Improving Policing," 236.

5. Goldstein, "Improving Policing," 251.

6. 396 N.Y.S.2d 974, 976 (1977).

7. See, for example, Laurie Woods, "Litigation on Behalf of Battered Women," *Women's Rights Law Reporter* 5, no. 1 (October, 1978): 7–32, weighing costs and benefits of arrest model.

8. Woods, "Litigation," 29.

9. See, e.g., Lisa G. Lerman, "Mediation of Wife Abuse Cases: The Adverse Impact of Informal Dispute Resolution on Women," *Harvard Women's Law Journal* 7, no. 1 (March 1984): 70, characterizing law enforcement as the feminist model.

10. Stephen J. Schulhofer, "The Feminist Challenge in Criminal Law," *University of Pennsylvania Law Review* 143, no. 6 (June 1995): 2163. See notes 109–15 of this chapter and accompanying text for a discussion of the escalation effect.

11. Barbara K. Finesmith, "Police Response to Battered Women: A Critique and Proposals for Reform," *Seton Hall Law Review* 14, no. 1 (1983–84): 107.

12. See Bruno v. Codd, 976: "The complaint, supported by sworn statements in dozens of actual cases, alleges that police officers called to the scene of a husband's assault on his wife, uniformly refuse to take action, even if the physical evidence of the assault is unmistakable and undenied; that, instead, they inform the battered wife that they are unable to render assistance or make an arrest, solely because the victim is the wife of her assailant."

13. Bruno v. Codd, 977.

14. Bruno v. Codd, 977.

15. Kathleen Waits, "The Criminal Justice System's Response to Battering: Understanding the Problem, Forging the Solutions," *Washington Law Review* 60, no. 2 (April, 1985): 310.

16. Woods, "Litigation," 32–33 (Appendix: Consent Judgement, *Bruno v. Codd*).

17. William Blackstone, *Commentaries on the Laws of England* (Oxford: Clarendon Press, 1765–69), book 11, ch. 15, 444. One publication, for example, noted "Blackstone's codification of the common law in 1768 asserted that a husband had the right to 'physically chastise' an errant wife, provided the stick was no bigger than his thumb." Murray A. Straus and Richard J. Gelles, "Societal Change and Change in Family Violence from 1975 to 1985 as Revealed by Two National Surveys," *Journal of Marriage and Family* 48, no. 3 (August 1986): 466.

18. Blackstone, *Commentaries,* 444–45. See also Henry Ansgar Kelly, "Rule of Thumb and the Folklaw of the Husband's Stick," *Journal of Legal Education* 44, no. 3 (September 1994): 346–56.

19. Blackstone, *Commentaries,* 433.

20. Fulgham v. State, 46 Ala. 143, 144 (1871).

21. Fulgham v. State, 146, quoting Blackstone, *Commentaries,* 444–45.

22. Fulgham v. State, 146.

23. For example, Straus and Gelles, "Societal Change," 46. See Kelly, "Rule of Thumb," 342: the phrase "has been given a phony origin as designating an allowable weapon for wife-beaters, and in consequence there has been an effort to boycott its traditional usage because of the supposedly sinister circumstances of its beginnings."

24. State v. Rhodes, 61 N.C. 453, 454 (1868). Kelly argues this was a misrepresentation of the judges' actual sentiments. Kelly, "Rule of Thumb," 346.

25. Elizabeth Pleck, *Domestic Tyranny: The Making of American Social Policy against Family Violence from Colonial Times to the Present* (Urbana: University of Illinois Press, 2004), xiv.

26. US Commission on Civil Rights (CCR), *Under the Rule of Thumb: Battered Women and the Administration of Justice* (Washington, DC: January 1982), 20, https://perma.cc/2HSG-8ZAP.

27. See generally Pleck, *Domestic Tyranny*; Reva B. Siegel, "'The Rule of Love': Wife Beating as Prerogative and Privacy," *Yale Law Journal* 105, no. 8 (June 1996): 2117–2207.

28. Ruth H. Bloch, "The American Revolution, Wife Beating, and the Emergent Value of Privacy," *Early American Studies* 5, no. 2 (October 2007): 248.

29. Siegel, "Rule of Love," 2139. See also Pleck, *Domestic Tyranny*, 107–20, discussing race and corporal punishment.

30. Bruno v. Codd, 396 N.Y.S.2d 974, at 975.

31. CCR, *Under the Rule*, 12–22.

32. Morton Bard, *Training Police as Specialists in Family Crisis Intervention* (Washington, DC: US Government Printing Office, 1970), 1.

33. CCR, *Under the Rule*, 13.

34. CCR, *Under the Rule*, 14.

35. CCR, *Under the Rule*, 12

36. CCR, *Under the Rule*, 12–13.

37. CCR, *Battered Women: Issues of Public Policy* (Washington, DC: US Government Printing Office, 1978), 49–50, https://perma.cc/EE3R-MFUW.

38. Bard, *Training Police*, 6–7.

39. Bard, *Training Police*, 15.

40. Bard, *Training Police*, 15.

41. Bard, *Training Police*, 26.

42. Bard, *Training Police*, 23, citing Hans Toch, *Violent Men* (Chicago: Aldine Press, 1969).

43. Terry L. Fromson, "The Case for Legal Remedies for Abused Women," *New York University Review of Law and Social Change* 6, no. 2 (Spring 1977): 142.

44. Bard, *Training Police*, 28.

45. CCR, *Under the Rule*, 16, quoting International Association of Chiefs of Police, Training Key No. 245.

46. CCR, *Battered Women*, 52.

47. See Okla. Stat. Ann. Tit. 22, § 196; Tex. Crim. Proc. Code Ann. § 14.01; State v. Reger, 148 N.M. 342, 346 (Ct. App. 2010).

48. Laurie S. Kohn, "The Justice System and Domestic Violence: Engaging the Case but Divorcing the Victim," *New York University Review of Law and Social Change* 32, no. 2 (January 2008): 213–15 and n109, citing statutes.

49. Del Martin, *Battered Wives* (San Francisco: Glide Publications, 1976), 93, quoting Oakland, CA, Police Department Training Bulletin on Techniques of Dispute Intervention.

50. Martin, *Battered Wives,* 94, quoting Oakland Police Department Training Bulletin.

51. See Complaint, Scott v. Hart, No. C76 2395 WWS (N.D. Cal. 1976). The suit also alleged that police were more willing to arrest when the victim was a white woman and therefore discriminated against black female victims based on race. Scott v. Hart, 7–8. See also Pauline W. Gee, "Ensuring Police Protection for Battered Women: The *Scott v. Hart* Suit," *Signs* 8, no. 3 (Spring 1983): 555, discussing the police's neutrality claim.

52. Gee, "Ensuring Police Protection," 560.

53. Waits, "Criminal Justice System's Response," 271.

54. Finesmith, "Police Response," 85.

55. Finesmith, "Police Response," 86.

56. CCR, *Under the Rule,* 15.

57. Finesmith, "Police Response," 80.

58. Sarah Mausolff Buel, "Mandatory Arrest for Domestic Violence," *Harvard Women's Law Journal* 11 (1988): 224.

59. Murray A. Straus, Richard J. Gelles, and Suzanne K.. Steinmetz, *Behind Closed Doors: Violence in the American Family* (New York: Doubleday, 1980), 202–21; Richard J. Gelles, "Violence in the Family: A Review of Research in the Seventies," *Journal of Marriage and Family* 42, no. 4 (November 1980): 878–79; Hamilton I. McCubbin, Constance B. Joy, A. Elizabeth Cauble, Joan K. Comeau, Joan M. Patterson, and Richard H. Needle, "Family Stress and Coping: A Decade Review," *Journal of Marriage and Family* 42, no. 4 (November 1980): 855–71.

60. CCR, *Battered Women,* 52.

61. Protesting Stanford University's liquor ban after the Brock Turner case, one activist stated, "By banning hard liquor, it sends the subliminal message that alcohol causes rape. Rapists cause rape." Irin Carmon, "What Advocates Are Doing to End Sexual Assault on Campus," NBC News, September 4, 2016, https://perma.cc/W7H9-X24L.

62. John E. Snell, Richard J. Rosenwald, and Ames Robey, "The Wifebeater's Wife: A Study of Family Interaction," *Archives of General Psychiatry* 11 (August 1964): 107–12.

63. Snell, Rosenwald, and Robey, "Wifebeater's Wife," 111.

64. Snell, Rosenwald, and Robey, "Wifebeater's Wife," 111.

65. Snell, Rosenwald, and Robey, "Wifebeater's Wife," 111.

66. Straus, Gelles, and Steinmetz, *Behind Closed Doors,* 24, reporting on study.

67. Straus, Gelles, and Steinmetz, *Behind Closed Doors,* 139, 202–21; see also Gelles, "Violence in the Family," 878–79; Elizabeth Cauble et al., "Family Stress and Coping," 855–71.

68. Straus, Gelles, and Steinmetz, *Behind Closed Doors,* xxiii, 36.

69. Murray A. Straus, "Women's Violence toward Men Is a Serious Social Problem," in *Current Controversies on Family Violence,* ed. Donileen Loseke, Richard J. Gelles, and Mary M. Cavanaugh (Thousand Oaks, CA: Sage Publications, 2005), 57, discussing 1975 study.

70. See Straus, Gelles, and Steinmetz, *Behind Closed Doors,* 37, finding that of the couples reporting violence, 27 percent involved male-only violence and 24 percent involved female-only violence, with the bulk involving mutual violence.

71. See CCR, *Battered Women,* 527, 450–55 (witnesses making these arguments); Donileen R. Loseke and Demie Kurz, "Men's Violence toward Women Is the Serious Problem," in Loseke, Gelles, and Cavanaugh, *Current Controversies,* 79–96. However, the self-defense theory ran up against the evidence that a quarter of violent relationships involved female violence only. Straus, Gelles, and Steinmetz, *Behind Closed Doors,* 37.

72. Straus, "Women's Violence," in Loseke, Gelles, and Cavanaugh, *Current Controversies,* 62.

73. Murray A. Straus, "Sexual Inequality, Cultural Norms and Wife-Beating," in *Victims and Society,* ed. Emilio C. Viano (Washington, DC: Visage Press, 1976), 545.

74. Murray A. Straus, "Wife Beating: How Common and Why?," *Victimology: An International Journal* 2, no. 3–4 (1978): 450.

75. Suzanne K. Steinmetz, "The Battered Husband Syndrome," *Victimology: An International Journal* 2, no. 3–4 (1977–78): 499.

76. Steinmetz, "Battered Husband Syndrome," 499.

77. Steinmetz, "Battered Husband Syndrome," 507–8.

78. Gary W. Peterson and Suzanne K. Steinmetz, *Pioneering Paths in the Study of Families: The Lives and Careers of Family Scholars* (Binghamton, NY: Haworth Press, 2002), 562.

79. Richard J. Gelles, "The Missing Persons of Domestic Violence: Battered Men," *Women's Quarterly* 6 (1999): 20.

80. Murray A. Straus and Richard J. Gelles, "Societal Change and Change in Family Violence from 1975 to 1985 as Revealed by Two National Surveys," *Journal of Marriage and Family* 48, no. 3 (August 1986): 465–79.

81. Gelles, "Missing Persons," 20.

82. Susan Schechter, *Women and Male Violence: The Visions and Struggles of the Battered Women's Movement* (Cambridge, MA: South End Press, 1982), 341n17.

83. Joan Erskine, "If It Quacks Like a Duck: Recharacterizing Domestic Violence as Criminal Coercion," *Brooklyn Law Review* 65, no. 4 (1999): 1208.

84. Lawrence W. Sherman and Richard Berk, "The Minneapolis Domestic Violence Experiment," Police Foundation Reports, April 1984, 1–7, https://perma .cc/4Y2T-6GSR (emphasis added).

85. Sherman and Berk, "Minneapolis Domestic Violence Experiment," 2–4.

86. Sherman and Berk, "Minneapolis Domestic Violence Experiment," 1.

87. Joan Zorza, "Criminal Law of Misdemeanor Domestic Violence, 1970–1990," *Journal of Criminal Law and Criminology* 83 no. 1 (Spring 1992): 64, noting that fifteen states mandated arrest for any instance of DV and nineteen mandated arrest for violation of a protection order. See also Emily J. Sack, "Battered Women and the State: The Struggle for the Future of Domestic Violence Policy," *Wisconsin Law Review,* no. 6 (November 2004): 1657–1739; Town of Castle Rock, Colo. v. Gonzales, 545 U.S. 748 (2005).

88. See Lawrence W. Sherman and Ellen G. Cohn, "The Impact of Research on Legal Policy: The Minneapolis Domestic Violence Experiment," *Law and Society Review* 23, no. 1 (1989): 123, table 1, for 10 percent statistic; see Lawrence W. Sherman, "Influence of Criminology on Criminal Law: Evaluating Arrests for Misdemeanor Domestic Violence," *Journal of Criminal Law and Criminology* 83, no. 1 (Spring 1992): 24, for 84 percent statistic.

89. Sherman and Cohn, "Impact of Research," 129.

90. Town of Castle Rock v. Gonzales, 545 U.S. 748, 780–81 (2005) (internal quotations omitted).

91. Waits, "Criminal Justice System's Response," 302.

92. Amy Eppler, "Battered Women and the Equal Protection Clause: Will the Constitution Help Them When the Police Won't?," *Yale Law Journal* 95, no. 4 (March 1986): 791 (emphasis added).

93. Buel, "Mandatory Arrest," 215 (emphasis added).

94. Radha Iyengar, "Does the Certainty of Arrest Reduce Domestic Violence? Evidence from Mandatory and Recommended Arrest Laws," Working Paper No. 13186, National Bureau of Economic Research, June 2007, 10, https://perma.cc/9M37-DGAB.

95. Cf. Iyengar, "Does the Certainty," 10. But see Laura Dugan, Daniel Nagin, and Richard Rosenfeld, "Exposure Reduction or Retaliation? The Effects of Domestic Violence Resources on Intimate-Partner Homicide," *Law and Society Review* 37, no. 1 (March 2003): 192, https://perma.cc/4QZW-W74V, finding that aggressive arrest policies correlated with fewer killings of unmarried intimates.

96. Thurman v. Torrington, 595 F.Supp. 1521, 1524–26 (D. Conn. 1984).

97. *A Cry for Help: The Tracey Thurman Story,* directed by Robert Markowitz (Dick Clark Productions, 1989), https://perma.cc/4UTX-6WBY.

98. Dirk Johnson, "Abused Women Get Leverage in Connecticut," *New York Times,* June 15, 1986, https://perma.cc/UQE2-G8BK; Connecticut Family Violence Prevention and Response Act of 1986, C.G.S.A. § 46b-38c (1986).

99. Sherman and Cohn, "Impact of Research," 120.

100. Sherman and Cohn, "Impact of Research," 120–21.

101. Sherman and Cohn, "Impact of Research," 121.

102. Sherman and Cohn, "Impact of Research," 120.

103. Richard Lempert, "From the Editor," *Law and Society Review* 18 (1984): 509.

104. Richard Lempert, "Spouse Abuse: Ann Arbor Rushed into Arrest Ordinance without Studying Side Effects," *Ann Arbor News,* June 21, 1987, B15.

105. There is contemporary evidence that this is the case. See Meghan A. Novisky and Robert L. Peralta, "When Women Tell: Intimate Partner Violence and the Factors Related to Police Notification," *Violence Against Women* 21, no. 1 (2015): 65–86.

106. Lempert, "From the Editor," 509; see also Richard Lempert, "Humility Is A Virtue: On the Publication of Policy-Relevant Research," *Law and Society Review* 23, no. 1 (1989): 148.

107. Sherman and Cohn, "Impact of Research," 142.

108. Sherman and Cohn, "Impact of Research," 142.

109. See Janell D. Schmidt and Lawrence W. Sherman, "Does Arrest Deter Domestic Violence?" *American Behavioral Scientist* 36, no. 5 (May 1993): 603, https://perma.cc/RUU2-T87W; see also Sherman, "Influence of Criminology," 37.

110. Schulhofer, "Feminist Challenge," 2163.

111. Schmidt and Sherman, "Does Arrest Deter," 606.

112. Schmidt and Sherman, "Does Arrest Deter," 605–6; Sherman, "Influence of Criminology," 29.

113. See, e.g., Lisa Broidy, Danielle Albright, and Kristine Denman, "Deterring Future Incidents of Intimate Partner Violence: Does Type of Formal Intervention Matter?," *Violence Against Women* 22, no. 9 (2016): 1127–28, finding that intervention type did not affect reoffending; Min Xie and James P. Lynch, "The Effects of Arrest, Reporting to the Police, and Victim Services on Intimate Partner Violence," *Journal of Research in Crime and Delinquency* 54, no. 3 (November 20, 2016): 358–60, finding that arrest was unrelated to repeat victimization.

114. Lawrence W. Sherman, Janell D. Schmidt, and Dennis P. Rogan, *Policing Domestic Violence: Experiments and Dilemmas* (New York: Free Press, 1992), 210.

115. Sherman, Schmidt, and Rogan, *Policing Domestic Violence,* 51.

116. Sherman, Schmidt, and Rogan, *Policing Domestic Violence,* 50.

117. Sherman, Schmidt, and Rogan, *Policing Domestic Violence,* 50.

118. Joel Garner, "Evaluating the Effectiveness of Mandatory Arrest for Domestic Violence in Virginia," *William and Mary Journal of Women and the Law* 3 (1997): 224, citing Virginia Commission on Family Violence Prevention, *Report of the Law Enforcement Subcommittee,* September 29, 1995.

119. Garner, "Evaluating the Effectiveness," 225.

120. Garner, "Evaluating the Effectiveness," 225.

121. Garner, "Evaluating the Effectiveness," 231.

122. Garner, "Evaluating the Effectiveness," 32, quoting Virginia Commission, *Report,* 57 (emphasis added).

123. Zorza, "Criminal Law," 72 (emphasis added).

124. Lisa A. Frisch, "Research That Succeeds, Policies That Fail," *Journal of Criminal Law and Criminology* 83, no. 1 (April 1992): 216.

125. Sherman, Schmidt, and Rogan, *Policing Domestic Violence,* 52.

126. Frisch, "Research That Succeeds," 216.

127. There is some evidence for this phenomenon in David Hirschel, Eve Buzawa, April Pattavina, Don Faggiani, and Melissa Reuland, "Explaining the Prevalence, Context, and Consequences of Dual Arrest in Intimate Partner Cases," US Department of Justice National Criminal Justice Reference Service, May 2007, 81, https://perma.cc/RM6L-WBD5.

128. Woods, "Litigation," 12n35.

129. Meda Chesney-Lind, "Criminalizing Victimization: The Unintended Consequences of Pro-arrest Policies for Girls and Women," *Criminology and Public Policy* 2, no. 1 (November 2002): 82.

130. Woods, "Litigation," 12n35.

131. Lawrence W. Sherman, Janell D. Schmidt, Dennis P. Rogan, and Douglas A. Smith, "The Variable Effects of Arrest on Criminal Careers: The Milwaukee Domestic Violence Experiment," *Journal of Criminal Law and Criminology* 83, no. 1 (Spring 1992): 160.

132. "Responses from the Field: Sexual Assault, Domestic Violence, and Policing," American Civil Liberties Union, October 2015, 30, https://perma.cc/VXU2-DHCW.

133. All quotes are from Evan Stark, "Mandatory Arrest of Batterers: A Reply to Its Critics," in *Do Arrests and Restraining Orders Work?*, ed. Eve S. Buzawa and Carl G. Buzawa (Thousand Oaks, CA: Sage Publications, 1996), 129.

134. Frisch, "Research That Succeeds," 213.

135. Statistics on arrest rates are discussed in chapter 2, note 20.

136. Mekha Rajan and Kathy A. McCloskey, "Victims of Intimate Partner Violence: Arrest Rates across Recent Studies," *Journal of Aggression, Maltreatment and Trauma* 15, no. 3–4 (2007): 37.

137. L. Kevin Hamberger and Theresa Potente, "Counseling Heterosexual Women Arrested for Domestic Violence: Implications for Theory and Practice," *Violence and Victims* 9, no. 2 (July 1994): 126.

138. Hirschel et al., "Dual Arrest," 12.

139. See Andrea D. Lyon, "Be Careful What You Wish For: An Examination of Arrest and Prosecution Patterns of Domestic Violence Cases in Two Cities in Michigan," *Michigan Journal of Gender and Law* 5, no. 2 (1999): 298.

140. See, e.g., Fla. Stat. Ann. § 784.03 (battery); Ind. Code Ann. § 35–42–2–1 (battery); Jones v. State, 213 Md. App. 208, 217 (2013) (intent-to-frighten assault).

141. Indeed, "Leniency toward women has become an almost accepted phenomenon among [criminal justice] scholars." Amy Farrell, Geoff Ward and Danielle Rousseau, "Intersections of Gender and Race in Federal Sentencing: Examining Court Contexts and the Effects of Representative Court Authorities," *Journal of Race, Gender, and Justice* 14, no. 1 (Fall 2010): 85–86; see also Laurie L. Ragatz and Brenda Russell, "Sex, Sexual Orientation, and Sexism: What Influence Do These Factors Have on Verdicts in a Crime-of-Passion Case?," *Journal of Social Psychology* 150, no. 4 (June 2010): 341–60.

142. Kathy A. McCloskey and Marilyn H. Sitaker, eds., *Backs against the Wall: Battered Women's Resistance Strategies* (New York: Routledge, 2009), 38, citing studies.

143. Meda Chesney-Lind, "Patriarchy, Crime, and Justice: Feminist Criminology in an Era of Backlash," *Feminist Criminology* 1, no. 1 (January 2006): 14, citing Federal Bureau of Investigation, "Crime in the United States, 2003," 2004, 275; Lawrence A. Greenfeld and Tracy L. Snell, "Women Offenders," Bureau of Justice Statistics: Special Report, December 1999, 2–3, https://perma.cc/3VEU-M7RL.

144. Jennifer Schwartz, Darrell Steffensmeier, and Ben Feldmeyer, "Assessing Trends in Women's Violence via Data Triangulation: Arrests, Convictions, Incarcerations, and Victim Reports," *Social Problems* 65, no. 3 (August 2009): 494.

145. See Sally F. Goldfarb, "Reconceiving Civil Protection Orders for Domestic Violence: Can Law Help End the Abuse without Ending the Relationship?," *Cardozo Law Review* 29, no. 4 (March 2008): 1510–13.

146. Xie and Lynch, "Effects of Arrest," 358–60, finding that use of services, but not offender arrest, reduced victimization; Novisky and Peralta, "When Women Tell," 66–67, theorizing that mandatory arrest policies may deter arrest-averse victims from reporting.

147. Franklin E. Zimring, *The Great Crime Decline* (New York: Oxford University Press, 2007), esp. 1.

148. See Zimring, *Great Crime Decline,* 49–52; Oliver Roeder, Lauren-Brooke Eisen, and Julia Bowling, "What Caused the Crime Decline?," *Brennan Center for Justice* (2015): 79, https://perma.cc/ZD65-VXET; Bruce Western, *Punishment and Inequality in America* (New York: Russell Sage Foundation, 2006), ch. 7.

149. Jennifer Truman and Rachel Morgan, "Nonfatal Domestic Violence, 2003–2012," U.S. Department of Justice, Bureau of Justice Statistics: Special Report, April 2014, 3, https://perma.cc/L2D3-EXM7; "UCR Domestic Violence," Florida Department of Law Enforcement, accessed March 15, 2019, https://perma.cc/TWR3–5V8G; Hirschel et al., "Dual Arrest," 4, https://perma.cc/RM6L-WBD5; David Hirschel, Eve Buzawa, April Pattavina, and Don Faggiani, "Domestic Violence and Mandatory Arrest Laws: To What Extent Do They Influence Police Arrest Decisions?," *Journal of Criminal Law and Criminology* 98, no. 1 (Fall 2007): 256–57, 258n11.

150. Studies are discussed in notes 118, 138, and 146 of this chapter. See also Robert C. Davis, Chris O'Sullivan, Donald J. Farole Jr., and Michael Rempel, "A Comparison of Two Prosecution Policies in Cases of Intimate Partner Violence: Mandatory Case Filing versus Following the Victim's Lead," *Criminology and Public Policy* 7, no. 4 (January 2009): 634; Eve S. Buzawa and Aaron D. Buzawa, "Courting Domestic Violence Victims: A Tale of Two Cities," *Criminology and Public Policy* 7, no. 4 (January 2009): 671–72.

151. Sherman et al., "Variable Effects of Arrest," 160.

152. Zorza, "Misdemeanor Domestic Violence," 66.

153. Lawrence W. Sherman and Janell D. Schmidt, "From Initial Deterrence to Long-Term Escalation: Short-Custody Arrest for Poverty Ghetto Domestic Violence," *Criminology* 29, no. 4 (November 1991): 843.

154. See Pleck, *Domestic Tyranny,* 116.

155. Lawrence W. Sherman and Heather M. Harris, "Increased Death Rates of Domestic Violence Victims from Arresting vs. Warning Suspects in the Milwaukee Domestic Violence Experiment," *Journal of Experimental Criminology* 11, no. 1 (March 2015): 1, https://perma.cc/VD2B-JH68.

156. Sherman and Harris, "Increased Death Rates," 1.

157. Belinda Luscombe, "When Not to Arrest an Abuser in a Domestic Violence Case," *Time* magazine, March 5, 2014, https://perma.cc/RBK5-NNCR. See also Sherman and Harris, "Increased Death Rates," 17–18.

158. Sherman and Harris, "Increased Death Rates," 17.

159. Sherman and Harris, "Increased Death Rates," 18.

160. Luscombe, "When Not to Arrest."

161. Luscombe, "When Not to Arrest."

4. THE WEAPON

1. Associated Press, "The Jiggles That Changed Television," *Today,* March 3, 2004, https://perma.cc/8BLP-YT2W.

2. Leslie Bennetts, "Beautiful People, Ugly Choices," *Vanity Fair,* August 25, 2009, https://perma.cc/Q5PV-V3JJ.

3. Corey Williams, "Francine Wilson, Subject of Major Spousal Abuse Case and Movie, Dies," *Herald Dispatch,* April 1, 2017, https://perma.cc/G3EN-VQAG.

4. Stephen Farber, "A Serious Farrah Fawcett Takes Control in '*Extremities,*'" *New York Times,* August 17, 1986, https://perma.cc/QTF6-RXB2.

5. *The Burning Bed,* directed by Robert Greenwald (Tisch/Avnet Productions, 1984), https://perma.cc/3B59-R3LM; See also Louise Knott Ahern, "'The Burning Bed': A Turning Point in Fight against Domestic Violence," *Lansing State Journal,* October 27, 2014, https://perma.cc/SPZ5-8MSP.

6. UPI, "'Burning Bed' Tops Prime Time Ratings," UPI Archives, October 17, 1984, https://perma.cc/NF4F-T7CL

7. Farber, "Serious Farrah Fawcett."

8. Ahern, "'Burning Bed,'"; Jay B. Rosman, "Domestic Violence: Recent Amendments to the Florida Statutes," *Nova Law Review* 20, no. 1 (September 1995): 125–26.

9. Emily Langer, "Francine Hughes Wilson, Whose 'Burning Bed' Became a TV Film Dies, at 69," *Washington Post,* April 1, 2017, https://perma.cc/ENW2–44PH.

10. Gioia Diliberto, "A Violent Death, a Haunted Life," *People,* October 8, 1984, https://perma.cc/95Z8-YKAY.

11. Diliberto, "Violent Death."

12. Diliberto, "Violent Death."

13. Scott Pohl, "'Burning Bed' Murder Case: Defense Attorney Looks Back," *WKAR-MSU,* March 30, 2017, https://perma.cc/2EKK-KE5U; Kelly Kazek,

"Woman Who Was Subject of Battered-Wife Film 'The Burning Bed' Dies in Alabama," AL.com, March 29, 2017, https://perma.cc/WA98-Y7PS.

14. Martha Minow, "Surviving Victim Talk," *UCLA Law Review* 40, no. 6 (August 1993): 1433.

15. Minow, "Surviving Victim Talk," 1433.

16. See Anne M. Coughlin, "Excusing Women," *California Law Review* 82, no. 1 (January 1994): 1–93; Mary Ann Dutton, "Update of the 'Battered Woman Syndrome' Critique," VAW.net, August 2009, https://perma.cc/4ST8-6BPU. I discuss the trope of ruined rape victims in chapter 5 in the section "Managing Myths."

17. Beth Richie, *Arrested Justice: Black Women, Violence, and America's Prison Nation* (New York: New York University Press, 2012), 90.

18. Marie Gottschalk, *The Prison and the Gallows: The Politics of Mass Incarceration in America* (Cambridge: Cambridge University Press, 2006), 97–114.

19. Jonathan Simon, "Megan's Law: Crime and Democracy in Late Modern America," *Law and Social Inquiry* 25, no. 4 (Autumn 2000): 1136.

20. Marlene Young and John Stein, "The History of the Crime Victims' Movement in the United States," Office for Victims of Crime Archive, December 2004, https://perma.cc/RBN8-WX9F.

21. Young and Stein, "History."

22. Gottschalk, *Prison and the Gallows,* 88–90; see generally Markus Dirk Dubber, *Victims in the War on Crime: The Use and Abuse of Victims' Rights* (New York: New York University Press, 2002); Aya Gruber, "Victim Wrongs: The Case for a General Criminal Defense Based on Wrongful Victim Behavior in an Era of Victims' Rights," *Temple Law Review* 76, no.4 (December 2003): 645–67.

23. See Elayne Rapping, "Television, Melodrama, and the Rise of the Victims' Rights Movement," *New York Law School Law Review* 43, nos. 3–4 (June 1999–2000): 670–72, discussing the prejudicial effect of victim impact statements in death penalty sentencing hearings; Gruber, "Victim Wrongs," 658–60.

24. Senate Committee on the Judiciary, Report on Crime Victims' Rights Amendment, S. Rep. 108–191 (2003), 85, quoting Patricia Perry.

25. Elizabeth E. Joh, "Narrating Pain: The Problem with Victim Impact Statements," *Southern California Interdisciplinary Law Journal* 10, no. 1 (September 2000): 28.

26. Arizona's Victims' Rights Amendment confers the "right" to "refuse an interview, deposition, or other discovery request by the ... *defendant's* attorney," a right all people *already have.* It does not confer the right to refuse to cooperate with police or prosecutors, which is basically compulsory. Arizona Constitution, Article II, §2.1(A)(5).

27. Gottschalk, *Prison and the Gallows,* 90, quoting Katherine Beckett and Theodore Sasson, *The Politics of Injustice: Crime and Punishment in America* (Thousand Oaks, CA: Pine Forge Press, 2000), 161 (internal quotation marks omitted).

28. Gottschalk, *Prison and the Gallows,* 90.

29. Dubber, *Victims in the War,* 335.

30. See chapter 2, in the section "Leniency versus Women's Liberation," for this discussion.

31. Lynne Henderson, "Co-opting Compassion: The Federal Victims' Rights Amendment," *Saint Thomas Law Review* 10, no. 3 (March 1998): 584.

32. Dubber, *Victims in the War,* 192.

33. Ronald W. Reagan, "Proclamation 4831—Victims Rights Weeks, 1981," Ronald Reagan: Presidential Library and Museum, April 8, 1981, https://perma.cc /YG7M-7R4J.

34. President Clinton stated, "We sure don't want to give criminals like gang members, who may be victims of their associates [any rights]." Henderson, "Co-opting Compassion," 585, quoting Clinton's announcement in support of a Victims' Rights Amendment, *Online News Hour,* June 25, 1996, PBS, https://www.pbs.org /newshour/politics/law-jan-june96-victim_06–25.

35. Bruce Shapiro, "Victims and Vengeance: Why the Victims' Rights Amendment Is a Bad Idea," *Nation,* February 10, 1997, 11–19.

36. Lynne Henderson, "Revisiting Victims' Rights," *Utah Law Review* 1999, no. 2 (March 1999): 408, arguing that participation in criminal litigation may not help victims heal.

37. Minow, "Surviving Victim Talk," 1434.

38. Janet Reno, "Remarks of the Honorable Janet Reno, Attorney General of the United States, to the Child Welfare League of America," United States Department of Justice Archives, March 13, 1998, https://perma.cc/WR42–3BU7.

39. Michelle Goldberg, "Trump's 'Angel Moms' Deserve Our Sympathy. But Their Message Is a Lie," *Slate,* September 1, 2016, https://perma.cc/GZX2-R27D.

40. See Ronald W. Reagan, "Remarks at the Annual Conference of the National Sheriffs' Association in Hartford, Connecticut," Ronald Regan Presidential Library and Museum, June 20, 1984, https://perma.cc/SU8G-V6A4, calling criminals a "privileged class."

41. Jon Kyl, Steven J. Twist, and Stephen Higgins, "On the Wings of Their Angels: The Scott Campbell, Stephanie Roper, Wendy Preston, Louarna Gillis, and Nila Lynn Crime Victims' Rights Act," *Lewis and Clark Law Review* 9, no. 3 (September 2005): 584 (emphasis added).

42. Alice Koskela, "Victim's Rights Amendments: An Irresistible Political Force Transforms the Criminal Justice System," *Idaho Law Review* 34, no. 1 (December 1997): 158 for both quotes.

43. Lois Haight Herrington, Garfield Bobo, Frank Carrington, James P. Damos, Doris L. Dolan, Kenneth O. Eikenberry, Robert J. Miller, Rev. Pat Robertson, and Stanton E. Samenow, "Recommendations for Government Action," *President's Task Force on Victims of Crime: Final Report,* December 1982, 32, https://perma.cc /FF4N-ESLQ. In 1987, Reagan appointed Herrington as "chairman" and executive director of the White House Conference for a Drug Free America.

44. Herrington et al., 114. The "Warren Court Era" extended from 1953 to 1969, when Earl Warren presided as chief justice. It is remembered for its distinctly civil libertarian bent.

45. Herrington et al., "Recommendations for Government Action."

46. William L. Hart et al., *Family Violence: Attorney General's Task Force Final Report,* September 1984, iii, https://perma.cc/CXN7-SX4D. Hart was later convicted of embezzling crime-fighting funds in a case that divided the community, with his supporters accusing federal officials of racism. See Robert Blau, "Detroit Divided over Trial of Police Chief of 'a Thousand Faces,'" *Chicago Tribune,* February 2, 1992, https://perma.cc/6QNT-LEXH.

47. See, e.g., David Crary, "Ashcroft Defends Abortion Subpoenas," *Boston Globe,* February 13, 2004, https://perma.cc/E6BD-6P7D; Eric Lichtblau, "Defending '03 Law, Justice Dept. Seeks Abortion Records," *New York Times,* February 12, 2004, https://perma.cc/G552-Q89F.

48. Ari Shapiro, "Ashcroft Defends Actions on Torture Memos," *All Things Considered,* July 17, 2008, NPR, https://perma.cc/9RS4–9A8M. I note that there were media reports that Ashcroft internally voiced objections to Bush about the torture program.

49. See Bob Egelko, "Domestic Violence Ruled a Reason for Political Asylum," *SFGate,* August 26, 2014, https://perma.cc/WS6U-ACLJ; Rachel L. Swarns, "Ashcroft Weighs the Granting of Political Asylum to Abused Women," *New York Times,* March 11, 2004, https://perma.cc/DH8V-F2NC; Department of Homeland Security Position on Respondent's Eligibility for Relief at 43, Alvarado-Pena, No. A 73 753 922 San Francisco (U.S. Department. of Justice Deportation Proceedings, February 19, 2004), https://perma.cc/S6TP-69U3; William Fisher, "Battered Women and the Contentious Immigration Debate," *National Ledger,* April 28, 2006, https://perma.cc/YP9Q-6ZFJ.

50. Daniella Silva, "ACLU Sues Jeff Sessions over Restricting Asylum for Victims of Domestic, Gang Violence," NBC News, August 7, 2018, https://perma.cc/SLM6–93MP.

51. Hart et al., *Family Violence,* vi.

52. Associated Press, "Fox News Host 'Judge Jeanine' Pirro Sued for Defamation By Black Lives Matter Activist," *USA Today,* December 13, 2017, https://perma.cc/P8W6–5D38.

53. Media Matters Staff, "Fox Host: Trump Sexual Assault Claim Is Just 'Locker Room Talk' and 'Frat House Language,'" *Media Matters,* October 10, 2016, quoting Judge Jeanine Pirro, *Fox and Friends,* October 10, 2016, https://perma.cc/A268–4D4S;

54. Hart et al., *Family Violence,* 11.

55. Lisa A. Frisch, "Research That Succeeds, Policies That Fail," *Journal of Criminal Law and Criminology* 83, no. 1 (1992): 210.

56. Hart et al., *Family Violence,* 23.

57. Melinda Cooper, *Family Values: Between Neoliberalism and the New Social Conservatism* (Brooklyn, NY: Zone Books, 2017), 21.

58. Cooper, *Family Values,* 21.

59. Hart et al., *Family Violence,* ii.

60. Hart et al., *Family Violence,* 119.

61. 98 Cong. Rec. E4 142–43 (October 2, 1984) (Remarks of Rep. Au Coin on H.R. 1904). Conservatives also sought to fund "faith-based" DV interventions. See, e.g., George W. Bush, "National Domestic Violence Awareness Month, 2005: A Proclamation by the President of the United States of America," The White House: President George W. Bush Archives, September 30, 2005, https://perma.cc /SJ8M-EFVU.

62. Hart et al., *Family Violence*, 118.

63. Concerned Women for America, "Our History," n.d., accessed November 24, 2018, https://perma.cc/H89T-6BRR.

64. Susan Faludi, *Backlash: The Undeclared War against American Women* (New York: Crown, 1991), 251.

65. Allan Carlson, *The Natural Family: A Manifesto* (Dallas, TX: Spence 2007), 7, https://perma.cc/F3ZM-KJC9.

66. Hart et al., *Family Violence*, 118.

67. John Ashcroft, "Prepared Remarks of Attorney General John Ashcroft. Annual Symposium on Domestic Violence," Department of Justice, October 29, 2002, https://perma.cc/6GLL-SZWK.

68. Elaine Chiu, "Confronting the Agency in Battered Mothers," *Southern California Law Review* 74, no. 5 (July 2001): 1258.

69. See Zelda B. Harris, "The Predicament of the Immigrant Victim/Defendant: 'Vawa Diversion' and Other Considerations in Support of Battered Women," *Saint Louis University Public Law Review* 23 (2004): 54, noting that "mandatory policies were sought to address ... coercive control tactics used by the abuser to prevent the victim from seeking assistance."

70. See Evan Stark, "Re-presenting Woman Battering: From Battered Woman Syndrome to Coercive Control," *Albany Law Review* 58, no. 4 (June 1995): 1006.

71. Laurie Woods, "Litigation on Behalf of Battered Women," *Women's Rights Law Reporter* 5 (October 1978): 29 (emphasis added).

72. Cheryl Hanna, "No Right to Choose: Mandated Victim Participation in Domestic Violence Prosecutions," *Harvard Law Review* 109, no. 8 (June 1996): 1891.

73. See chapter 3, notes 95, 105, and 146.

74. Cynthia Grant Bowman, "The Arrest Experiments: A Feminist Critique," *Journal of Criminal Law and Criminology* 83, no. 1 (Spring 1992): 203.

75. Hanna, "No Right to Choose," 1900.

76. See Ruth Jones, "Guardianship for Coercively Battered Women: Breaking the Control of the Abuser," *Georgetown Law Journal* 88, no. 4 (April 2000): 609.

77. Donna Wills, "Domestic Violence: The Case for Aggressive Prosecution," *UCLA Women's Law Journal* 7, no. 2 (Spring/Summer 1997): 179.

78. Prentice L. White, "Stopping the Chronic Batterer through Legislation: Will It Work This Time?," *Pepperdine Law Review* 31, no. 3 (April 2004): 725.

79. White, "Stopping the Chronic Batterer," 725.

80. White, "Stopping the Chronic Batterer," 725.

81. I discuss the prevalence of specialized DV courts in chapter 2, note 19.

82. Adam Liptak, "Threats and Responses: The Detainees; For Post-9/11 Material Witness, It Is a Terror of a Different Kind," *New York Times,* August 19, 2004, https://perma.cc/SD7J-BU44.

83. Hanna, "No Right to Choose," 1898, for both quotes.

84. Hanna, "No Right to Choose," 1898.

85. One battered women's advocate argued in 1992, "Even if a law enforcement approach fails to result in specific deterrence . . . [it] sends an appropriate message to the community—that domestic violence is not acceptable." Lisa G. Lerman, "The Decontextualization of Domestic Violence," *Journal of Criminal Law and Criminology* 83, no. 1 (April 1992): 224–25.

86. Alice M. Miller and Mindy Jane Roseman, introduction to *Beyond Virtue and Vice: Rethinking Human Rights and Criminal Law,* ed. Alice M. Miller and Mindy Jane Roseman (Philadelphia: University of Pennsylvania Press, 2019), 13.

87. Bernard E. Harcourt, "Joel Feinberg on Crime and Punishment: Exploring the Relationship between the Moral Limits of the Criminal Law and the Expressive Function of Punishment," *Buffalo Criminal Law Review* 5, no. 1 (September 2001): 168.

88. Marion Wanless, "Mandatory Arrest: A Step toward Eradicating Domestic Violence, but Is It Enough?," *University of Illinois Law Review* 1996, no. 2 (March 1996): 533–61. See also Frisch, "Research That Succeeds," 216: mandatory arrest policies are necessary to "show just how advanced we truly are."

89. Claire Houston, "How Feminist Theory Became (Criminal) Law: Tracing the Path to Mandatory Criminal Intervention in Domestic Violence Cases," *Michigan Journal of Gender and Law* 21, no. 2 (July 2014): 252.

90. Lenore Walker, *The Battered Woman* (New York: Harper and Row, 1979), 69. See also R. Emerson Dobash and Russell P. Dobash, *Women, Violence and Social Change* (London: Routledge, 1992), 218.

91. Susan L. Miller, "Arrest Policies for Domestic Violence and Their Implications for Battered Women," in *It's a Crime: Women and Justice,* ed. Roslyn Muraskin and Ted Alleman (Upper Saddle River, NJ: Prentice Hall 1993), 247, citing studies.

92. Miller, "Arrest Policies," 247; see also Jeffrey Ackerman and Tony P. Love, "Ethnic Group Differences in Police Notification about Intimate Partner Violence," *Violence Against Women* 20, no. 2 (2014): 166–67, 177.

93. Donna Coker, "Shifting Power for Battered Women: Law, Material Resources, and Poor Women of Color," *U.C. Davis Law Review* 33, no. 4 (June 2000): 1018.

94. American Civil Liberties Union, *Responses from the Field: Sexual Assault, Domestic Violence, and Policing,* New York: American Civil Liberties Union, October 2015, 10, https://perma.cc/VXU2-DHCW.

95. American Civil Liberties Union, *Responses from the Field,* 25.

96. American Civil Liberties Union, *Responses from the Field,* 28.

97. American Civil Liberties Union, *Responses from the Field,* 29.

98. See, e.g., S.C. Code Ann. § 23-3-430 (2018); Wash. Rev. Code § 9A.44.130 (2018); Miss. Code Ann. § 45-33-25 (2018).

99. Stanley Cohen, *Folk Devils and Moral Panics: The Creation of the Mods and Rockers,* 3rd ed. (London: Routledge, 2002), xxii.

100. See Darkness to Light, "Child Sex Abuse Statistics: Perpetrators," updated December 22, 2015, https://perma.cc/MP3U-EKWD; Sarah W. Craun and Matthew T. Theriot, "Misperceptions of Sex Offender Perpetration: Considering the Impact of Sex Offender Registration," *Journal of Interpersonal Violence* 24, no. 12 (December 2009): 2057–72; Naomi J. Freeman and Jeffrey C. Sandler, "The Adam Walsh Act: A False Sense of Security or an Effective Public Policy Initiative?," *Criminal Justice Policy Review* 21, no. 1 (March 2010): 46, noting that "several recent studies . . . have found registration and notification laws to be ineffective methods of reducing sexual victimizations" and that "there is some evidence to suggest that these types of laws are increasing recidivism" and citing studies.

101. See William J. Clinton, "Remarks on Signing Megan's Law and an Exchange with Reporters," govinfo, Administration of William J. Clinton, 1996, May 17, 1996, 763, https://perma.cc/PFD9-92L2.

102. Wayne A. Logan, "Megan's Laws as a Case Study in Political Stasis," *Syracuse Law Review* 61, no. 3 (April 2011): 378–79; see also People v. Ross, 646 N.Y.S.2d 249, 250 n.1 (N.Y. Sup. Ct. 1996), listing registration statutes.

103. Jonathan Simon, "Introduction: Crime, Community, and Criminal Justice," *California Law Review* 90, no. 5 (October 2002): 1417.

104. Associated Press, "Adam Walsh Case Transformed Missing Kid Searches," Fox News, December 17, 2008, https://perma.cc/625X-X42P, quoting Richard Moran.

105. William J. Stuntz, "The Pathological Politics of Criminal Law," *Michigan Law Review* 100, no. 3 (December 2001): 505–600.

106. Stuntz, "Pathological Politics," 532.

107. Stuntz, "Pathological Politics," 532.

108. Colo. Rev. Stat. §§ 16–13–801 to 16–13–812 (1998). See also Jessica Fender, "Family Members of Sex Offenders Organize Lawsuit against Colorado's Indeterminate Sentences," *Denver Post,* August 13, 2011, https://perma.cc/66TD-RA4M; Wayne A. Logan, "Populism and Punishment: Sex Offender Registration and Community Notification in the Courts," *Criminal Justice* 26, no. 1 (Spring 2011): 44.

109. Rapping, "Television, Melodrama," 675–76, quoting Van Gordon Sauter, "Rating the Reality Shows and Keeping Tabs on the Tabloids," *TV Guide,* May 2, 1992, 18.

110. White House, "President Signs H.R. 4472, the Adam Walsh Child Protection and Safety Act of 2006," press release, July 27, 2006, https://perma.cc/JM5G-2V9J.

111. Jon M. Sands, "Re: Adam Walsh Child Protection and Safety Act of 2006, Pub. L. 109–248," *Federal Public Defender District of Arizona* (November 16, 2006): 12–13, https://perma.cc/CU6M-S358; See also Robert Ecoffey et al., "Report of the Native American Advisory Group on the Organizational Sentencing Guidelines," US Sentencing Commission (2003), 32, https://perma.cc/QQY8-JV4B.

112. Mark Motivans and Tracey Kyckelhahn, "Federal Prosecution of Child Sex Exploitation Offenders, 2006," US Department of Justice, *Bureau of Justice Statistics Bulletin,* December 2007, https://perma.cc/6H25-5DCB.

113. Motivans and Kyckelhahn, "Federal Prosecution."

114. See, e.g., Jeffrey Kofman, "Sex Offenders Live in Village under Miami Bridge," ABC News, September 3, 2009, https://perma.cc/66S9-3CSL; Isaiah Thompson, "Sex Offenders Set Up Camp," *Miami New Times,* December 13, 2007, https://perma.cc/3VMW-Q6SZ; Greg Allen, "Bridge Still Home for Miami Sex Offenders," *All Things Considered,* July 21, 2009, NPR, https://perma.cc/KK7S-2Y5U.

115. Thompson, "Sex Offenders."

116. Greg Allen, "Sex Offenders Forced to Live under Miami Bridge," *All Things Considered,* May 20, 2009, NPR, https://perma.cc/5NU4-TBUJ.

117. Terrence McCoy, "Miami Sex Offenders Live on Train Tracks Thanks to Draconian Restrictions," *Broward-Palm Beach New Times,* March 13, 2014, https://perma.cc/E2C3-SGV7.

118. David Finkelhor, Richard Ormrod, and Mark Chaffin, "Juveniles Who Commit Sex Offenses against Minors," US Department of Justice, Office of Juvenile Justice and Delinquency Prevention, December 2009, 1–2, https://perma.cc/C93A-P9WR.

119. Finkelhor, Ormrod, and Chaffin, "Juveniles," 2.

120. Sarah Stillman, "List," *New Yorker,* March 14, 2016, https://perma.cc/42EB-B7R2; see also Hal Arkowitz and Scott O. Lilienfeld, "Once a Sex Offender, Always a Sex Offender? Maybe Not," *Scientific American: The Sciences,* April 1, 2008, https://perma.cc/2FUM-VWU7.

121. Stillman, "List."

122. Stillman, "List." See also "Son of Child-Welfare Crusader Accused of Sex Offense," *Columbus Dispatch,* May 31, 2007, https://perma.cc/UUZ2-JQ5A.

123. Stillman, "List."

124. Stillman, "List," quoting psychologist Mark Chaffin.

125. Puck Lo, "Sex-Offender Laws Are Ineffective and Unfair, Critics Say," Al Jazeera America, October 17, 2004, https://perma.cc/KN7S-Y46A.; Wayne Logan, "Challenging the Punitiveness of 'New-Generation' SORN Laws," *New Criminal Law Review* 21, no. 3 (August 2018): 426–57.

126. Stillman, "List," quoting Minnesota Sexual Violence Prevention Program, *Sexual Violence Prevention.*

127. See, e.g., Michelle J. Anderson, "Campus Sexual Assault Adjudication and Resistance to Reform," *Yale Law Journal* 125, no. 7 (May 2016): 1954.

128. Leigh B. Bienen, "Defining Incest," *Northwestern University Law Review* 92, no. 4 (June 1998): 1563–64.

129. Kerwin Kaye, "Sexual Abuse Victims and the Wholesome Family: Feminist, Psychological, and State Discourses," in *Regulating Sex: The Politics of Intimacy and Identity,* ed. Elizabeth Bernstein and Laurie Schnaffer (New York: Routledge, 2005), 143, 147–48.

130. Camille Gear Rich, "Innocence Interrupted: Reconstructing Fatherhood in the Shadow of Child Molestation Law," *California Law Review* 101, no. 3 (June 2013): 658.

131. Rich, "Innocence Interrupted," 659.

132. Freedman, "Redefining Rape," 279; Barbara Burrell, *Women and Politics: A Quest for Political Equality in an Age of Economic Inequality* (New York: Routledge, 2018), 126; Jessica R. Pliley, "Why Is It Congress Seems Concerned with Families Only When Sex Trafficking is at Issue?," *George Washington University History News Network,* December 7, 2014, https://perma.cc/6NZM-JTHW; Anne Valk, "Remembering Together: Take Back the Night and the Public Memory of Feminism," in *U.S. Women's History: Untangling the Threads of Sisterhood,* ed. Leslie Brown, Jacqueline Castledine, and Anne Valk (New Brunswick, NJ: Rutgers University Press, 2017), 186.

133. Cleo M. Harrington, "Take Back the Night," *Harvard Crimson,* May 5, 2017, https://perma.cc/3KVG-548Y.

134. William R. Smith and Marie Torstensson, "Gender Differences in Risk Perception and Neutralizing Fear of Crime: Toward Resolving the Paradoxes," *British Journal of Criminology* 37, no. 4 (October 1997): 608–34. See also Roxanne Lieb, Vernon Quinsey, and Lucy Berliner, "Sexual Predators and Social Policy," *Crime and Justice* 23 (January 1998): 49 ("Fear of sexual assault is an influential aspect of women's psychology and often leads women to make adjustments in the kinds of activities they engage in and in their perceptions of situations").

135. Anderson, "Campus Sexual Assault," 1957–58, quoting the National Alliance to End Sexual Violence.

136. Elisabeth Einaudi and Peggy Mason, "WOMEN: Take Back the Night," *Harvard Crimson,* November 6, 1980, https://perma.cc/GA42-WNKH.

137. Einaudi and Mason, "WOMEN."

138. Mary P. Koss, "Rape: Scope, Impact, Interventions and Public Policy Response," *American Psychologist* 48, no. 10 (October 1993): 1062, asserting that "uniting all women is the fear of rape."

139. Catharine A. MacKinnon, *Are Women Human? And Other International Dialogues* (Cambridge, MA: Harvard University Press, 2006), 88, for both quotes; see also Catharine A. MacKinnon, "Prostitution and Civil Rights," *Michigan Journal of Gender and Law* 1, no. 1 (1993): 30.

140. 148 Cong. Rec. H916 (2002), Rep. Green remarking on the Two Strikes and You're Out Child Protection Act).

141. Paul Brest and Ann Vandenberg, "Politics, Feminism, and the Constitution: The Anti-pornography Movement in Minneapolis," *Stanford Law Review* 39, no. 3 (February 1987): 623. Original testimony reprinted in Catherine A. MacKinnon, *Butterfly Politics* (Cambridge, MA: Harvard University Press, 2017), 101.

142. Brest and Vandenberg, "Politics, Feminism," 629.

143. Alice Echols, "The Taming of the Id: Feminist Sexual Politics, 1968–83," in *Pleasure and Danger: Exploring Female Sexuality,* ed. Carole S. Vance (Boston: Routledge, 1984), 61.

144. Brest and Vandenberg, "Politics, Feminism," 629.

145. Brest and Vandenberg, "Politics, Feminism," 641, quoting MacKinnon.

146. Brest and Vandenberg, "Politics, Feminism," 629–30, quoting a member of the Minneapolis gay community (emphasis added).

147. Kathleen Barry, *Female Sexual Slavery* (New York: New York University Press, 1979), 40.

148. Barry, *Female Sexual Slavery,* 9.

149. Barry, *Female Sexual Slavery,* 10, for both quotes.

150. Barry, *Female Sexual Slavery,* 11.

151. Barry, *Female Sexual Slavery,* 11, for both quotes.

152. Ronald Weitzer, "Sex Trafficking and the Sex Industry: The Need for Evidence-Based Theory and Legislation," *Journal of Criminal Law and Criminology* 101, no. 4 (October 2011): 1338.

153. Barry, *Female Sexual Slavery,* 39.

154. Cynthia L. Wolken, "Feminist Legal Theory and Human Trafficking in the United States: Towards a New Framework," *University of Maryland Law Journal of Race, Religion, Gender and Class* 6, no. 2 (2006): 410.

155. Julie Burchill, *Damaged Gods: Cults and Heroes Reappraised* (London: Arrow, 1987), 9. Catharine MacKinnon's stance was more moderate: "Criminal laws against prostitution make women into criminals for being victimized as women.... This is not to argue that prostitutes have a sex equality right to engage in prostitution." MacKinnon, "Prostitution and Civil Rights," 20.

156. Aya Gruber, Amy J. Cohen, and Kate Mogulescu, "Penal Welfare and the New Human Trafficking Intervention Courts," *Florida Law Review* 68, no. 5 (September 2016): 1364–67.

157. Lauren Hersh, "Sex Trafficking Investigations and Prosecutions," in *Lawyer's Manual on Human Trafficking: Pursuing Justice for Victims,* ed. Jill Laurie Goodman and Dorchen A. Leidholdt (Report of the New York State Judicial Committee on Women in the Courts: N.Y. Sup. Ct. App. Div.1d, 2013), 260.

158. See Elizabeth Bernstein, *Brokered Subjects: Sex, Trafficking, and the Politics of Freedom* (Chicago: University of Chicago Press, 2019).

159. See Miller and Roseman, *Beyond Virtue and Vice;* Janet Halley, Prabha Kotiswaran, Hila Shamir, and Chantal Thomas, "From the International to the Local in Feminist Legal Responses to Rape, Prostitution/Sex Work, and Sex Trafficking: Four Studies in Contemporary Governance Feminism," *Harvard Journal of Law and Gender* 29, no. 2 (2006): 335–423; Prabha Kotiswaran, "Born unto Brothels: Toward a Legal Ethnography of Sex Work in an Indian Red-Light Area," *Law and Social Inquiry* 33, no. 3 (July 2008): 579–629; Bernstein, *Brokered Subjects,*

160. Gruber, Cohen, and Mogulescu, "Penal Warfare," 1339–43.

161. Duncan Kennedy, "Sexual Abuse, Sexy Dressing and the Eroticization of Domination," *New England Law Review* 26, no. 4 (Summer 1992): 1314.

162. Judy Klemesrud, "Joining Hands in the Fight against Pornography," *New York Times,* August 26, 1985, https://perma.cc/RD3B-RZP8.

163. Andrea Dworkin, *Letters From a War Zone* (London: Secker and Warburg, 1988), 13–14, https://perma.cc/87P3-LRCP.

164. See Christina E. Wells and Erin Elliott Motley, "Reinforcing the Myth of the Crazed Rapist: A Feminist Critique of Recent Rape Legislation," *Boston University Law Review* 81, no. 1 (February 2001): 189.

165. Sharon Marcus, "Fighting Bodies, Fighting Words: A Theory and Politics of Rape Prevention," in *Gender Struggles: Practical Approaches to Contemporary Feminism,* ed. Constance L. Mui and Julien S. Murphy (Lanham, MD: Rowman and Littlefield, 2002), 170–71; see also Janet Halley, *Split Decisions: How and Why to Take a Break from Feminism* (Princeton, NJ: Princeton University Press, 2006), 199.

5. THE NEW FRONT

1. The statistics regarding how much nonmarital sex occurred before the sexual revolution are conflicting. Some studies estimate that nonmarital sex was a fairly constant phenomenon over time, while others show steep increases during and after the sexual revolution era. However, the studies do consistently show an increase over time and a decrease in the age of premarital sex after the sexual revolution. Compare Lawrence L. Wu, Steven P. Martin, and Paula England, "Reexamining Trends in Premarital Sex in the United States," *Demographic Research* 38, no. 27 (February 2018): 733–34, https://perma.cc/BNP7–4YBF (finding that premarital sex rates for women born in the 1960s and 70s were 32 percentage points higher than for women born in the 1940s), with Lawrence B. Finer, "Trends in Premarital Sex in the United States, 1954–2003," *Public Health Report* 122, no. 1 (January-February 2007): 73–78, https://perma.cc/4UTZ-QXSM (finding consistently high levels of premarital sex with a slight increase for women born in the 1960s and '70s compared to women in the 1940s). The important point is that feminists in the 1970s found themselves in a new sexual *culture,* regardless of whether more nonmarital sex occurred.

2. I discuss the "sex wars" over pornography in chapter 4, in the section "Predators and Prey."

3. Kathryn Abrams, "Sex Wars Redux: Agency and Coercion in Feminist Legal Theory," *Columbia Law Review* 95, no. 2 (March 1995): 318.

4. Kathleen Barry, "'Sadomasochism': The New Backlash to Feminism," *Trivia,* no. 1 (Fall 1982): 83–84.

5. Morrison Torrey, "Feminist Legal Scholarship on Rape: A Maturing Look at One Form of Violence against Women," *William and Mary Journal of Women and the Law* 2, no. 1 (1995): 38, for both quotes.

6. bell hooks, *Feminist Theory: From Margin to Center* (Boston: South End Press, 1984), 118.

7. Aviva Orenstein, "'MY GOD!': A Feminist Critique of the Excited Utterance Exception to the Hearsay Rule," *California Law Review* 85, no. 1 (January 1997): 196.

8. Catharine A. MacKinnon, *Toward a Feminist Theory of the State* (Cambridge, MA: Harvard University Press, 1989): 109 (emphasis added), 128. See also Catharine A. MacKinnon, *Feminism Unmodified: Discourses on Life and Law* (Cambridge, MA: Harvard University Press, 1987), 45–49.

9. Catharine A. MacKinnon, "Feminism, Marxism, Method, and the State: An Agenda for Theory," *Signs* 7, no. 3 (Spring 1982): 516.

10. MacKinnon, *Toward a Feminist Theory,* 116.

11. See Wendy Brown, *States of Injury: Power and Freedom in the Late Modernity* (Princeton, NJ: Princeton University Press, 1995), 86.

12. Catharine A. MacKinnon, *Women's Lives, Men's Laws* (Cambridge, MA: Belknap Press, 2007), 246.

13. See Lenore Walker, *The Battered Woman* (New York: Harper and Row, 1979), 69, calling women "accomplices" to their own battering.

14. Susan Brownmiller, *Against Our Will: Men, Women, and Rape* (New York: Fawcett Books, 1975), 377 (emphasis added).

15. Gayle S. Rubin, "Thinking Sex: Notes for a Radical Theory of the Politics of Sexuality," in *Pleasure and Danger: Exploring Female Sexuality,* ed. Carole S. Vance (Boston: Routledge, 1984), 150.

16. This is discussed in chapter 4, in the section "Predators and Prey."

17. Catharine A. MacKinnon, "Rape Redefined," *Harvard Law and Policy Review* 10, no. 2 (Summer 2016): 469.

18. See Commonwealth v. Rhodes, 510 A.2d 1217 (Penn., 1986), 1218–20.

19. Commonwealth v. Rhodes, 481 A.2d 610, 613 (Sup. Ct. Penn., 1984), reversed by 510 A.2d 1217 (Penn., 1986).

20. Rhodes, 481 A.2d at 613.

21. Rhodes, 481 A.2d at 613.

22. Rhodes, 510 A.2d at 1225–26.

23. MacKinnon, "Rape Redefined," 469, for all quotes (emphasis added).

24. Rhodes, 510 A.2d at 1226.

25. Rhodes, 510 A.2d at 1226.

26. See Estelle B. Freedman, *Redefining Rape: Sexual Violence in the Era of Suffrage and Segregation* (Cambridge, MA: Harvard University Press: 2013), 274–75. See also American Law Institute, Model Penal Code (Official Draft and Revised Comments 1980) [MPC] § 213.1 cmt. 3 (discussing racial history of rape law).

27. MPC §§ 213.6(5) (credibility and corroboration instructions) & (4) (prompt complaint) (Am. Law Inst., Official Draft and Revised Comments 1980).

28. MPC §§ 213.1(1). I discuss these rules in chapter 1, in the section "Sex, Policing, and Sex Policing."

29. Susan Estrich, "Rape," *Yale Law Journal* 95, no. 6 (May 1986): 1087–1184; Susan Estrich, *Real Rape: How the Legal System Victimizes Women Who Say No* (Cambridge, MA: Harvard University Press, 1987).

30. Brownmiller, *Against Our Will,* 15.

31. Vernon R. Wiehe and Ann L. Richards, *Intimate Betrayal: Understanding and Responding to the Trauma of Acquaintance Rape* (Thousand Oaks, CA: Sage Publications, 1995), 43–45.

32. See American Law Institute, Model Penal Code: Sexual Assault and Related Offenses Tentative Draft No. 1 (April 30, 2014), 86–91, surveying state and federal law on the status of prompt complaint, corroboration, and Lord Hale; see also Estrich, "Rape," 1123–24.

33. See, e.g., State v. Eskridge, 526 N.E.2d 304, 306 (Ohio 1988) ("Force . . . can be subtle and psychological"); People v. Iniguez, 872 P. 2d 1183, 1189 (Cal. 1994).

34. See Johnson v. State, 328 P.3d 77, 89 (Alaska 2014) ("The criminal prohibition on rape has as its goal preventing the loss of autonomy, dignity, free will, and bodily integrity"); People v. Soto, 245 P.3d 410, 418 (Cal. 2011) (rape is violation of "sexual autonomy").

35. Estrich, "Rape," 1095.

36. Joshua Dressler, "Where We Have Been, and Where We Might Be Going: Some Cautionary Reflections on Rape Law Reform," *Cleveland State Law Review* 46, no. 3 (June 1998): 423.

37. Meredith J. Duncan, "Sex Crimes and Sexual Miscues: The Need for a Clearer Line between Forcible Rape and Nonconsensual Sex," *Wake Forest Law Review* 42, no. 4 (December 2007): 1112; Ian Ayres and Katharine K. Baker, "A Separate Crime of Reckless Sex," *University of Chicago Law Review* 72, no. 2 (Spring 2005): 599–666; Donald A. Dripps, "Beyond Rape: An Essay on the Difference between the Presence of Force and the Absence of Consent," *Columbia Law Review* 92, no. 7 (November 1992): 1805.

38. MacKinnon, "Rape Redefined," 465.

39. Catharine A. MacKinnon, "Feminism, Marxism, Method, and the State: Toward Feminist Jurisprudence," *Signs: Journal of Women in Culture and Society* 8, no. 4 (Summer 1983): 647.

40. Commonwealth v. Berkowitz, 641 A.2d 1161 (Pa. 1994).

41. Commonwealth v. Berkowitz, 609 A.2d 1338, 1340 (Pa. Super. Ct. 1992), order aff'd in part, vacated in part, 641 A.2d 1161 (1994).

42. Berkowitz, 609 A.2d at 1340.

43. Berkowitz, 609 A.2d at 1341.

44. Berkowitz, 641 A.2d at 1164.

45. Berkowitz, 641 A.2d at 1164.

46. "The domination Mr. Berkowitz exercised with his body over and into her body and the atmosphere of intimidation he created with the locked door were not seen as probative. . . . If sex inequality was regarded as a potential form of force, they could have been, along with her expressions of disinclination." MacKinnon, "Rape Redefined," 468.

47. 18 Pa. C.S.A. § 3101 & § 3124.1 (West 1995).

48. Jan Ackerman, "Two Protests by NOW Take Judges to Task on Rape Ruling," *Pittsburgh Post-Gazette,* June 7, 1994, available at 1994 WLNR 2265884.

49. Peter B. Woods, "Lock Up Rapists Longer," letter to the editor, *Morning Call,* June 14, 1994, available at 1994 WLNR 1956414.

50. *Berkowitz,* 641 A.2d at 1164–65. Mario F. Cattabiani, "Berkowitz Surrender Delayed ESU Student in 'No Is Not Enough' Case Gets Extension to Aug. 1," *Morning Call,* July 19, 1994, https://perma.cc/Z5QD-WENG; Associated Press, "Wherein 'No' Is Not Enough," *New York Times,* May 29, 1992, https://perma.cc /JTJ8-LAUV.

51. 18 Pa. C.S.A. § 3101 & § 3124.1 (West 1995).

52. See Aya Gruber, "Consent Confusion," *Cardozo Law Review* 38, no. 2 (December 2016): 424–29, describing the sexual consent formula.

53. See Martha R. Burt, "Cultural Myths and Supports for Rape," *Journal of Personality and Social Psychology* 38, no. 2 (February 1980): 217–30, finding that gender-stereotypic beliefs are linked to acceptance of rape myths; Gary D. LaFree, Barbara F. Reskin, and Christy A. Visher, "Jurors' Responses to Victims' Behavior and Legal Issues in Sexual Assault Trials," *Social Problems* 32, no. 4 (April, 1985): 389–407, finding that victims' drinking, drug use, and adultery, but not sex-role conformity, led jurors to question defendants' guilt; Valerie P. Hans and Neil Vidmar, *Judging the Jury* (New York: Plenum Press, 1986), 205–15, discussing the studies. Cf. Christy A. Visher, "Juror Decision Making: The Importance of Evidence," *Law and Human Behavior* 11, no. 1 (March 1987): 1–17, finding the strength of evidence to be the most important factor. For a modern survey of the literature, see Sokratis Dinos, Nina Burrowes, Karen Hammond, and Christina Cunliffe, "A Systematic Review of Juries' Assessment of Rape Victims: Do Rape Myths Impact on Juror Decision-Making?," *International Journal of Law, Crime and Justice* 43, no. 1 (March 2015): 36–49.

54. Aviva A. Orenstein, "No Bad Men! A Feminist Analysis of Character Evidence in Rape Trials," *Hastings Law Journal* 49 (March 1998): 678.

55. Leigh Bienen, "Rape Reform Legislation in the United States: A Look at Some Practical Effects," *Victimology* 8, no. 1–2 (1983): 139.

56. Dan M. Kahan, "Culture, Cognition, and Consent: Who Perceives What, and Why, in Acquaintance-Rape Cases," *University of Pennsylvania Law Review* 158, no. 3 (February 2010): 729–813. See also David P. Bryden, "Redefining Rape," *Buffalo Criminal Law Review* 3, no. 2 (January 2000): 417.

57. This may be because many of the rape myth studies looked at the correlation between believing myths and acquitting but not the prevalence jurors who believed rape myths or whether such myths survived the deliberation process. Cf. David J. Giacopassi and R. Thomas Dull, "Gender and Racial Differences in the Acceptance of Rape Myths within a College Population," *Sex Roles* 15, nos. 1/2 (1986): 63–75, finding that "only a minority of respondents subscribe to the myths and stereotypes." Indeed, "The multiple ways in which those abstract attitudes interact with the details of a case, as well as with the applicable legal tests and burdens of proof and the group dynamics within the jury room, are not capable of observation through surveys or scales." Louise Ellison and Vanessa E. Munro, "A Stranger in the Bushes, or an Elephant in the Room? Critical Reflections upon Received Rape Myth Wisdom in the Context of a Mock Jury Study," *New Criminal Law Review: An International and Interdisciplinary Journal* 13, no. 4 (Fall 2010): 799.

58. "Felony Defendants in Large Urban Counties, 1990" (Statistical Tables), US Department of Justice, May 1993, 13 (table 15), https://perma.cc/383B-8RTF.

59. "Felony Defendants in Large Urban Counties, 2009—Statistical Tables," US Department of Justice, December 2013, 24 (table 21), https://perma.cc/92GQ-QXHF.

60. See "Felony Defendants 1990," 17 (table 20); "Felony Defendants 2009," 29 (table 24).

61. See Cassia C. Spohn, Dawn Beichner, Erika Davis Frenzel, and David Holleran, "Prosecutors' Charging Decisions in Sexual Assault Cases: A Multi-site Study, Final Report," National Criminal Justice Reference Service, no. 197048 (October 2002), 74, quoting David Neubauer, *America's Courts and the Criminal Justice System*, 3rd ed. (Pacific Grove, CA: Brooks/Cole, 1988).

62. There are rape courts in other countries, such as South Africa. Cynthia Grant Bowman and Elizabeth Brundige, "Child Sex Abuse within the Family in Sub-Saharan Africa: Challenges and Change in Current Legal and Mental Health Responses," *Cornell International Law Journal* 47, no. 2 (March 2014): 280–82.

63. Beatrice Diehl, "Affirmative Consent in Sexual Assault: Prosecutors' Duty," *Georgetown Journal of Legal Ethics* 28, no. 2 (June 2015): 508.

64. Charlene L. Muehlenhard and Lisa C. Hollabaugh, "Do Women Sometimes Say No When They Mean Yes? The Prevalence and Correlates of Women's Token Resistance to Sex," *Journal of Personality and Social Psychology* 54, no. 5 (May 1988): 875.

65. Muehlenhard and Hollabaugh, "Do Women Sometimes Say No," 875. For more recent studies, see Charlene L. Muehlenhard, "Examining Stereotypes about Token Resistance to Sex," *Psychology of Women Quarterly* 35, no. 4 (2011): 676–83; Susan E. Hickman and Charlene L. Muehlenhard, "'By the Semi-mystical Appearance of a Condom': How Young Women and Men Communicate Sexual Consent in Heterosexual Situations," *Journal of Sex Research* 36, no. 3 (1999): 258–72; Lucia O'Sullivan and Elizabeth Allgeier, "Feigning Sexual Desire: Consenting to Unwanted Sexual Activity in Heterosexual Dating Relationships," *Journal of Sex Research* 3, no. 3 (1998): 234–43.

66. See Charlene L. Muehlenhard, Terry P. Humphreys, Kristen N. Jozkowski, and Zoë D. Peterson, "Complexities of Sexual Consent among College Students: A Conceptual and Empirical Review," *Journal of Sex Research* 53, nos. 4–5 (May 2016): 477.

67. See American Law Institute, Model Penal Code: Sexual Assault and Related Offenses Preliminary Draft No. 5, September 8, 2015, 53–54 (discussing the "No means no" debate); Ill. Comp. Stat. 5/12–17 (2003) (establishing "No means no" law); United States v. Simpkins, No. ARMY20160263, 2018 WL 4055915, at *2 (A. Ct. Crim. App. Aug. 22, 2018); Commonwealth v. Lefkowitz, 481 N.E.2d 227, 232 n.1 (Mass. App. 1985) (Brown, J., concurring) ("'No' must be understood to mean precisely that"); United States v. Carr, 18 M.J. 297, 302 (C.M.A. 1984) (disallowing reasonable mistake of consent defense when victim said "no").

68. American Law Institute, Model Penal Code: Sexual Assault and Related Offenses Tentative Draft No. 2 (April 15, 2016), 1. (Article 213.0(3)(d) states, "A clear verbal refusal—such as 'No,' 'Stop,' or 'Don't'—suffices to establish the lack of consent." I am an adviser to the MPC revision project and have followed the many proposals and ongoing debates.

69. See, e.g., Lois Pineau, "Date Rape: A Feminist Analysis," *Law and Philosophy* 8, no. 2 (August 1989): 217–43; Robin D. Wiener, "Shifting the Communication Burden: A Meaningful Consent Standard in Rape," *Harvard Women's Law Journal* 6 (March 1983): 143–61; Stephen J. Schulhofer, "Taking Sexual Autonomy Seriously: Rape Law and Beyond," *Law and Philosophy* 11, nos. 1–2 (1992): 35–94.

70. Amanda Marcotte, "Slutwalk, #MeToo and Donald Trump: A Grim but Hopeful Season for Feminism," *Salon,* October 3, 2018, https://perma.cc/T2CF-HXZ4.

71. The MPC reporters surveyed rape statutes in every jurisdiction and determined that nine jurisdictions—Florida, Hawaii, New Jersey, Oklahoma, Oregon, Pennsylvania, Vermont, Wisconsin, and the Uniform Code of Military Justice—had felony sexual assault statutes that expressly require affirmative permission, positive agreement, or active cooperation, and five—Colorado, D.C., Kansas, Minnesota, and the United States—had misdemeanor affirmative consent statutes. American Law Institute, Model Penal Code: Sexual Assault and Related Offenses Tentative Draft No. 3, April 6, 2017, 41 n93.

72. Wis. Stat. Ann. § 940.225.

73. State v. Lederer, 299 N.W.2d 457, 460 (Wis. Ct. App. 1980).

74. Terry P. Humphreys and Mélanie M. Brousseau, "The Sexual Consent Scale—Revised: Development, Reliability, and Preliminary Validity," *Journal of Sexual Research* 47, no. 5 (2010): 422. See also Muehlenhard et al., "Complexities of Sexual Consent."

75. State in the Interest of M.T.S., 609 A.2d 1266, 1269 n.1 (N.J. Super. Ct. App. Div. 1992), quoting N.J. Stat. Ann. § 2C:14–2c(1).

76. M.T.S., 609 A.2d at 1274–75.

77. M.T.S., 609 A.2d at 1276

78. M.T.S. 609 A.2d at 1276, quoting Perna v. Pirozzi, 457 A.2d 431, 462 (N.J. 1983).

79. M.T.S., 609 A.2d at 1276.

80. N.J. Stat. § 2C:14–2 (1978).

81. N.J. Stat. § 2C:14–2 (1978); State v. Cabana, 716 A.2d 576, 578 (N.J. Super. Ct. App. Div. 1997).

82. Perna v. Pirozzi, 457 A.2d 431, 439 (N.J. 1983).

83. M.T.S., 609 A.2d at 1278.

84. M.T.S., 609 A.2d at 1279.

85. M.T.S., 609 A.2d at 1267.

86. M.T.S., 609 A.2d at 1268.

87. M.T.S., 609 A.2d at 1268.

88. State In the Interest of M.T.S., 588 A.2d 1282, 1283 (reversed by M.T.S., 609 A.2d 1266).

89. M.T.S., 588 A.2d 1283.

90. M.T.S., 588 A.2d 1283.

91. Humphreys and Brousseau, "Sexual Consent Scale," 421, citing studies.

92. One author who called tonic immobility a "common" and typical" response relied on a single study involving interviews with seven women who described their

dissociative response to a sexual attack. Kimberly Peterson, "Victim or Villain? The Effects of Rape Culture and Rape Myths on Justice for Rape Victims," *Valparaiso University Law Review* 53 (2019): 508, 513, citing Sunda Friedman, Te Bockhorst, Mary Sean O'Halloran, and Blair N. Nyline, "Tonic Immobility among Survivors of Sexual Assault," *Psychological Trauma: Theory, Research, Practice, and Policy* 7, no. 2 (March 2015); see also Michelle J. Anderson, "Reviving Resistance in Rape Law," *University of Illinois Law Review,* no. 4 (1998): 1011, discussing frozen fright; Martin Symonds, "The Rape Victim: Psychological Patterns of Response," *American Journal of Psychoanalysis* 36, no. 1 (1976): 29, discussing psychological infantilism.

93. Mitchell A. Watsky and Samuel Gruber, "Induction and Duration of Tonic Immobility in the Lemon Shark, *Negaprion brevirostris,*" *Fish Physiology and Biochemistry* 8, no. 3 (May 1990): 207–10; "Explorer of the Week: Samuel 'Doc' Gruber," *National Geographic,* July 26, 2012, https://perma.cc/Z69R-VSZG.

94. Symonds, "Rape Victim," 27–34. See Marlene A. Young, "A History of the Victims' Movement in the United States," United Nations Asia and Far East Institute for the Preventions of Crime and the Treatment of Offenders, Resource Material Series No. 70 (n.d.), 72, https://perma.cc/FT6G-CDAT, discussing Symonds's study.

95. Symonds, "Rape Victim," 29.

96. Symonds, "Rape Victim," 29.

97. Symonds, "Rape Victim," 31.

98. Symonds, "Rape Victim," 33.

99. Symonds, "Rape Victim," 33. See also Brian P. Marx, John P. Forsyth, and Jennifer M. Lexington, "Tonic Immobility as an Evolved Predator Defense: Implications for Sexual Assault Survivors," *Clinical Psychology: Science and Practice* 15, no. 1 (March 2008): 74, 79, theorizing that sexual assault may produce tonic immobility but that it "ought to be more likely only after several behavioral strategies (i.e., escape, screaming, and fighting back) have failed and general feelings of fear have escalated into extreme fear or panic."

100. Commentators rely on Anderson's cursory 1998 observation that "some women" freeze in fright (Anderson, "Reviving Resistance," 1011) as proof that frozen fright is a typical response in dating scenarios. See, e.g., Kristen L. Stallion, "Missouri Abolishes the Corroboration Rule and the Destructive Contradictions Doctrine: A Victory for Victims of Sexual Assault?," *Missouri Law Review* 80 no. 2 (Spring 2015): 622. Anderson, indeed, later cited herself for the broader proposition that "frozen in fright, *many* women . . . remain passive in the face of a sexual attack." Michelle J. Anderson, "All-American Rape," *St. John's Law Review* 79, no. 3 (Summer 2005): 625–44 (emphasis added).

101. Melissa Hamilton, "The Reliability of Assault Victims' Immediate Accounts: Evidence from Trauma Studies," *Stanford Law and Policy Review* 26, no. 1 (January 2015): 303. See Stallion, "Missouri," 622; Michal Buchhandler-Raphael, "The Failure of Consent: Re-conceptualizing Rape as Sexual Abuse of Power," *Michigan Journal of Gender and the Law* 18, no. 1 (July 2011): 160 ("A complainant is *often* unable to verbally express refusal, a *common* response that psychologists refer to as "'frozen fright'") (emphasis added).

102. See, e.g., Stephen J. Schulhofer, *Unwanted Sex: The Culture of Intimidation and the Failure of Law* (Cambridge, MA: Harvard University Press, 1998), 266.

103. Humphreys and Brousseau, "Sexual Consent Scale," 422, citing studies.

104. See Bethany Saltman, "We Started the Crusade for Affirmative Consent Way Back in the '90s," *New York Magazine: The Cut,* October 22, 2014, https://perma.cc/T7DK-2S2L; Aya Gruber, "Rape, Feminism, and the War on Crime," *Washington Law Review* 84, no. 4 (2009): 634–35; Katharine K. Baker, "Sex, Rape, and Shame," *Boston University Law Review* 79, no. 3 (June 1999): 687, discussing these events.

105. The Canadian legislature first adopted an affirmative consent definition of sexual assault in 1992, defining consent as "the voluntary agreement of the complainant to engage in the sexual activity in question." In 1999, the Canadian Supreme Court made clear that the defendant "cannot rely on the complainant's silence or ambiguous conduct to initiate sexual contact." Kyla Barranco, "Canadian Sexual Assault Laws: A Model for Affirmative Consent on College Campuses?," *Michigan State International Law Review* 24, no. 3 (2016): 821–22, 830–31, quoting Criminal Code [of Canada], R.S.C. 1985, c. C-46, § 273.1(1) & R. v. Ewanchuk (1999) 1 S.C.R. 330, para. 42 (Can.).

106. See, e.g., Melanie Ann Beres, "Rethinking the Concept of Consent for Anti-sexual Violence Activism and Education," *Feminism and Psychology* 24, no. 3 (August 2014): 373–389; Nicole Bedera, "Moaning and Eye Contact: College Men's Negotiations of Sexual Consent in Theory and in Practice" (PhD diss., University of Michigan, 2017), https://perma.cc/XAL4-KFRZ; Jena Nicols Curtis and Susan Burnett, "Affirmative Consent: What Do College Student Leaders Think about 'Yes Means Yes' as the Standard for Sexual Behavior?," *American Journal of Sexuality Education* 12, no. 3 (2017): 201–14.

107. I discuss slut-shaming in chapter 1, in the section "Rape as a Racial Phenomenon." See also Kathleen A. Bogle, *Hooking Up: Sex, Dating, and Relationships on Campus* (New York: New York University Press, 2008), 109, performing a qualitative study of sexual behavior on college campuses and finding that men labeled seductively dressed women "easy" or "stupid."

108. See, for example, Lani Anne Remick, "Read Her Lips: An Argument for a Verbal Consent Standard in Rape," *University of Pennsylvania Law Review* 141, no. 3 (January 1993): 1103–51.

109. See Fed. R. Evid. 412 (1988) (federal rape shield law); GA. Code Ann. § 24-4-412 (West 2014) ("Evidence of past sexual behavior includes, but is not limited to, evidence of the complaining witness's marital history, mode of dress, general reputation for promiscuity, nonchastity, or sexual mores contrary to the community standards."). See generally Jack E. Call, David Nice, and Susette M. Talarico, "Analysis of State Rape Shield Laws," *Social Science Quarterly* 72, no. 4 (December 1991): 774–88; Bienen, "Rape Reform Legislation."

110. For example, most shield laws permit the introduction of past sexual conduct evidence relevant to identity. See, e.g., Ind. Code § 35-37-4-4. Many also incorporate catch-all provisions that allow the introduction of otherwise prohibited

evidence when exclusion would be unconstitutional. See, e.g., Conn. Gen. Stat. Ann. § 54–86F; D.C. Code § 22–3022. Feminists have fought against this constitutional catch-all for years. See, e.g., Anderson, "From Chastity Requirement," 83–84; Harriett R. Galvin, "Shielding Rape Victims in the State and Federal Courts: A Proposal for the Second Decade," *Minnesota Law Review* 70, no. 4 (April 1986): 886.

111. Michelle J. Anderson, "From Chastity Requirement to Sexuality License: Sexual Consent and a New Rape Shield Law," *George Washington Law Review* 70, no. 1 (February 2002): 94.

112. Anderson, "From Chastity Requirement," 94.

113. Catharine A. MacKinnon, "Reflections on Sex Equality under Law," *Yale Law Journal* 100, no. 5 (March 1991): 1294.

114. Anderson, "From Chastity Requirement," 92.

115. Privacy Protections for Rape Victims Act of 1978: Hearing on H.R. 4727, 96th Cong. 36256 (1978) (statement of Senator Biden).

116. Ilene Seidman and Susan Vickers, "The Second Wave: An Agenda for the Next Thirty Years of Rape Law Reform," *Suffolk University Law Review* 38, no. 2 (2005): 473.

117. Doe v. Purdue Univ., No. 17–3565, 2019 WL 2707502, at *7 (7th Cir. June 28, 2019).

118. See, e.g., Berkowitz, 641 A.2d at 1165–66 (excluding defense evidence that the complainant and her jealous boyfriend had argued over her infidelity in the past, which the defense intended to use to rebut the prosecution's insistence that the complainant had no reason to lie).

119. People v. Lucas, 408 N.W.2d 431, 432 (1987), reversed by Michigan v. Lucas, 500 U.S. 145 (1991).

120. Hall v. State, 500 So.2d 1282, 1286 (Ala. Crim. App. 1986).

121. Fed. R. Evid. 413 (1996).

122. Katharine K. Baker, "Once a Rapist? Motivational Evidence and Relevancy in Rape Law," *Harvard Law Review* 110, no 3 (January 1997): 578–79, discussing recidivism statistics.

123. "Report of the Judicial Conference of the United States on the Admission of Character Evidence in Certain Sexual Misconduct Cases," *Federal Rules Decisions* 159 (1995): 52.

124. Brownmiller, *Against Our Will*, 387; Eugene J. Kanin, "False Rape Allegations," *Archives of Sexual Behavior* 23, no. 1 (February 1994): 84.

125. See David Lisak, Lori Gardinier, Sarah Nicksa, and Ashley Cote, "False Allegations of Sexual Assault: An Analysis of Ten Years of Reported Cases," *Violence Against Women* 16, no. 12 (December 2010): 1318–34, finding a false reporting rate of 5.9 percent in a small New England town and citing studies putting rate at 2 to 10 percent. The FBI reported in 1997 that 8 percent of rape accusations were "unfounded." This was apparently the last time the FBI reported statistics on "unfounded" rapes. Federal Bureau of Investigation, *Uniform Crime Reports for the United States: Crime Index Offenses Reported* (1997), 26, https://perma .cc/82E9-7YDH.

126. See William Donohue, Gwendolyn C. Carlson, Lorraine T. Benuto, and Natalie M. Bennett, "Examining the Scientific Validity of Rape Trauma Syndrome," *Psychiatry, Psychology and Law* 21, no. 6 (2014): 858–76, arguing that RTS was never meant to comment on the truth of rape allegations. See, e.g., Ann Wolbert Burgess and Lynda Lytle Holmstrom, "The Rape Victim in the Emergency Ward," *American Journal of Nursing* 73, no. 10 (October 1973): 1740–45 (original study).

127. Patricia A. Resick, "The Psychological Impact of Rape," *Journal of Interpersonal Violence* 8, no. 2 (June 1993): 223–55: "An overall pattern has emerged with reasonable consistency in all of these studies. Most rape victims experience a strong acute reaction that lasts for several months. By 3 months post-crime, much of the initial turmoil has decreased and stabilized" (225), citing studies. See also Julie A. Allison and Lawrence S. Wrightsman, *Rape: The Misunderstood Crime* (Newbury Park, CA: Sage Publications, 1993); Maria Crespo and Violeta Fernandez-Lansac, "Memory and Narrative of Traumatic Events: A Literature Review," *Psychological Trauma: Theory, Research, Practice, and Policy* 8, no. 2 (March 2016): 155, concluding that "there is not enough support to conclude that the memories in PTSD depend on special mechanisms, as the cognitive models argue."

128. See chapter 7, text accompanying note 54.

129. I discuss the current count of affirmative consent statutes in note 71 of this chapter.

130. Judith Butler, "Against Proper Objects," in *Feminism Meets Queer Theory,* ed. Elizabeth Weed and Naomi Schor (Bloomington: Indiana University Press, 1997), 14.

131. Andrea Dworkin and Catherine A. MacKinnon, *Pornography and Civil Rights: A New Day for Women's Equality* (Minneapolis, MN: Organizing Against Pornography, 1988), 23.

132. Martha Minow, "Between Vengeance and Forgiveness: Feminist Responses to Violent Injustice," in *Feminist Legal Theory: An Anti-essentialist Reader,* ed. Nancy E. Dowd and Michelle Jacobs (New York: New York University Press, 2003), 385.

133. Janet Halley, "The Politics of Injury: A Review of Robin West's *Caring for Justice,*" *Unbound: Harvard Journal of the Legal Left* 1 (2005): 89.

134. See Katherine M. Franke, "Theorizing Yes: An Essay on Feminism, Law, and Desire," *Columbia Law Review* 101, no. 1 (January 2001): 206–7.

135. Janet Halley, *Split Decisions: How and Why to Take a Break from Feminism* (Princeton, NJ: Princeton University Press, 2006), 362.

136. Halley, "Politics of Injury," 82.

137. Robin West, "Desperately Seeking a Moralist," *Harvard Journal of Law and Gender* 29 (2006): 16.

138. Rubin, *Thinking Sex,* 150 (emphasis added).

139. See text accompanying notes 82–83 of this chapter. See also Stephen J. Schulhofer, "The Feminist Challenge in Criminal Law," *University of Pennsylvania Law Review* 143, no. 6 (June 1995): 2181; Nicholas J. Little, "From No Means No to Only Yes Means Yes: The Rational Results of an Affirmative Consent Standard in

Rape Law," *Vanderbilt Law Review* 58 no. 4 (May, 2005): 1349n174; Estrich, "Rape," 1126.

140. Andrea Dworkin, *Intercourse* (New York: Free Press, 1987), 123.

141. Christina Cauterucci, "Trump Will Tap Woman Who Thinks Birth Control Doesn't Work to Lead U.S. Birth Control Program," *Slate: XX Factor,* May 2, 2017, https://perma.cc/M8YL-LAMG.

142. "Sexual Risk Avoidance (SRA) Education and LGBTQ Teens," *Ascend Report,* 2016, https://perma.cc/7DDV-JQHP.

143. Ezra Klein, "'Yes Means Yes' Is a Terrible Law, and I Completely Support It," *Vox,* October 13, 2014, https://perma.cc/9355-M22M.

144. Compare Deborah Tuerkheimer, "Affirmative Consent," *Ohio State Journal of Criminal Law* 13, no. 2 (Spring 2016): 441–68, studying appellate cases and hypothesizing that prosecutors do not strictly apply affirmative consent, and Gruber, "Consent Confusion," 140–41, arguing that appellate cases would not reflect affirmative consent prosecutions that resulted in pleas.

145. See Dorothy E. Roberts, "Race, Vagueness, and the Social Meaning of Order-Maintenance Policing," *Journal of Criminal Law and Criminology* 89, no. 3 (Spring 1999): 775–836; William J. Stuntz, "Unequal Justice," *Harvard Law Review* 121, no. 8 (June 2008): 2012; Loïc Wacquant, "Race as Civic Felony," *International Social Science Journal* 57, no. 183 (March 2005): 128.

146. Ruth D. Peterson and John Hagan, "Changing Conceptions of Race: Towards an Account of Anomalous Findings of Sentencing Research," *American Sociological Review* 49, no. 1 (February 1984): 57; Robert W. Hymes, M. Leinart, S. Rowe, and W. Rogers, "Acquaintance Rape: The Effect of Race of Defendant and Race of Victim on White Juror Decisions," *Journal of Social Psychology* 133, no. 5 (October 1993): 627–34 (finding mock jurors more likely to convict black defendants in stranger rape cases and black and white defendants who offended cross-racially in date rape cases).

147. Darrell Steffensmeier, Jeffrey Ulmer, and John Kramer, "The Interaction of Race, Gender, and Age in Criminal Sentencing: The Punishment Cost of Being Young, Black, and Male," *Criminology* 36, no. 4 (November 1998): 768.

148. See Christopher Hartney and Linh Vuong, *Created Equal: Racial and Ethnic Disparities in the U.S. Criminal Justice System,* Report for the National Council on Crime and Delinquency (March 2009), https://perma.cc/2L2A-DQN4, 11, finding that the 2006 relative rate of incarceration on rape charges for blacks was over three times higher than for whites; Howard N. Snyder, "Arrest in the United States 1990–2010," US Department of Justice: Bureau of Justice Statistics (October 2012), https://perma.cc/Q9HJ-Q68T, reporting that 13,210 whites, 6,300 blacks, 290 American Indian or Alaska Native, and 280 Asian or Pacific Islanders had been arrested for forcible rape; "Perpetrators of Sexual Violence: Statistics," RAINN, accessed November 4, 2018, https://perma.cc/QHE5-X53S, reporting that 50 percent of identified perpetrators were white while 27 percent were black. The foregoing studies likely understate the disparity because they count Hispanics in the white category. See also Casey T. Harris et al., "Are Blacks and Hispanics Disproportion-

ately Incarcerated Relative to Their Arrests? Racial and Ethnic Disproportionality between Arrest and Incarceration," *Race and Social Problems* 1, no. 4 (November 2009): 187–99; Gary D. LaFree, "The Effect of Sexual Stratification by Race on Official Reactions to Rape," *American Sociological Review* 45, no. 5 (October 1980): 842–54; Nazgol Ghandnoosh, "Race and Punishment: Racial Perceptions of Crime and Support for Punitive Policies," The Sentencing Project, September 2014, https://perma.cc/JK6Z-GRZZ.

149. Darren Lenard Hutchinson, "Ignoring the Sexualization of Race: Heteronormativity, Critical Race Theory and Anti-racist Politics," *Buffalo Law Review* 47, no. 1 (Winter 1999): 85 ("The construction of black women as promiscuous causes jurors in sexual assault prosecutions to doubt black women's credibility").

150. Bureau of Justice Statistics, number of rape/sexual assaults, 1993–2017, generated using the NCVS Victimization Analysis Tool at www.bjs.gov. June 30, 2019. The number dipped to a low of 207,760 in 2005 and thereafter fluctuated between 200,000 and 400,000.

151. See chapter 3, the section "What If Arrest Is Not Best?," for a discussion of the "great crime decline."

152. Carole Goldberg-Ambrose, "Unfinished Business in Rape Law Reform," *Journal of Social Issues* 48, no. 1 (1992): 184, surveying studies; see also Jody Clay-Warner and Callie Harbin Burt, "Rape Reporting after Reforms: Have Times Really Changed?," *Violence Against Women*, 11 no. 2 (February 2005): 150–76, surveying conflicting studies on increases in reporting and finding that rapes after 1990 were more likely to be reported than those before 1974.

153. "Felony Defendants 1990," 13 (table 15); "Felony Defendants 2009," 24 (table 21).

154. See Pheny Z. Smith, "Felony Defendants in Large Urban Counties, 1990," US Department of Justice, Office of Justice Programs, Bureau of Justice Statistics (May 1993), https://perma.cc/6K4P-FG6E, 17; Brian A. Reaves, "Felony Defendants in Large Urban Counties, 2009—Statistical Tables," US Department of Justice, Office of Justice Programs, Bureau of Justice Statistics (December 2013), https://perma.cc/7JN5-KTLP, 24. There are similar reports for 1992, 1994, 1996, 1998, 2000, 2002, 2004, and 2006.

155. University at Albany School of Criminal Justice, Hindelang Criminal Justice Research Center, *Sourcebook of Criminal Justice Statistics,* https://perma.cc/3URJ-YKZD, table 6.0023.2013, showing a prison population percentage of 0.8 in 1980 and 6.2 in 2013.

156. Violent Crime Control and Enforcement Act of 1994, Pub. L No. 103–322, 108 Stat 1796 (hereafter Crime Control Bill).

157. Dennis Shea, "Clinton and the GOP Options: Winning Back Reagan Democrats," *Washington Post,* February 16, 1993, available at 1993 WLNR 5643877.

158. Harry A. Chernoff, Christopher M. Kelly, and John R. Kroger, "The Politics of Crime," *Harvard Journal on Legislation* 33, no. 2 (1996): 544.

159. T. J. Raphael, "How One Political Ad Held Back a Generation of American Inmates," *Takeaway: Justice,* May 18, 2015, https://perma.cc/UD8U-ZQ7P.

160. Chernoff, Kelly, and Kroger, "Politics of Crime," 538.

161. See Hearing on Federal Cocaine Sentencing Laws: Reforming the 100:1 Crack Powder Disparity before the Senate Committee on the Judiciary, 110th Cong. (2008) (statement of Sen. Joseph R. Biden, Chairman, S. Comm. on the Judiciary), https://perma.cc/J864-MP35.

162. Guy Gugliotta, "Crime Bill a Hostage of Politics," *Washington Post,* August 5, 1992, https://perma.cc/8UMS-592G.

163. Chernoff, Kelly, and Kroger, "Politics of Crime," 538.

164. ABC News/WP poll, January 30–February 2, 1992, available in LEXIS, Market Library, Rpoll File (Democrats 39 percent, Republicans 35 percent).

165. Violent Crime Control and Law Enforcement Act of 1994, H.R. Rep. No. 103–123 (1994) (Conf. Rep.) (statement of Rep. Biden), https://perma.cc /VN2F-JXHJ.

166. William J. Clinton, "Remarks on Signing the Violent Crime Control and Law Enforcement Act of 1994," in *Public Papers of the Presidents of the United States: William J. Clinton, 1991, Book II* (Washington, DC: Government Printing Office, 1994), 1540, https://perma.cc/B89S-ECRR.

167. Clinton, "Remarks on Signing," 1539–40.

168. Crime Control Bill §§ 60001–600025, 70001–70002, 90101–90107, 100001–100003, 110501–110518, 160001–160003, 170101, 170201, 230101–230102, 250001–250008, 280001–280006, 32101–32109.

169. Greg Krikorian, "Federal and State Prison Populations Soared under Clinton, Report Finds," *Los Angeles Times,* February 19, 2001, https://perma.cc /CQ5L-QHWV,

170. Carrie Johnson, "20 Years Later, Parts of Major Crime Bill Viewed as Terrible Mistake," *Morning Edition,* September 12, 2014, NPR, https://perma.cc /XD53-7EM3.

171. Peter Baker, "Bill Clinton Concedes His Crime Law Jailed Too Many for Too Long," *New York Times,* July 15 2015, https://perma.cc/Y8JZ-JD4K.

172. Crime Control Bill § 40121(a)(3) ("Part T—Grants to Combat Violent Crimes against Women").

173. Crime Control Bill §§ 40111, 40112, 40113, 40121, 40501–40505, 40701–40703.

174. See, e.g., Leigh Goodmark, *A Troubled Marriage: Domestic Violence and the Legal System* (New York: New York University Press, 2011), 21–22; Mimi Kim, Donna Coker, Sujatha Baliga, and Alisa Bierria, "Plenary 3—Harms of Criminalization and Promising Alternatives," *University of Miami Race and Social Justice Law Review* 5, no. 2 (2015): 378 (remarks of Mimi Kim); Rachel E. Rosenbloom, "Beyond Severity: A New View of Crimmigration," *Lewis and Clark Law Review* 22 , no. 3 (December 2018): 700.

175. Crime Control Bill, §§ 40301–40303.

176. *Crimes of Violence Motivated by Gender: Hearing before the Subcomm. on Civil and Constitutional Rights of the House Comm. on the Judiciary,* 103d Cong., 1st Sess. 80 (1993) (statement by Conference of Chief Justices on S. 15, Violence Against

Women Act of 1991, adopted by the State-Federal Relations Committee of the Conference of Chief Justices at meeting in Scottsdale, Arizona, on January 31, 1991).

177. United States v. Morrison, 529 U.S. 598 (2000).

178. Judith Resnik, "Reconstructing Equality: Of Justice, Justicia, and the Gender of Jurisdiction," *Yale Journal of Law and Feminism* 14, no. 2 (2002): 404.

179. Sarah F. Russell, "Covering Women and Violence: Media Treatment of VAWA's Civil Rights Remedy," *Michigan Journal of Gender and Law* 9, no. 2 (2003): 333.

180. William J. Clinton, "Remarks in Observance of National Domestic Violence Awareness Month," in *Public Papers of the Presidents of the United States: William J. Clinton* (Washington, DC: Government Printing Office, 1995), 1750, https://perma.cc/RM76-8NPR.

181. *Providing for Further Consideration of H.R. 4092, Violent Crime Control and Law Enforcement Act of 1994*, 103rd Cong., 2d sess., H. Res. 401 (1994), https://perma.cc/XWD2-NG5X.

182. Clinton, "Remarks on Signing," 1540.

183. Clinton, "Remarks on Signing," 1540.

184. *Domestic Violence in America*, H5182–5, 103rd Cong., 2d sess. *Congressional Record* 140 (June 28, 1994): 5128 (statement of Rep. Bernie Sanders), available at 1994 WL 287907.

185. Vanessa Williams, "1994 Crime Bill Haunts Clinton and Sanders as Criminal Justice Reform Rises to Top in Democratic Contest," *Washington Post*, February 12, 2016, https://perma.cc/8E7M-T86L.

186. "Sanders Voted for 1994 Crime Bill to Support Assault Weapons Ban, Violence against Women Provisions," *Bern Report*, February 25, 2016, https://perma.cc/9T3X-PXMZ.

6. FROM THE SEXUAL COLD WAR TO THE NEW SEX PANIC

1. Claire Gordon, "When America Started Caring about Rape," Al Jazeera America, March 20, 2015, https://perma.cc/335S-RUNQ, quoting Susan Brownmiller.

2. The report was called "extremely powerful" by Julia Coffman, Judy Miller, and Victor Acquah, "Digital Transitions: Nonprofit Investigative Journalism: Evaluation Report on the Center for Public Integrity," May 2010, 10, https://perma.cc/SF7F-WF4P. For the report itself, see Kristen Lombardi and Kristin Jones, "Sexual Assault on Campus: A Frustrating Search for Justice," Center for Public Integrity, 2010, 7, https://perma.cc/9GNN-44KU. NPR's coverage includes Kristen Lombardi, "How College Campuses Handle Sexual Assaults," interview by Rebecca Roberts, *Talk of the Nation*, December 3, 2009, NPR, https://perma.cc/ZT76-RZ8T; Joseph Shapiro, "Campus Rape Victims: A Struggle for Justice," *Morning Edition*, February 24, 2010, NPR, https://perma.cc/R5UZ-LYHQ, quoting Russlynn Ali.

3. Shapiro, "Campus Rape Victims."

4. Lombardi and Jones, "Sexual Assault on Campus," 73.

5. 20 U.S.C. §§ 1681–1688 (2002).

6. Dawn R. Matthias, Office for Civil Rights, to Laura Dunn, August 6, 2008 (hereafter OCR Letter), 1, https://perma.cc/933P-84Y6.

7. Lombardi and Jones, "Sexual Assault on Campus," 73.

8. OCR Letter, 2–3, 5, 6, 7–8.

9. OCR Letter, 12.

10. Christina Hoff Sommers, "The Media Is Making College Rape Culture Worse," *Daily Beast,* January 23, 2015, https://perma.cc/5LWE-H4XF, describing an interview between Sommers and Kristin Jones.

11. Shapiro, "Campus Rape Victims," quoting Russlynn Ali.

12. Lombardi and Jones, "Sexual Assault on Campus"; Russlynn Ali, Office for Civil Rights, US Department of Education, "Dear Colleague Letter: Sexual Violence," April 4, 2011 (hereafter Dear Colleague Letter), https://perma.cc /WJD3-ZED5.

13. Ali, "Dear Colleague Letter," 2, citing Christopher P. Krebs, Christine H. Lindquist, Tara D. Warner, Bonnie S. Fisher, and Sandra L. Martin, "The Campus Sexual Assault (CSA) Study," National Institute of Justice, December 2007, https:// perma.cc/VGB8-XXH7.

14. Ali, "Dear Colleague Letter," 12.

15. "Title IX: Tracking Sexual Assault Investigations," *Chronicle of Higher Education,* n.d., accessed March 18, 2019, https://perma.cc/2E8L-LTUJ.

16. Walt Bogdanich, "A Star Player, and a Flawed Rape Investigation," *New York Times,* April 16, 2014, https://perma.cc/5EQ8-ARES; Julia Dahl, "Inside the Jameis Winston Rape Case File," CBS News, December 6, 2013, https://perma.cc/QYN8-SYJ7; Heisman Trophy Committee, "Heisman Winner 2013: Jameis Winston," Heisman Trophy, December 2013, noting Winston's record-breaking age of nineteen years and 342 days—but no accusation of rape, https://perma.cc/UAL8-K2Q9. As of the writing of this book, Winston is a star quarterback for the Tampa Bay Buccaneers and has settled two federal civil lawsuits with his accuser Erica Kinsman, who had already received a settlement of $950,000 from FSU. See Marc Tracy, "Jameis Winston and Woman Who Accused Him of Rape Settle Lawsuits," *New York Times,* December 15, 2016, https://perma.cc/25AU-BVMV; Marc Tracy, "Florida State Settles Suit over Jameis Winston Rape Inquiry," *New York Times,* January 25, 2016, https://perma.cc/4PMM-HZS5.

17. Roberta Smith, "In a Mattress, a Lever for Art and Political Protest," *New York Times,* September 21, 2014, https://perma.cc/ABW6-542J; Alexandra Svokos, "Students Bring Out Mattresses in Huge 'Carry That Weight' Protest against Sexual Assault," *Huffington Post,* October 29, 2014, https://perma.cc/J4S2-HUPX.

18. Charlotte Alter, "Columbia University Activist Emma Sulkowicz Is Going to the State of the Union," *Time,* January 20, 2015, https://perma.cc/T9XB-3WNS; Lizzie Crocker, "Emma Sulkowicz: From Mattress to Therapist's Couch," *Daily Beast,* January 19, 2017, https://perma.cc/2PTZ-X4RF.

19. Kate Taylor, "Columbia Settles with Student Cast as a Rapist in Mattress Art Project," *New York Times,* July 14, 2017, https://perma.cc/P6Z3-NHMA.

20. Taylor, "Columbia Settles with Student."

21. Sabrina Rubin Erdely, "A Rape on Campus: A Brutal Assault and Struggle for Justice at UVA," *Rolling Stone,* November 19, 2014, https://perma.cc /K8LV-FUPT.

22. Eamon McNiff, Lauren Effron, and Jeff Schneider, "How the Retracted Rolling Stone Article 'A Rape on Campus' Came to Print," *20/20,* June 13, 2017, ABC, https://perma.cc/BFA3-ZKJA.

23. Anthony Zurcher, "Rolling Stone Apologises for Virginia Rape Story," BBC News, December 5, 2014, https://perma.cc/45CM-ZRG3. The fraternity eventually settled with *Rolling Stone* for $1.65 million. Michael Edison Hayden, "University of Virginia Fraternity Settles with Rolling Stone over Retracted Campus Rape Story," ABC News, June 13, 2017, https://perma.cc/J2RW-SH7C.

24. McNiff, Effron, and Schneider, "'Rape on Campus.'"

25. Responding to Tucker Carlson's argument that the accused students were otherwise law-abiding, she said, "Hitler never beat his wife either." "'The Situation with Tucker Carlson' for June 5," NBC News, updated June 6, 2006, https://perma .cc/XPE6-MSMW.

26. Seth Cline, "Playboy: UVA Is Nation's Top Party School," *U.S. News and World Reports,* September 26, 2012, https://perma.cc/2K2E-VXWM.

27. T. Rees Shapiro, "Jury Finds Reporter, Rolling Stone Responsible for Defaming U-Va. Dean with Gang Rape Story," *Washington Post,* November 4, 2016, https://perma.cc/GSC9-564U, quoting Scott Sexton, attorney for *Rolling Stone,* in his closing statement.

28. Erdely, "Rape on Campus."

29. Erdely, "Rape on Campus."

30. Erdely, "Rape on Campus."

31. Erdely, "Rape on Campus."

32. Erdely, "Rape on Campus."

33. See McNiff, Effron, and Schneider, "'Rape on Campus'"; T. Rees Shapiro, "'Catfishing' over Love Interest Might Have Spurred U-Va. Gang Rape Debacle," *Washington Post,* January 8, 2016, https://perma.cc/NPK4-P2D7.

34. Haven Monahan to Ryan Duffin, text messages, September 5–7, 2012 (Haven-Ryan texts), https://perma.cc/P7WV-FZYE.

35. Haven-Ryan texts, September 5, 2012.

36. Haven-Ryan texts, September 13, 2012.

37. Shapiro, "'Catfishing'"; Kaitlyn Schallhorn, "Attorneys Release Texts Connected to Infamous UVa Rape Hoax—And They Claim the Messages Reveal Shocking Twist," *Blaze,* February 10, 2016, https://perma.cc/YP3A-AUNK.

38. Haven-Ryan texts, September 27, 2012.

39. Shapiro, "'Catfishing.'"

40. "'Jackie' Testifies: Rolling Stone Story Was 'What I Believed to Be True at the Time,'" *Guardian,* October 24, 2016, https://perma.cc/797A-3FHN.

41. McNiff, Effron, and Schneider, "'Rape on Campus.'" Renda's full testimony before the Senate Committee on Health, Education, Labor, and Pensions, "Sexual

Assault on Campus: Working to Ensure Student Safety," June 26, 2014, can be found at https://perma.cc/2AXN-96KU.

42. T. Rees Shapiro, "Attorneys for 'Jackie' in Rolling Stone Lawsuit Protest under Oath Deposition, Saying It Could 'Re-traumatize' Her," *Washington Post,* March 30, 2016, https://perma.cc/3XSZ-AVD3.

43. Shapiro, "Attorneys for 'Jackie.'"

44. "'Jackie' Testifies."

45. Kirby Dick and Amy Ziering, directors, *The Hunting Ground,* CNN Films, released February 27, 2015, https://perma.cc/4XVW-NQTP.

46. Ann Hornaday, "Review: 'The Hunting Ground' Lucidly Investigates the Issue of Campus Rape," *Washington Post,* March 12, 2015, https://perma.cc /SH5H-6SS7.

47. Lady Gaga (Stefani Germanotta), "'Til It Happens to You,' Performance at the 88th Academy Awards, February 28, 2016," YouTube video, February 29, 2016, https://perma.cc/G7ZC-5RBU.

48. Korin Miller, "Lady Gaga's Emotional Oscar Performance Has Inspired Hope and Admiration," *Women's Health,* February 29, 2016, https://perma.cc /P4R6-U8SH.

49. Jon Krakauer, *Missoula: Rape and the Justice System in a College Town* (New York: Doubleday, 2015).

50. Jon Krakauer and Laura L. Dunn, "Don't Weaken Title IX Campus Sex Assault Policies," *New York Times,* August 3, 2017, https://perma.cc/L4P4-ZSAM.

51. Scott Jaschik, "After 'Rolling Stone,'" *Inside Higher Ed,* December 8, 2014, https://perma.cc/CK28-VPAA, quoting Dunn.

52. Jaschik, "After 'Rolling Stone,'" quoting Dunn.

53. Sofi Sinozich and Lynn Langton, "Rape and Sexual Assault Victimization among College-Age Females, 1995–2013," US Department of Justice, Bureau of Justice Statistics, December 2014, 3, https://perma.cc/MQ8V-9VJK, showing general decline in rapes on and off campus in figure 2, p. 3; Michael Planty, Lynn Langton, Christopher Krebs, and Marcus Berzofsky, "Female Victims of Sexual Violence, 1994–2010," US Department of Justice Bureau of Statistics, March 2013, https:// perma.cc/ZD3F-NJ5E, showing the same general decline in figure 1; Howard N. Snyder, "Arrest in the United States, 1990–2010," US Department of Justice Bureau of Statistics, October 2012, https://perma.cc/Q9HJ-Q68T, reporting that the forcible rape arrest rate fell 59 percent between 1990 and 2010.

54. Sinozich and Langton, "Rape," 1 (figure 1).

55. See, for example, Mary P. Koss, Christine A. Gidycz, and Nadine Wisniewski, "The Scope of Rape: Incidence and Prevalence of Sexual Aggression and Victimization in a National Sample of Higher Education Students," *Journal of Consulting and Clinical Psychology* 55, no. 2 (1987): 162–70 (original one-in-five study).

56. Gina Vivinetto, "What 'Hookup Culture'? Millennials Having Less Sex Than Their Parents," NBC News, August 2, 2016, https://perma.cc/HBK5-NP28.

57. Gregg Jarrett, "Every College Parent's Fear: Campus Rape," Fox News, September 25, 2014, https://perma.cc/D3DX-H5Z9.

58. Alexa St. John, "Survey Indicates Female Students Fear Walking Home Alone," *Michigan Daily,* November 13, 2016, https://perma.cc/69UZ-EHCW.

59. St. John, "Survey Indicates."

60. St. John, "Survey Indicates" (emphasis added).

61. Clery Act, 20 U.S.C. § 1092(f) (1990). See also Jacob Gersen and Jeannie Suk, "The Sex Bureaucracy," *California Law Review* 104, no. 4 (August 2016): 881–948.

62. Suzanne Le Mignot, "Some Northwestern Students Rattled by Date-Rape Allegations," CBS News Chicago, February 7, 2017, https://perma.cc/R2ZD-XLXS.

63. David Cantor, Bonnie Fisher, Susan Chibnall, Reanne Townsend, Hyunshik Lee, Carol Bruce, and Gail Thomas, "Report on the AAU Campus Climate Survey on Sexual Assault and Sexual Misconduct," Westat, September 21, 2015, https://perma.cc/V8DQ-ECL7.

64. Sinozich and Langton, "Rape," 3 (figure 2).

65. Sinozich and Langton, "Rape," 15. Notably, "The survey does not specifically ask about incidents in which the victim was unable to provide consent because of drug or alcohol consumption" (14).

66. Krebs et al., "Campus Sexual Assault (CSA) Study," viii–ix.

67. Krebs et al., "Campus Sexual Assault (CSA) Study," 5–1: the percentage of "women who reported being a victim of attempted or completed sexual assault of any type before entering college . . . [was] 15.9%, . . . and since entering college [was] 19.0%."

68. Krebs et al., "Campus Sexual Assault (CSA) Study," 5–1. The one-in-five statistic included completed and attempted assaults.

69. Krebs et al., "Campus Sexual Assault (CSA) Study," vii, showing that 93 percent of cases involving drugs and alcohol were situations of voluntary intoxication.

70. Krebs et al., "Campus Sexual Assault (CSA) Study," vii: "The primary implications of the CSA Study are the relative rarity of cases of [involuntary intoxication] and the need to incorporate alcohol and drug messages into sexual assault prevention and risk reduction programming."

71. Ali, "Dear Colleague Letter," 2.

72. University of Colorado, Boulder, "Overview: Sexual Misconduct Survey," n.d., accessed November 18, 2018, https://perma.cc/E2XD-6RXC.

73. University of Colorado, Boulder, "Phase Two—Data Summary," July 2016, https://perma.cc/Y2WM-EQ6M; "2015 Campus Sexual Assault Survey," on file with author.

74. Author's discussions with Teresa Wroe, director of education and prevention and deputy Title IX coordinator, University of Colorado, May 23, 2016, and May 15, 2017.

75. Charlotte Bowditch, "Inside CU's Attempt to Combat On-Campus Sexual Assault," *CU Independent,* April 26, 2016, https://perma.cc/443H-BPDJ, quoting University of Colorado, Boulder.

76. University of Colorado, Boulder, "2015 Campus Sexual Assault Survey."

77. Author's discussions with Teresa Wroe.

78. Author's discussions with Teresa Wroe.

79. For examples of the campaign posters, originally created by Canadian nurses, see "Just Because She's Drunk . . . Doesn't Mean She Wants To . . . ," *Truth about Nursing,* August 29, 2012, https://perma.cc/GC7M-N28A. See also Sarah Kuta, "CU-Boulder Embraces 'It's on Us' Campaign from White House," *Daily Camera,* September 19, 2014, https://perma.cc/NNF8-CVF9; Mary-Lynn Elliott, "Wardenburg Promoting Sexual Assault Awareness at CU Boulder," *CU Independent,* October 3, 2013, https://perma.cc/SCX7-CTYU.

80. Cantor et al., "Report," 16–17. See also Nick Anderson and Susan Svrluga, "What a Massive Sexual Assault Survey Found at 27 Top U.S. Universities," *Washington Post,* September 21, 2015, https://perma.cc/R88G-VMSB.

81. Cantor et al., "Report," 18 (figure 5). See also Emily Yoffe, "The Problem with Campus Sexual Assault Surveys," *Slate,* September 24, 2015, https://perma.cc/JN8V-Z6GS, quoting survey author Cantor that there was "some indication that people who did not respond were less likely to be victims."

82. Sarah Kuta, "Survey: 28% of CU–Boulder's Female Undergrads Sexually Assaulted While in College," *Daily Camera,* February 9, 2016, https://perma.cc/4Q4M-HEYP.

83. Claire Gordon, "Conservatives Slam Expanded Definition of Rape," Al Jazeera America, June 30, 2014, https://perma.cc/JCB4-A2JD.

84. Aziza Ahmed, "Women Who Punish: Feminist Technocracy and Violence against Women," unpublished manuscript, 2014, on file with author.

85. Sarah Kuta, "'Healthy Outrage' Fuels Attorney Suing CU, Other Schools on Behalf of Men Accused of Sexual Assault," *Daily Camera,* September 2, 2016, https://perma.cc/L2WZ-H2R4.

86. Yoffe, "Problem."

87. See Dave Gustafson, "Serial Rapists Commit 9 of 10 Campus Sexual Assaults, Research Finds," Al Jazeera America, October 28, 2013, https://perma.cc/Z24U-ML5P.

88. David Lisak and Paul M. Miller, "Repeat Rape and Multiple Offending among Undetected Rapists," *Violence and Victims* 17, no. 1 (2002): 73–84, https://perma.cc/SS78-UTQB.

89. Lisak and Miller, "Repeat Rape," 76.

90. Lisak and Miller, "Repeat Rape," 78.

91. John Lauerman, "College Serial Rapists Evade Antiquated Campus Responses," *Bloomberg,* June 12, 2013, https://perma.cc/53B3-GESJ,

92. Jock Young, "Moral Panic: Its Origins in Resistance, Ressentiment and the Translation of Fantasy into Reality," *British Journal of Criminology* 49, no. 1 (January 2009): 13.

93. Fred Thys, "At Summit on Sexual Assault, Administrators Learn Strategies to Stop Serial Rapists," WBUR News, July 16, 2014, https://perma.cc/2VZJ-3XLL.

94. See, e.g., Jill Filipovic, "17 Beliefs about Sexual Assault That Are Totally Wrong," *Cosmopolitan,* August 28, 2014, https://perma.cc/YA9P-GAEP (stating that the number one "misconception" is that college rapists are not predators).

95. Davidlisak.com, accessed December 1, 2018, www.davidlisak.com/; David Lisak, "Predators: Uncomfortable Truths about Campus Rapists," *Connection,* Summer 2004, 19–21, https://perma.cc/3XU5-DRJS.

96. Gail Schontzler, "Expert Blames Most 'Date Rapes' on Serial Predators," *Bozeman Daily Chronicle,* August 13, 2013, https://perma.cc/5SHJ-KSPX, summarizing the statement of David Lisak at Montana State University, August 2013.

97. This profile came from interviews in the 1980s with a handful of confessed assaulters. Linda LeFauve, "The Misleading Video Interview with a Rapist at the Heart of the Campus Sexual Assault Freakout," *Reason,* November 20, 2015, https://perma.cc/93H8-BYQW. See also Jesse Singal, "*The Hunting Ground* Uses a Striking Statistic about Campus Rape That's Almost Certainly False," *New York Magazine: The Cut,* November 23, 2015, https://perma.cc/WHQ9-SMQT; Megan McArdle, "Campus Rape Debate Needs Better Numbers," *Bloomberg,* July 28, 2015, perma.cc /EC86-PNLZ.

98. See, e.g., Krakauer, *Missoula,* 131–37, relying on one of the interviews to characterize a typical repeat offender.

99. Amelia Thomson-DeVeaux, "What If Most Campus Rapes Aren't Committed by Serial Rapists?," *FiveThirtyEight,* July 13, 2015, https://perma.cc/8ARB-9MJ2.

100. Kevin M. Swartout et al., "Trajectory Analysis of the Campus Serial Rapist Assumption," *JAMA Pediatrics* 169, no. 12 (December 2015): 1149.

101. Swartout et al., "Trajectory Analysis," 1149.

102. Swartout et al., "Trajectory Analysis," 1150–51.

103. Swartout et al., "Trajectory Analysis," 1152.

104. Swartout et al., "Trajectory Analysis," 1153.

105. Swartout et al., "Trajectory Analysis," 1153.

106. Tyler Kingkade, "Researchers Push Back on Criticisms of Well-Known Serial Rapist Study," *Huffington Post,* October 28, 2015, https://perma.cc/SS4M-LHSZ; James W. Hopper, David Lisak, and Allison Tracy, "Letter to Editor, concerning Swartout et al., 'Trajectory Analysis of the Campus Serial Rapist Assumption,'" October 23, 2015, https://perma.cc/2UEZ-2TBM.

107. James W. Hopper, "Comment on "Trajectory Analysis of the Campus Serial Rapist Assumption," *Pubpeer,* 2015, https://perma.cc/Y3AW-AA97; Jim Hopper, "Does Posting on PubPeer Count as Prior Publication? Journal Says Yes, Rejects Letter Rebutting Campus Sexual Assault Data," *Retraction Watch,* April 26, 2016, https://perma.cc/43P8-BQJR.

108. "University Says No Misconduct in Campus Rape Paper," *Retraction Watch,* August 16, 2016, https://perma.cc/F2NA-RFWD, quoting Swartout.

109. "University Says No Misconduct." See also Robby Soave, "Adherents of Junk Campus Rape Science Are Retaliating against Critics," Reason.com, February 9, 2016, https://perma.cc/QP4A-VLT9.

110. Alicia Oeser, statement at Harvard Law School Campus Sexual Assault "Teach-In," September 2014. I should note that the suffering of veteran soldiers is also highly variable. See Sebastian Junger, "How PTSD Became a Problem Far beyond the Battlefield," *Vanity Fair,* May 7, 2015, https://perma.cc/RP72-RB3K.

111. Patricia Frazier and Laura Schauben, "Causal Attributions and Recovery from Rape and Other Stressful Life Events," *Journal of Social and Clinical Psychology* 13, no. 1 (1994): 1–14; Patricia Frazier, "Victim Attributions and Post-rape Trauma," *Journal of Personality and Social Psychology* 59, no. 2 (January 1990): 298–304; Patricia A. Frazier, "The Role of Attributions and Perceived Control in Recovery from Rape," *Journal of Personal and Interpersonal Loss* 5, nos. 2–3 (January 2008): 203–25. There is a current debate over the effects of "characterological" versus "behavioral" self-blame. See Kimberly Hanson Breitenbecher, "The Relationships among Self-Blame, Psychological Distress, and Sexual Victimization," *Journal of Interpersonal Violence* 21, no. 5 (May 2006): 597–611.

112. Harter Secrest & Emery LLP, "Conducting Trauma-Informed and Legally-Compliant Investigations, Hearings, and Appeals," August 2, 2016, https://perma .cc/294F-R2VE; Michael Henry et al., "The 7 Deadly Sins of Title IX Investigations," Association of Title IX Administrators (ATIXA), 2016, https://perma .cc/2J7G-RMC2; Kate Watson, "Trauma-Informed Approach to Working with Survivors of Sexual Assault," New York State College Health Association, January 1, 2015, https://perma.cc/3XHS-P5TV.

113. Sheila Coronel, Steve Coll, and Derek Kravitz, "Rolling Stone and UVA: The Columbia University Graduate School of Journalism Report," *Rolling Stone,* April 5, 2015, https://perma.cc/V965-KPZZ.

114. Frazier, "Role of Attributions," 220.

115. Coronel, Coll, and Kravitz, "Rolling Stone and UVA."

116. See Herbert L. Packer, "Two Models of the Criminal Process," *University of Pennsylvania Law Review* 113, no. 1 (November 1964): 9–10.

117. William Blackstone, *Commentaries on the Laws of England,* vol. 4 (Oxford: Clarendon Press, 1769), 352.

118. Cathy Young, "Weekly Standard: The Feminine Lie Mystique," National Public Radio, July 29, 2011, https://perma.cc/BT9F-QRX3, quoting Wendy Murphy.

119. Alex Burness, "Boulder Rep. Jared Polis: 'I Misspoke' on Campus Rape," *Daily Camera,* September 15, 2015, https://perma.cc/H5VJ-4W6J.

120. Emily Shugerman, "Men Sue in Campus Sexual Assault Cases," *Ms.* magazine, June 18, 2014, https://perma.cc/34V7-28NP, quoting Caroline Heldman.

121. US Department of Education, Office for Civil Rights, "School Climate and Safety: Data Highlights on School Climate and Safety in Our Nation's Public Schools," (2015–16 Civil Rights Data Collection), April 2018, https://perma.cc /N8VM-YXT3.

122. US Department of Education, "School Climate and Safety," 3.

123. Antoinette Campbell, "Police Handcuff 6-Year-Old Student in Georgia," CNN, April 17, 2012, https://perma.cc/8CPM-Z5QZ.

124. Priyanka Boghani, "Salecia Johnson, 6, Handcuffed and Arrested by Georgia Police," *Public Radio International,* April 17, 2012, https://perma.cc/S72B-CJUG.

125. Campbell, "Police Handcuff 6-Year-Old."

126. Gersen and Suk, "Sex Bureaucracy," 944.

127. Corey Mitchell, "Schools 'Less Safe for Black and Brown Children,' Civil Rights Advocates Say," *Education Week,* April 24, 2018, https://perma.cc/S2WJ-KQVT.

128. Krakauer and Dunn, "Don't Weaken Title IX."

129. Burness, "Polis: 'I Misspoke.'"

130. Tyler Kingkade, "Students Punished for Sexual Assault Should Have Transcripts Marked, Title IX Group Says," *Huffington Post,* September 24, 2015, https://perma.cc/L3AJ-FFR5; CS Staff, "Bill Would Leave Sexual Misconduct Mark on Student Transcripts," *Campus Safety Magazine,* December 13, 2016, https://perma.cc/9JYM-YVWM; Shannon Crane Fiedler, "Mandatory Transcript Notations for Crimes of Violence on Campus: Scarlet Letter or Saving Grace?," *Syracuse Law Review* 67, no. 3 (July 2017): 711–40; Jake New, "Requiring a Red Flag," *Inside Higher Ed,* July 10, 2015, https://perma.cc/2JSV-FH44.

131. Gersen and Suk, "Sex Bureaucracy," 929, quoting the University of Wyoming, "Where Is Your Line: Consent Is Sexy!" For more examples, see Gersen and Suk, "Sex Bureaucracy," 928–29.

132. We-Consent, mobile ed., ISCE Software, ISCE.edu, 2015, screenshots on file with author.

133. See Meg Graham, "New Apps Urge Mutual Consent, 'Yes Means Yes,' When It Comes to Sex," *Chicago Tribune,* July 20, 2015, https://perma.cc/QMF7-GLQE.

134. Beth McMurtrie, "Why Colleges Haven't Stopped Binge Drinking," *Chronicle of Higher Education,* December 2, 2014, https://perma.cc/MU8H-U26S.

135. Susan Svrluga, "Despite Scandals and Bad Ink, More and More Students Want to Go Greek," *Washington Post,* January 20, 2015, https://perma.cc/9286-MV3T.

136. Elisha Fieldstadt and Katie Wall, "UVA Sorority Members Plan to Skip Parties but Still Don't Agree with Policy," NBC News, January 31, 2015, https://perma.cc/Q3TZ-28BN.

137. Suzannah Weiss, "College's Anti-drinking Poster Victim-Blames Sexual Assault Survivors," *Teen Vogue,* September 2, 2017, https://perma.cc/PZN3-9AVC. Cf. Michael Karson, "Is So-Called Victim Blaming Always Bad?," *Psychology Today,* September 13, 2014, https://perma.cc/42F3-CHLJ.

138. Cal. Education Code § 67386 (West, 2016).

139. Samantha Stendal, "A Needed Response," YouTube, March 22, 2013, https://perma.cc/EU72–6K6C. See also Sarah Beston, "The Powerful Antirape PSA That Everyone Needs to Watch," Takepart, May 18, 2014, https://perma.cc/L3YH-N9MH.

140. Jana Lynn French, "Interview with Sam Stendal, Creator of 'A Needed Response,'" Peabody Awards, December 15, 2014, https://perma.cc/97Z7-ANTF.

The college student who created the video was also featured in *Glamour* magazine's "Women of the Year" issue; see Emily L. Foley, "Hometown Heroes: 50 Phenomenal Women of the Year Who Are Making a Difference," *Glamour,* November 17, 2014, https://perma.cc/8CWU-Z8DT.

141. Tanya Somanader, "President Obama Launches the 'It's on Us' Campaign to End Sexual Assault on Campus," ObamaWhiteHouse.gov, September 19, 2014, https://perma.cc/58PM-7F6B.

142. Gabe LaMonica, "Biden Urges Men to Be Part of Fight against Campus Rape," CNN, April 30, 2014, https://perma.cc/CM3E-CJ96.

7. ENDLESS WAR?

1. E.g., Danielle Keats Citron and Mary Anne Franks, "Criminalizing Revenge Porn," *Wake Forest Law Review* 49, no. 2 (June 2014): 345–91; Allow States and Victims to Fight Online Sex Trafficking Act of 2017, Pub. L. No. 115–164, 132 Stat. 1253 § 2421A (2018) [FOSTA] ("Whoever . . . owns, manages, or operates an interactive computer service . . . with the intent to promote or facilitate the prostitution of another person shall be fined under this title, imprisoned for not more than 10 years, or both"); Alafair S. Burke, "Domestic Violence as a Crime of Pattern and Intent: An Alternative Reconceptualization," *George Washington Law Review* 75, no. 3 (April 2007): 552–612, calling for criminalizing coercive control; Deborah Tuerkheimer, "Recognizing and Remedying the Harm of Battering: A Call to Criminalize Domestic Violence," *Journal of Criminal Law and Criminology* 94, no. 4 (July 2004): 959–1031; Melissa Marie Blanco, "Sex Trend or Sexual Assault? The Dangers of 'Stealthing' and the Concept of Conditional Consent," *Penn State Law Review* 123, no. 1 (2018): 245, advocating prosecuting "stealthing" as sexual assault; cf. Alexandra Brodsky, "'Rape-Adjacent': Imagining Legal Responses to Nonconsensual Condom Removal," *Columbia Journal of Gender and Law* 32, no. 2 (March, 2017): 183–210, proposing a civil tort for this conduct.

2. Aja Romano, "A New Law Intended to Curb Sex Trafficking Threatens the Future of the Internet as We Know It," *Vox,* July 2, 2018, https://perma.cc/Z832-WPXY, arguing that the FOSTA bill, which shut down backpage.com, threatens internet speech and diminishes sex worker safety.

3. E. Ann Carson and Elizabeth Anderson, "Prisoners in 2015," US Department of Justice, Bureau of Justice Statistics, December 2016, 14, https://perma.cc/LQ8V-KY3N.

4. Doe v. Town of Jupiter Police Department, Case No. 9:19-cv-80513-DMM (S.D. Fla. 2019), 6 (class action privacy suit by spa customers detailing these facts).

5. Doe v. Jupiter.

6. Doe v. Jupiter.

7. Doe v. Jupiter, 7–8. See also Terry Spencer, "Customers Videotaped at Orchids of Asia Spa File Class-Action Lawsuit," CBS Boston, April 22, 2019, https://perma.cc/N9K3-MX26.

8. Ken Belson, "Robert Kraft and Others Ask to Have Evidence Kept Private in Florida Case," *New York Times,* March 20, 2019, https://perma.cc/K4DE-HZV6; Daniel Moritz-Rabson, "Sex Worker Advocates Livid about 'Pretext of Rescue' after Authorities Arrest Women Related to Robert Kraft Investigation," *Newsweek,* April 26, 2019, https://perma.cc/8USY-L9BS.

9. Diana Moskovitz and Hallie Lieberman, "When the Robert Kraft Case Fell Apart, the Women Were Left to Pay the Price," *Deadspin,* June 20, 2019, https://perma.cc/T83P-LNF4.

10. Marc Freeman, "'Bungled from the Beginning': How Robert Kraft's Sex Sting Was Marred by Cops' Missteps," *South Florida Sun Sentinel,* May 18, 2019, https://perma.cc/C463-FJMS; Video: Human Trafficking 'Evil in Our Midst,' Aronberg Says in Announcing Prostitution Arrests," *Palm Beach Post,* February 25, 2019, https://perma.cc/QDE9-BWLJ. Video plays at https://youtu.be/tISLGkHGlYI.

11. "Video: Human Trafficking."

12. "Video: Human Trafficking."

13. Ruth Brown, "Prosecutors Concede No Human Trafficking in Kraft Spa Case," *New York Post,* April 12, 2019, https://perma.cc/SMV7-KTWE.

14. Patricia Mazzei, "'The Monsters Are the Men': Inside a Thriving Sex Trafficking Trade in Florida," *New York Times,* February 23, 2019, https://perma.cc/T3KU-6LYE?type=image.

15. Moskovitz and Lieberman, "Women Were Left."

16. Moskovitz and Lieberman, "Women Were Left."

17. Grace Chang and Kathleen Kim, "Reconceptualizing Approaches to Human Trafficking: New Directions and Perspectives from the Field(s)," *Stanford Journal of Civil Rights and Civil Liberties* 3, no 1 (August 2007): 343.

18. Detective Michael Fenton, "Affidavit and Application for Search Warrant Authorizing the Monitoring and Recording of Visual, Non-audio Conduct" (Case No. 4DCA 19–1499, Florida v. Kraft), September 21, 2018, https://perma.cc/UT2S-YNZ6.

19. Jaxon Van Derbeken and Ryan Kim, "Alleged Sex-Trade Ring Broken Up in Bay Area / Police Say Koreans in Massage Parlors Were Smuggled In," *SF Gate,* July 2, 2005, https://perma.cc/BAV7-3Q5H.

20. Derbeken and Kim, "Alleged Sex-Trade Ring."

21. Derbeken and Kim, "Alleged Sex-Trade Ring."

22. Carol Leigh, "Behind the Moral Panic, an Opportunity to Work," *SF Gate,* July 22, 2005, https://perma.cc/P9WD-M4CV.

23. Chang and Kim, "Reconceptualizing Approaches," 334.

24. Max Ehrenfreund, "When Rhode Island Accidentally Legalized Prostitution, Rape Decreased Sharply," *Washington Post,* July 17, 2014, https://perma.cc/2ZV5-CFSH, describing the 31 percent drop in reported rapes after the decriminalization of prostitution in 2003.

25. See COYOTE v. Roberts, 502 F.Supp. 1342 (D.R.I., 1980), COYOTE v. Roberts, 523 F.Supp. 352 (D.R.I., 1981).

26. Lynn Arditi, "How R.I. Opened the Door to Prostitution," *Providence Journal,* May 31, 2009, https://perma.cc/46D3-W4E6; Ray Henry, "RI Lawmakers Reach Deal to Ban Indoor Prostitution," Associated Press, October 28, 2009; Amanda Milkovits, "Legislators Drop Bid to Outlaw Brothels," *Providence Journal,* June 16, 2005, A1.

27. See Scott Cunningham and Manisha Shah, "Decriminalizing Indoor Prostitution: Implications for Sexual Violence and Public Health," National Bureau of Economic Research, Working Paper 20281, July 2014, 10, https://perma.cc/RJ2Z-UZFJ, citing Judge Elaine Bucci's order; Arditi, "How R.I. Opened the Door." Meanwhile, the police continued to raid massage parlors and arrest women, but on immigration charges. Amanda Milkovits, "Brothels Survive on Weak R.I. Law," *Providence Journal,* August 19, 2006, A3.

28. Milkovits, "Legislators Drop Bid"; "R.I. Massage Workers Sore over Prostitution Crackdown," Fox News, July 18, 2005, https://perma.cc/E44E-4DCQ; Amanda Milkovits and Tracy Breton, "Bill Aims to Crack Down on Massage Parlors," *Providence Journal,* June 28, 2005, B1. Civil libertarians pushed back well into 2009. See, e.g., Family Life Center, "Rethinking Arrest: Street Prostitution and Public Policy in Rhode Island," July 2009, https://perma.cc/5LE9-EK9J.

29. Sarah Schweitzer, "Many Seek Ban as Prostitution Thrives in R.I.," *Boston Globe,* August 13, 2009, https://perma.cc/A3L8-ZG79; Lynn Arditi, "Tougher Sex Laws Gain Backing," *Providence Journal,* June 12, 2009, B1.

30. Cynthia Needham, "Bill Targets Loophole in Prostitution Law," *Providence Journal,* April 9, 2009, B1.

31. Needham, "Bill Targets Loophole"; Lynn Arditi, "R.I. in 'Eye of the Storm' in Sex Trafficking, Prostitution," *Providence Journal,* April 19, 2009, https://perma.cc/5KMW-Q8G9.

32. Arditi, "Eye of the Storm"; Ray Henry, "Advocates Urge Defeat of RI Indoor-Prostitution Ban," *South Coast Today,* June 10, 2009, https://perma.cc/BG7X-A6NC ("To prosecute human traffickers, investigators sometimes need to arrest low-level prostitutes and pressure them to testify against higher-ups, State Police Col. Brendan Doherty said"); Lynn Arditi, "Closing a Loophole," *Providence Journal,* October 28, 2009, at A01, quoting Giannini as stating that the bill "mean[s] police will no longer be powerless."

33. Henry, "Advocates Urge Defeat"; Steve Peoples, "Prostitutes Speak Out against Bill to Close Loophole," *Providence Journal,* October 26, 2009, A1.

34. Donna M. Hughes and Robert P. George, "Not a Victimless Crime," *National Review,* August 10, 2009, https://perma.cc/7V2J-9VKF.

35. Peoples, "Prostitutes Speak Out."

36. Peoples, "Prostitutes Speak Out"; Lynne Arditi, "RI: Sex Workers Testify at Senate Hearing on Prostitution Bill," *Providence Journal,* June 22, 2009, https://perma.cc/9QXH-N6QU.

37. "RI Lawmakers Hear from Critics of Criminal Prostitution," Associated Press, May 1, 2019, https://perma.cc/ZT7S-Z92R.

38. Jaclyn Friedman, "Consent Is Not a Lightswitch," *Amplify*, November 9, 2010, https://web.archive.org/web/20101119203249/http://amplifyyourvoice.org/u/Yes_Means_Yes/2010/11/9/Consent-Is-Not-A-Lightswitch.

39. Jacob Gersen and Jeannie Suk, "The Sex Bureaucracy," *California Law Review* 104, no. 4 (August 2016): 931.

40. National District Attorneys Association, Women Prosecutors Section, "National Sexual Assault Investigation and Prosecution Best Practices Guide," January 3, 2018, 15, https://perma.cc/8UQF-U3AT.

41. National District Attorneys Association, "National Sexual Assault Investigation," 15 (emphasis added).

42. Cassia C. Spohn, Dawn Beichner, Erika Davis Frenzel, and David Holleran, "Prosecutors' Charging Decisions in Sexual Assault Cases: A Multi-site Study, Final Report," US Department of Justice, October 28, 2002, 3, https://perma.cc/5J45-4GVZ, citing studies.

43. Brady v. Maryland, 373 U.S. 83, at 88 (1963).

44. Brady, 373 U.S. at 88.

45. See Jones v. Chicago, 856 F.2d 985, 995 (7th Cir. 1988).

46. Joanna Archambault, Heather Huhtanen, and Kimberly Lonsway, "The Earthquake in Sexual Assault Response: Implementing VAWA Forensic Compliance," EVAWI, May 2013, updated December 2018, 23, https://perma.cc/XV4K-WMQU.

47. EVAWI, "About EVAW International," EVAWI.org, n.d., accessed October 13, 2018, https://perma.cc/K3C4-28TH.

48. EVAWI, "Grants," EVAWI.org, n.d., accessed October 13, 2018, https://perma.cc/3NJ9-QGX8.

49. Joanna Archambault and Kimberly Lonsway, "Effective Report Writing: Using the Language of Non-consensual Sex," EVAWI, February 2006, updated February 2019, https://perma.cc/7DYX-T9ZG.

50. Archambault and Lonsway, "Effective Report Writing," 30.

51. Archambault and Lonsway, "Effective Report Writing," 13.

52. Archambault and Lonsway, "Effective Report Writing," 33.

53. Archambault and Lonsway, "Effective Report Writing," 32.

54. Archambault and Lonsway, "Effective Report Writing," 33.

55. Deborah Tuerkheimer, "#MeToo Comes to the Cosby Courtroom," *New York Times*, April 9, 2018, https://perma.cc/JAU3-XR5S.

56. This occurred through a reading of the "common scheme" exception to Pennsylvania's prior bad acts rule, Pa. R. Evid. 404. See Commonwealth v. Cosby Jr., No. 3314 EDA 2018, 2019 WL 2157653, at 43–48 (Pa. Com. Pl. May 14, 2019) (trial court defending the ruling); Chris Francescani, "Cosby Judge Will Allow 5 Additional Accusers to Testify against the Comedian," ABC News, March 15, 2018, https://perma.cc/9WJJ-YRY9.

57. Callie Marie Rennison and Mary J. Dodge, *Introduction to Criminal Justice: Systems, Diversity, and Change,* 2nd ed. (Thousand Oaks, CA: Sage Publications, 2017), 20.

58. Prachi Gupta, "Brock Turner Is Now the Textbook Definition of 'Rape' in Criminal Justice Classes," *Jezebel,* September 13, 2017, https://perma.cc/KQ5Y-9A6L.

59. See United States v. Alexander, 471 F.2d 923, 959–65 (D.C. Cir. 1972) (Bazelon, J. dissenting) (discussing possibility of an exculpatory "rotten social background" principle); see generally Richard Delgado, "Rotten Social Background: Should the Criminal Law Recognize a Defense of Severe Environmental Deprivation?" *Law and Inequality* 3, no. 1 (July 1985): 9–90.

60. Jacqueline Lee, "Witness: Stanford Rape Defendant Brock Turner Had Victim's DNA on Hands," *Mercury News,* March 21, 2016, https://perma.cc/97U3-7TMB.

61. Katie J. M. Baker, "Here's the Powerful Letter the Stanford Victim Read Aloud to Her Attacker," *BuzzFeed News,* June 3, 2016, https://perma.cc/TJ2H-5HW8.

62. Baker, "Here's the Powerful Letter."

63. Tim Baysinger, "How BuzzFeed Became the Outlet That Made the Stanford Rape Victim's Letter Go Viral," *Adweek,* June 7, 2016, https://perma.cc/QLD8-JR3U.

64. Baysinger, "How BuzzFeed Became the Outlet."

65. Frank Pallota, "Why Ashleigh Banfield Read Stanford Rape Victim's Letter on CNN," CNN Business, June 6, 2016, https://perma.cc/WH4K-D46Z.

66. Emma Reynolds, "'To Girls Everywhere, I Am with You': Women Read Viral Rape Victim Impact Statement," News.com.au, June 10, 2016, https://perma.cc/B7H3-QVTU.

67. Lee, "Stanford Rape Defendant."

68. Cal. Penal Code § 1203.065(b) (West 2016) (at that time, applying the "interests of justice" exception to assault with intent to rape, § 220, and penetration of an intoxicated/unconscious person, §§ 289(d) & (e)).

69. Monica Lassettre, "Probation Report," People v. Brock Allen Turner (Case No. B1577162), June 2, 2016, 13–16, https://perma.cc/95NM-EJQJ; Jeffrey F. Rosen, "People's Sentencing Memorandum," People v. Brock Allen Turner (Case No. B1577162), May 27, 2016, 25, http://documents.latimes.com/people-v-brock-allen-turner-59/.

70. Sam Levin, "Stanford Sexual Assault: Read the Full Text of the Judge's Controversial Decision," *Guardian,* June 14, 2016, https://perma.cc/ZL5F-JYK2.

71. Tyler Kingkade, "Secretive Feminist Group Is Uniting To Recall the Judge in Brock Turner Case," *Huffington Post,* August 2, 2016, https://perma.cc/ZR69-7X5V; Phoenix Tso, "Meet the Secret Society That's at War with Rape Culture," *UPROXX,* June 29, 2016, https://perma.cc/F288-NN5U.

72. Lassettre, "Probation Report," 12.

73. Lassettre, "Probation Report," 5.

74. Baker, "Here's the Powerful Letter."

75. Lassettre, "Probation Report," 7.

76. Lassettre, "Probation Report," 7.

77. Lassettre, "Probation Report," 11.

78. Judith Levine, "Brock Turner and the Problem of Punishment," *Boston Review,* June 16, 2016, https://perma.cc/WJ67-JS64.

79. Rosen, "People's Sentencing Memorandum," 15.

80. Gabriella Paiella, "Here Is Brock Turner's Statement to the Judge," *New York Magazine: The Cut,* June 8, 2016, https://perma.cc/3BQ4–6DEF; Michael W. Armstrong, "Defendant's Sentencing Memorandum," People v. Brock Allen Turner (Case No. B1577162), May 31, 2016, https://perma.cc/EL9B-ULVY.

81. Samantha Stendal, "A Needed Response," YouTube video, May 22, 2013, https://perma.cc/EU72–6K6C.

82. Armstrong, "Defendant's Sentencing Memorandum."

83. Elle Hunt, "'Twenty Minutes of Action': Father Defends Stanford Student Son Convicted of Sexual Assault," *Guardian,* June 6, 2016, https://perma.cc/6MFM-DDZJ.

84. Michele Dauber (@mldauber), "#brockturner father: son not 'violent' only got '20 mins of action' shouldn't have to go to prison," Twitter, June 4, 2016, https://perma.cc/8WHD-JFZE.

85. Tyler Kingkade, "Letter from Brock Turner's Father," *Huffington Post,* June 6, 2016, https://perma.cc/G6KD-XVS3.

86. Bryan Stevenson, *Just Mercy: A Story of Justice and Redemption* (New York: Spiegel and Grau, 2014), 17–18.

87. Maria Ruiz, "Remove Judge Aaron Persky from the Bench for Decision in Brock Turner Rape Case," Change.org, 2016, https://perma.cc/4XQE-J4Q P (showing 1,323, 466 signatures).

88. Tyler Kingkade, "Public Defenders Stick Up for Judge Persky amid Recall Effort," *Huffington Post,* June 24, 2016, https://perma.cc/MZ8S-B2ZX, quoting letter from Sajid Khan et al., Public Defender, Santa Clara County (June 15, 2016).

89. Sajid Khan, "A Letter in Support of Judge Aaron Persky and Judicial Discretion," Change.org, June 2016, https://perma.cc/X8CK-NVL6.

90. Kingkade, "Public Defenders"; Sajid Khan, "Letter in Support" (Change.org shows 444 total signatures on Khan's petition).

91. Akiva Freidlin et al., "Stanford Law School Graduates Submit Letter to Reconsider Recall Effort to Judge Persky," Albert Cobarrubias Justice Project, June 22, 2016, https://perma.cc/A4N9-VC4E.

92. Freidlin et al., "Stanford Law School Graduates."

93. Freidlin et al., "Stanford Law School Graduates."

94. Jenn Hoffman, "Brock Turner Going Free Is the Best Thing to Happen to Rape Awareness," *xoJane,* September 5, 2016, https://perma.cc/SDK4-YM57.

95. Hoffman, "Brock Turner Going Free."

96. Cal. Penal Code § 290 (West 2012).

97. Cal. Penal Code § 290; Amy B. Wang, "Brock Turner Is Now Registered as a Sex Offender in Ohio after Spending Three Months in Jail," *Washington Post,* September 6, 2016, https://perma.cc/JR6Q-L2UW.

98. Mitchell Byars, "Woman Raped by Austin Wilkerson Calls Sentence 'Light,' but Found Legal Process 'Therapeutic,'" *Boulder News,* August 12, 2016, https://perma.cc/KKM6-HJM3.

99. Byars, "Woman Raped."

100. Kate Hogan, "People's 25 Women Changing the World: Kendra Heuer," *People* magazine, November 3, 2016, https://perma.cc/VE8P-P76R.

101. Hogan, "People's 25 Women."

102. Colorado Sex Offender Lifetime Supervision Act of 1998, Colo. Rev. Stat. § 18–1.3–1004 (2016).

103. Tracey Kaplan, "Brock Turner: A Sex Offender for Life, He Faces Stringent Rules," *Mercury News,* September 2, 2016, https://perma.cc/P3BK-SWC7.

104. Amy Goodman, "Debate: Is Recalling Judge Persky a Victory for Sexual Assault Survivors or a Dangerous Precedent?," *Democracy Now!,* August 30, 2016, https://perma.cc/SZ3P-V5EM.

105. Carson and Anderson, "Prisoners in 2015," 14 (reporting that 52.9 percent of prisoners are incarcerated for violent offenses).

106. Robin Abcarian, "Recall Effort of Judge in Stanford Rape Case Gains Steam and Political Allies," *Los Angeles Times,* July 8, 2016, https://perma.cc/AAV7-CH2P.

107. See Roper v. Simmons, 543 U.S. 551, 575 (2005).

108. "2015 Hate Crime Statistics," U.S. Department of Justice, Federal Bureau of Investigation: Criminal Justice Information Service Division (2016), https://perma.cc/88RY-93U2, measuring "known" offenders and finding that 24.3 percent were black and 48.4 percent were white, not factoring in Latino ethnicity; Michael Bronski, Ann Pelligrini, and Michael Amico, "Hate Crime Laws Don't Prevent Violence against LGBT People," *Nation,* October 2, 2013, https://perma.cc/CX9L-CKLW.

109. Elahe Izadi, "Louisiana Is the First State to Offer Hate Crime Protections to Police Officers," *Washington Post,* May 26, 2016, https://perma.cc/FDG2–4EQ4.

110. Isabela Bumanlang, "Stanford Law Grads Write Open Letter, Question Judge Persky Recall," *Stanford Daily,* June 25, 2016, https://perma.cc/8CDF-E5SU.

111. This has been demonstrated exhaustively in the capital punishment context. See Matthew B. Robinson, "The Real Death Penalty: Capital Punishment According to the Experts," *Criminal Law Bulletin* 45, no. 2 (2009): 3 (84 percent of death penalty experts believe that "the racial bias in capital punishment does not pertain to race of defendant but rather to race of victim"); Michael L. Radelet and Glenn L. Pierce, "Race and Death Sentencing in North Carolina, 1980–2007," *North Carolina Law Review* 89, no. 6 (September 2011): 2145; Samuel R. Gross and Robert Mauro, "Patterns of Death: An Analysis of Racial Disparities in Capital Sentencing and Homicide Victimization," *Stanford Law Review* 37, no. 1 (November 1984): 105.

112. Jason Doiy, "Stanford Sex Assault Case Judge Aaron Persky Accused of Leniency for an Athlete Again," CBS News, October 19, 2016, https://perma.cc/U493–9QNG.

113. Paul Elias, "Judge in Stanford Rape Case Often Follows Sentencing Report," *AP News*, June 17, 2016, https://perma.cc/G6TS-AAPQ.

114. Susan Svrluga, Elahe Izadi, and Sarah Larimer, "'Repugnant'—Or 'Fair'? Debate Erupts over Judge's Decision in Stanford Sexual Assault Case," *Washington Post*, June 8, 2016, https://perma.cc/A4R2-WMGR.

115. Svrluga, Izadi, and Larimer, "'Repugnant.'"

116. Svrluga, Izadi, and Larimer, "'Repugnant.'"

117. Tracey Kaplan, "Brock Turner Case Fallout: Prospective Jurors Refuse to Serve under Judge," *Mercury News*, June 9, 2016, https://perma.cc/P6B4-AMSQ.

118. Tracey Kaplan, "Brock Turner: D.A. Gets Judge Kicked Off New Sex Case," *Mercury News*, June 14, 2016, https://perma.cc/7ZAS-ZG2D.

119. Phil Helsel, "Judge in Controversial Brock Turner Case Removed from New Sex Assault Case," *NBC News*, June 15, 2016, https://perma.cc/WC7U-8QQN.

120. Kaplan, "D.A."

121. Shaun King, "Brock Turner and Cory Batey, Two College Athletes Who Raped Unconscious Women, Show How Race and Privilege Affect Sentences," *New York Daily News*, June 7, 2016, https://perma.cc/6FG3–82M8.

122. King, "Brock Turner."

123. King, "Brock Turner."

124. The author himself specified that Batey should not have "been given a break" like Turner. King, "Brock Turner."

125. Stacey Barchenger, "Cory Batey Sentenced to 15 Years in Vanderbilt Rape Case," *USA Today*, July 14, 2016, https://perma.cc/H5ZK-2D5L.

126. Stacey Barchenger, "What Message Does Vanderbilt Rape Case Send?," *USA Today*, July 16, 2016, https://perma.cc/B8UD-42JM.

127. Irene Hooks, "Brock Turner and Corey Batey: Same Crime, Different Sentence," *Odyssey*, June 13, 2016, https://perma.cc/DDR8-H9M7.

128. Sam Levin, "Stanford Trial Judge Overseeing Much Harsher Sentence for Similar Assault Case," *Guardian*, June 27, 2016, https://perma.cc/XN7K-E5S3.

129. Levin, "Stanford Trial Judge."

130. Levin, "Stanford Trial Judge."

131. Levin, "Stanford Trial Judge."

132. 20A Cal. Jur. 3d Criminal Law: Pretrial Proceedings § 899 (in California, judges are permitted to reject plea bargains, but only if they articulate why the plea is contrary to the public interest); see People v. Loya, 1 Cal. App. 5th 932 (Cal. App. 5th Dist. 2016).

133. Although the DA might respond that Ramirez was sober and used physical force. See Levin, "Stanford Trial Judge."

134. Lizzie Crocker, "Feminists Put Judge Aaron Persky on Trial," *Daily Beast*, August 14, 2016, https://perma.cc/W3HN-9T42.

135. Levin, "Stanford Trial Judge," quoting Dauber.

136. Svrluga, Izadi, and Larimer, "'Repugnant'"

137. Svrluga, Izadi, and Larimer, "'Repugnant.'"

138. Sex Crimes: Mandatory Prison Sentence, A.B. 2888, 2016 Leg., Reg. Sess. (Cal. 2016), https://perma.cc/3CCG-NWZJ.

139. Rosen, "People's Sentencing Memorandum," 15; Jessica Calefati, "Brock Turner Case: Bills to Mandate Prison for Sexually Assaulting Unconscious Victims, Redefine Rape Clear Committee," *Mercury News,* June 28, 2016, https://perma.cc /U2TU-JB23.

140. Calefati, "Brock Turner Case."

141. Cal. Penal Code § 261 (West 2013).

142. Sex Crimes: Rape, A.B. 701, 2016 Leg., Reg. Sess. (Cal. 2016), https:// perma.cc/5KSG-TTXT.

143. Jazmine Ulloa, "Spurred by Brock Turner Case, Gov. Jerry Brown Signs Laws to Toughen Laws against Rape," *Los Angeles Times,* September 30, 2016, https://perma.cc/VD93-KYZ4.

144. Sarah Larimer, "In Aftermath of Brock Turner Case, California's Governor Signs Sex Crime Bill," *Washington Post,* September 30, 2016, https://perma.cc /C633-B8W8.

145. Maggie Astor, "California Voters Remove Judge Aaron Persky, Who Gave a 6-Month Sentence for Sexual Assault," *New York Times,* June 6, 2018, https:// perma.cc/N332–5MN2.

146. Christina Cauterucci, "The Armed Protests outside Brock Turner's Home Are Dangerously Counterproductive," *Slate: XXFactor,* September 6, 2016, https:// perma.cc/AGD7-JK3P; see also Will Garbe, "Protesters Gather outside Brock Turner's Parents' Home," *Dayton Daily News,* June 12, 2016, https://perma.cc /H4VU-KA3P.

147. Sam Levin, "Armed Anarchists Rally at Brock Turner's Home: 'Try This Again, We'll Shoot You,'" *Guardian,* September 6, 2016, https://perma.cc/J2AK-BXML.

148. Levin, "Armed Anarchists."

149. Levin, "Armed Anarchists."

150. Will Garbe, "Brock Turner Registers in Greene County as Tier III Sex Offender," *Dayton Daily News,* September 6, 2016, https://perma.cc/42AC-4NR2.

151. Garbe, "Brock Turner Registers."

CONCLUSION

1. David Cole, "Turning the Corner on Mass Incarceration?," *Ohio State Journal of Criminal Law* 9, no. 1 (Fall 2011): 50.

2. Cole, "Turning the Corner," 50.

3. Cole, "Turning the Corner," 50.

4. E. Ann Carson and Elizabeth Anderson, "Prisoners in 2015," US Department of Justice, *Bureau of Justice Statistics Bulletin,* December 2016, 3, https://perma.cc /ED52-KMX5.

5. Carson and Anderson, "Prisoners in 2015," 8.

6. E. Ann Carson, "Prisoners in 2016," US Department of Justice, *Bureau of Justice Statistics Bulletin,* January 9, 2018, 10, https://perma.cc/N2CY-MDVQ; Oliver Hinds, Jacob Kang-Brown, and Olive Lu, "People in Prison 2017," Vera Institute of Justice, May 2018, 1, https://perma.cc/F5JM-6JK9.

7. Sentencing Reform and Corrections Act of 2015, S.2123, 114th Congress (2015–2016).

8. Rebecca R. Ruiz, "Attorney General Orders Tougher Sentences, Rolling Back Obama Policy," *New York Times,* May 12, 2017, https://perma.cc/28V7-TXFP.

9. Sentencing Reform and Corrections Act of 2015, S.2123, 114th Congress (2015–2016); Sentencing Reform and Corrections Act of 2017, S.1917, 115th Congress (2017); Jonathan Keim, "The Sentencing Reform and Corrections Act of 2015: Post-markup Reactions and Analysis," *National Review,* October 28, 2015, https://perma.cc/5J99-T7EM; Justin George, "Can Bipartisan Criminal-Justice Reform Survive in the Trump Era?," *New Yorker,* June 6, 2017, https://perma.cc/5PV2-AUMS.

10. Sentencing Reform and Corrections Act of 2017, S.1917, 115th Congress (2017).

11. Aya Gruber, "Neofeminism," *Houston Law Review* 50, no. 5 (2013): 1325–90; Aya Gruber, "A Neo-feminist Assessment of Rape and Domestic Violence Law Reform," *Journal of Gender, Race, and Justice* 15, no. 3 (Spring 2012): 583–615.

12. Ian Halley, "Queer Theory by Men," *Duke Journal of Gender Law and Policy* 11 (2004): 30.

13. Jorge L. Esquirol, "The Failed Law of Latin America," *American Journal of Comparative Law* 56 (2008): 89.

14. Janet Halley, Prabha Kotiswaran, Rachel Rebouché, and Hila Shamir, *Governance Feminism: An Introduction* (Minneapolis: University of Minnesota Press, 2018), 254.

15. Halley, Kotiswaran, and Rebouché, *Governance Feminism,* 67–68.

16. See Richard Delgado and Jean Stefancic, *Critical Race Theory* (New York: NYU Press, 2001), 5; Deborah L. Rhode, "Feminism and the State," *Harvard Law Review* 107, no. 6 (April 1994): 1184, noting feminism's "commitment to a more egalitarian distributive structure and a greater sense of collective responsibility."

17. See chapter 3, the section "What If Arrest Is Not Best?," and chapter 4, the section "The Ideal Battered Woman," for this discussion.

18. See Aya Gruber, "Murder, Minority Victims, and Mercy," *Colorado Law Review* 85 (2014): 170–76.

19. See, for example, Sharon Lamb, "Sex Education as Moral Education: Teaching for Pleasure, about Fantasy, and against Abuse," *Journal of Moral Education* 26, no. 3 (September 1997): 301–3; Moira Carmody et al., "Framing Best Practice: National Standards for the Primary Prevention of Sexual Assault through Education," National Sexual Assault Prevention Education Project for NASASV (2009), https://perma.cc/CT3A-B2HD; Pennsylvania Coalition Against Rape, *Literature Review: Healthy Sexuality Education as Sexual Abuse Prevention* (Enola: Pennsylvania Coalition Against Rape, 2016), https://perma.cc/6QM7-Q8MS.

20. CBC News, "Ontario Sex-Ed Dispute: Why 1 Mother Will Keep Her Kids Home," CBC News, September 9, 2015, https://perma.cc/K7FT-M9G3.

21. See chapter 5, the section "The Sexual Cold War," for this discussion.

22. Cheryl Corley, "HBCUs Move to Address Campus Sexual Assaults, but Is It Enough?," National Public Radio, September 29, 2014, https://perma.cc/SY6C-FFV8, describing a Title IX orientation session for freshmen at Howard University where the administrator stated, "Repeat after me—an enthusiastic yes."

23. I discuss the "invasion" view of rape's harms in chapter 5, in the section "The Sexual Cold War."

24. See Jeannie Suk, "The Trouble with Teaching Rape Law," *New Yorker,* December 15, 2014, https://perma.cc/5ZNJ-KUG3; Jenny Jarvie, "Trigger Happy," *New Republic,* March 3, 2014, https://perma.cc/HF6S-PASJ.

25. See Lorna Veraldi and Donna M. Veraldi, "Is There a Research Basis for Requiring Trigger Warnings?," *Forensic Psychology* 1 (March 2015): 5–7, https://perma.cc/4KAN-8AEZ.

26. Veraldi and Veraldi, "Is There a Research Basis," 6.

27. One of the stranger responses I have heard to my analysis of the trigger culture is that it simply does not exist. See, e.g., Tyler Kingkade, "Despite Fears about Trigger Warnings, Survey Suggests Few Faculty Are Forced to Use Them," *Huffington Post,* June 23, 2015, https://perma.cc/9PYZ-QK75. I do not doubt that professors in many disciplines need not worry about trigger warnings, but for those of us who teach rape, homicide, racial profiling, gay panic, and other "sensitive" topics, the issue is all too real.

28. Thomas Mathiesen, *The Politics of Abolition Revisited* (London: Routledge, 1974), 31–32 (emphasis in original).

29. Thomas Mathiesen, "The Politics of Abolition," *Contemporary Crises* 10 (1986): 87, https://perma.cc/J847-CT4F.

30. Mathiesen, "Politics of Abolition," 87.

31. Chuck Grassley, "Sen. Chuck Grassley: Sentencing Reform Bill Will Fight Crime," Fox News, April 27, 2018, https://perma.cc/9C5U-JA2L; First Step Act, H.R.5682, 115th Congress (2018).

32. D Dangaran and Anna Nathanson, "Thank You So Much for Joining Us for the Fighting the (Q)arceral State Conference," email, October 24, 2018.

33. Dangaran and Nathanson, "Thank You So Much." For a discussion of the Trump memo, see Erica L. Green, Katie Benner, and Robert Pear, "'Transgender' Could Be Defined Out of Existence under Trump Administration," *New York Times,* October 21, 2018, https://perma.cc/33TU-EMFK.

34. Dangaran and Nathanson, "Thank You So Much." For the resources on each of these, see Aaron Rose, "What to Do Instead of Calling the Police," Aaronxrose.com, July 8, 2016, https://perma.cc/RP46-AATC; "Black Lives Matter Boston," accessed November 20, 2018, https://perma.cc/QQK2-Y4GZ; Black and Pink Boston Chapter, Facebook page, accessed November 20, 2018, https://perma.cc/4THD-T7VT; "We Are Because She Was," Sisters Unchained, n.d., accessed March 16, 2019, https://perma.cc/8WFG-DCTA; Key Jackson and Malcolm Shanks, "Practical POC Tips for

Fighting the Trump Administration's Latest Assault on Trans People," *Color Lines,* October 22, 2018, https://perma.cc/5E4P-DRRL.

35. Mathiesen, "Politics of Abolition," 81.

36. Mathiesen, "Politics of Abolition," 84.

37. Mathiesen, "Politics of Abolition," 84.

38. Mathiesen, "Politics of Abolition," 84.

39. "NLG Adopts Resolution Supporting Prison Abolition," National Lawyers Guild, December 17, 2015, https://perma.cc/788N-7VQ5.

40. Ruairí Arrieta-Kenna, "'Abolish Prisons' Is the New 'Abolish ICE,'" *Politico,* August 15, 2018, https://perma.cc/773G-MYEF.

41. Alexandria Ocasio-Cortez, "Alexandria Ocasio-Cortez on Her Catholic Faith and the Urgency of a Criminal Justice Reform," *America: The Jesuit Review,* June 27, 2018, https://perma.cc/3NH9-6JSX.

42. Floyd v. City of New York, 959 F.Supp.2d 540 (S.D.N.Y. 2013); Floyd v. City of New York 959 F.Supp.2d 668 (S.D.N.Y. 2013).

43. Ligon v. City of New York, 538 Fed.Appx. 101 (2d Cir. 2013).

44. Benjamin Weiser and Joseph Goldstein, "Mayor Says New York City Will Settle Suits on Stop-and-Frisk Tactics," *New York Times,* January 30, 2014, https://perma.cc/WK6Z-8B7C.

45. "Stop-and-Frisk Data," New York Civil Liberties Union, accessed November 20, 2018, https://perma.cc/58HT-ZAFW.

46. I arrived at this percentage by adding up felonies and misdemeanors in 2011 and those in 2017 and calculating the change. I did not adjust for population changes. The counts come from "Historical New York City Crime Data," New York Police Department, accessed March 17, 2019, https://perma.cc./R8B5-SAKN.

47. "Chicago BLM Activist: 'We Need to Abolish the Police,'" *Fox News Insider,* July 12, 2016, https://perma.cc/Q5CJ-YAKP, video available at http://bit.ly/29NgR80.

48. See Maya Dukmasova, "Abolish the Police? Organizers Say It's Less Crazy Than It Sounds," *Chicago Reader,* August 25, 2016, https://perma.cc/9T6X-UUGR.

49. Dukmasova, "Abolish the Police?"

50. INCITE!, "Welcome!," n.d., accessed March 16, 2019, https://perma.cc/5EJK-MW5Z.

51. INCITE!, "Statement on Gender Violence and the Prison Industrial Complex (2001)," accessed November 20, 2018, https://perma.cc/H899-ATED.

52. INCITE!, "Statement on Gender Violence," all quotes in paragraph.

53. Ellen Carol DuBois and Linda Gordon, "Seeking Ecstasy on the Battlefield: Danger and Pleasure in Nineteenth-Century Feminist Sexual Thought," in *Pleasure and Danger: Exploring Female Sexuality,* ed. Carole S. Vance (Boston: Routledge, 1984), 42.

54. Nils Christie, *Crime Control as Industry: Towards GULAGS, Western Style?* (London: Routledge, 1993), 13.

INDEX

in, 7; on mandatory arrest, 88; on mandatory prison sentences for sex offenses, 6; marriage equality movement in, 51; on plea bargains, 268n132; on sex offender registration, 183; and Turner sentencing, 179–82

Campaign for Adequate Welfare Reform, 46–47

Campaign for California Families, 51

campus antirape movement, 151–69; American Association of Universities on, 159, 161; campus serial rapist assumption, 163; Campus Sexual Assault Study (2007, CSA Study), 153, 159, 161; climate surveys by universities, 159–62; Columbia University case (2014), 153–54; CPI report (2010) on, 151–53, 157; Florida State University case (2013), 153; and incarceration, 164–69; media coverage of, 8; and predator panic, 158–59; "rapists cause rape" argument, 223n61; *Rolling Stone* on, 164; and serial college rapist narrative, 162–64; and "slut shaming," 39, 213–14n118, 246n107; Title IX, Education Amendments (1972, Department of Education), 152–53, 159–61, 166; Turner case, 178–90; University of Virginia case (*Rolling Stone* story), 154–58, 164. *See also* neofeminism

Campus Sexual Assault Study (2007, CSA Study), 153, 159, 161

Canada: on affirmative consent, 246n105; sexuality education in, 195–96

capitalism. *See* race and class issues

capital punishment: Clinton Crime Bill (Violent Crime Control and Enforcement Act of 1994), 146–48; death penalty, 22, 38–39, 267n111; McGee case, 38, 125

Carby, Hazel, 35

carceral feminism, defined, 7, 118

Carlson, Allan, 103–4

Carlson, Tucker, 254n25

"Carry That Weight" performance art, 154

La Casa de las Madres, 53

Center for Constitutional Rights, 201

Center for Court Innovation, 215n19

Center for Public Integrity (2010, CPI Report), 151–53, 157

Chang, Grace, 172–73

Change.org, 182

Chappell, Marisa, 46–47

chastity and morality: affirmative consent and modern-day moralism, 174–78; children as "unchaste," 22, 209n22; "hue and cry" rule, 208n7; legal feminists on police attitudes, 70–71; moral panic, defined, 109; seduction, 24, 26; sexual revolution and changing norms of, 121–23, 239n1; and "slut shaming," 39, 137, 213–14n118, 246n107

Chen, Lei, 172

Chesney-Lind, Meda, 86–87

Chicago Reader, on police abolition movement, 202

children: age-of-consent reform (1920), 26–27, 32; "forcible compulsion" of, 124–25; juvenile defendants, 32, 112–13, 166, 184; school discipline and incarceration rates, 166; sexuality education for, 195–97; as "unchaste," 22, 209n22; as victims of sexual crimes, 109–12, 235n100. *See also* consent

Chinese Exclusion Act of 1882, 30

Chinese immigrants. *See* Asian Americans

Chiu, Elaine, 104

Christie, Nils, 204

Citizens' Crusade Against Poverty, 46–48

Citron, Danielle Keats, 261n1

City University of New York (CUNY), 73–76

civil commitment of sex offenders, 109, 111

civil protection order, 2, 205

class issues. *See* race and class issues

climate surveys by universities, 159–62

Clinton, Bill: Clinton Crime Bill (Violent Crime Control and Enforcement Act of 1994), 146–48; on victims' rights, 100, 231n34

coercion, consent *vs.,* 14, 123–28

coercive control, 57, 97, 104–6, 118, 135, 170

Cohen, Stanley, 109

Coker, Donna, 62, 66, 108

Coker v. Georgia (1977), 38–39

Cole, David, 191

119–20; rape reform, rape prosecution, and incarceration, 146–50; rape trauma syndrome, 141–42; sex-positive feminist view, defined, 121; sexual revolution and cultural change, 121–23, 239n1; and shield laws, 137–40, 246–47n110; stranger rape *vs.* date rape, 125; tonic immobility, 135–36, 244–45n92, 245n99–100. *See also* fear of rape; neofeminism

Dauber, Michelle, 179–82, 184–85, 187–88

Daughters of Bilitis, 50

Davis, Martha, 49

"Dear Colleague Letter" (DCL, Obama administration), 153

death penalty (capital punishment), 22, 38–39, 267n111

DeBlasio, Bill, 201

decriminalization of sex work, 118, 174

Delaware, punishment for domestic violence (1901), 33

Department of Education, 152–53, 157, 159–61, 166

Department of Homeland Security, 102

Department of Justice, 111

deterrence, 81–93

DeVos, Betsy, 157

Dick, Kirby, 157

discrimination. *See* race and class issues

distributional analysis, 194

"distributional" *vs.* "formalist" approaches, 192–95

District of Columbia (D.C.): affirmative consent statutes, 244n71; on domestic violence first-time offenders, 4; on warrantless arrest for domestic violence, 215n19

Disu, Jessica, 201–2

Doe, Emily, 178–83, 185

domestic violence (DV), 67–93; aggressive prosecution policy (1990s), 106–7, 234n85; antistate and antipoverty feminists on, 45–59; battered women's syndrome, 105, 141; coercive control, 57, 97, 104–6, 118, 135, 170; criminal justice example (Jamal and Britney), 1–5; deterrence and proarrest stance, 81–93; dual arrest in incidents of,

88–89; and everywoman claim, 52–53, 56–58, 62, 87, 108; family violence research on, 68, 76–81, 224n71; hotlines for help, 95; incarceration statistics (1980s to present), 44–45; "injury-adjusted" rates of, 78–81; legal feminists on, 45–46, 59–66; and mediation training for police, 68, 73–76, 77; neoliberalism and effect on, 64–66; no-drop prosecution, 44, 89, 106, 130, 155; and police criticism, 67–68; proarrest stance and *Bruno,* 68–76, 221n12; proarrest stance and escalation effect, 68–69, 84–88, 91–93; punishment for, nineteenth-century/turn of twentieth century punishment, 25, 33, 92; "rule of thumb," 71–72, 222n23; social stressors as cause of, 77–78, 92. *See also* historical perspective of gender crimes; neofeminism; victimhood narratives and victims' rights

dominance feminists: on coercion *vs.* consent, 123–28; defined, 121; and gendered power in society, 142–44; on sexual revolution, 121–23, 239n1. *See also* date rape and rape reform

Douglass, Frederick, 35

Driver, Minnie, 11

Dubber, Markus, 99

DuBois, Ellen, 203–4

due process, 10–11, 100–101, 138, 153, 162, 165–67, 176

Dukakis, Michael, 147

Duke University, 154, 165–66

Dunn, Laura, 151–53, 157–58, 167

Dworkin, Andrea, 119, 144

economic issues. *See* welfare issues

Education Amendments (Title IX, 1972, Department of Education), 152–53, 159–61, 166

Eggman, Susan, 188–89

Ellison, Louise, 242n57

End Domestic Abuse Wisconsin, 92–93

End Violence Against Women International (EVAWI), 176–77

Eramo, Nicole, 154–58

Erdely, Sabrina, 154–58, 164

Mathiesen, Thomas, 197–98, 199
McGee, Willie, 38, 125
McGuire, Danielle, 38
mediation training for police, 68, 73–76, 77
Memorial United Methodist Church, 50
"Memory and Narrative of Traumatic Events" (Crespo and Fernandez-Lansac), 248n127
mens rea, defined, 128–29
#MeToo movement, 5–12
Miami (Florida), sexual offenders in, 111–12
Michigan, *People v. Lucas* (1987), 139
Milano, Alyssa, 10–11
Milkovits, Amanda, 263n27
millennial feminism, defined, 5
Miller, Alice, 107
Miller, Paul, 162–64
Milwaukee study (1980s), on arrest, 58
Mingbi, Shen, 172
Minneapolis Domestic Violence Experiment (Sherman and Berk), 81–87, 91–93
Minnesota: affirmative consent statutes, 244n71; Minneapolis antipornography ordinance (1983), 115–17; Minneapolis Domestic Violence Experiment (Sherman and Berk), 81–87, 91–93; Sexual Violence Prevention Program, 113; St. Paul women's shelter, 47, 64
Minow, Martha, 97, 100, 143
Mississippi: McGee case (1951), 38, 125; on warrantless arrest for domestic violence, 215n19
Missoula (Krakauer), 157, 163
Model Penal Code (MPC), 125, 243n68, 244n71
morality. *See* chastity and morality
moral panic, 109
Moran, Richard, 110
Morning Call (Allentown, Pennsylvania), on rape incarceration, 128
Morrison, Toni, 49
Mothers Against Senseless Killing, 202
"Moynihan Report" (*The Negro Family: The Case for National Action,* Johnson administration), 41, 91
Ms., on class issues of feminism, 48

M.T.S. case (1992), 132–35, 144, 176
Munro, Vanesa E., 242n57
murder, 21, 52–54, 82
Murphy, Wendy, 154, 166, 254n25

Nadasen, Premilla, 49
Nash, Jennifer, 52
Nathanson, Anna, 199
National Center on Women and Family Law, 91
National Crime Victimization Surveys (Bureau of Justice Statistics), 145–46, 159, 215n20
National District Attorneys Association of Women Prosecutors Section, 175
National Family Violence Surveys, 79
National Lawyers Guild (NLG), 200
National Organization of Women (NOW): antipoverty position of, 49; on *Commonwealth v. Berkowitz* (1994), 128; and lesbian issues, 50, 52, 116; on sex trafficking, 174
National Public Radio (NPR), campus rape report of (2010), 151–53, 157
National Welfare Rights Organization, 48
National Women's Suffrage Association, 24
Native Americans, Adam Walsh Children Protection Act (2006) and effect on, 111
Naziri, Micah, 189
Negro Family: The Case for National Action, The ("Moynihan Report," Johnson administration), 41, 91
neofeminism, 191–204; defined, 193; "formalist" *vs.* "distributional" approaches, 192–95; for gender justice, 198–99; and incarceration reduction, 191–92, 197–204; and sexuality education effort, 195–97; stance against policing, prosecution, and punishment, 199–204
neoliberalism: defined, 65; and domestic violence, 64–66; and victims' rights, 99–104
Nevada, on warrantless arrest for domestic violence, 215n19
New Abolitionists, 27, 117–18
New Jersey: affirmative consent statutes, 244n71; *Perna v. Pirozzi* (1983), 133;

proarrest stance. *See* law enforcement

progressive prosecution, 171, 192

Prohibition, temperance movement and, 20, 23–28, 32, 35–36

prostitution: and corroboration requirement, 20–23; decriminalization of sex work, 118, 174; defined, 208n50; and Kraft, 171–72; massage parlors and sex trafficking, 171–74, 263n27; Online Trafficking Act (2017), 261n1; Operation Gilded Cage, 173; prostitution abolition, 122, 170; recriminalization of, 174; temperance movement on, 26; victimhood narratives and victims' rights, 117–19, 238n155; "white slavery," 27–28, 31–32, 37; "yellow slavery," 28–31

protection order, 2, 205

Providence Journal, on prostitution, 263n27

"Psychological Impact of Rape, The" (Resick), 248n127

Psychological Trauma, on rape trauma, 248n127

PTSD (post-traumatic stress disorder), 157, 165, 248n127

punishment: age-of-consent reform and punishment of young girls, 32; capital punishment, 22, 38–39, 267n111; *Coker v. Georgia* (1977) on, 38–39; life sentences, 90, 183, 187; mandatory minimum sentences, 6, 86, 148–89, 192; nineteenth-century/turn of twentieth century punishment for domestic violence, 25, 33, 92; rape-based lynching of black men, 34–37; sex offender registration, 180, 183–84, 188. *See also* capital punishment

Quinn, Mae, 32

race and class issues: consent and "Lord Hale instruction," 20–23, 125; and everywoman narrative, 52–53, 56–58, 62, 87, 108; hate crime legislation, 184–85; of immigration, 28–31, 39, 102, 170, 171–74, 263n27; and incarceration rates, 7–8, 166, 191–92, 249–50n148;

Latinas, shelters for, 53–57, 62; lynching, 34–37; mandatory arrest issues of, 86–88; and Mann Act, 31–33; #Me Too movement inception, 10; race of jurors, 249n146; rape as racial phenomenon, 32–40; and rape reform as selective enforcement, 144–45; second wave feminists on, 48–59; sexuality of "privileged young white women," 14–15; and Turner-Batey disparity, 185–86; of victimhood narratives and victims' rights, 107–8; white privilege, 62; "white slavery," 27–28, 31–32, 37; white supremacy, 54; "yellow slavery," 28–31

radical feminism, 42–46, 63–64, 103, 118–19, 198, 202

Ramirez, Paul, 187–88

rape: child predator laws, 109–12, 235n110; definitions, 163, 189; false reporting rates, 140, 247n125; incest *vs.,* 113; "Lord Hale instruction" on, 20–23, 125; pregnancy of rape victims, 37–38; rape trauma syndrome, 141–42, 165, 177, 248n127; "rapists cause rape" argument, 223n61; Rule 413 (federal evidentiary rule), 139–40; sexual assault, definitions, 159, 160; and shield laws, 137–40, 246–47n110; Take Back the Night (TBTN), 43–44; trigger warnings, 196–97, 271n27. *See also* children; date rape and rape reform; historical perspective of gender crimes; neofeminism; victimhood narratives and victims' rights

"Rape on Campus, A" (Erdely), 154–58

rape reform. *See* date rape and rape reform

Rapping, Elayne, 110

Reagan, Ronald: neoliberalism and Reagan Revolution, 64–66; on victims' rights, 99–104

"Real Men" video, 168–69

Renda, Emily, 157

Reno, Janet, 100, 101–4

"Repeat Rape and Multiple Offending among Undetected Rapists" (Lisak and Miller), 162–64

Resick, Patricia A., 248n127

Resnik, Judith, 148

revenge pornography, 13, 170, 195

South Dakota, on warrantless arrest for domestic violence, 215n19
Southern Strategy, 41–42, 65
Sparks, Glenn, 76
Speeth, Susan, 114
Spitzer, Eliot, 31
St. Paul (Minnesota), first women's shelter, 47, 64
Stanford University. *See* Turner, Brock
Stark, Evan, 87
State v. Cabana (1997), 133
State in Interest of M.T.S. (1992), 132–34, 144, 176
State v. Rhodes (1868), 71
statistics: Assault Victimization Survey (2014), 159; campus rape decline, 255n53; decline in incarceration (since 2014), 191; domestic violence incarceration statistics (1980s to present), 44–45; guilty verdicts in rape cases, 129–30, 242n57; juveniles as sex offenders, 112; National Crime Victimization Surveys, 145–46, 159, 215n20; race of arrestees for rape, 249–50n148; rape/sexual assault statistics (1993–2017), 250n150; sex offenders *vs.* other types of offenders in prison population, 170–71; victim mortality from nonviolent causes, 92; violent crime arrest and incarceration statistics, 91
stay-away orders, 2–4, 89
stealthing, 170, 197, 261n1
Steinmetz, Suzanne, 78–81
Stevenson, Bryan, 182, 184, 190
stop-and-frisk policies, 201
"Stranger in the Bushes, or an Elephant in the Room, A?" (Ellison and Munro), 242n57
stranger rape, 43, 114–15, 119–20, 125–26, 242n57
Straus, Murray, 78–81
Students for a Democratic Society (SDS), 74
Study of Family Violence (Straus, Gelles, Steinmetz), 78–81
Stuntz, William, 110
suffrage movement, 23–26
Suk, Jeannie, 167, 175

Sulkowicz, Emma, 153–54
Supreme Court (US), on Minneapolis Experiment, 82. *See also individual case names*
Swartout, Kevin, 163–64
Symonds, Martin, 135–36
Symposium on Domestic Violence (2002), 104

Take Back the Night (TBTN), 43–44, 114–19, 237n134
temperance movement, 20, 23–28, 32, 35–36
Tennessee, sex offense sentencing in, 186–87
Tennessee Coalition to End Domestic and Sexual Violence, 187
Tesler, Michael, 57
Thomasson, Randy, 51
Throwaway Children, The (Richette), 55
Thurman, Tracey, 82–83
Till, Emmett, 35
Tillmon, Johnnie, 48, 49–50
Title IX, Education Amendments (1972, Department of Education), 152–53, 159–61, 166
Toch, Hans, 74
Toland, Hugh, 29
tonic immobility, 135–36, 244–45n92, 245n99–100
Torrington (Connecticut) Police Department, Tracey's Law and, 82–83
Tracey's Law, 82–83, 88
Tracy, Allison, 164
trauma: PTSD (post-traumatic stress disorder), 157, 165, 248n127; rape trauma syndrome, 141–42, 165, 177, 248n127; *Rolling Stone* story, 154–58, 164; trauma-informed investigations, 165, 170, 176; trial as second rape, 138, 196; trigger warnings, 196–97, 271n27
Travis, Jeremy, 148
trigger warnings, 196–97, 271n27
Trump, Donald: Angel Moms and victims' rights, 100; on campus antirape movement, 157; First Step Act of, 197–98; on "immigrant rapists," 39; on immigration, 9; Johnson pardoned by,

33; on LGBT issues, 199; Pirro on, 102; on Sentencing Act, 191–92, 197–98; on sex trafficking, 170; sexual assault complaints against, 8; on sexuality education, 196

Tuerkheimer, Deb, 178

Turner, Brock: conviction and sentencing of, 178–82; judicial recall efforts in case of, 182–89; presentence recommendation about, 179; "rapists cause rape" argument, 223n61; release of, 189–90; in textbook, 178; victim impact statement in, 178

Turner, Dan, 181–82, 184

Under the Rule of Thumb (Commission on Civil Rights), 71–72, 222n23

Uniform Code of Military Justice, affirmative consent statutes, 244n71

University of California, Toland and, 29

University of Colorado: campus climate survey, 159–61; fraternities of, 168

University of Michigan, 158

University of Virginia, 154–58, 164, 168

University of Wisconsin, 151–53

U.S. v. Holte (1915), 31–32

U.S. v. Morrison (2000), 148–49

U.S. v. Wiley (1974), 21

Utah, on warrantless arrest for domestic violence, 215n19

Vandenberg, Ann, 116

Vaughan, Sharon Rice, 47, 64

Vermont, affirmative consent statutes, 244n71

victimhood narratives and victims' rights, 94–120; *The Burning Bed* (made-for-TV movie), 94–96, 104; children as juvenile offenders, 112–13; children as victims, 109–12, 235n100; credibility tests of victims, 140–42; and domestic violence prosecution, 106–7, 234n85; "ideal victim" image, 96–98; learned helplessness, 105–6; legal feminists on family violence research, 68, 76–81, 224n71; race and class issues of, 107–8; Reagan on victims' rights, 99–104; survivors *vs.* victims, 97; Take Back the

Night on, 114–19, 237n134; victim blaming, 11, 77–78, 104–6, 135, 140, 168, 181; victim impact statements, 99; victims' advocates, 8, 45, 59–60, 77, 89, 100, 106, 142, 163, 176; victim's movements in United States *vs.* Europe, 98; victims' rights organizations, 17, 93, 98–101. *See also* date rape and rape reform

victim mortality from nonviolent causes, 92

Victim Rights Law Center, 161

Victims' Rights Amendment (Arizona), 230n26

Victims' Rights Amendment (federal), 100

Vindication of the Rights of Woman, A (Wollstonecraft), 23

Violence Against Women Act (VAWA), 148–50

Violent Crime Control and Enforcement Act (1994), 146–48

Virginia, on mandatory arrest, 85

Waits, Kathleen, 69–70

Wake Forest Law Review, on sex trafficking, 261n1

Walker, Lenore, 107

Walsh, Adam, 109–12, 114

Walsh, John, 110–12, 114

Wang, Lei, 172

War on Crime, 41–42, 65

War on Drugs, 101

Washington Post: on campus antirape movement, 157; on domestic violence, 95

Washington Post, on crime, 147

Washington (state), on warrantless arrest for domestic violence, 215n19

Way, Katie, 12

We-Consent App, 167

Weinstein, Harvey, 8, 10

Weitzer, Ronald, 117

welfare issues: antistate and antipoverty feminists' sentiments of, 41–43, 45–52, 57, 59; arguments against arrest for domestic violence, 72; economic rights of women, 25; legal feminists on economic position of families, 61–62; neoliberalism and Reagan Revolution,

Founded in 1893,
UNIVERSITY OF CALIFORNIA PRESS
publishes bold, progressive books and journals
on topics in the arts, humanities, social sciences,
and natural sciences—with a focus on social
justice issues—that inspire thought and action
among readers worldwide.

The UC PRESS FOUNDATION
raises funds to uphold the press's vital role
as an independent, nonprofit publisher, and
receives philanthropic support from a wide
range of individuals and institutions—and from
committed readers like you. To learn more, visit
ucpress.edu/supportus.